CHAPLAINS
OF THE
UNITED STATES ARMY

By

Roy J. Honeywell
Colonel, Ret., USAR

Professor of History: Boston University
1920–33

A Chaplain since 5 July 1918

OFFICE OF THE CHIEF OF CHAPLAINS

DEPARTMENT OF THE ARMY

WASHINGTON 25, D. C. 1958

Preface

The influence of religious faith upon fighting men and military events is conspicuous through all history. This has been very true in the development of the United States. If the history of our country is to be understood fully, this vital factor in our national life must be seen in its true perspective. The beliefs and practices of the chaplains who have guided the religious and moral thinking of successive generations of American soldiers indicate the faith which animated them in battle and the ideals with which they returned to civil life.

Recognizing the value of a history of the Army chaplaincy both for the education of the Army and the information of the American public, the Chief of Chaplains initiated such a study early in the Great War. Several research workers compiled much valuable information in his office. After his retirement, the present writer was given the task of completing these investigations and writing a systematic narrative. In this task he has been greatly indebted to those who have done so much of the preliminary work and to many others who have helped him solve specific problems as they have appeared. He hopes that this study may contribute to an appreciation of intelligent faith among people of all creeds and to a strengthening of the forces which promote integrity and honor among members of the armed forces.

In general, citations of authorities for paragraphs are grouped together, though more than one reference number is used in some instances to avoid possible confusion. If the abbreviation *ibid.* is used after a group of citations, it refers only to the last. When successive paragraphs are derived from the same group of sources, that fact is indicated. Some important facts, especially those concerning the years 1941–48, are known to the author from his own observation. In many cases no documentary records exist. A number of factual paragraphs derived from sources of this nature appear without any citations. The author vouches for the accuracy of such facts. A few instances of contradictory records have been found. If a critical study failed to remove all doubt, that fact has been stated in the text. Some important sources have been colored by the strong partisan attitude of the writers. If such statements are quoted or summarized, it is to show how these persons viewed a situation at the time and does not imply an indorsement of these views.

Contents

Chapter		Page
I.	EARLY CONCEPTS	1
II.	IN COLONIAL DAYS	10
III.	THE SPIRIT OF 76	30
IV.	FROM CONCORD TO NEWBURGH	54
V.	FROM WASHINGTON TO LINCOLN	75
VI.	THE TRUMPET THAT SHALL NEVER CALL RETREAT	88
VII.	OF LAWS AND MEN	104
VIII.	SUMTER TO APPOMATTOX	126
IX.	GRANT TO PERSHING	152
X.	HOW CHAPLAINS WERE MADE IN 1918	170
XI.	CANTONMENT AND TRENCH	183
XII.	BETWEEN WORLD WARS	198
XIII.	NINE THOUSAND MEN	214
XIV.	ADMINISTRATIVE PROBLEMS	230
XV.	TRAINING FOR THE GREAT WAR	243
XVI.	EQUIPMENT AND SUPPLY	253
XVII.	PEARL HARBOR TO TOKYO BAY	271
XVIII.	COUNSELING AND WELFARE	295
XIX.	COLD WAR	307
XX.	KOREA	329
XXI.	ACHIEVEMENTS	337
	BIBLIOGRAPHY	345
	INDEXES	371

CHAPTER I

Early Concepts

Two facts must be recognized by the person who would understand the chaplaincy in the American Army. One is that the methods and immediate objectives of the chaplains reflected the religious convictions of their time and varied in some particulars from 1776 to 1861 and 1942. It is no less necessary to consider that the men of the Revolution, who fixed a general pattern for later years, were steeped in the Hebrew Scriptures and believed them a guide book for all times and places. They consciously imitated the acts of Moses or Samuel, expecting similar results to follow. A Massachusetts chaplain was selected by the precise method used in choosing Saul to be King of Israel, and a Connecticut captain changed his campaign plans at the behest of his chaplain as confidently as David had done the same on the advice of Abiather.[1] Many practices observed reverently by American chaplains grew directly out of the usages of the primitive church and of the prophets, priests, and judges of Israel.

Almost universal, and older than the writing of history, is the belief that superhuman forces are decisive in the outcome of battles. Among the earliest Hebrew stories is that of Melchizedek assuring Abram that his remarkable victory over the kings of the East was due to the intervention of Jehovah. Deborah and many others believed that God sent storms and in other ways discomfited the enemies of the Chosen People. Events like the defeat at Ai and the loss of the Ark by the sons of Eli raised a question about the divine favor being absolute and led to the realization that it was conditioned upon the righteousness of the nation and its rulers.[2]

Through the centuries this idea adapted itself to changing concepts of right and justice. The crusaders were so sure of their cause that they took their victories as a matter of course. Victories in other

---

[1] *Vide post*, Ch. II.
[2] Genesis 14:20; Judges 5; Joshua 7–8; I Samuel 4:4–11.

wars, especially of the few over the many, were accepted as vindicating the cause of the victors, and defeats could be rationalized in a way which saved the faith of the vanquished.   When the wind changed and froze the mud so that Washington could save his cannon the night of his march to Princeton, it was hailed as a special providence by many. The successive Confederate victories in 1862 left many Union chaplains sorely perplexed by the apparent triumph of the government which upheld slavery, and two years later their Southern brethren could not understand the desertion by Providence of a cause whose justice they held to be axiomatic.   Chaplains and other devout people felt that the American victories with slight losses in 1898 plainly showed the hand of Providence.   Abraham Lincoln stated this basic faith as strongly as he challenged a rival concept when he said that he was not so concerned that God should be on the side of the Union as that the Government should be on God's side of the struggle.[3]

Once the idea is accepted that God is likely to favor one side in a war, either permanently or at intervals, it becomes supremely important to know which side will be aided and the conditions under which this help may be expected.   If this belief includes the confidence that helpful information can be obtained through superhuman channels, there can be no doubt of the importance of the person who can obtain and interpret such revelations.   It may be that this function of the military chaplain was recognized even before others which were old before the Exodus.

Moses directed Joshua to inquire of the priest before starting military operations.   When the Danites planned to conquer their inheritance in the north, they consulted Micah's chaplain and were assured of success.   After a number of defeats in their punitive war against the Benjamites, the Hebrew leaders consulted Phinehas, their chaplain in an earlier expedition, and were promised the victory on the morrow.[4] Divination seems to have been a major function of Ahijah when he was in Saul's camp at Gibeah with religious equipment of special sanctity, and his inability to get a revelation was attributed to Jonathan's unconscious violation of Saul's vow.[5]   Several times while Abiathar was David's chaplain he obtained revelations of the future by means of an ephod.[6]   In the period of the Divided Kingdom there

---

[3] *Vide post*, Chs. VI, IX.
[4] Numbers 27:21; Judges 18:5–6; 20:27–28.
[5] I Samuel 14.
[6] I Samuel 23:6–14, 30:7–8.

are several instances of the outcome of military enterprises being fore-told, but these are uniformly the declarations of prophets speaking in the name of Jehovah, and these men do not seem to have accompa-nied the army as chaplains.[7]   Judas Maccabaeus not only led his sol-diers in prayer, but he frequently interpreted dreams which were understood to forecast the outcome of impending battle.[8]

Thucydides says that "soothsayers brought forth the usual vic-tims" on the eve of battle between Athenians and Spartans, and the implication is that they had accompanied the army in the field.[9] Among the early Romans the augurs determined such matters as the favorable time for military operations according to the occult lore of their profession.   These practices continued long after the educated Roman had lost all faith in their efficacy.   Diocletian forbade augury, and Constantius made it a capital offense.   The Eastern Empire in-cluded a similar prohibition in the Codex of Justinian.[10]

Though the cruder forms of divination might be repudiated or outlawed, humanity never has lost faith in the possibility of gaining reve-lations of the divine will.   Once that will was determined, it was easy to infer how Providence might be expected to operate.   Whether the prophet or apostle, priest or parson spoke by the inspiration of an inner light or by authority of his office, his dicta were received with great respect.   Often his method was to interpret an ancient writing or deci-sion and apply it to the present situation.   This enabled the chaplains of the Revolution and Civil War to preach convincingly on the certain triumph of their cause because of its essential justice as revealed by Scripture, and the same emphasis was not lacking in 1918.

A different but related concept also is older than recorded history. This is the belief that military and religious leaders can obtain super-human aid by proper observances.   These might be at the beginning of a campaign or battle or at a moment of crisis during the fight.   The story of the Hebrews being victorious while Moses held up his hands is well known.   During the journey through the wilderness Moses made two silver trumpets and placed them in the care of the priests. Besides other uses, it was directed that they be sounded on the eve of battle, with the positive assurance that this would bring the victory. When Moses sent a force against the Midianites, he sent Phinehas with

---

[7] II Samuel 5:23–25; I Kings 12:21–24, 20:13–15; 22:1–28; Jeremiah 42–43.
[8] II Maccabees 15.
[9] Thucydides—*The Peloponnesian War*, Book VI, Ch. XVIII, p. 377.
[10] *The New Oxford Classical Dictionary*, pp. 120, 292.

these trumpets and other religious equipment. This seems to make him the earliest military chaplain whose name has survived. Already this grandson of Aaron had been highly honored for his zeal and initiative. Many years later during a battle between the armies of Israel and Judah the latter found themselves ambushed and overwhelmingly outnumbered. At this moment their chaplains sounded the ancient trumpets. The men of the South responded with a great shout, and their Northern kinsmen fled.[11]

The march around Jericho with the Ark in the midst of the army was unusual, but sacrifices before battle "to entreat the favor of Jehovah" were common and were believed to bring storms and other calamities upon the enemy.[12] A similar faith seems to have been general among the peoples of antiquity. A good example of how it gained expression among the more enlightened Greeks is found in Thucydides' account of the sailing of the expedition to Sicily in 415 B. C.:

> The ships now being manned, and everything put on board with which they meant to sail, the trumpets commanded silence, and the prayers customary before putting out to sea were offered, not in each ship by itself, but by all together to the voice of a herald; and bowls of wine were mixed through all the armament, and libations made by the soldiers and their officers in gold and silver goblets. In their prayers joined also the crowds on the shore, the citizens and all others that wished them well. The hymns sung and the libations finished, they put out to sea.[13]

The Romans inherited a faith in which offerings to departed ancestors and other spirits were believed to retain their favor but do not seem to have developed special ceremonies for applying this to military needs. When the Fetiales decided that war should be declared upon some nation and gained the approval of the elders, they went to the frontier, threw a spear or pointed stake across the boundary, and recited this traditional prayer, though it asked for help in the war only by implication:

> Hear me, Jupiter and Quirinus, and all other gods. I call you to witness that this nation is unjust and does not practice righteousness, and our elders will consider by what means we may secure our dues.[14]

In the early middle ages some of these threads of tradition met and took on Christian forms. An anonymous Greek writer of about 583 has

---

[11] Exodus 17; Numbers 10:9, 25:13, 31:6; II Chronicles 13:12–15.
[12] I Samuel 7:7–11, 13:8–15.
[13] Thucydides, *loc. cit., ad fin.*
[14] *The New Oxford Classical Dictionary*, p. 361; Tenny Frank—*Roman Imperialism*, p. 8.

preserved a description of the army of Belisarius.   He mentions standards which were blessed and carried into battle and makes a revealing
statement about the influence of the ideal leader:

> Intelligence, calmness, prudence, severity without excess, tem-
> perance, all of these are indispensable; the art of war is identified
> with Wisdom.   But above all piety is necessary for the leader,
> which will bring the blessings of heaven upon the General.   Next
> to God, he is the soldier of Providence, terror of the unbelievers,
> grand priest of the army, whose prayers not less than his military
> science will merit the victory.[15]

This emphasis upon the piety of the leader and his prayers as a
guarantee of victory is significant.   So is another statement by this
writer:

> Finally come the chaplains.   They play an important role in
> the army where exercises of piety were so assiduously practiced.
> In the morning and the evening they chant the trisagion, "Holy God,
> Strong God, Immortal God", and in the moment of the combat to the
> cry of the combatants, *"Adjuva"*, the multitude cry out, *"Deus."*[16]

The story of St. Martin illustrates another phase of this belief.   It
is told that he divided his military cloak, giving a large piece to a beg-
gar and wearing the remainder as a cape.   This *capella* became a
famous relic and was taken on military enterprises for the benefit its
presence would confer.   Its custodian came to be called the *cappellanus,*
which became *chapellain* in Old French and *chaplain* in English.   The
place where the relic was kept and where religious rites were performed
was known as the *chapel.*   The French king's chaplain was made grand
almoner.   This title prevailed over the other, and in modern France
the military chaplain is known as the *aumonier.*[17]

Through the centuries a change in emphasis can be discerned in
the observances designed to gain success in war.   Waning faith in the
efficacy of sacrifices and libations, amulets and ceremonies left prayer
as the chief reliance of devout soldiers who hoped to obtain superhuman aid.   It might be associated with a time of fasting or with elaborate ritual or might be the simplest form of petition.   Washington
deprecated profanity, warning that the favor of Providence could not
be expected if the Divine Name were constantly dishonored; and
Lincoln emphasized this negative aspect of prayer.   Stonewall Jackson

---

[15] *The Strategicon,* quoted by Ferdinand Lot—*L'Art Militaire et Les Armees au moyen age en Europe
et dans les proche Orient,* I, 46.

[16] *Ibid.,* p. 49.

[17] Lot, *op. cit.,* pp. 80–82, quoting the *Gesta Dei Per Francos* of St. Gregory of Tours; *Encyclopedia Britannica,* 11th Ed., V, 852.

prayed earnestly on the eve of battle and invariably attributed the victory of the morrow to the blessings of Heaven.[18]   No function of the modern chaplain is more natural than prayers for victory according to the usages of his faith.

From earliest times the efficacy of prayer against the enemy has seemed as logical as supplications for victory.   When Balak hired Balaam to curse the Hebrews, both parties looked upon his words as a potent oracle, although he disappointed his employer.[19]   From early Britain come stories of chieftains employing a druid to curse their opponents, while the rival leader countered with the services of a Christian saint.   Solemn anathemas were powerful weapons when both armies believed in their potency.   This element can be distinguished in the prayers of some modern chaplains.   An uncompromisingly direct supplication is attributed to Samuel Dunbar, a chaplain in the French and Indian War.   When it was reported that a hostile fleet was about to attack Boston, he prayed that the Lord would "put a bit in their mouths and jerk them about, send a strong northeast gale and dash them in pieces on Cohasset Rock." [20]

Parallel with these concepts across the centuries has run the thought that chaplains could enhance the effectiveness of the troops by encouraging them, demonstrating the justice of their cause, and stimulating their patriotic loyalty.   When the code of Deuteronomy was written, it included what has been called the law of the chaplaincy in the Hebrew army.   While the emphasis is upon the continuing divine favor, the immediate purpose is the encouragement of the men:

> When thou goest out to battle against thine enemies, and seest horses and chariots and a people more than thou, be not afraid of them; for the Lord thy God is with thee, which brought thee up out of the land of Egypt.   And it shall be, when ye are come nigh unto the battle, that the priest shall approach and speak unto the people, and shall say unto them, Hear, O Israel, ye approach this day unto battle against your enemies: let not your hearts faint, fear not, and do not tremble, neither be ye terrified because of them; for the Lord your God is he that goeth with you, to fight for you against your enemies, to save you.[21]

A striking comment on the functions of chaplains appears in a letter of James Lainez, the Jesuit General, to Juan la Cerde, a Spanish officer leading an expedition against the Turks in North Africa.   The

---

[18] *Vide post*, Chs. IV, VII, IX.
[19] Numbers 22–24; Deuteronomy 23:3–6; Joshua 24:9–10.
[20] *Yale Biographies and Annals*, Ser. 2, 1745–63.
[21] Deuteronomy 20:1–4.

whole passage expresses the ideals and objectives of today.   It recognizes the fact, never forgotten since, that soldiers fight better when they are sure that their cause is morally right and when they are sustained by religious faith, and it stresses the duty of chaplains to promote both of these ends:

> I believe that our Lord will be very well served and your Excellency much consoled if you send some good religious along on this expedition, men who will be true servants of God and who will seek the salvation of souls.   By prayer and good example, by preaching and hearing confessions, by nursing the sick and helping the dying, these men will do a tremendous amount of good.   They will teach the soldiers proper motives for fighting, keep them from quarreling among themselves and will call them to task for blasphemies and gambling.   Finally, I know that the soldiers will profit from this, for by their peace of mind and confidence in God they will better fulfill their duties in war.[22]

The belief that it is inconsistent with their sacred office for chaplains to carry arms and use them against the enemy is very old.   Canon 2 of the Council of Ratisbon (Regensburg) in 742 relaxed a more sweeping prohibition only to the extent of allowing chaplains to accompany the army for strictly religious functions:

> We prohibit the servant of God in every way from bearing arms or fighting in the army or going against the enemy, except those alone who because of their sacred office, namely, for celebrating of mass and caring for the relics of the saints, have been designated for this office; that is to say, the leader may have with him one or two bishops with their priest chaplains, and each captain may have one priest, in order to hear the confessions of the men and impose upon them the proper penance.[23]

Feudalism brought some departures from this noncombatant rule. When lands were given to monasteries or other religious foundations, it became necessary for the abbots or bishops to assume their full responsibilities to their vassals.   Often this meant both religious and military leadership, and numbers of these suzerain-chaplains died with sword or axe in hand.   The rise of the military orders still further challenged the idea that a clergyman must not fight for the cause he supports with his prayers.   During the Civil War large numbers, both North and South, served as line officers or in the ranks, and several chaplains joined in the fighting.   Even in the Second World War the

---

[22] Josepn H. Fichter—*James Lainez, Jesuit*, p. 277.
[23] *Lexikon fur Theologie und Kirche*, "Militarseesorg"; Lot, *op. cit.; Cambridge Medieval History*, IV, "Capitularies."

military zeal of some chaplains was such that it was necessary to remind them that the rights established by the Geneva Convention belong to all chaplains and must not be endangered by the bellicose conduct of a few.[24]

Two ancient concepts have come to be so interwoven that they are
all but inseparable.   It is a truism that chaplains are in the Army to
serve God, but this purpose has become so fully identified with service
to humanity that the two are seldom distinguished.   This is true
whether a chaplain tries to strengthen the home church by enlisting
soldiers in its support or hopes to make them better citizens by teaching ideals of civic integrity.   It is still more true when his immediate
purpose is to promote the moral and spiritual life of individuals.   This
must remain his ultimate objective, but it coincides with lesser ends, for
it has been demonstrated repeatedly that better men make better
soldiers.

The Great Awakening of the period about 1740 had a lasting
effect upon the American church, and this affected the methods and
objectives of chaplains.   Intended to quicken the seriousness of those
whose faith had become perfunctory, it stimulated an evangelistic
movement which became more emotional than many of the leaders
wished.   Jonathan Edwards, the early leader of this movement, was
the son of one distinguished chaplain and the grandfather of another.
Benjamin Pomeroy, who was barred from his pulpit in Hebron, Connecticut, for 7 years because of his New Light convictions, was a chaplain in the French wars and again in the Revolution.   Undoubtedly
this movement prepared the way for the tremendous growth of the
evangelical churches, which dominated the chaplaincy of the Civil
War and made evangelism more than ever before the chaplain's first
responsibility.[25]

Out of the great immigration of the 1850's grew several factors
which brought changes of policy.   A large number of these people
were of the Roman Catholic faith.   Many of them located in the
eastern cities, with the result that certain regiments enrolled in these
localities for the Civil War contained a majority of Catholic men.
This made it imperative that they should have Catholic chaplains.
Others were attached to higher headquarters so that they might serve
the men of their faith in various units.[26]   This hastened recognition
of the fact that minority groups, especially those having distinctive

---

[24] *Vide post, passim.*
[25] William Warren Sweet—*The Story of Religions in America, passim.*
[26] D. P. Conyngham—*The Soldier of the Cross, passim.*

beliefs and practices, should be provided with their own forms of worship whenever possible. The "Three Major Faiths" have long been recognized, usually with the assumption that organized bodies in America which were neither Jewish nor Catholic could be classified as Protestant. By the time of the Second World War this concept was challenged by several other groups holding principles so different from those of the Three that identification with any of them seemed illogical and contradictory.

Another result of the immigration was the settlement in America of great numbers of devout people whose sincere belief about such matters as temperance and sabbath observance was materially different from the standards generally considered obligatory by great numbers of their new neighbors. Perplexity, if not mutual distrust, was apt to follow when soldiers of these faiths found themselves in a regiment with a chaplain of one of the stricter groups. His attack upon worldly indulgence seemed to them a pharisaical insistence upon trifling matters. Sometimes both points of view were modified.[27]

This rapid survey of three millenia of human thought and practice shows that both primitive and enlightened people have believed persistently that military events can be influenced by a superhuman power. They have employed the recognized experts and equipment of the time to reveal the future or gain the aid of higher powers. Gradually the former gave place to an interpretation of a present or former revelation of the divine will, which in turn was often accomplished by a demonstration of the justice of a cause. When moral and patriotic grounds for loyalty were seen to coincide, the chaplain aided the cause by exhorting the men to do their duty to God and country and by strengthening individual character, which is the ultimate basis of trustworthiness. Finally, recognition that moral and spiritual values transcend all others made their cultivation the chaplain's supreme task.

---

[27] Marcus Lee Hansen—*The Immigrant in American History*, pp. 107–25.

CHAPTER II

In Colonial Days

Transplanted to America with the earliest settlers, the chaplaincy made important adaptations to conditions in the New World before it reached a measure of standardization during the Revolution. Clergymen who accompanied some of these parties ministered to soldiers and civilians alike, whether they were employed by king, proprietor, or trading company. The advance of the frontier placed some chaplains in remote forts where they were expected to influence the Indians as well as serve the garrison. Further development brought the militia system under which a settled minister sometimes marched with the men of his parish as their chaplain. Long before the Revolution most provincial governments, especially those of New England, considered chaplains a necessary part of their defensive organization.

In the long story of Spanish conquest few names are worthy of higher honor than that of Bartolomé de Las Casas, who went to Cuba with Velasquez in 1511 and strove earnestly but with small success to restrain the cruelty of his associates. In striking contrast is Mendoza's defense of the excesses of Menendez. La Loutre and Rouband were primarily missionaries, but they exerted great political influence among the French and Indians and accompanied their war parties at times. When Champlain and De Monts led their Catholic and Protestant followers to Acadia, they brought clergymen of both faiths to minister to the settlers and their defenders. It is recorded that these spiritual leaders sometimes emphasized their theological differences with their fists. Robert Hunt was chaplain at Jamestown during the first year of the settlement. John Smith called him "an honest, religious, and courageous Divine; during whose life our factions were oft qualified, our wants and great extremities so comforted, that they seemed easie in comparison of what we endured after his memorable death." [1]

---

[1] *Encyclopedia Britannica*,"Las Casas"; Francis Parkman—*Pioneers of France in the New World*, pp. 120–22, 222–23, *Montcalm and Wolfe*, I, 493; George Bancroft—*History of the United States*, II, 589; *The Army Chaplain*, April 1931, p. 3.

The first dominies at New Amsterdam were not regarded as military chaplains, but their church stood inside the fort, and it was Megapolensis who dissuaded Stuyvesant from firing on the English fleet in 1664 and precipitating a hopeless battle. A generation later the English chaplain at Fort James seems to have been the only clergyman conducting Episcopal services on Manhattan Island.[2]

What appears to have been the first instance in the English colonies of settled civilian pastors being selected officially to serve as military chaplains in an emergency was in the spring of 1637. The Pequots roused the enmity of more peaceable tribes by seizing their hunting grounds east of the Thames, then turned against the English and killed several people in Wethersfield and other settlements. The magistrates of Connecticut immediately called the first general court of the infant colony, and on the first of May it was resolved "that there shalbe an offensive war agt the Pequoitt." A draft of 90 men was ordered from the 3 villages which composed the colony, and 9 days later this force sailed down the river in 3 boats with Captain John Mason in command and Samuel Stone of Hartford as chaplain and advisor to the leader. The chaplain was 35 years of age. A graduate of Emmanuel College, Cambridge, he had been suspended in the Established Church for nonconformity and came to America with Thomas Hooker.[3]

At the mouth of the river the expedition met Uncas and the friendly Mohegans. Mason's orders were to proceed to the Thames and attack overland, but the readiness of Uncas to help against the common enemy impressed him with the value of similar aid from the Narragansetts, and he proposed that the expedition get reinforcements from that tribe and attack the Pequots in the rear. As the officers opposed Mason's plan, the matter was referred to the chaplain. Stone spent the night in devotion and prayer and in the morning approved the captain's departure from his original instructions. The surprise and slaughter of the Indians followed. Mason declared, "We had sufficient light from the Word of God for our proceedings." What the chaplain thought of the merciless annihilation of the tribe is not known, but many saw the hand of Providence in the victory which followed the change of plan so prayerfully decided by him.[4]

---

[2] John Fiske—*Dutch and Quaker Colonies in America*, I, 183, 290; John R. Brodhead—*Documents Relating to the Colonial History of the State of New York*, III, 415.

[3] Charles M. Andrews—*The Colonial Period of American History*, II, 92–93; Harris E. Starr—"Two Early Chaplains," *The Army Chaplain*, January 1934.

[4] *Ibid.*

Returning to the Thames, the expedition found a force from Massachusetts with their chaplain, John Wilson, pastor of the First Church of Boston.   Fourteen years older than Stone, he had been in Boston for 7 years and had become a leading minister of the colony.   Though the son of a clergyman of the Established Church, he had been graduated from Kings College, Cambridge, and converted to Puritan principles.   William Hubbard called him "that holy man of God, . . . the chariots and horsemen of our Israel, by whose faith and prayer . . . the country was preserved, so it was confidently believed that no enemy should break in upon a place whilst he survived, which some have observed, accordingly came to pass." [5]

When Connecticut asked the help of her neighboring colonies against the Pequots, the request to Plymouth was sent so late that news of the victory came before her troops were ready to march.   So far as material needs were concerned, Massachusetts completed her preparations promptly.   As a chaplain was considered as necessary as a captain, the ministers chose two of their number who were deemed to be well qualified for this duty, then cast lots between them in a solemn invocation of Providence, and the lot fell upon Wilson.   When the force was mustered, it was found that some "were still under a Covenant of Works, and that the Blessing of God could not be implored or expected to crown the Arms of such unhallowed Men with Success."   When the "Unclean" were cast out, 160 men marched, with their chaplain now confident of success.   Like the Spartans at Marathon, they were true to their faith but arrived after the battle was over.   Another tradition concerns a Pequot who was carrying off an English maid in a canoe. The soldiers were afraid to fire lest they should injure the prisoner, but the chaplain cried, "God will direct the bullet".   If any doubted, they were reassured when the first shot killed the Indian and the girl escaped unharmed.   Both Stone and Wilson were given land for their services in the Indian war. [6]

In 1676 during Philip's War, Hope Atherton, minister at Hatfield, went as chaplain of Captain Turner's force which attacked an Indian camp near the falls of the Connecticut which bear the captain's name. Many of the natives were slain, and their forges and other equipment for making weapons and munitions were destroyed.   Before Turner could complete this task, he was attacked by strong parties from other camps.   The commander and one-fourth of his men were killed in the

---

[5] *Ibid;* William Hubbard—*Narrative of the Indian Wars in New England,* II, 19–20.
[6] *Ibid;* A. W. M'Clure—*Lives of John Wilson, John Norton, and John Davenport.*

retreat. The chaplain lost his horse, was separated from his comrades, and wandered in the forest for 3 days without food before he came in sight of the river and was able to find his way home.[7]

Few tales involving army chaplains have more romantic interest than the story of the expedition sent by Massachusetts against Quebec in 1690 under the command of her knighted ship-carpenter, Sir William Phips, fresh from the sack of Port Royal. An account of this enterprise was sent to Increase Mather, president of Harvard and colonial agent in England, by John Wise, one of the chaplains. He was the sturdy parson of Ipswich who had been fined, imprisoned, and deposed 3 years before for resisting the tyranny of Andros. His associate chaplains were John Emerson, of the distinguished family which gave numerous chaplains to the service in later emergencies; Grindall Rawson, student of Indian languages; and John Hale, who later acquiesced in the witchcraft prosecution until his own wife was accused, when he recognized the folly of the movement and preached and wrote to show it in its true light. They were chosen for this duty by the General Court, the deputies and magistrates voting separately.[8]

Phips was commissioned general in command of troops and ships by Simon Bradstreet, Massachusetts' 87-year-old governor, and John Wally was made lieutenant general. In his instructions to Phips the governor directed him to show due respect and kindness to the reverend and worthy divines who were to go with the expedition and to be guided by the advice of his council, which would consist of the lieutenant general, the majors of regiments, the chaplains, and the captains of ships and companies. Another admonition of the venerable governor was: "Let all cursing, swearing, drunkenness debauchery and all manner of Prophaneness be Suppressed and duly punished," and his closing words were, "and in all let your Reliance and dependance be on the Wisdome Conduct and Arme of the Lord of Hosts, with whom alone it is to give Success." [9]

The Force, consisting of about 2,500 soldiers and seamen in 32 vessels, sailed from Hull on 9 August and anchored before "Kebecque" on 6 October. Explaining why the attack failed, Wise said that there was some truth in the reasons alleged: the lack of provisions, ammunition, and time. Landing below the Charles River with many barriers

---

[7] James Russell Trumbull—*History of Northampton,* I, 325–36; John Gorham Palfrey—*History of New England,* III, 193–95.

[8] John Fiske—*The Beginnings of New England,* p. 271; John Wise—*Two Narratives of an Expedition Against Quebec, A. D. 1690,* pp. 20–21; William B. Sprague—*Annals of the American Pulpit,* I, 168; Benjamin K. Emerson—*The Ipswich Emersons,* p. 64.

[9] Wise, *op. cit.,* pp. 20–21.

between them and the town he deemed a serious blunder, but the town could have been taken without serious difficulties but for the cowardice of certain officers, especially the lieutenant general. Wise went with the landing party led by Wally. Feeble French resistance was quickly overcome, and the chaplain urged the men not to pursue fugitives into the forest but to advance against the town. Finding the lieutenant general with some difficulty, Wise urged an attack while the men were still warm with such vehemence that they were sent as far as the river; but Wally would not cross, although there was no visible opposition.[10]

The night was spent in "padling and fooling," and nothing was done in the morning, though the disgusted chaplain said that the town could have been taken if the men had been allowed to sleep during the night and had been given a biscuit and a good round dram. A small party of French attacked but were driven away while the lieutenant general and chaplain were on the flagship for a conference with Phips. This unnerved Wally still more and made him fear a night attack, but Wise pointed out the security of their position and strength of their field artillery, exclaiming, "Let them come! We will fight with all Canada if they come." At a council of war he urged that the North Town be occupied at once so that the men could have shelter and that supplies be drawn from the Isle of Orleans and the attack pressed with vigor. The junior officers approved, but the lieutenant general and majors insisted that the men must be reembarked at once. Though there was no sign of danger and the men were sleeping comfortably in barns and haystacks, Wally called them out an hour before midnight and left them on the cold sand of the river bank till morning. Then they were sent to the ships, Wally saying that the guns must be left to save the men and striking over the head some men who tried to bring them to the boats, although there was still no sign of the enemy. The stalwart chaplain made no comment upon the conduct of the enterprise by Phips, though it was not above criticism; but he declared that Wally's cowardly incompetence, culminating in the needless abandonment of five cannon, was worthy of death.[11]

The ships were back in Boston on 19 November. It is probable that the trepedation of the lieutenant general subsided more quickly than the wrath of the bellicose chaplain, who wrote his evaluation of

---

[10] *Ibid.*, pp. 4–18.
[11] *Ibid.*

the second in command on 23 December.   After his death 35 years later, an unknown writer made this comment upon his service at Quebec: "Not only the Pious Discharge of his Sacred Office, but his Heroick Spirit, and Martial Skill and Wisdom did greatly distinguish him".   Forty-six years after his military service the Massachusetts legislature voted 300 acres of unappropriated land to his family.[12]

Not only were chaplains considered necessary for major enterprises, but they frequently accompanied small parties or were stationed at isolated posts in time of nominal peace.   On 27 June 1702, Massachusetts appropriated 20 pounds toward the support of a chaplain at Brookfield, a garrisoned place which was being resettled after devastation by the Indians but was unable to support itself without help. Joseph Smith served for 3 years under this arrangement.   In 1711 Timothy Edwards was chosen by the Connecticut legislature as one of the chaplains of a force starting for Canada.   He became sick at Saratoga on the upper Hudson and was taken as far as Stillwater by boat. From there he was conveyed to Albany on a bed in a wagon.   As the campaign soon was abandoned, he was able to return to his home. What is now Concord, N. H., was established as a Massachusetts town in 1726 and called Penny-Cook Plantation.   Enoch Coffin, one of the proprietors, went with the pioneers as their chaplain.[13]

The story of Queen Anne's Chapel at Fort Hunter, New York, illustrates the association of other functions with those of the military chaplaincy.   As early as 1702 the Society for the Propagation of the Gospel in Foreign Parts sponsored a clergyman of the Church of England as a missionary to the Mohawks.   After two others had met with scant success, Thomas Barclay, chaplain of the fort at Albany, was assigned to this work in 1708.   For 4 years he performed his duties at the mission, once a month conducting Episcopal services in the Dutch church at Schenectady, 24 miles to the east, and frequently preaching in Dutch to the Episcopalians of Albany, 17 miles beyond.   Some accounts of his work during this period imply that he kept his residence in Albany, making periodic trips westward for his ministrations in Schenectady and among the Mohawks.   The fact that he acted as pastor of an Episcopal congregation which met in the Lutheran chapel in Albany after 1709 gives some support to this supposition.   On the other

---

[12] *Ibid.*, p. 39 and Introduction.

[13] Josiah Howard Temple—*History of North Brookfield, Massachusetts*, p. 159; Sprague, *op. cit.*, I, 230; Arthur C. McGiffert—*Jonathan Edwards*, p. 3; John C. Thorne—*Granite State Monthly*, n. d.

hand, it seems doubtful if the missionary society which sponsored his work would have been satisfied with a permanent residence so far from the Mohawk villages.[14]

In 1708 Peter Schuyler conducted a party of Mohawk chiefs to London and presented them to the Queen. She promised to comply with their request that she build them a fort and chapel. Soon afterwards Governor Hunter arrived in New York under orders to carry out this promise. The palisaded fort built in 1712 at the confluence of Schoharie Creek with the Mohawk was named in his honor. At various times until the Revolution, this post was garrisoned by English troops. Even as an Indian fort it was a link in the British defensive chain, as it guarded the most direct route by which the friendly Mohawks could be attacked from Canada. The stone chapel inside the palisades, built as a part of the original contract, was 24 feet square. The Queen sent altar linens, Bibles and prayer books, and a silver communion service. When the Mohawks abandoned the valley early in the Revolution, they buried most of these articles. Ten years later, they recovered the silver and took it to their new home in Ontario, where it has been preserved as a priceless heirloom. About 1820 the chapel was demolished in the construction of the Erie Canal.[15]

Among those who followed Barclay in his missionary-chaplain-pastor office was John Ogilvie, who interrupted his 15 years at Fort Hunter in 1758 to serve in the field as chaplain of the Royal American Regiment and whose ministrations were welcomed not only by the men of that unit but by the large body of Indians who accompanied the British army.[16]

At times the unusual status of some of these clergymen occasioned no little perplexity to the provincial governors, but few stories equal that which the Earl of Bellomont, Governor of New York, wrote to the Secretary of the Board of Trade on 19 October 1700. He had dismissed Symon Smith, chaplain at New York, for what he considered unmitigated roguery, but the impudent chaplain had challenged his authority to remove him. During his absence, wrote the governor, the chaplain had induced the lieutenant governor to sign a marriage license bearing the name of Adam Ball. Later he changed the last name to Baldridge and married this notorious pirate to a woman who had been married previously to another pirate by a New Jersey

---

[14] Sprague, *op. cit.*, V, 91.
[15] W. Max Reid—*The Mohawk Valley*, pp. 78–97.
[16] Sprague, *op. cit.*, V, 134–35.

justice of the peace. Further difficulties for the poor governor grew out of the abortive attempt to establish an independent American Episcopate at this time, as the English minister at New York refused to recognize his authority in certain matters until specific orders were received from London. He urged the selection of ministers who would not be a scandal to the church, English rather than Scotch, and friendly to the present royal house. He had been informed that an allowance of 80 pounds each for five missionaries to the Iroquois was being considered on condition that Harvard men be chosen. He much preferred ministers of the Church of England because those of New England "pray ex tempore and mightily decry set forms of prayers insomuch that they never use the Lord's Prayer." [17]

In 1690 King William found that there would be a small surplus in the military funds of New York because of the disparity between the values of Sterling and provincial money. He directed Governor Sloughter to appoint a chaplain for the two military companies recently organized and to pay him 6 shillings 8 pence a day from these surplus funds. The daily pay of the "chirurgeon" was fixed at 2 shillings 6 pence. Nine years later Governor Bellomont forwarded to the Board of Trade a petition from the chaplain and officers of the four companies at Albany, asking to be relieved from the 30 percent discount on colonial money, which "grevious burthen," said the Earl, " . . . hath been all this while a great discouragement to the service in this scarce country, where all things both for the belly and back are very near treble the rates they are in England." Eight months later he wrote that the men were deserting and that he feared the officers soon must do the same or starve, as the pay office had used them so barbarously. It had been necessary for him to lend 20 pounds each to the chaplain and lieutenants, which had put him more than 400 pounds in debt.[18]

In 1725 Captain Henry Dwight was in command of Fort Dummer, situated in what is now southeastern Vermont but maintained by Massachusetts at that time. Soon after taking command he wrote, "We shall lead a heathenish life unless a chaplain be allowed." This request led to the appointment of Daniel Dwight, who served for 2 years at a salary of 100 pounds. In 1756 the general court fixed the monthly pay of chaplains at 6 pounds 8 shillings, Massachusetts currency, which was 1 pound more than the pay of a captain and half that of a colonel. Samuel West was paid 4 pounds a month, with

---

[17] Brodhead, *op. cit.*, IV, 766.
[18] *Ibid.*, pp. 377, 522.

rations, in 1761–62 while on duty at Fort Pownal on the Penobscot. New Hampshire gave land to Samuel Langdon for his share in the expedition of 1745 and to Henry True for his services in 1759 and 1762.[19]

It would be interesting to know the terms under which Jonathan Frye, a young man just graduated from Harvard, joined Lovewell's third expedition against the Abenakis in 1725. About 300 settlers had been killed on the frontier by these allies of the French at a time when England and France were at peace. Regarding the savages as predatory beasts to be exterminated, Massachusetts paid a bounty for Indian scalps. Doubtless the chaplain shared this view, and his appointment may have been only Lovewell's invitation to share the fortunes of the party.[20]

Marching from that part of Nashua which is still called The Harbor from its being the site of Lovewell's fortified house, the company reached a lake in western Maine near the town which bears the chaplain's name. Morning prayers were interrupted by a shot, and an Indian was seen on the shore. Though they feared he might be a decoy, the English pressed forward and soon were surrounded by a large force under Chief Paugus. In the long battle Lovewell and a third of his men were slain, and more than half of the others were wounded. One of these was the chaplain, who soon found that he could not keep up with the others on their night retreat and insisted that they leave him in the forest. He sent an affectionate message to his father, but nothing more was ever heard of him.[21]

The Indians themselves suffered heavy losses, and this battle did much to end their depredations on the New England frontier. The relief of the English found expression in a number of ballads which were popular for many years. At the centennial celebration of this battle a poem which he had written for the occasion was read by Congressman Enoch Lincoln, soon afterward governor of Maine. One of the earlier ballads included the following lines:

> Our worthy Captain Lovewell among them there did die;
> They killed Lieutenant Robbins, and wounded good young Frye,
> Who was our English chaplain; he many Indians slew,
> And some of them he scalpéd, when bullets round him flew.[22]

---

[19] Trumbull, *op. cit.*, pp. 21, 605; Parkman—*Montcalm and Wolfe*, I, 386; Sprague, *op. cit.*, VIII, 51; *Dictionary of American Biography*, X, 588; Harriet Eliza Noyes—*A Memorial History of the Town of Hampstead, New Hampshire*, p. 322.

[20] Everett S. Stackpole—*History of New Hampshire*, I, 259; Palfrey, *op. cit.*, IV, 441–44; Lewis Clinton Hatch, Ed.—*Maine; A History*, I, 189–90; Fiske—*New France and New England*, pp. 233–48.

[21] Same as 20.

[22] *Ibid.*

The story of Stephen Williams, pastor at Longmeadow, Massachusetts, for 36 years, illustrates vividly the shadow of Indian warfare
that hung over the northern frontier for a century after it had ceased
to be an internal problem.   In the winter of 1704 when he was nearly
11 years of age, his home at Deerfield was destroyed and, with his parents and their family, he was carried into captivity by Indians from
Canada.   His mother could not keep up with their captors and was
slain.   He was separated from the others and did not see his father for
14 months.   An exchange of prisoners brought him back to Massachusetts after 21 months.   A factual account of his return has been published both with a similar narrative by his father and separately.[23]

In 1745 he served as a chaplain at Louisbourg but lay ill for many
weeks in Boston on his way home.   Ten years later he was chaplain
of the regiment commanded by his kinsman, Colonel Ephraim Williams, whose legacy founded Williams College.   The day before the
colonel's death in the battle of Lake George the chaplain preached from
the text, "Which remain among the graves and lodge in the mountains"—Isaiah 65:4.   It is said that his long Calvinistic sermon to the
Indians about this time sorely taxed the resourcefulness of the interpreter who was to turn it into Mohawk.   The next year he was chaplain
of a regiment commanded by Dr. Thomas Williams, but ill health
forced him to leave the army before the end of the campaign.   On 21
April 1775, at the age of 82, we find him praying with the troops who
were about to march for Boston; and at a public fast 3 weeks later he
was humiliated because he fell asleep during the sermon of his guest
preacher.[24]

John Norton's adventures in 1746 are quite similar to those of
Stephen Williams 40 years before.   First minister of the church at
Bernardston, he was made chaplain to the forts on the Massachusetts
frontier in 1745 with headquarters at Shirley.   In August of the next
year he went to Fort Massachusetts, near Williamstown, intending to
spend a month at that post.   The next day the fort was surrounded
by several hundred French and Indians.   Besides the chaplain, the
fort contained a sergeant, 20 men, 3 women, and 5 children, and more
than half of the men were sick.   By the second day one man had
been killed and two wounded, and there remained only four bullets
for each soldier.   The chaplain had been firing buckshot and con-

---

[23] George Sheldon, Ed.—*What Befell Stephen Williams in His Captivity;* John Williams—*The
Redeemed Captive Returning to Zion.*
[24] Sprague, *op. cit.,* I, 285; Parkman—*Montcalm and Wolfe,* I, 295; Ellen Chase—*Beginning of
the American Revolution,* III, 290–92.

cluded that his efforts had not been futile when the French complained of the use of such unmilitary munitions. To avoid the massacre which usually followed an Indian assault, the sergeant determined to surrender, though the chaplain was one of those who "would willingly have stood it out to the last." The French officers were very considerate of their prisoners. The sergeant and chaplain were treated as guests by the two officers next in rank to the general. Those unable to walk were carried on litters, including the little girl born soon after the march began and christened "Captivity" by the chaplain. He saw a number of his fellow prisoners die during their winter in Canada, but he was exchanged about a year after his capture. He left an account of his experiences called *The Redeemed Captive*.[25]

The struggle often called King George's War had a significance out of proportion to its military results. It quickened the rivalries which brought the decisive contest with France a few years later and demonstrated what provincials could do by their own resources. Similarly, it gave a group of chaplains the experience of association in a daring enterprise, the Louisbourg campaign, and seems to have introduced some degree of supervision by one of their number. Samuel Moody of York (Maine) is called the chief of chaplains of this expedition by a careful modern writer. He was a near neighbor of Sir William Pepperell, the commanding general, and it may well be that his influence over the activities of his colleagues was little more than an easier access to their commander.[26]

Of the 10 chaplains known to have served in this war, at least 7, and probably 9, went to Louisbourg. They were described as a "goodly company of preachers." Simon Backus served the large Connecticut regiment until his death at Louisbourg in May 1746. Samuel Langdon, later president of Harvard, went with the men of New Hampshire. Moses Coffin doubled as a drummer and was called "the drum ecclesiastic." His life was saved when a pocket Bible stopped a bullet. Joseph Hawley served the artillerymen, still under a slight shadow of distrust on moral grounds from the early times when the use of gunpowder was considered akin to witchcraft. After the surrender Moody demolished the images and altar in the French church with an axe, no doubt believing that he was following the example of Gideon in a protest against idolatry. It may be that

---

[25] Arthur L. Perry—*Origins in Williamstown*, pp. 124–42.

[26] Fairfax Downey—"Yankee Gunners at Louisbourg," *American Heritage*, February 1955, p. 54.

his zeal was quickened by the failure to find what he would have considered the legitimate spoils of war. A silver cross was taken home and presented to Harvard College, but the chaplains seem to have returned empty handed. Apparently it was considered proper that the chaplain of a victorious force should appropriate captured religious articles. When Fort Frontenac surrendered to Colonel John Bradstreet in 1758, he authorized the chaplain to take the ornaments and sacred vessels of the chapel. Soon after the triumphal return from Louisbourg Joseph Emerson accepted a call to a church in a new community thirty-odd miles from Boston and induced his neighbors to name their town for the victorious general under whom his father and grandfather served as chaplains.[27]

The war of 1755–63 made little change in the status of chaplains. In general they were assigned to regiments, but in some instances to forts where they remained although the personnel of the garrison might change. Appointment was normally by the governor of the province which raised the troops or where the fort was situated. Thomas Barton, missionary to the Episcopal congregations recently organized in Huntington, Carlisle, and York, Pennsylvania, frequently led his parishioners to defend the settlements from Indian attacks during the 3 years following the defeat of Braddock. When Forbes marched against Fort Duquesne in 1758, the young men offered to join the army if their pastor would go with them. The general concurred in the proposal that he serve as their chaplain, but the actual appointment may have come from the governor, who was colonel-in-chief of the regiment to which the chaplain was assigned.[28]

Daniel Emerson kept a journal of his experiences in the summer of 1755 which gives a revealing picture of camp life and the perplexities of chaplain duty at that time. He was a distant kinsman as well as the son-in-law of the Chaplain Emerson who had served at Louisbourg 20 years before and thus belonged to the distinguished family which gave New England several chaplains and many clergymen in successive generations. His biographer states that he was considered the ranking officer of his regiment because of his family coat of arms bearing three lions. He had been called to the church in Hollis, New Hampshire, 12 years earlier just at the time when that frontier community was separated from Massachusetts by the survey of the colonial

---

[27] *Ibid.*, pp. 54, 113; William W. Backus, *A Genealogical Memoir of the Backus Family*, p. 121; Sprague, *op. cit.*, I, 243; Brodhead, *op. cit.*, X, 825; *Journal of American History*, III, 119.

[28] Sprague, *op. cit.*, V, 169.

boundary. A New Light in theology, he set a high value upon education and at one time conducted a school attended by a son of Governor Wentworth. Before the Revolution he helped to send 12 boys to college from his little town. Like many Emersons, he was a Harvard graduate. For a time he was chaplain of Rogers' Rangers, but most of his service was with a regiment raised near his home. Three years later he served another summer with the army.[29]

The journal begins on 9 July when he left home, committed to God in prayer "in which Br. Emerson was greatly enlarged". This may refer to his brother-in-law and neighbor, the younger Joseph. Traveling north along the Merrimac, he joined his regiment beyond Concord on the fourth day. He had preached with "great enlargement" in two villages on his way but had little when first he prayed with the regiment. This led him to yearn to "be delivered from the fear of men which brings a snare." The next day he saw the need for more wisdom, zeal, and courage than in any position in which he ever had been placed. Though he did not mind sleeping on the ground after 2 days, he soon was down with fever and ague. The colonel took his place at evening prayers and urged the chaplain to sleep on his couch. Three days later he rose early and "endeavored to pour out my soul in secret, tho' 'tis difficult to get alone with God." Orders came for him to join the army at Albany, and he left camp on 21 July with leave to spend some days at home. In a village along the way he preached with great enlargement and became very warm. He attributed the great cold he took, to riding in this condition that evening. As he thought his "clay tabernakle was bowing toward the earth," he prayed that he might be prepared for death. Notwithstanding this gloomy outlook, he was able to traverse the 40 miles to his home the next day.[30]

Refreshed in mind and body after a week at home, he set out for Albany. His route crossed New Hampshire to the Connecticut Valley, which he followed far to the south, skirting the wilderness of western Massachusetts and reaching the Hudson at Kinderhook. Two weeks after leaving home, he was in Albany, having traveled about 200 miles between points little more than half that distance apart. Everywhere he was hospitably received, spending only one night in the forest but catching a severe cold at that time. He was enlarged preaching in a crowded stockade on the New Hampshire frontier,

---

[29] Emerson, *op. cit.*, pp. 83–91.
[30] *Ibid.*

though he felt deep pity for the unfortunate people who had fled there from an expected Indian attack.[31]

From Albany he hastened northward to join his regiment. He prayed with the troops several times daily, as they were camped on both sides of the river, and preached against profanity with great plainness but meagre results. He became sick as well as discouraged, but was treated with great kindness by Colonel Schuyler. Early in September the troops moved to the north. At Stillwater the chaplain killed two waterfowl, which gave him a supper worthy of record. He reached Fort Lyman late on the seventh, and the journal ends abruptly with a brief note of the alarm caused the next morning by the booming of Johnson's cannon at Lake George. It is recorded that it was the chaplain's custom at regimental inspections to hold up his Bible as his only weapon. He served his church at Hollis for more than half a century, but in the 78th year of his age his granddaughter's husband was associated with him in the pastorate.[32]

For nearly 2 years George Washington tried vainly to obtain a chaplain for the troops under his command on the Virginia frontier. On 23 September 1756 he wrote to Governor Dinwiddie an account of the drunkenness and demoralization of the troops and added:

> The want of a chaplain does, I humbly conceive, reflect dishonor upon the regiment, as all other officers are allowed. The gentlemen of the corps are sensible of this, and did propose to support one at their private expense. But I think it would have a more graceful appearance were he appointed as others are.[33]

Apparently services for the troops were conducted regularly, notwithstanding the lack of a regular chaplain, for the next day the youthful commander ordered that they be paraded at ten the following Sunday and marched as usual to the fort to attend divine services. Six weeks later he assured the governor that a person of merit could be obtained by the officers if the government would grant a subsistence, "as it is highly necessary we should be reformed from those crimes and enormities we are so universally accused of." The same day he explained to John Robinson, Speaker of the House of Burgesses and Treasurer of Virginia, that the troops were debauched and made unfit for duty by the number of tippling houses in Winchester and that "a chaplain for the Regiment ought to be provided, that we may at least have the show if we are said to want the substance of Godli-

---

[31] *Ibid.*
[32] *Ibid.*
[33] *Writings of George Washington*, Bicentennial Ed., I, 470.

ness!"   The governor replied with a touch of irritation that Washington had not even named the person he wished to be appointed though he should know that a statement of his qualifications and the bishop's letter of license must be submitted to the commissary and to himself before any action could be taken.   Washington explained that he had no individual in mind but had thought there would be no offense in his suggestion.   The next spring he reiterated more strongly his request that "a gentleman of sober, serious and religious deportment be chosen for this important trust," but without success.[34]

A year later Dinwiddie was gone, and the resolute colonel reminded John Blair, President of the Council and acting governor, that the assembly had provided for a chaplain, stated his expectation that "a sober, serious man" would be appointed, and concluded with a touch of irony.   "Common decency, Sir, in a camp calls for the services of a divine, and which ought not to be dispensed with, altho' the world should be so uncharitable as to think us void of religion and incapable of good instructions."[35]

Thus, at the age of 24, George Washington demonstrated the respect for religion and confidence in its salutary influence among soldiers which led him to support the efforts of the chaplains throughout the Revolution with the full weight of his authority and prestige. Seven weeks before his death he wrote to General Morgan and to the Secretary of War supporting the appointment of a chaplain for the troops to be stationed at Harper's Ferry.[36]

Abercromby's chaplains at Lake George gave a fine example of the fraternal spirit which usually exists among chaplains of various faiths.   Episcopalians, Presbyterians, and Congregationalists held prayer meetings together twice a week.   John Cleaveland left a diary in which he tells of a call he and eight other chaplains made upon the General.   They were received very cordially and urged to teach the men to do their duty and be courageous.   Abercromby told an anecdote of a chaplain he had known in Germany who told the men just as the battle was about to begin that he had time to say only, "Be courageous; for no cowards go to heaven."   When Cleaveland and his abler colleagues preached, regulars as well as provincials came to hear. It would be interesting to know how Chaplain Newell in this situation applied the text, "Love your enemies."   Caleb Rea, a young surgeon

---

[34] *Ibid.*, I, 473, 498 and Note, 505, 510, II, 33, 56.
[35] *Ibid.*, II, 178.
[36] *Ibid.*, XXXVII, 406, 413.

in Cleaveland's unit, organized a regimental chorus, which contributed greatly to the chaplain's services. The pious surgeon was much grieved by the profanity of the soldiers, especially of the regulars, and believed it was the reason for the defeat at Ticonderoga. Three years earlier Colonel Williams had feared a similar result from the prevalent wickedness, especially of the New York and Rhode Island troops. A typical chaplain's program during this campaign included sermons twice a week, morning and evening prayers each day, and frequent psalm-singing in the intervals of military drill.[37]

Three chaplains on duty at Fort Edward in 1758 are striking examples of the varieties of personality found in this service. John Graham, the gloomy minister of Suffield, Connecticut, reached the fort after a period of illness at Albany. He soon concluded that there was little a chaplain could do and that the office was held in contempt by many. Breakfasting with General Lyman, he was grieved because no blessing was asked. Still more wicked seemed the conduct of the general and his chief officers who sat in his tent drinking punch and disturbing the worshipers at evening prayers by their conversation and laughter. Though the general never used it himself, he did not rebuke profanity in his presence. In such a situation, the despairing chaplain could but exclaim, "Lord, make me know my duty and what I ought to do!"[38]

William Crawford of Worcester failed to bring money with him and complained loudly of neglect and privation. Inadvertently he preserved for us in a letter to a member of the General Court nearly all we know about a brother chaplain—"As for Mr. Weld, he is easy and silent whatever treatment he meets with, and I suppose they thought to find me the same easy and ductile person; but may the wide yawning earth devour me first!" Colonel Frye mentions the forlorn state in which Weld reached the camp. Crawford, somewhat more fortunate, was decently clothed but did not have even a blanket until the colonel lent him one and got a captain to take him into his tent. Usually a chaplain had his own tent or shared that of the colonel. Whether Chaplain Weld's amiability was a more wholesome influence than the demanding self-assertion of Crawford or the desponding melancholy of Graham must be left to inference, for on this point the records are silent. The irreligion which troubled these chaplains existed in spite of General Winslow's order against "Curseing and

---

[37] Parkman—*Montcalm and Wolfe,* I, 292, 296, II, 116–17.
[38] *Ibid.,* I, 402–05.

swareing" and that requiring attendance at daily prayers and, "in a decent manner, clean and shaved," at the two Sunday sermons.[39]

Benjamin Franklin has preserved a delightful anecdote of Charles Beatty, chaplain of the force led by Franklin to guard the northwest frontier of Pennsylvania after the defeat of Braddock:

> We had for our chaplain a zealous Presbyterian minister, Mr. Beatty, who complained to me that the men did not generally attend his prayers and exhortations.   When they enlisted, they were promised, besides pay and provisions, a gill of rum a day, which was punctually serv'd out to them, half in the morning, and the other half in the evening; and I observ'd they were as punctual in attending to receive it; upon which I said to Mr. Beatty, "It is, perhaps, below the dignity of your profession to act as steward of the rum, but if you were to deal it out and only just after prayers, you would have them all about you."   He liked the tho't, undertook the office, and, with the help of a few hands to measure out the liquor, executed it to satisfaction, and never were prayers more generally and punctually attended; so that I thought this method preferable to the punishment inflicted by some military laws for non-attendance on divine service.[40]

Chaplain Beatty had been very active in raising forces to repel the Indian attacks of 1755.   He served for several years with Pennsylvania troops, but it is not recorded that he received from other commanders such practical support in promoting attendance at his religious ministration.[41]

In a few instances chaplains acted as company commanders or led frontier parties in defense or attack, but this never seems to have been on account of their status as chaplains.   The nearest approach to such service which has been found is the assignment of Eli Forbes and John Brainard at the end of the 1759 campaign to conduct 400 invalids to Albany in the dual capacity of chaplains and officers. Because this duty was tedious and expensive, Forbes received special compensation from the General Court of Massachusetts.[42]

Very little is known of the British chaplains and their activities. If no better provision was made for them than during the Revolution, several of the new regiments came to America without any.   In 1768 William Smith of Philadelphia was appointed chaplain pro tempore of the Royal Regiment of Ireland by Colonel Wilkins and seems to have ministered to that unit until it left the city later in that year.

---

[39] *Ibid.*

[40] Sprague, *op. cit.*, III, 121; *Benjamin Franklin's Autobiography*, pp. 215–16.

[41] Sprague, *op. cit.*, III, 121.

[42] John J. Babson—*History of the Town of Gloucester, Cape Ann*, p. 403.

Presumably this was because the regiment had no regular chaplain. Thomas Brown, apparently a deacon who came to America as a chaplain, served with his regiment in 1762. Later he took priestly orders and was rector of St. Peter's, Albany, and of a church in Maryland.[43]

The presence of chaplains with the French forces was not without influence upon those who ministered to their foes. Because of the predominance of the Roman Catholic faith in France and Canada, all were priests of that church. Many post and unit chaplains do not seem to have gone beyond their normal religious functions, but it was firmly believed in New England and other colonies that the missionary priests among the Indians incited them to attack the English settlements in times of peace as well as of war. This belief accounts for the bitterness against Father Rale which led to his death at Norridgewock in 1724. Much the same hostility was felt toward Father Picquet, who established a mission in northern New York. He organized several war parties and accompanied French and Indian forces in a number of attacks upon English posts. Thus he may be considered a chaplain, though this was incidental to his basic enterprise of bringing the Iroquois under his religious influence and attaching them to the political and military interests of France. The remark that he was worth 10 regiments, attributed to the Marquis du Quesne, is an index of his success.[44]

This close association of religious and political ends had the unfortunate result of injecting into religious differences the antipathies engendered by war, a situation in which few people are capable of regarding their enemies with dispassionate justice. The Thanksgiving sermon preached at Brookfield at the end of the war by Eli Forbes, a chaplain in 1759 and again during the Revolution, is typical of the thought of many colonial parsons, though it is easy to see meanings in some of his florid phrases which the chaplain may not have intended:

> God has given us to sing this day the downfall of New France, the North American Babylon, New England's rival . . . . We had to lament the fall of the valiant and good General Wolfe, whose death demands a tear from every British eye, a sigh from every Protestant heart . . . . He [Amherst] transplants British liberty to where till now it was unknown. He acts the General, the Briton, the Conqueror, and the Christian. What fair hopes arise from the peaceful and undisturbed enjoyment of this good land, and the blessings of our gracious God with it! Methinks I see towns enlarged, settlements increased, and this howling wilderness become a fruitful

---

[43] Sprague, *op. cit.,* V, 161, 135, Note.

[44] Stackpole, *op. cit.,* I, 257; Parkman—*Conspiracy of Pontiac,* I, 56; *Montcalm and Wolfe, passim;* Phileas S. Garand—*History of the City of Ogdensburg,* p. 65.

field which the Lord hath blessed; and to complete the scene, I see churches rise and flourish in every Christian grace where has been the seat of Satan and Indian idolatry.[45]

A number of incidents from this period illustrate the continuity in spirit and devotion which has characterized the chaplaincy during the years. In 1757 Jonathan French was disabled by illness and discharged. When he recovered his health, he reenlisted, was stationed at Castle William near Boston, and soon was made a sergeant. As he was ambitious to become a minister, the chaplains at the fort helped him in his preparation for college. Ten years later he was on duty at the same post as a chaplain. During the war Chaplain Kirkpatrick passed through the Iroquois country with his regiment and was impressed with the character and potentialities of the Six Nations. Largely through his influence Samuel Kirkland undertook his mission to the eastern tribes. During the Revolution Kirkland kept the Oneidas and Tuscaroras friendly and served as chaplain to the American forces.[46]

Still more striking is the story of John Steel, an Irish Presbyterian of Mercersburg and Carlisle, Pennsylvania. In 1752 he led his people to repel an Indian attack and showed such ability that he was commissioned a captain in the militia. This appointment, which he held for 21 years, did not prevent a term as chaplain in 1757. His leadership is shown in 1774 when his congregation met and declared themselves in favor of national independence. Two years later he was placed in command of a company of Carlisle minutemen, but his health and age would not permit him to take the field. On 29 July 1947 officers of the Chaplain School observed the anniversary of the chaplaincy in the American Army by conducting a service in his honor at his grave. Among those participating were clergymen of the Congregational, Roman Catholic, Evangelical-United Brethren, Lutheran, and Jewish faiths.[47]

Thirty-one men are known to have served colonial troops in 1755–63. Nearly half were from Massachusetts, and a fourth were on duty with Pennsylvania regiments. Congregationalists were the most numerous, with a considerable number of Presbyterians and some Episcopalians. Several of these men were destined to serve again in the Revolution and to be known as ardent champions of in-

---

[45] Parkman—*Montcalm and Wolfe*, II, 378–79.
[46] Samuel K. Lothrop—"Life of Samuel Kirkland," *Library of American Biography*, Jared Sparks, Ed., Series 2, Vol. 15, pp. 147–48.
[47] *Pennsylvania Archives*, Ser. 5, I; *The Army and Navy Chaplain*, October 1947, pp. 3–4.

dependence. John Cleaveland and Gad Hitchcock, through pulpit or press, delivered withering attacks upon British policy before the appeal to arms. This uncompromising spirit and transcendent confidence were expressed in striking terms by Samuel Dunbar in a time of great anxiety when he prayed that the Redcoats might return to the land whence they came, "for Thou knowest, O God, that their room is better than their company." [48]

---

[48] Alice Baldwin—*The New England Clergy and the American Revolution*, pp. 157–58, 181; *Yale Biographies and Annals*, Ser. 2, 1745–63.

CHAPTER III

The Spirit of 76

The story of the chaplaincy in the American Revolution is a fascinating tale. The men who served were a group more varied than is often found working for a common end and dedicated to a common ideal. Among them were men chosen for their knowledge of the Indian, French, or German languages or for their political influence. Some acted as surgeons or unit commanders. Terms of service ranged from a few days to 8 years. Many were young men, but one sturdy old patriot volunteered in his 73d year and served for 18 months before admitting that he was not equal to field duty. One lost 3 sons in the service, another 2. Several lost their health, their homes, or their possessions. At least 10 were captured and held as prisoners, one being drowned in an attempt at escape. Three are listed as killed and 2 as wounded in battle, and at least 8 died from other causes.

The records of these men are far from complete. State or Federal archives give a skeleton of some military careers. Church and college publications and local histories are major sources of information. Some of these, depending in part upon unconfirmed traditions, are not authorities of the first order. Doubtless some clergymen who conducted services in camp without any official status were spoken of as chaplains in later years. About 20 men called chaplains in some records have not been counted in this study because of contradictory evidence. Perhaps a few others would be in the same class if all facts were known, but 179 have been accepted with some confidence as having been on duty with Continental or State troops at some time during the war. A modern writer reckons that 111 of these were in the Continental service.[1]

The number who were furnished by various States is significant. Crediting a man to the State from which he entered the service, we have: New Hampshire 13, Massachusetts 42, Rhode Island 4, Connecticut 38, New York 8, New Jersey 12, Delaware 3, Pennsylvania 22, Maryland 2, Virginia 15, North Carolina 5, South Carolina 3,

---

[1] Charles H. Metzger—"Chaplains in the American Revolution," *The Catholic Historical Review*, April 1945, p. 51.

Georgia 4, Canada 1, and 7 uncertain.   As more than half came from New Hampshire, Massachusetts, and Connecticut, it is not surprising that the largest group were Congregationalists.   They numbered at least 72, with 32 Presbyterians, 18 Episcopalians, and 9 Baptists.   The affiliation of some is not known, and the record is confused by the failure of some writers to distinguish the Dutch and German Reformed Churches.   Others called any Protestant a Presbyterian if he was not an Anglican.   Several of these men had served in the French wars, among them Benjamin Pomeroy of Hebron, Connecticut, who resigned at the age of 74 and returned to the civilian pastorate.

The place and influence of American chaplains in the army of the Revolution cannot be appreciated without some understanding of the outlook and activities of the clergy, political as well as moral and spiritual.   Important in every colony since its beginning, their political leadership was especially evident in New England, where the revolutionary philosophy was given an early and emphatic expression.   As the church was almost the only meeting place for the people, the custom of reading proclamations and announcements of general interest from the pulpit became common.   In some towns the minister was in the habit of giving a weekly lecture.   This gave him the opportunity to deal with subjects scarcely appropriate in a Sunday sermon.

Not only prayers but sermons by the local pastor were common at town meetings, military musters, and similar events.   Even more influential were the election sermons customary in several colonies at the annual election of the governor's council.   As the preacher of the day was chosen by the assembly and his sermon usually was printed and distributed, his words carried great prestige.   Quite similar were the sermons at the annual election of the Ancient and Honorable Artillery Company of Boston.   That preached by Oliver Peabody on 5 June 1732 and many later ones are extant.   Sixty-seven Connecticut election sermons, beginning with that of James Fitch in 1674, have survived; and John Norton's 1661 discourse seems to be the earliest of the Massachusetts series which has been preserved.   These sermons, expounding the political philosophy of the time and declaring the moral and religious implications of contemporary questions, became political textbooks and shaped immeasurably the thinking of the people for generations.[2]

Remembering that the founders of virtually all the colonies came to the new world to escape some form of restriction upon their politi-

---

[2] Alice M. Baldwin—*The New England Clergy and the American Revolution*, pp. 4–6.

cal, economic, social, or religious freedom, it is not surprising to find
them and their children on guard against anything which could impair
their hard-won liberties.   Their clergymen, being mostly American in
birth and education, naturally shared this view.   Many of them were
as familiar with the political philosophy of John Locke and others who
had justified the opposition to three generations of Stuarts as were
Otis, Adams, Henry, or Jefferson.   They quoted scripture to show that
these principles were a part of the law of God and thus gave a divine
sanction to resistance whenever they were threatened with encroach-
ment from any source.

Of the struggle with Andros in 1688 it was said, "The men of
Massachusetts did much quote Lord Coke."   This eminent jurist, who
had lost his office by defying a tyrant, had declared that a law contrary to the constitution or against common right or reason was void
and would be controlled by the Common Law.   Ebenezer Pendleton
proclaimed and applied this doctrine in the election sermon of 1710.
Thirty-seven years later Charles Chauncy declared that the British
constitution protected the prerogatives of Lords and Commons as well
as of the King and that those of the colonial governments were equally
sacred.   During the French Wars the people were urged to defend
free British institutions against French tyranny.   The Stamp Act drew
from Stephen Johnson, afterward a chaplain, the warning that such
violations of the constitution threatened the British empire, because
"A kingdom divided against itself cannot stand."   Nonimportation
and home manufactures were urged from many pulpits.   John Cleaveland told the women of his parish who were spinning at his home that
they might help "prevent the ruin of the whole British empire."
Oliver called the dissenting clergy "Mr. Otis's black regiment" and
said they were "set to work to preach up manufactures instead of
gospel."   While stationed at Boston, General Haldimand wrote, *"Leurs
pretres Presbiteriens sont les plus dangereux de tous les Etres."* [3]

As early as 1717 John Wise, who had been a chaplain in 1690,
used the social compact doctrine in opposition to the formation of
synods among Congregationalists.   An American episcopate, long
dreaded as a peril to free compact between pastor and people, seemed
to some an imminent danger after the passage of the Quebec Act in
1774.   Ebenezer Devotion asserted in 1766 that nothing but compact
held the colonies to the British empire and the whole compact would
be destroyed if one part of it were annulled.   In 1774, J. Lathrop de-

---

[3] *Ibid., passim;* David Hutchison— *The Foundations of the Constitution,* p. 256, citing Quincy—
Massachusetts Reports; Allen French—*The First Year of the American Revolution,* p. 175.

clared it treason against the state which should be resisted even by
war when a ruler violated his compact and leaped the bounds of the
constitution.   In the Massachusetts election sermon of that year Gad
Hitchcock, afterward a chaplain, urged opposition to every form of
oppression and tyranny, notwithstanding the unexpected presence of
General Gage in the congregation.   On the very day when the general
was sending his troops and ships against Bunker Hill, John Cleaveland
launched against him a fiery attack, soon afterward published in the
Essex *Gazette:*

> Thou profane, wicked monster of falsehood and perfidy, . . .
> your late infamous proclamation is as full of notorious lies as a toad
> or rattlesnake of deadly poison—you are an abandoned wretch.
> . . .   Without speedy repentance, you will have an aggravated
> damnation in hell. . . .   You are not only a robber, a murderer,
> and usurper, but a wicked Rebel: A rebel against the authority of
> truth, law, equity, the English Constitution of Government, these
> colony states, and humanity itself.[4]

It was said of Cleaveland that he preached his whole parish into
the army, then went himself.   Several clergymen, including Cotton
Mather Smith, frankly advocated independence long before 1776.
His neighbor chaplain, Thomas Allen, fought the Tory sentiment of
Western Massachusetts for 2 years before he brought Pittsfield to his
side.   In 1778 William Gordon was dismissed from his legislative
chaplaincy because he attacked the Massachusetts Assembly for draft-
ing a constitution, as he believed it should have been prepared by a
convention chosen for that purpose so that it might rest upon a real
compact.   These sentiments are typical of the convictions of great
numbers of the clergy and of the way in which they applied their concept of moral law to the public questions of the day.[5]

In some of the larger towns, laymen were influential leaders, but
in many of the small communities the ministers had little competition
in shaping the opinions of the people.   Popular leaders frequently
used arguments which had long been heard from the pulpit.   The
formula with which Samuel Adams could clinch any argument against
encroachments upon the mores of the centuries, "The constitution
ought to be fixed," runs through his writings with an iteration scarcely
surpassed by the *Carthago delenda est* of Cato.   Though it was quoted
from Vattel, it is a restatement of the "unalterable principles, fixed
rules, and established constitution" proclaimed in Pemberton's election

---

[4] Baldwin, *op. cit., passim.*
[5] *Ibid.*

sermon of 1710 and of the unalienable rights which Devotion saw in the English constitution in 1766.[6]

Adams asked Dr. Samuel Cooper to give him his views on public questions frequently, promising to`use them for the benefit of the country. He and Hancock were guests of Jonas Clark, a leading exponent of the religious imperatives behind the revolutionary doctrines, on the night when the British march to Lexington abruptly changed words and argument into deeds. Many clergymen were active in support of the Revolution. At least 13 sat in the Massachusetts Constitutional Convention of 1779–80, and large numbers served on town committees and provincial congresses or were active in recruiting or in raising supplies. Philip Fithian and Andrew Hunter, both chaplains a short time afterward, are said to have been in the group of young men who burned a cargo of tea in New Jersey about the time of the Boston Tea Party.[7]

An enumeration of religious organizations shows 3,105 congregations in the 13 colonies in 1775. These included 658 Congregational, 543 Presbyterian, 498 Baptist, 480 Anglican, 295 Quaker, 261 German and Dutch Reformed, 151 Lutheran, and 50 Catholic. Besides these there were a number of Jewish congregations and the beginnings of the Methodist and other movements. Several of these groups were held by administrative or other strong ties to European churches, but the Congregational and Presbyterian churches were notably free from such limitations. In the Northern and middle colonies most of the Anglican clergy were loyalists, but in Virginia, the Carolinas, and especially in Georgia, a considerable number supported the American cause notwithstanding their ordination vow of loyalty to the King as head of the church. Doubtless they were helped by the doctrine that true loyalty required resistance to those enemies of the King in the British government who were abusing his power. James Madison, president of William and Mary College and afterward the first bishop of Virginia, was so ardent that he could not endure the implications of royalty in the phrase, "The Kingdom of Heaven" but substituted such expressions as "that great republic where there is no distinction of rank and where all men are free and equal."[8]

In most parts of the country, the loyalist clergy and those who

---

[6] *Ibid.*

[7] *Ibid.;* J. T. Headley—*The Chaplains and Clergy of the Revolution*, p. 56; *Dictionary of American Biography*, IX, 399.

[8] Harry J. Carmen and Samuel McKee—*A History of the United States*, I, 286; Alexander C. Flick, Ed.—*History of the State of New York*, III, 56; H. J. Eckenrode—*The Revolution in Virginia*, p. 107; L. G. Tyler—*College of William and Mary* (Bulletin; X, No. 4, p. 58).

advocated nonresistance to British policy were a distinct minority.
When the respected leaders of the churches which had been interpret-
ing the moral law since the earliest settlement threw the vast weight
of those institutions behind the Revolution, great numbers of the people
had no further doubt where their duty lay.   When scores of these
ministers went into the army as chaplains, they animated great numbers of citizen soldiers with the conviction that they were fighting for
a holy cause and that in the end they could not fail.   It is hard to ex-
aggerate the significance of such an influence in holding together the
nucleus of any army through those trying times when the American
cause seemed hopeless.   The amazing pertinacity of George Washington may have been sustained in no small degree by the confidence of
the chaplains who stood by him through these trying years.[9]

When the war began, numbers of clergymen marched with their
parishioners or hastened to the camp near Boston, but the militia system had not been developed to the point where many of them could
properly be regarded as unit chaplains.   Many of these clergymen
ministered to the troops for longer or shorter periods without formal
appointment and without pay.   As an army organization evolved,
some of these ministers were chosen to be chaplains of the various
regiments or brigades.   The governor of Connecticut appointed chaplains to regiments.   One was chosen for each brigade of Rhode Island
troops by the brigade officers.   New Hampshire chaplains were chosen
in much the same way and assigned sometimes to brigades, but more
frequently to regiments.   Virginia law authorized one chaplain to
each regiment to be chosen by the field officers and captains, but none
seem to have been appointed until 1776.[10]   Some New York and
Pennsylvania chaplains were chosen by the legislatures.   The Massachusetts Provincial Congress adopted a proposal of the local ministers
that they should serve in rotation for a month at a time, but this plan
did not prove satisfactory and was modified so that nine of their number would be chosen by the general and field officers for regular duty
while their pulpits would be supplied by neighboring ministers.   Apparently the usual practice was for each man to serve two regiments.[11]

Massachusetts, Connecticut, and New Hampshire at the outset
paid their chaplains 6 pounds a month; but by 1777 the latter was
paying 10 pounds, with a higher rate for brigade chaplains.   In that
year Delaware chaplains were paid $40.   With the pound valued at

---

[9] Baldwin, op. cit., passim.
[10] Donald A. Thompson—American Army Chaplaincy, p. 5; New Hampshire State Papers, I–II,
passim; Clarke and Force—American Archives, 4 Ser., III, 398, 411, IV, 134
[11] New York Archives. I, 17; Baptist Encyclopedia, p. 1009; French, op. cit., p. 175–76.

$3.75, these rates of pay do not differ greatly from those established by Congress for Continental chaplains. These pay scales compare strikingly with those of the British Army. At that time the pay and subsistence allowance for British chaplains of all arms amounted to 11 shillings 8 pence a day, or 17 pounds 10 shillings for a month of 30 days. This was more than the pay of a lieutenant, but considerably less than that of a captain of infantry. It was 10 times the pay of a private, though the latter would receive important allowances. When Congress authorized captain's pay for chaplains, it was three times the amount allowed to privates.[12]

The "adoption" of the New England armies brought several chaplains into the Continental service, but it is difficult to state exactly when or by what means this important action was taken. On 16 May 1775, the Provincial Congress of Massachusetts wrote to the Continental Congress a request for advice about establishing a government and suggested that it would be well for Congress to take the "regulation and general direction" of the army then gathering for the common defense. On 2 June, John Hancock presented the matter to Congress. A week later Massachusetts was advised to form a government, but the other proposition was not mentioned. Apparently, however, an understanding had been reached, for on 3 June the delegates from New York wrote to the Congress of that colony about "the Continental army in our province, which is to be maintained at the general charge."[13] The same day Congress bought powder for the "Continental Army."

About this time, but on an unknown date, John Adams moved that the Congress adopt the army at Cambridge and name a commander, but action was postponed. On 10 June he expected that 10,000 men would be maintained in Massachusetts and half that number in New York at Continental expense. Four days later a committee was named to prepare rules "for the government of the army," and Washington was chosen commander-in-chief the next day. On the 17th the delegates were free to report that Congress had undertaken to raise and maintain 15,000 men. As more than 10,000 actually were besieging Boston, but were insufficient to man the lines, Washington was authorized to maintain such force as he deemed necessary if it did not exceed 22,000 men. This action, taken in a

---

[12] *Ibid.;* Johnston—*Connecticut Men in the Revolutionary War; N. H. State Papers,* I, 48–49, II, 14; *Delaware Archives,* I, 96: Edward A. Curtis—*The Organization of the British Army in the American Revolution,* p. 158; *Journals of the Continental Congress* (hereafter cited as *Journals*), II, 220.

[13] Louis Clinton Hatch—*The Administration of the American Revolutionary Army,* p. 6, citing Force, 4:2:621, 898, and *Journals,* I, 115.

resolution of 21 July, is the earliest formal vote of which we have a clear record.[14]

The transfer of chaplains from State to Continental service seems to have been as indefinite as the transfer of the troops themselves. Enlistment in various State regiments had been for different periods, in most cases expiring late in 1775. By great exertion Washington was able to enroll a considerable proportion of the men in the new Continental regiments for service in 1776. Beginning with that year, the Continental Army was truly a distinct entity, though it was still customary to designate regiments by the States of origin.[15]

On 29 July 1775 Congress adopted a scale of pay for the army. Chaplains were allowed $20 a month, the amount authorized for captains. As this is the earliest national legislation known to recognize the chaplaincy in the Army of the United States, the date has been established officially as that of the origin of the Federal chaplaincy. In August 1775, Washington reported that 15 chaplains were serving 23 regiments, but 29 had none. In December, 19 regiments had chaplains and 22 did not. Apparently several chaplains left the service at this time, for the army returns for 8 January 1776 show 16 Continental regiments served by 8 chaplains and 11 not provided for.[16]

In a measure this situation can be attributed to a pending change in policy. On the last day of 1775 Washington called the attention of Congress to the inadequacy of chaplains' pay, stating that some of them were paying substitutes in their parishes more than they received from the government. As he felt that the current rate of pay would not attract the men of ability needed in the army, he recommended a substantial increase, suggesting that each chaplain serve two regiments if Congress could not provide for a larger number. On 16 January Congress adopted this suggestion, fixing the pay at $33⅓ a month. Three weeks later the general directed brigade commanders to arrange for the assignment of 14 chaplains to 28 regiments, giving preference to those who had served in 1775. After 2 more weeks it was necessary to remind the brigadiers that they had not complied with this order and that an immediate reply was expected.[17]

This arrangement was fairly satisfactory while the troops remained in one camp, but much confusion arose when the spring campaign placed parts of the army in Boston, New York, and Canada. The

---

[14] French, *op. cit.*, pp. 750–52.

[15] Hatch, *op. cit.*, pp. 6–7.

[16] *Journals*, II, 220; *Bulletin No. 112*, PID, WD, 4 Aug. 1947; Headley, *op. cit.*, p. 62–63.

[17] *Writings of George Washington*, Bicentennial Edition (hereafter cited as *Writings*), IV, 197–98, 307, 341.

general told Congress frankly that the only remedy was to appoint one chaplain to each regiment and provide adequate pay.   Regimental chaplains were authorized immediately, their pay being continued at $33⅓ a month.   Washington directed regimental commanders to procure chaplains, "persons of good character and exemplary lives," and to see that they were treated with proper respect and that military personnel attended religious services.[18]

On 11 April 1777 the pay of regimental chaplains was advanced to $40 a month, but on 27 May Congress ordered that only one chaplain be allowed to a brigade and that he should receive the pay and allowances of a colonel of the same corps.   It was further provided that these chaplains should be appointed by Congress on recommendation of brigade commanders, but that only clergymen of experience and established public character for piety, virtue, and learning should be nominated.   The President of Congress informed Washington of this action, saying that it was necessary as a means of attracting men of superior learning and virtue.   He stressed the increased pay and assignment to larger units as these inducements without indicating whether the appeal of the latter was expected to result from the dignity of belonging to the staff of a higher echelon or from the opportunity to minister to a greater number of men.[19]   The honorable aspect of the new arrangement seemed important to Daniel Roberdeau, a member of Congress.   His letter to the general shows quite fully what the government hoped at that time might be accomplished by its chaplains:

> Congress has this day made a new arrangement of the Chaplain's department, by reducing that part of the Staff to one for each Brigade to be recommended by the Brigadiers and appointed by Congress, with the pay rations and Forrage allowed to Colonels. This new and honorable Establishment is designed to suppress the horrid sins of Cursing swearing and other Vices with which, I am sorry to say, our Army Vies with the most abandoned of the English Troops; to strengthen the Officers hands by publick and private exortations to obedience of General and Regimental Orders; to discourage Disertions by recommending the Service; to encourage Enlistments; to recommend cleenlyness as a virtue conducive to health, and to reprehend the neglect of it.   These and other valuable Ends with the Countenance and concurrence of General Orders by the blessing of heaven I doubt not may be answered by a careful choice and recommendation of pious Clergymen zealously

---

[18] *Ibid.,* V, 192; Headley, *op. cit.,* p. 66.
[19] Journals, VIII, 256, 390, 421; Edmund C. Burnett—*Letters of Members of the Continental Congress,* II, 376.

attached to our glorious Cause, who will not begrudge the exertion of every nerve in the Service; but if Drones induced by the loaves and Fishes should creep into the Army the designs of Congress will be entirely defeated; to prevent which I frankly confess has induced me to step out of my line on this occasion, and I beg you will not look upon it as an impertinent intrusion on you, when I assure you the honor of God my Countries welfare your Comfort and that of every sober Officer and man in the Army are my only motives.[20]

Washington protested the resolution which gave only one chaplain to a brigade, pointing out that the arrangement of the preceding year which assigned each chaplain to two regiments had worked badly in several ways. He stated that the brigade commanders were unanimous in the opinion that the new plan could not be followed without great dissatisfaction. He felt that adequate service to a brigade was too great a task for one man but placed major emphasis upon the danger of rousing discord and jealousy by forcing the men to participate in a form of worship they did not profess. As regiments were raised locally, he assumed that the members would be accustomed to a common form of worship and would obtain a chaplain satisfactory to virtually all the men. Brigades, on the other hand, consisted of 4 or 5 regiments, and some of them 6.[21]

As the Army was organized in the following winter, 70 regiments were grouped in 16 brigades. Seven of the latter consisted of 4 regiments each, with 2, 3, 5, 6 or 9 of the other regiments brigaded together. Apparently three regiments to the brigade was considered a normal plan of organization. When the northern Army was reorganized in 1782, all but 2 brigades consisted of 3 regiments.[22]

The actual relationship between this system of organization and Washington's analysis of sectarian grouping in terms of local geography may be doubtful. With scarcely an exception, a brigade was composed of regiments from the same State. In the more homogeneous States differences of religious practice, if localized at all, prevailed in communities too small to raise more than a company at most. Had such differences appeared among the troops, they would have been within the regiments, not between them. The general's principle had more relevance in those States where large numbers of immigrants

---

[20] *Ibid.*

[21] *Writings*, VIII, 138, 203.

[22] Francis B. Heitman—*Historical Register of Officers of the Continental Army during the War of the Revolution*, pp. 11–12; Edward C. Boynton—*General Orders of George Washington, Commander-in-Chief of the Army of the Revolution, issued at Newburgh on the Hudson, 1782-1783*, pp. 46–47.

firmly attached to their religious usages had settled together in large areas of the back country.   Without considering language barriers which existed in some cases, a regiment enrolled, for example, on the Virginia frontier might not have responded wholeheartedly to the ministrations of a brigade chaplain of the prevailing faith of the Tidewater regions.   There seems to be little evidence that tensions of the kind feared by the general actually existed in those cases where one chaplain served a whole brigade.

On 19 July 1777, Washington remarked in a letter to General Heath that nothing had been done to reduce the number of chaplains and he doubted if the plan to have one serve three regiments would ever be carried out.   Three days earlier Congress had voted that regimental chaplains who chose to continue in the service might remain with their regiments under their present pay and appointments.   The first draft of this resolution applied only to the North Carolina Brigade, the one composed of nine regiments, and authorized the discharge of chaplains who wished to return home, but it was made general in application before it was adopted.   On an unknown date in the following year it was voted to dismiss regimental chaplains and to make assignments to brigades with the unanimous consent of the brigadiers. On 8 May 1781, the commanders of the northern and southern armies were directed to rearrange the chaplains of the various State lines so as to retain in service only as many chaplains of each line as there were brigades in that line.   Surplus chaplains were to be retired on the half-pay of captains for life.   Early in 1783 Congress offered 5 years' full pay instead of the half pay for life which had been promised to all officers, and the offer was accepted generally by the Army.   In the case of chaplains, this was interpreted to be captain's pay.[23]

The action of Congress on 8 May 1781, grew directly out of the comparative claims of Chaplains William Rogers and Robert McMurdie to the chaplaincy of a Pennsylvania brigade.   After more than 2 years of service, Rogers was appointed chaplain of the Third Pennsylvania Brigade on 1 June 1778.   A year later he was sent on Sullivan's expedition as a brigade chaplain. For reasons which do not appear, McMurdie, who had served a year less than Rogers, felt that he should have been advanced to this brigade chaplaincy and appealed to Congress.   The Board of War decided that he had no ground for

---

[23] *Writings*, VIII, 438, XXII, 135; *Journals*, VIII, 557, XII, Appendix, XXIV, 345–46; Hatch, *op. cit.* 178.

complaint, but soon afterward he was made chaplain of the Second Brigade and was transferred to the First in July 1780.[24]

Apparently the reorganization of the Pennsylvania troops into two brigades left Rogers without an assignment, and in some manner the situation involved a dispute between the two chaplains. Rogers asked Congress to settle the matter, and it was decided that he was still in the army and entitled to pay because he had not been certified as surplus by the commander of the southern army. He retired the same month, but the records do not show whether this was from necessity or choice. At this same time McMurdie was trying to collect back pay for a period with the 11th Regiment, "which regiment I suppose he never saw during that time, nor indeed labored very much in any vineyard towards gathering into the sheepfold," to quote the paymaster. The question hinged upon whether the resolution of 27 May 1777 operated to vacate appointments to regiments. By implication Congress decided in the negative, but it was determined to avoid similar difficulties in future by ordering the implementation of the earlier resolution for the disposal of surplus chaplains.[25]

Another episode may have been related to the selection of brigade chaplains and the dismissal of others. John Elliot, Chaplain of the Second Connecticut Regiment (not to be confused with John Eliot of Massachusetts), resigned or was dismissed on 20 February 1778 after 10 months of service. Washington wrote that because of this and other disappointments he went over to the enemy. It may be that his dismissal and failure to be selected for a brigade chaplaincy were these disappointments, but this is pure conjecture. After nearly 2 years he came to the American lines, asking that he might throw himself on the mercy of his home State of Connecticut, and Washington acceded to this request. The degree of disloyalty involved in his going into the British lines after his separation from the American service need not be determined, and the action of Connecticut in his case is not known.[26]

On 18 September 1777, hospital chaplains were authorized and allowed 60 dollars a month, 3 rations a day, and forage for 1 horse, but 3 years later they were discontinued and brigade chaplains were directed to attend the hospitals from time to time. Late in 1778 a chaplain was appointed to the various posts in the Highlands of the Hudson

---

[24] *Journals*, XIV, 773, XVII, 615, XX, 483, 486; *Pennsylvania Archives*, 5 Ser., II, 257, 574, 632, III, 574, 591; Thomas R. Saffell—*Records of the Revolutionary War*, p. 78.

[25] Same as 24.

[26] *Writings*, XVII, 154.

and was allowed the pay and subsistence of a brigade chaplain.[27]   A few days before regimental chaplains were abolished, Washington wrote a delightful combination of seriousness and banter to the commander of a cavalry unit:

> A chaplain is part of the establishment of a corps of cavalry, and I see no objection to your having one, unless you suppose yours will be too virtuous and moral to require instruction.   Let him be a man of character and conversation, and who will influence the manners of the corps both by precept and example.[28]

Apparently the foregoing statements by the Commander-in-Chief and by the Congress are as definite pronouncements on the qualifications of chaplains as were made.   Both placed the quality of character which would command and hold respect above every other consideration.   This reiterates Washington's statement of 20 years before that a chaplain should be "a gentleman of sober, serious, and religious deportment." [29]   There is no reason to believe that any number of chaplains were found wanting in this particular.

Although it was normally taken for granted, it is evident that ordination was not an absolute prerequisite for appointment to the chaplaincy.   Joel Barlow, a Yale graduate of recognized ability who had served for a time as a volunteer, was induced to apply for appointment by the need for chaplains and by the urging of Chaplain Abraham Baldwin.   Though he had no intention of making the ministry his profession, he studied theology for 6 weeks, was licensed to preach, and became chaplain of the Fourth Massachusetts Brigade in 1780 through the influence of Colonel Humphreys and General Greene.   Soon after his arrival in camp he witnessed the execution of Major Andre and was moved to preach a "flaming political sermon" by Arnold's treachery.   This remarkable man served for 3 years, writing several of the patriotic songs which had a wide influence in the army and among civilians.   In later years he had a distinguished literary and diplomatic career.   He died on 22 December 1812 in Poland while on a mission to Napoleon.[30]

Chaplain Baldwin was a tutor at Yale during Barlow's student years.   His sister Ruth married Barlow during his first year as a chaplain.   In 1783 Baldwin became a lawyer and moved to Georgia.   For

---

[27] *Journals,* VIII, 754, XII, 1091; *Writings,* XX, 376, Note.

[28] To Col. George Baylor, 23 May 1777, *Writings,* VIII, 109.

[29] To Robert Dinwiddie, 29 April 1757, *Writings,* II, 33.

[30] *Dictionary of American Biography,* I, 610; Headley, *op. cit.,* p. 208; Charles Burr Todd—*Life and Letters of Joel Barlow, passim.*

many years before his death in 1807 he represented his State in the Congress of the Confederation or in the national House or Senate. His vote in the Federal Convention broke the inexorable majority of the large States which was forcing its plan of representation and threatening to drive the small States from the Union. He was the organizer and first president of the college which grew into the University of Georgia. The county where the State capital was located at that time was named in his honor.[31]

Few questions seem to have been raised about the theological fitness of chaplains of the various faiths. The fact that several great religious bodies, though differing in certain points of belief and polity, had been fully established in some colonies from the earliest settlement, made a high degree of tolerance necessary. Other churches, brought to this country by distinct bodies of immigrants, were equally recognized within those groups. The propriety of a Roman Catholic chaplain serving the Canadian regiments seems to have been recognized. However, there arose a distinct opposition among the chaplains to the appointment of John Murray, Father of Universalism in America. During the summer of 1775 he was chaplain of the Rhode Island troops, gaining the lasting esteem of the officers and exerting a salutary influence among the men. As had been his custom in civil life, he refused to accept pay for his services. When opposition developed, he was supported strongly by General Greene and others; and on 17 September Washington announced his appointment as chaplain of the Rhode Island regiments and ordered that he be respected as such. Ill health limited his service to less than a year. Later he organized a church in Boston and played a leading part in the development of the Universalist movement.[32]

Several chaplains were chosen for special assignments because of linguistic abilities. Christian Streit, a Lutheran, whose name appears in several spellings, was appointed to the German-speaking Eighth Virginia Regiment in the summer of 1776 and served for a year. About the same time John Conrad Bucher of the German Reformed Church was appointed chaplain of a Pennsylvania German Regiment. He served for a year, when his health compelled him to resign. He had come to America with the German troops under Braddock, serving

---

[31] Henry Clay White—*Abraham Baldwin: One of the Founders of the Republic and Father of the University of Georgia, the First of American State Universities, passim.*

[32] Appleton's *Cyclopedia of American Biography;* John Murray—*Life of John Murray,* pp. 214, 408; Boston *Traveler,* 9 Sept. 1941.

through the French and Pontiac's wars and rising to the grade of captain. In 1780 he was chaplain in the Lancaster County militia.[33]

After some prior service with Pennsylvania troops, Henry Miller was appointed chaplain of the German Brigade in 1777. On 18 May of the next year at the request of a number of German officers, he was made chaplain to the Germans in the main army without being confined to any particular brigade, which position he resigned after another 15 months. Johann Daniel Gros of the German Reformed Church was a chaplain to the Levies under Colonel Marinus Willet on the New York frontier from 1780 to the end of the war. The large number of Germans in these forces make it probable that a knowledge of the language was an important consideration.[34]

In July 1775, John Peter Tetard was employed as French interpreter to General Schuyler and chaplain of a French Canadian regiment, and his pay for both services was to be that of a major. Another interpreter chaplain was Samuel Kirkland. On 19 June 1766, some months before his graduation from Princeton, he was ordained and appointed a missionary to the Oneida Indians under the sponsorship of a Scottish missionary society. With some interruptions, this work continued for 30 years. At the outbreak of the Revolution he exerted himself to keep the Six Nations friendly to the American cause but succeeded only in the case of the Oneidas and Tuscaroras. Washington attached great importance to his activities and urged Congress to give him adequate support. He served as chaplain at Fort Schuyler and with Sullivan's expedition against the Senecas.[35]

On 16 October 1779, in recognition of his services among the Indians, Congress voted to pay Kirkland "six thousand dollars and that the clothier general be instructed to provide him with a suit of cloaths, a hatt, linnen sufficient for four shirts, two pair of stockings, and a pair of shoes, to be in full for his past services and expences." This seems to show a higher valuation of these services than was anticipated in January 1777 when the Board of War recommended to Congress that he be paid $444 for his services during the current year as missionary to the Indians and $300 for his extra services as chaplain and interpre-

---

[33] *Virginia Historical Magazine*, Jan. 1933, p. 11; Heitman, *op. cit.; Dictionary of American Biography*, III, 220, IX, 48.

[34] *Journals*, VII, 284, XI, 507, XIV, 933; *Penn. Archives*, Ser. 5, II, 513; Heitman, *op. cit.; N. Y. Archives*, I, 256, 258, 259, 537.

[35] *Ibid.*, p. 17, 140; *Journals*, VII, 72, XV, 1181; *Writings*, III, 527; *Papers of the Continental Congress*, I, 51; S. K. Lothrop—*Life of Samuel Kirkland* in Jared Sparks, Ed.—*Library of American Biography*, 2 Ser., XV, 255; William B. Sprague—*Annals of the American Pulpit*, I, 625.

ter.   This may imply that his diplomatic services were considered his most important contribution or may be a recognition of the loss of his salary from Scotland.   After the war the missionary society paid his back salary except for the period when he was actually serving those in arms against Great Britain.   In 1785 Congress paid him 250 pounds for special services during the war, and in 1788 the Indians and the State of New York gave him a joint grant of land.[36]

In 1784 Kirkland acted as interpreter at the Fort Stanwix Council and influenced the Indians to accept the terms of peace.   His influence led to the conversion of Cornplanter to the Christian faith.   He founded Hamilton College for the education of Indian and white boys; and his son was a distinguished president of Harvard.[37]

The efforts of Congress to gain support in Canada led to the organization of two Canadian regiments.   On 26 January 1776, Father Louis Eustace Lotbiniere, although more than 60 years of age, was appointed chaplain of one of these regiments by Benedict Arnold and became the first Roman Catholic chaplain in the Army of the United States.   He was promised 14 pounds 10 shillings a month, including rations, at a time when the pound was worth $3.75, but later he was paid at the rate of $41.33 a month until the pay of chaplains was increased in 1777.   With the failure of the Canadian expedition, this regiment, commanded by Colonel Livingston, was transferred to the vicinity of Philadelphia.   After his retirement in 1781, Father Lotbiniere was paid with fair regularity for 3 years, but he died in poverty in October 1786.   In support of American independence he had given up his pastorate and family associations, incurred ecclesiastical censure and discipline, and spent his declining years among a strange people whose language he could scarcely use.[38]

Father P. R. Floquet of Montreal also incurred the censure of his bishop by administering the sacraments to Hazen's Canadian regiment, but there is no evidence that he ever was a chaplain.   Father Pierre Huet de la Valiniere also served this regiment, but the records do not show that he was its chaplain.   Father Pierre Gibault of Kaskaskia rendered invaluable services to George Rogers Clark in his Illinois campaign but seems to have had no official status.   Speaking the French language and being priests of the Roman Catholic Church were both necessary

---

[36] *Journals, loc. cit.*

[37] *Ibid.;* Sprague, *op. cit.,* I, 624.

[38] *Journals,* V, 645 *et passim;* A. H. Germain—*Catholic Military and Naval Chaplains,* 1776–1917, pp. 2–10; *Records American Catholic Historical Society of Philadelphia,* XV, 70; *History Magazine,* 1867, p. 103.

to the service of these clergymen.   About 100 chaplains were on duty with the French Army or Navy in America, but little is known of their activities.   Apparently all returned to France except the Carmelite Father, Paul de St. Pierre, who died in the Illinois country; Father Rossiter, who located in Philadelphia; and the Franciscan priest, Charles Whalen, who remained in New York.[39]

Several chaplains acted as surgeons either during their chaplaincy or at another time.   David Jones was paid more than $1,000 a year for his extra services as surgeon while he was chaplain of the 4th Pennsylvania regiment.   David Griffith, who had studied medicine as well as theology, was appointed to this dual role by Congress, though it was emphasized that this should not be considered a precedent.   Years afterward he had Washington as a parishioner at Alexandria.   Though elected the first Episcopal bishop of Virginia in 1786, he was unable to go to England for consecration and resigned.[40]

Joseph Thaxter likewise served as surgeon to some extent during his chaplaincy.   When news of the British march to Lexington came, he galloped away, armed with a brace of pistols, and was in time to take part in the battle at Concord Bridge.   He acted as chaplain of Prescott's regiment at Bunker Hill and was commissioned by the Massachusetts legislature the following January.   Wounded during his service, he was lame for the rest of his life.   At the laying of the cornerstone of the Bunker Hill Monument in 1825, he was chosen to offer the prayer.   He had been mentioned as the only surviving chaplain of the Revolution at that time, but several were still alive, among them William Plumb, who lived until 1843.[41]

Another soldier of Bunker Hill has been mentioned as chaplain and surgeon, though no record has been found of his appointment to either office.   This was John Martin, who prayed with the troops before the battle, took a musket and fought through the engagement, and soon afterward preached to the defeated regiment on Nehemiah 4:14, the text dear to the heart of many chaplains in the hour of danger, "Be ye not afraid of them."   David Avery has been called an assistant surgeon, though this may reflect no more than the fact that he ministered tirelessly to the physical as well as the spiritual needs of the

[39] Germain, *op. cit.*, pp. 6, 12, 24; *Catholic Historical Researches*, XXIII, 299; *The Catholic Builders of the Nation*, III, 289; *Dictionary of American Biography*, VII, 234–35.

[40] *Journals*, V, 602, XIV, 685; Lamb—*Biographical Dictionary*, III, "David Griffith"; Sprague, *op. cit.*, V, 271; *Virginia Historical Magazine*, 1933.

[41] Sprague, *op. cit.*, VIII, 84–86; Banks—*History of Martha's Vineyard*, p. 161; *History of Hingham*, I, 281; *Massachusetts Soldiers and Sailors in the War of the Revolution*.

wounded after Bunker Hill and other battles. Though he was present, praying for victory, it is not recorded that he fought at Bunker Hill. A few days earlier he had gone with the expedition to Noddle Island. After the fight he prayed and exhorted the men, then stood guard for 2 hours. The next year he crossed the Delaware with Washington, prayed for victory in the attack on Trenton, seized the musket of a fallen soldier, and fired on the enemy until he was wounded himself.[42]

Equally striking is the record of John Lyth, a Virginia Episcopalian, born and educated in England, who was a resident of Harrodsburg as early as 1775 and is said to have been the first clergyman in Kentucky. That year he was a representative to the legislature of the shortlived colony of Transylvania. This body adopted nine laws, of which the Act to Prevent Profane Swearing and Sabbath Breaking may reflect the influence of the clerical member. He served as chaplain of Virginia militia in the expedition against the Cherokees. After 3 months' service as surgeon of the 13th Virginia, he was killed by the Indians on 15 January 1778. Apparently he was not acting as chaplain at the time of his death, for Alexander Balmaine was regimental chaplain at that time.[43]

Another chaplain who served in other ways gave his life for American independence. This was James Caldwell, graduate of Princeton and minister of the Presbyterian Church of Elizabeth, N. J. His parishioners included some of the most prominent men of the time, and about 40 were commissioned officers. One of them, Colonel Dayton, commanded a local battalion and nominated Caldwell to be its chaplain, expecting that he would serve the New Jersey Brigade. Reporting this action to Congress, presumably for confirmation, he stated that it might have been proper to request this action from the New Jersey Committee of Safety if that body had been in session. Ordered to Canada, Dayton proceeded to the Mohawk Valley of New York. At Johnstown, home of the late Indian Commissioner, Sir William Johnson, news was received of the Declaration of Independence, and the chaplain gave the toast to the "harmony, honour, and prosperity" of the new nation.[44]

Returning to New Jersey, Caldwell was made deputy quartermaster general. Whether he held a specific appointment as chaplain

---

[42] Headley, *op. cit.*, pp. 72, 293ff.

[43] U. S. Shaler—*Kentucky: A Pioneer Commonwealth*, pp. 69–71; *Virginia Historical Magazine*, 1933.

[44] Headley, *op. cit.*, p. 218ff; Edwin T. Hatfield—*Elizabeth, New Jersey, passim; American Archives*, 5:3:1095; Ebenezer Elmer—*Journal, passim;* Nicholas Murray—"Memoir of the Rev. James Caldwell," *New Jersey Society Proceedings*, III, 79ff; *Dictionary of American Biography*, III, 408.

during the next 5 years is uncertain.   As his church was near the American camp and in the area where he was best known, he was constantly active in religious ministrations to his parishioners and the troops while he obtained supplies and information for Washington. A camp joke of the time tells how a friend was perplexed by the initial letters D. Q. M. G. over the door of his office in Chatham, saying that the only meaning he could see in them was "Devilish Queer Minister of the Gospel."   His zeal and activities made him the object of especial hostility by the enemy.   His house was burned in February 1779 and his church the next year.   In June 1780 Knyphausen marched against Morristown but was beaten back.   During the retreat Mrs. Caldwell was shot through the window of the house where she was staying.   Her husband and friends believed the act was deliberate.   Three weeks later Clinton tried to retrieve Knyphausen's failure and marched to Springfield.   At the height of the battle the Americans' supply of wadding gave out.   The Chaplain hurried to the nearby church, brought out an armful of Isaac Watts' hymn books, and shouted as he distributed them, "Now, put Watts into them, boys." [45]   Ninety-three years later Bret Harte told the story of the "rebel high priest" in a typical ballad, which includes the following lines:

> They were left in the lurch
> For the want of more wadding.   He ran to the Church,
> > Broke the door, stripped the pews, and dashed out on the road
> > With his arms full of hymn-books, and threw down his load
> At their feet.   Then above all the shouting and shots
> Rang his voice: "Put Watts into 'em, boys; give 'em Watts!" [46]

It is said that the chaplain often preached with his pistols beside him and a guard outside the door, but what his enemies failed to do openly was accomplished through treachery.   On 24 November 1781, he went to Elizabeth Point to meet a Miss Murray who was coming from New York under a flag of truce to visit relatives.   The American sentinal raised a question about a package she was bringing, and in the discussion another soldier shot the chaplain.   The man was hanged, as the trial brought out no justification for his act and the evidence convinced the court that he had been bribed.   Lafayette adopted the chaplain's eldest son and educated him in France.   He became a distinguished philanthropist and was one of the founders of the American Bible Society. [47]

---

[45] Same as 44.
[46] *Harte's Complete Poems*, p. 31.
[47] Same as 44.

Several other chaplains gave their lives for American independence. The first was Amos Adams, chaplain of Brewer's Massachusetts Regiment during the siege of Boston, who succumbed to the hardships of the service on 5 October 1775. To William Emerson belongs a different priority. His home was the old manse immortalized by Hawthorne which still stands just across a narrow field from Concord Bridge. On the morning of the battle he encouraged the troops and cared for women and children who had fled from their homes. That evening he wrote a vivid account of the day's events, implying by his use of pronouns that he was with the alarm company which prepared to defend the town after the Minute Men had advanced toward Lexington and that he retreated across the river when the British appeared in force and was with the party which made the final advance to and across the bridge. This supposition is in harmony with a tradition that he appeared that morning with a firelock in his hands and encouraged one timid man by placing a hand on his shoulder and saying, "Don't be afraid, Harry; God is on *our* side." However, some writers believe that he was at his house during the fight at the bridge.[48]

These facts and the record of his ministrations to the troops at a muster in the preceding month make it seem quite probable that he was recognized as the chaplain of the local militia in the informal way which was common at the time. This gives plausibility to the statement that he was the first chaplain to serve in the Revolution. Two future chaplains were active that day but both as fighting men. Emerson was in the camp at Charlestown for a time that summer and the next year was chaplain of the troops at Ticonderoga for some months. Becoming ill with a disease that threatened to grow worse, he started for home but could go no farther than Gookins Falls on Otter Creek near Rutland, Vt. Here he died in the home of the local minister. He was a son of the Joseph Emerson who was a chaplain at Louisbourg in 1745. Ralph Waldo, the best known of the Emersons, was his grandson.[49]

Philip Vickers Fithian served with the New Jersey militia and Ebenezer Baldwin with a Connecticut regiment. Both died of camp fever in the vicinity of New York in 1776. Sylvanus Ames died at Valley Forge and Caleb Barnum at Pittsfield as he returned from Ticonderoga. Soon afterward Ebenezer David died in a southern hospi-

---

[48] Heitman, *op. cit.;* Ralph L. Rusk—*The Life of Ralph Waldo Emerson,* pp. 44–48; Marion Macone to Author, 23 Dec. 1955.

[49] Rusk, *loc. cit.*

tal. Several writers mention Whitman Welch as a chaplain in Arnold's expedition to Quebec or with a relieving force sent after the death of Montgomery. This has been questioned because no record of his appointment has been found, but there is no doubt that he ministered to the sick in the American camp near Quebec and that he died there of smallpox in March or April 1776.[50]

Fortunately we have more information about John Rosbrugh, though his name appears in several spellings. According to these records he was born in Ireland in 1717, graduated from Princeton at the age of 44, and was ordained to the Presbyterian ministry 3 years later. When Washington's army seemed hopelessly defeated late in 1776, he joined a company of his Pennsylvania neighbors and marched to Philadelphia, where he was made chaplain of the regiment to which it was attached. During a skirmish near Trenton early in January 1777 he fell into the hands of a party of Hessians, who killed him with a bayonet or sword while he knelt, praying for his family and enemies. A parishioner succeeded in giving his body a temporary burial, and Chaplain George Duffield had it removed to the churchyard of First Church in Trenton.[51]

Another Princeton Presbyterian to die for independence was Moses Allen. Pastor at Midway, Georgia, he was outspoken in his support of the American cause and served as chaplain of the Georgia troops who invaded Florida. His church and home were burned in retaliation by Tories. At the capture of Savannah he encouraged the men in the front lines but was made prisoner with the others. Because of his political influence he was denied the parole given to other officers and was confined in a prison ship. Attempting to escape by swimming, he was too weak to reach the shore and drowned on 8 February 1779.[52]

Other captured chaplains were more fortunate. John Cordell, though held a prisoner for 15 months, later served a Virginia regiment for 2 years. Daniel McCalla was paroled after some months on a prison ship in Canada. Because he prayed publicly for the success of the United States, he was accused of breaking his parole, but fled to Virginia until exchanged. Charles Thompson was captured when

---

[50] Heitman, *op. cit.;* Wm. S. Stryker—*New Jersey in the Revolution,* p. 379; cf. John Calvin Thorne—*A Monograph on the Rev. Israel Evans,* p. 3; *Dictionary of American Biography,* I, 242; Franklin B. Dexter—*Biographical Sketches of the Graduates of Yale College,* II, 157, III, 4–8; *Yale Biographies and Annals,* 2 Ser., p. 775; cf. A. L. Perry—*Origins in Williamstown;* Metzger, *loc. cit.*

[51] Heitman, *op. cit.;* Sprague, *op. cit.,* III, 254; Headley, *op. cit.,* p. 161; Wm. H. Egle—*History of Pennsylvania;* Appleton—*Cyclopedia of American Biography,* V, n. p.

[52] Headley, *op. cit.,* p. 331ff; Heitman, *op. cit.*

his Rhode Island home and church were burned.   Confined on a
guard-ship at Newport for about a month, he was released for reasons
which he never understood.   John Hurt was paroled after detention
for 7 months.   Hezekiah Ripley crept away from his drowsy guards
soon after his capture.   Little is known about the captivity of Andrew
Hunter or Thomas Davis.   Early in 1780 an agreement was reached
by British and American authorities for the immediate release of all
chaplains who might be captured, and this policy was maintained
until the end of the war.[53]

It is evident that no obligation for chaplains to refrain from bel-
ligerent acts was recognized during the early years of the war.   On
several occasions they encouraged wavering men in the front lines,
assuming temporary command in a few instances.   They obtained
information by scouting or by questioning prisoners.   Samuel West
solved the code and translated an important captured letter for Washington.   Several led militia companies, acting as their chaplains at
the same time.[54]

Thomas Allen, elder brother of the chaplain drowned at Savannah, was one of the most warlike of these fighting chaplains.   A
Harvard graduate, he located in Pittsfield and strongly championed
the American cause during the years before the war when Tory sentiment was strong in western Massachusetts.   After serving as chaplain
during the disastrous campaign near New York in 1776 and along
Lake Champlain the next summer, he joined Stark at Bennington.
It is recorded that he advanced alone and was recognized by the
Tories in the advanced intrenchments south of the Walloomsac.   He
called upon the enemy to surrender and avoid needless loss of life but
retired when he was fired upon and a bullet passed through his hat.
Being a better marksman, he is reported to have said to a brother or
friend who was fighting with him, "Joe, you load and I'll fire."
When the Americans stormed the German works, he is said to have
been one of the first men over the intrenchments.   Finding some
surgeon's supplies, he turned immediately to the care of the wounded.[55]

During the siege of Charleston, Robert Smith, later an Episcopal
bishop, left the hospital where he was chaplain and fought in the lines.
After the surrender he was banished to Philadelphia.   Few stories of

[53] *Ibid.;* Headley, *op. cit.,* p. 276; Sprague, *op. cit., passim; Virginia Historical Magazine,* 1933;
Mary P. Root—*Patron Saints;* Hurt to Washington, 24 Sept. 1781, Ms. Lib. of Cong.; *Writings,*
XVIII, 202, 216, 475, XXII, 344, XXIII, 139, XXV, 38, 196.

[54] Hurt to Washington, *loc. cit.; Writings,* XIII, 71; Sprague, *op. cit., passim.*

[55] Headley, *op. cit.,* p. 150; Sprague, *op. cit.,* I, 607; Lamb—*Biographical Dictionary,* I, 70; Hoffman Nickerson—*The Turning Point of the Revolution,* pp. 252-54.

this nature equal in dramatic interest that of James Hall, a Scotch-Irish Presbyterian and graduate of Princeton, who settled in North Carolina.   He went with Rutherford's expedition against the Cherokees and preached a famous sermon, the men sitting around him in the shade of green boughs cut from the forest trees.   As this was the first sermon preached in northern Georgia, the locality was named Hall County.   In 1779 and again 2 years later Hall took the field as commander and chaplain of a company of cavalry.   When Davidson was killed guarding the fords of the Catawba, Greene selected Hall for his successor with the grade of brigadier general, but he declined for the same reason he had refused a position as teacher of mathematics at Princeton after his graduation, a prior obligation as a minister of religion.   He was a skilled swordsman, a scientist, teacher, and organizer of ability.   He is credited with the independent invention of a steamboat and of a "little clock" for measuring distances by the revolution of wagon wheels.   Less is known about the devices for submarine navigation invented by Abner Benedict for the destruction with torpedoes of the British vessels attacking New York.[56]

An especial interest surrounds two chaplains because of their subsequent appointment to the Regular Army by the government under the constitution.   John Hurt of Virginia served with credit for about 7 years during the war.   On 4 March 1791, the day after the authorization of one chaplain for the new Army, he was appointed.   On his resignation in 1794, David Jones, a Baptist and native of Delaware, succeeded him.   He had served from the spring of 1776 till the end of the war, much of the time with General Wayne.   He was with his old commander in the Indian wars and remained in the army till 1800.   In 1812 he volunteered his services and was appointed by the Secretary of War, General Armstrong, an old comrade in arms.   After more than 2 years of active duty, he was honorably discharged some weeks after his 79th birthday.   Benjamin Balch and Andrew Hunter later served as chaplains in the Navy.   The latter seems to have been appointed, at the age of 69, partly for his ability as a mathematician, and he is said to have been the first chaplain schoolmaster in the Navy.   General David Hunter was his son.[57]

Such were the men who kept the light of faith bright in the camps of the Continental Army and among the farmer soldiers of the War

---

[56] Sprague, *op. cit.*, III, 383, V, 172; Headley. *op. cit.*, pp. 164, 246; *Dictionary of American Biography*, VIII, 133; William H. Foote—*Sketches of North Carolina*, p. 315ff.

[57] *Journals*, IX, 1057, XI, 749, 810, 850; Heitman, *op. cit.*; *Dictionary of American Biography*, IX, 399.

for Independence.   They taught a generation that religious and political freedom and responsibility are inseparable.   They gave to patriotic zeal a power that the tragedies of Long Island and Brandywine
could not overwhelm and which lived through the dreary months of
Valley Forge and Morristown.   They won the respect of men like
Nathanael Greene and George Washington, who knew their worth.
Later generations saw in their devotion a challenging example which
impelled the Church in every emergency to give of her best for the
spiritual leadership of those whom the country has called into her
armed forces.

CHAPTER IV

From Concord to Newburgh

The chaplains of the Revolution went everywhere with their men. They comforted the wounded in the snows of Quebec and the forests of Kentucky. They braced the wavering line at Savannah and led the charge at Bennington. They crossed the Delaware with Washington and stood beside him at Yorktown. The records abound in facts of unusual interest about these men and what they did, but only a representative few of these varied experiences can be told.

On one occasion George Duffield was conducting a service in an orchard on the Jersey shore, standing in the fork of a tree so he could be seen and heard by all. Attracted by the singing, the British guns on Staten Island opened fire, and cannon balls crashed through the tree tops till the congregation found safety behind a neighboring hill. Manassah Cutler describes his feelings when a cannon ball just missed him and La Fayette during the attack on Newport: "Was pleased with his firmness, but found I had nothing to boast of my own, and as I had no business in danger concluded to stay no longer lest I should happen to pay too dear for my curiosity." He is described as an engineer who made powder for the army and is the same clergyman who led a migration from Massachusetts to Ohio after the war.

His advice led to the inclusion of provisions in the Ordinance of 1787 which prohibited slavery in the Northwest Territory and set apart certain lands for the support of education. Samuel McClintock, the chaplain of the French wars who lost 3 of his 4 sons in the Revolution, was the clergyman whom Trumbull showed in clerical garb in his picture of the battle of Bunker Hill.[1]

At the news of the surrender of Burgoyne, Timothy Dwight preached a famous sermon on Joel 2:20—"I will remove far off from you the northern army"—but General Putnam would not believe that the words were in the Bible until they were shown to him. The chaplain, a grandson of Jonathan Edwards, was afterward president of Yale

---

[1] William B. Sprague—*Annals of the American Pulpit*, I, 527, III, 190; W. P. and J. P. Cutler—*Life, Journals, and Correspondence of Rev. Manassah Cutler*, I, 2; Lamb—*Biographical Dictionary*, II, V; *Journal of American History*, II, 531; J. T. Headley—*Chaplains and Clergy of the Revolution*, p. 71.

for more than 20 years. David Sandford is remembered for donating his entire salary toward war expenses and because he was the best horseman in his brigade. John Nevelling sold all his property for $25,000 and lent the whole amount to Congress, but the loan never was repaid. Stephen Peabody later became a brother-in-law of President Adams. Samuel Eakin was described as the most eloquent preacher, with the sole exception of Whitefield, who had ever been in this country.[2]

Several of the chaplains had been influenced in their youth by the preaching of that great evangelist. When Arnold's Quebec expedition was about to leave Newburyport, Samuel Spring preached a moving sermon in the church where Whitefield had been buried 5 years before, taking Exodus 33:15 for his text—"If thy presence go not with me, carry us not up hence." After the service the officers induced the sexton to open the crypt that they might look upon the remains of the famous preacher and take some memento to carry on their perilous campaign. Spring endured the toil, cold, rain, and hunger which characterized the march to the St. Lawrence. In the attack he helped carry the wounded Arnold to the rear. After his return he was called to the pastorate of the church where he had preached so eloquently over the bones of Whitefield.[3]

One of the most remarkable stories of the time concerns Washington and John Gano, a distinguished chaplain of the Baptist faith. It is related that the general one day sought out the chaplain, told him that he had become convinced through study that immersion was the scriptural form of baptism, and demanded the ordinance at his hands. The general wished no publicity given to the ceremony, though it is said to have taken place in the presence of 42 witnesses. In 1926 the story was published with affidavits procured at an earlier date from 2 aged grandchildren of the chaplain and other members of the family alleging that they remembered hearing the chaplain's children say that their father told them of his baptism of Washington.[4]

Thus substantiated, the story gained a considerable currency; but some writers, without imputing dishonesty to any person, find it incredible. They point out that it depends upon old people's memories of

---

[2] *Ibid.*, pp. 182, 362; Hershner and Liest—*History of St. John's Reformed Church in Lower Heidelburg;* William C. Todd—*Rev. Stephen Peabody and Wife of Atkinson, N. H.*, pp. 4, 10; Appleton—*Cyclopedia of American Biography.*

[3] Headley, *op. cit.*, pp. 90–102.

[4] I. M. Haldeman—*A History of the First Baptist Church in the City of New York*, pp. 8–9; L. G. Barnes—*The John Gano Evidence of George Washington's Religion; Time,* 6 Sept. 1932, p. 30; Rupert Hughes—*George Washington*, pp. 277–80; Headley, *op. cit.*, p. 252.

what they had been told many years before about a statement by a third person.   Different tellings of the story name the Potomac, Valley Forge, and Newburgh as the scene of the baptism.   An artist's conception of the scene shows the chaplain as 3 or 4 inches taller than the general, while in reality he was several inches shorter.   Washington's general respect for religion but evident indifference to specific doctrines and practices are cited, and full weight is given to the improbability that he would find time for abstract studies amid the burdens and perplexities of the revolutionary years.   A Baptist minister, who says he would be delighted to believe the story if he could, points to the low esteem in which Baptists were held by many in the established churches before they had developed an educated ministry as a reason why Washington would not have been attracted to their distinctive belief. Finally, it seems more than human, notwithstanding the general's dislike of publicity, that 42 persons could witness the baptism of so prominent a man without any subsequent reference to the event.[5]   While some of these arguments have little evidential value, in the aggregate they establish a probability that this story is similar to others which have come down to us through channels of unquestioned sincerity but have no foundation in fact.

Who was the first chaplain in the Army of the United States?   It means little to name John Hurt, though he was definitely the first chaplain in the Regular Army as organized in 1791 by the Federal Government.   His 38 months of service under that appointment, though he was a pioneer in the peace-time chaplaincy, have left few records by which they can be compared with his 81 months in the revolutionary army.   A plausible criterion is the rule that chaplains assigned on 1 January 1776 to the regiments newly enrolled in the Continental service should be accorded this distinction, for the transition from State armies to a force under the control of Congress, in process for 7 months, was virtually complete at that time.

Trustworthy records show at least 18 chaplains in the Continental Army on that date: David Avery, Samuel Blair, Benjamin Boardman, Joseph Buckminster, John Carnes, Ebenezer Cleaveland, Noah Cooke, Ebenezer David, John Ellis, Jacob Forster, John Gano, Abiel Leonard, Isaac Mansfield, Oliver Noble, Josiah Payne, Elias Smith, Hezekiah Smith, and Eleazer Sweetland.   It is significant to note that these chaplains were from the following States: New Hampshire 2; Massachusetts 9; Rhode Island 1; Connecticut 4; New York 1; and Pennsyl-

---

[5] Same as No. 4.

vania 1. Forster resigned in 2 months, but Ellis served until the end of the war.[6]

More significant is the fact that half of these men had been on duty for several months. It seems just to credit individuals with such periods of duty with State troops when they continued in the Continental Army without a break. Apparently Avery, Boardman, Cleaveland, Leonard, Mansfield, and Hezekiah Smith joined the army near Boston within a few days after the battle of Lexington, and others appeared soon afterward. Several were recorded as present for duty on the first day of May. Records admittedly incomplete and not consistent in every detail seem to give a slight priority to David Avery. He is said to have formed a company among his parishioners in Windsor, Mass., on the Sunday after the 19th of April, which was the 23d in 1775, and to have marched at once to Cambridge. Though one writer tells of his activities on 3 Sundays within a period of 10 days and another confuses his home town with Windsor, Vt., there seems no reason to question the statement that he arrived in Cambridge on the 29th and preached on the Common the next afternoon. When the roll of Colonel John Patterson's regiment was made up to 7 May, he was recorded as engaged on 22 April. This date may be a mistake of one day in computation or, as published, a misreading of script for the 23d, the day on which he and his neighbors volunteered. To add another element of confusion, his name on this roll is crossed off without any explanation. There is no doubt that he was paid from 7 May nor that some official of the regiment considered that he had been on duty for 16 days at that time. The honor due to Avery for his 57 months of faithful service is not impaired by these flaws in the record of its beginning nor by the fact that the same honor should be accorded to others who took up their duties a few days or many months later but fulfilled them with the same fidelity.[7]

More significant as an index of their influence is the time some of these men were on duty. Recognizing that minor errors may result from the character of the records, it seems probable that John Ellis and Israel Evans had the longest periods of service, lacking about 1 month of 8 years. There is some indication that Ellis was in the army a few days longer than his colleague, though a tradition that Evans was the only chaplain to serve through the war without interruption still survives in New Hampshire. David Jones, Enos Hitch-

---

[6] Francis B. Heitman—*Historical Register of Officers of the Continental Army;* Headley, *op. cit.,* pp. 289–92; *Massachusetts Soldiers and Sailors,* I; *Yale Biographies and Annals,* 3 Ser., p. 307.

[7] Same as No. 6.

cock, and James Tate were on duty for 7 years or longer.   Six years
and some months are credited to John Hurt, Abraham Baldwin, and
Andrew Hunter, and more than 5 to William Barton, Hezekiah
Smith, John Mason, and Louis Lotbiniere.   William Plumb, William
Rogers,. David Avery, John Gano, Noah Cooke, and Samuel Kirk-
land served more than 4 years.[8]

In the performance of their duties the chaplains received notable
support from higher authority.   The Massachusetts anticipatory regulations of early April 1775 required officers and soldiers to attend
services and to deport themselves properly, the former on pain of
court-martial and reprimand, the latter of a monetary fine.   Congress
included substantially the same regulation in the Articles of War
adopted on 30 June 1775 and retained this provision when the Articles were revised on 20 September 1776.   The penalty for disorder
or manifest irreverence was court-martial and reprimand for officers
and a fine of one-sixth of a dollar for noncommissioned officers and
privates.   In June, General Ward ordered strict attendance at morning and evening prayers and at Sabbath services, enjoined quiet after
the chaplain had taken his place, forbade plays on Sunday, and
required that wood for Sunday's fires be prepared on Saturday.[9]

Immediately on taking command Washington informed the officers and men that they were required and expected to attend services
punctually, and similar orders were issued frequently in later years.
The order of 28 June 1777, announcing services on succeeding Sundays, was unusually pointed:

> The commanding officers of corps are to see that they attend;
> themselves, with officers of all ranks, setting the example.   The
> Commander in Chief expects an exact compliance with this order,
> and that it be observed in future as an invariable rule of practice—
> and every neglect will be considered not only a breach of orders,
> but a disregard of decency, virtue and religion.[10]

The general followed his own prescription with creditable fre-
quency.   There are numerous references to his attendance at services,
usually accompanied by 2 or 3 division or brigade commanders.   To
give the troops an opportunity both for worship and for rest, he issued
a standing order excusing them from all but the most pressing fatigue
duties on Sunday.   This was suspended on the eve of the battle of Long

---

[8] Heitman *op. cit.*

[9] Allen Franch—*The First Year of the American Revolution,* p. 175; *Journals of the American Congress,* I, 90, 482.

[10] *The Writings of George Washington,* Bicentennial Ed. (hereafter cited as *Writings*), III, 309,
VII, 407, VIII, 77, 114, 308, IX, 275.

Island when Howe's troops were in front of his meager defenses but was reissued later. As the situation during the campaign near Philadelphia often interfered with services on Sunday, he directed the chaplains to arrange a plan for conducting them at other times.[11]

The general fought vice and immorality of every kind and urged brigade and regimental commanders to support the chaplain's services as a helpful counterinfluence. Gaming was expressly forbidden and declared to be the foundation of evil and the cause of ruin to many gallant and brave officers. He added that this did not apply to games of exercise for amusement, which were to be encouraged. Against nothing did he wage more persistent but fruitless warfare than the habit of profane and coarse speech. The Massachusetts regulations of 1775 had imposed fines for oaths or execrations. The Articles of War enacted by Congress made the penalty one-sixth of a dollar for enlisted men and double this amount for officers.[12]

Washington's first general order required obedience to this rule, an admonition which he repeated several times in succeeding years. The order of 31 May 1777 stressed the responsibility of officers to discourage profanity by example and by punishing offenders and enjoined the regular holding of religious services as a restraining influence. It was issued immediately after the receipt of a letter from Congressman Roberdeau in which he stressed the new dignity given to the chaplains by elevating them to a position on the brigade staff. He thought this would help to suppress cursing and swearing and would strengthen the officers' hands by exhortations to obedience.[13] On 29 July 1779 the general issued still another order in a mood more of despair than of hope:

> Many and pointed orders have been issued against that unmeaning and abominable custom of *swearing*, notwithstanding which, with much regret the General observes that it prevails, if possible more than ever. His feelings are constantly wounded by the oaths and imprecations of the soldiers wherever he is in hearing of them.
>
> The name of that Being, from whose bountiful goodness we are permitted to exist and enjoy the comforts of life is incessantly imprecated and profaned in a manner as wanton as it is shocking. For the sake therefore of religion, decency and order the General hopes and trusts that officers of every rank will use their influence and

---

[11] *Ibid.*, V, 367, 490, XI, 343, XXVI, 250, IX, 329.

[12] *Ibid.*, VIII, 129, X, 242; French, *op. cit.*, p. 175; *Journals of the American Congress*, I, 91, 482.

[13] *Writings*, III, 309, V, 367, VIII, 77; Edmund C. Burnett—*Letters of Members of the Continental Congress*, II, 373.

authority to check a vice which is as unprofitable as it is wicked and shameful.

If officers would make it an invariable rule to reprimand, and if that does not do, punish soldiers for offences of this kind, it could not fail of having the desired effect.[14]

The records show a few attempts to impose the penalties prescribed by law. As early as August 1775, Captain William H. Ballard of Fry's Massachusetts regiment was convicted by court-martial of profane swearing and beating and abusing his men on two occasions and was fined 4 shillings for each offense. The following May, Joseph Child of the New York Train of Artillery was tried for "defrauding Christopher Stetson of a dollar, also for drinking Damnation to all Whigs and Sons of Liberty and for profane cursing and swearing." He was found guilty of profane cursing and swearing and speaking contemptuously of the American Army and was sentenced to be drummed out of the Army. At the same time Thomas Watkins was found guilty of being out of his quarters at unseasonable hours and making a disturbance and of profane cursing and swearing. He was sentenced to confinement on bread and water for 6 days and to be fined one-sixth of a dollar for profane swearing as provided by the third Article. In each of these instances some other objectionable action was associated with the profanity, and it is doubtful how much weight the court attached to each offense.[15]

On special occasions Washington always made conspicuous and appropriate use of his chaplains. When news of the surrender of Burgoyne was received, he ordered a celebration. Chaplains were to present short discourses, followed by cannon salutes and a *feu-de-joie*. The French alliance, after the bitter winter at Valley Forge, called forth deeper expressions of gratitude. The chaplains announced the good news, offered up a thanksgiving, and delivered suitable discourses in all major units. The army was formed in two lines. Three salutes of 13 guns were fired, each followed by a running musketry fire down one line and back the other, and this by directed cheers for the King of France, for the friendly European powers, and for the American States. The nature of the event being celebrated probably accounts for the prominence given the generals who held or claimed European titles. The right and left were commanded by Lord Sterling and the Marquis de Lafayette, the second line by Baron de Kalb, and the whole by Baron von Steuben.[16]

---

[14] *Writings*, XVI, 13.
[15] *Writings*, III, 410, V, 32.
[16] *Writings*, IX, 391, XI, 354.

Comparatively few chaplains of the Revolution belonged to the liturgical bodies to whom altar furnishings and similar equipment are important. The English Bible, to be interpreted and applied to personal and national problems, was the one necessity, carried in the chaplain's knapsack or stored in his memory. The place of the Bible in the colonial literature of the century is illustrated by the fact that 143 of the 179 chaplains had been given biblical names. On the eve of the disbanding of the Army, Chaplain John Rodgers suggested that Bibles be presented to the troops. Washington assured him that this project would have received especial support from him if proposed in time.[17]

Chaplains conducted their services where they could. Barlow mentions preaching in a great Dutch barn. In the Maine woods Spring preached from a pile of knapsacks, and both Langdon and Avery spoke from an inverted rum hogshead on Cambridge Common.[18] What seems to have been the first Army chapel was built in the camp near Newburgh during the first months of 1783.

This structure, usually called "The Temple" or "The New Public Building," was sponsored by Chaplain Israel Evans, who had a measure of supervision over its planning and construction. This remarkable man might be called the father of the Army chapel system. A native of Pennsylvania, he graduated from Princeton in 1772 in a class of 22, of whom 14 became ministers. Besides Evans, five were chaplains: Moses Allen, Philip Fithian, Andrew Hunter, Robert Keith, and William Linn. Evans served with distinction to the end of the war and seems to have had an especially close relation with the Commander-in-Chief. A miniature, believed to have been painted at Valley Forge by Kusciusko, is inscribed "Washington's Chaplain." In 1825 this was shown to Lafayette, who recognized it at once and said, "That is our worthy chaplain." A portrait in the Capitol at Concord calls him "Chaplain to Gen. Stark." After Sullivan's campaign against the Indians, Evans preached a notable sermon in which he declared that the expedition had opened savage lands to liberty and religion, which would extend to the western ocean. The next day a committee consisting of 1 general and 4 field officers waited on him and asked a copy of the sermon so that it might be printed and distributed to the army.[19]

---

[17] *Writings*, XXVII, 1.

[18] Todd, *loc. cit.;* Headley, *op. cit.,* pp. 95, 291.

[19] John C. Thorne—*Monograph of Rev. Israel Evans*, pp. 1–12, 20–30; Israel Evans—*A Discourse Delivered at Easton on 17 Oct. 1779.*

Probably the chaplain's long service with New Hampshire troops paved the way for his call to the pastorate of the First Church in Concord in 1788, the invitation being a joint action by the church and the town. His use of the bass viol and flute in church roused serious opposition. For 4 years he was chaplain of the general court. A sentence from his election sermon of 2 June 1791, addressed to that body and to the whole country, deserves to be remembered: "Fear the affluence of gold; fear a too unequal distribution of riches; secure yourselves against the spirit of conquest; have arms for your defense, but none for offense." He resigned in 1797 and died 10 years later. He left funds to endow a chair of oratory and belles-lettres at Dartmouth, and it still is known as the Evans Foundation. It is related that on the verge of battle he prayed that the Lord would lead the army to victory; but if this should not be according to the divine will, that He would stand neutral and let flesh and blood decide the issue. During his last illness he was visited by a brother minister who prayed that he might sit down with Abraham, Isaac, and Jacob in the kingdom of heaven. Evans whispered, "and with Washington, too." [20]

On Christmas Day 1782, Washington approved Evans' plan for the erection of a house of worship and announced the Chaplain's request that interested general and field officers meet the next morning at General Gates' quarters. As the weather was very bad, the meeting was not held; but Gates called another for the following day. Probably the weather improved, and it may be that the major general's order carried more weight than the chaplain's request. Be that as it may, the brigade and regimental commanders met on Friday, the 27th, named a committee to determine a proper site, and called another meeting for the following Monday. Again the weather was bad, but enough officers were present to set the project in motion. Major Rochefontaine, the engineer, gave out estimates of the timber and shingles each unit should supply. As a plan to build brigade hospitals had been abandoned, it was determined to use certain boards drawn for this purpose. Colonel Tupper was chosen to superintend the work, and Chaplain Evans to handle necessary demands upon the Quarter Master General. [21]

From this point the progress of the building is recorded with a regularity worthy of a ship log in a series of orders, chiefly issued by Gates, the senior major general.

---

[20] Thorne, *loc. cit.*

[21] Edward C. Boynton—*General Orders of George Washington,* pp. 53–54; Amos E. Corning—*Washington at Temple Hill,* pp. 108–09.

January 5—   All materials, except shingles, to be on the spot by the 8th; boards, nails and nail rods will be issued by the Quarter Master General; a ration and a half will be given daily to those constantly employed.

January 9—   Lieutenant Nelson to assist Colonel Tupper, and both "are to be overslaughed from all other duty until the Building is finished." A sergeant and corporal from each wing and a sergeant from each brigade to superintend, 2 carpenters, 1 mason, and 3 attendants from each regiment, and 1 noncommissioned officer and 12 men from each regiment to collect stones to report on the 10th; the latter to receive a gill of rum and half-ration.

January 14—   Underpinning completed; most of the timber on the spot; dilatory regiments urged to furnish their share without delay.

January 15—   Foremen of blacksmiths to draw nail rods tomorrow.

January 17—   By the 22d each regiment to deliver its share of shingles and 80 split pole ribs 8½ feet long and 2½ inches wide at the top; 1 ration and 1½ gill of rum to be paid for every 50 shingles or 10 ribs.

January 21—   By the 24th each regiment to deliver 270 split lath 4 feet long, 2 inches wide, 1 inch thick on one edge and at least one-third inch on the other; a gill of rum and half-ration to be given for every 50 lath. A sergeant and 2 men from each regiment to report tomorrow to complete filling in the frames, each regiment to receive 22 gills of rum and 22 half-rations for an estimated 2 days of work; masons and tenders to report tomorrow.

January 25—   Nails to be delivered on the morning of the 27th.

January 26—   Each regiment to send five carpenters tomorrow morning to finish shingling during soft weather.

January 29—   Quotas of shingles, lath, and ribs to be completed by tomorrow.

February 4—   Artisans employed on the building to be excused from Thursday's review; each regiment to deliver by ten on Thursday 4 benches 8 feet 4 inches long, 11 inches wide, and 18 inches high; a gill of rum and half-ration to be given for each bench delivered on time.

February 8—   Lieutenant Nelson to have full authority during the absence of Colonel Tupper.

March 6—   Each brigade to send two lime burners tomorrow to erect a kiln and burn lime for finishing the building.

March 31—   Each brigade to send 2 masons, 1 carpenter, and 4 other men to continue as long as wanted.[22]

---

[22] Boynton, *op. cit.* pp. 54–58; *Writings,* XXVI, 278.

These data give much information about the building but leave several questions unanswered. On 10 January, Gates, apparently using round numbers, wrote that 5,120 feet of hewn timber, 3,000 lath, 21,000 shingles, and 1,000 split ribs had been delivered and that one half-ration and a gill of rum had been given for each 10 feet of timber. At that time the army consisted of 14 regiments, grouped in 6 brigades, and a detachment recently arrived from Maryland. Each week one regiment was ordered to duty on the lines, leaving only 14 units in camp at one time.[23] It is assumed that the detachment received a regimental requisition and that absent regiments were excused from particular calls made while they were out of camp. On this basis, if the indicated quotas were filled, the following costs in rum and rations would result:

Materials	Gills of rum	Rations
Timber, 5,120 feet	512	256
Ribs, 1,120	168	112
Lath, 3,780	75.6	37.8
Shingles, 21,000	630	420
Benches, 56	56	28

Manifestly this aggregate of 45 gallons and 854 rations does not include the cost of nails, lime, or other materials not specified. Extra inducements to laborers must be computed even more guardedly. Filling the frames would be at a cost of 154 gills and 77 rations a day, and gathering stones for the foundation would call for a daily expenditure, possibly for 2 days, of 182 gills and 91 rations. The 2 officers, 10 noncommissioned officers, 28 carpenters, 14 masons, and 42 attendants requisitioned on 9 January would be entitled to 144 rations daily, but there is slight indication of the number of days any of them worked. A labor cost of 21 gallons of the more popular form of legal tender seems probable, but the number of rations paid for work cannot be estimated. Temple Hill must have been a busy place on the Friday when the work began with 168 men hauling stones on sleds, 14 masons laying the foundation, 28 carpenters framing timbers, 42 men helping, and all under the supervision of 24 sergeants or corporals and 2 officers.

What kind of building did these men make from these materials? About 1850, Benson Lossing studied faint traces of the foundation and estimated a size of 80 by 40 feet. From information given him by Major Burnet, a Revolutionary officer living in the vicinity, he concluded that the structure was made of hewn logs and had many unglazed windows about the size of portholes in a man-of-war. Other

---

[23] Corning, *op. cit.*, p. 109; *Writings, passim.*

parts of his description were more accurate, but these points are contradicted by evidence which seems more reliable than the memory of
a very old man trying to describe what he had not seen for 67 years.
A contemporary account of what was to be built gives 110 by 30 feet
as the dimensions.[24]   William Tarbell, a soldier of the 7th Massachusetts Regiment, made a drawing of the camp in the spring of 1783.   A
copy in Washington's Headquarters at Newburgh, though conventionalized in some particulars, shows a building which might be something
more than 100 feet long with a door in the middle of one side and several large windows like those of a church to the right and left.   The
roof is the simple meeting of two planes, with a gable of equal height
over the door.   Not more than 15 years later General Heath, who
commanded the camp that spring, wrote our best description of the
building:

> Upon an eminence the troops erected a building handsomely
> finished with a spacious hall, sufficient to contain a brigade of troops
> on Lord's days for public worship, with an orchestra at one end; the
> vault of the hall was arched; at each end of the hall were two rooms
> conveniently situated for the issuing of the general orders, for the
> sitting of Boards of Officers, Court Martials, etc.   And an office
> and store for the Quarter Master and Commissary departments.
> On the top was a cupola and flag staff, on which a flag was hoisted
> occasionally for signals, etc.[25]

A few inferences can be drawn from Gates' orders.   The shingles
described by him on 10 January would cover about 4,666 square feet.
The roof in Tarbell's drawing would measure from 4,400 to 4,600.
The order of 21 January shows that the walls were built in a manner
common in those days, the spaces in the timbered frame being filled
with some available material.   It is possible that clods could be used,
even in midwinter, for the exceptionally mild weather was mentioned
4 days later.   The plan of 6 March for making a large supply of lime
suggests the plastering of the inner walls.   General Heath's reference
to the vault of the hall being arched seems to imply a form different
from that shown by Tarbell, and his use of the word *cupola* does not
describe satisfactorily the simple gable of the drawing; but neither of
these objections is conclusive, and some details of construction must remain in the field of conjecture.

There is no doubt that the Temple was built primarily as a house
of worship.   This thought was uppermost in General Heath's mind,

---

[24] Benson J. Lossing—*Pictorial Fieldbook of the Revolution*, I, 685; New York *Packet*, 16 Jan. 1783,
cited by Corning, *op. cit.*, p. 114.

[25] William Heath—*Memoirs*, pp. 329–30.

though he mentioned other purposes for which parts of it were used. Colonel Pickering wrote at the time that the chaplain expected to preach there on Sundays and the officers to use the building for dancing parties.[26]   No evidence has been found to confirm the tradition that it was designed for Masonic meetings.

Though it was not ready for religious services until the middle of February, it was used socially in celebrating the anniversary of the French alliance on the 6th.   Believing that the approach of peace justified a degree of leniency, Washington ordered the release of all military prisoners and their return to their regiments.   After a review and the firing of salutes and a *jeu-de-joie,* the officers assembled at the Temple, where they and their guests, numbering more than 500, listened to an oration by Chaplain Evans and partook of a cold collation.   The benches requisitioned for delivery before ten that morning, at a cost of 7 quarts and 28 rations, would have seated rather more than half the company.   It is not recorded that this function was considered at the time to be a dedication, but that term was used in later years.   A newspaper reported that "the company concluded one day with the greatest demonstrations of fascination and good humor." [27]   At nine that night Timothy Pickering was writing to his wife:

> I have returned from the "Temple of Virtue."   Alas! how little will it deserve the name! for how little virtue is there among mankind!   How small the number whose actions are not dictated by their interest or passion. . . . Some such will occasionally enter the Army's public building and give *color* for the title the good Doctor has chosen for it.[28]

He mentioned Mrs. Washington, Mrs. Knox, Mrs. Hand, and other ladies being present, assured his wife that she had lost nothing by her absence, and added that even the chaplain's oration fell short of his expectations.   The next morning Major Lansdale of the Maryland detachment offered "four silver dollars and no questions asked" for the return of a pair of silver plated stirrup irons lost at the Temple the previous evening.   In 1850 Lossing was told of the "orgies" of that evening and felt it appropriate that the latter part of the name was dropped at that time.[29]

It was at this time that Washington felt it necessary to address

---

[26] *Ibid.;* Octavius Pickering—*The Life of Timothy Pickering,* I, 399, quoting letter of 5 Feb. 1783; cf. Boynton, *op. cit.,* p. 59, Note.

[27] *Writings,* XXVI, 75–76, 103; New York *Packet,* 13 Feb. 1783, quoted by Corning, *op. cit.,* p. 110; cf. Lossing, *op. cit.,* I, 685.

[28] Pickering, *op. cit.,* I, 400.

[29] *Ibid.;* Boynton, *op. cit.,* p. 57; Lossing, *op. cit.,* I, 685.

what seems to have been his sharpest rebuke to the chaplains as a group. After stating that the New Building could be used for services and directing them to arrange a schedule so that it would be available to all brigades at some time on Sunday, he expressed his surprise at finding that the chaplains had considered their presence in camp during the winter so unimportant that nearly all of them had frequently been away at the same time. He directed that those absent at that time should be called back at once, that future leaves should be given only with his approval, and that chaplains arrange among themselves so that not more than one-third of them should be away at one time. He urged that, in addition to their public functions, they constantly visit the sick and added the assurance that "while they are thus publickly and privately engaged in performing the sacred duties of their office they may depend upon his utmost encouragement and support on all occasions, and that they will be considered in a very respectable point of light by the whole Army." [30]

Six weeks after Washington's reprimand to the chaplains he was happy to commend their zeal and ability and the decorum and regularity with which services were conducted on Sundays. He felt this would "reflect great credit on the army in general, tend to improve the morals, and at the same time, to increase the happiness of the soldiery, and must afford the most pure and rational entertainment for every serious and well disposed mind." This suggests how generally the conduct of preaching services was considered the chief function of the chaplains. Early in 1779 the brigade chaplain of the Light Dragoons applied to the Board of War for his pay. The Board pointed out that, because of the detached situation of these troops, the chaplain "may be able to perform divine service among them scarcely once a year" and recommended that he be discharged. Twenty-seven months later Congress carried out this proposal.[31]

Not only did some chaplains see little value in remaining with their units for ministrations to the sick and other individuals, but a number seem to have been rather careless about obtaining leave when they wished to be absent. When Congress revised the Articles of War in the autumn of 1776, a special rule for chaplains was adopted. If absent without leave or because of sickness, they should be tried by court-martial and were liable to discharge or to a fine not exceeding 1 month's pay and the loss of pay for the time of absence. Clearly

---

[30] *Writings,* XXVI, 136.
[31] *Ibid.,* p. 250; *Journals of the Continental Congress,* XIV, 659.

this special legislation was designed to meet a demonstrated need and to remedy a defect in the Articles of 1775 which made enlisted men absent without leave punishable at the discretion of the court but did not mention officers, probably with the expectation that their sense of responsibility would prevent such negligence.   One chaplain whom Washington held in high esteem was found guilty of unauthorized absence and subjected to the full penalty.   This he felt was a personal disgrace and a dishonor to his church.   He brooded over the situation until he became so depressed that he attempted suicide by cutting his throat.   Fortunately, the wounds were superficial and he recovered.[32]

Some chaplains, however, recognized the value of service to individuals.   During Arnold's march through the forests of Maine, Samuel Spring tried earnestly and with some success to lead a condemned man to a spirit of repentance for his crime.   Two members of Sullivan's force were convicted of inciting other soldiers to desert and were sentenced to be hanged.   Samuel Kirkland and William Rogers ministered to them, finding one deeply penitent but the other sullen and defiant.   The chaplains reported this to the general and were assured that he intended to pardon the former under the gallows because of his family and previous good conduct and the recommendation of the court.   At the time of execution three chaplains walked with the prisoners, talking seriously with them.   Rogers wrote that he addressed the spectators and Kirkland prayed, after which the one condemned man was "turned off" and the general ordered the release of the other.[33]

Three years before this when he was chaplain at Fort Stanwix, Kirkland had written to his wife about the difficulty of having public prayers more than once a day because the men were working so hard. He added, "I aim to be faithful in improving opportunities of personal intercourse with the troops, to enliven their love of God and of liberty, and their readiness to *do* and to *suffer* for the cause of the Country." [34]

On 5 July 1779, while Sullivan's expedition paused for a short time at Wyoming during his march against the western tribes of the Iroquois, Kirkland described his situation in terms of unusual interest. As he was attached to army headquarters, he had intimate contact

---

[32] *Journals of the American Congress*, I, 482; Charles H. Metzger—"Chaplains in the American Revolution," *The Catholic Historical Review*, April, 1945, p. 48, and to the Author, February 15, 1956.

[33] Robert J. Plumb—"Chaplain of Arnold's Expedition to Quebec," *The Chaplain*, July–Aug., 1949, p. 12; "Journal of Rev. William Rogers, D. D.," *Journals of the Military Expedition of Major General John Sullivan*, pp. 249–50.

[34] S. K. Lothrop—*Life of Samuel Kirkland*, in Jared Sparks, Ed.—*Library of American Biography*, 2 Ser., XV, 245–46.

with the general and with the other chaplains.   His letter reveals John
Sullivan in a most unusual light and shows much about the chaplain
himself:

> I am at present, in many respects, happily situated; have part
> of a large marquee to myself, and live in the General's family.
> Conversation in the family, for some days past, has been chiefly on
> religious subjects, such as the authenticity of the Scriptures, the na-
> ture and consequences of Deism.   The General has undertaken to
> convince any Deist (of which there is no want in the army), from
> principles of reason, that the Scriptures are of divine original, at
> least the doctrinal and preceptive parts.   In less than a day he has
> wrote thirty pages in quarto, to prove the existence of a Supreme
> Being, the truth of the Bible, and that Jesus is the promised Messiah
> and Savior of the world.   He had read the greatest part to me last
> evening and this morning.   I cannot but admire the ingenuity of
> the man, and the justness of many of his sentiments.   He frankly
> owned to me, that he was once a perfect Atheist, then a complete
> Deist, but at length became convinced, by fair and impartial rea-
> soning, of the existence of the Supreme Being, and the perfection of
> his character, of the inspiration of Holy Writ, and the mediatorial
> undertaking of Christ, and the general truths of the gospel, except
> this doctrine, viz., the depravity of human nature, which, he says,
> he must deny, or charge the Deity with imperfection, or, what is
> worse, with being the author of sin.   O that God may give me wis-
> dom and faithfulness to bear a suitable testimony to the *truth,* and
> never be left to deny the Lord! [35]

In March of that last winter of the war the Temple was the
scene of one of the most dramatic events in American history.   An
ominous situation had developed within the Army.   Pay, even in de-
preciated currency, was far in arrears.   Congress was bankrupt, and
the Army feared that it would be discharged and sent home in poverty.   Certain regiments had mutinied and tried to obtain redress from
Congress or their State governments by threats of force.   The proposal
that Washington set up a military dictatorship and correct the Nation's
wrongs drew from him a veto from which there could be no appeal.
A committee of officers visited Congress but returned with nothing but
some indefinite resolutions.   On 10 March an able but inflammatory
paper, calling a meeting the next day to adopt a course of action, was
circulated unsigned among the officers.   The Commander-in-Chief
deprecated this covert move but called a meeting for the 15th and
directed that the senior officer present should preside.   This was log-

---

[35] *Ibid.,* pp. 246–47.

ical, but he may have felt that Horatio Gates was safer in the chair than on the floor.[36]

When the officers were assembled, Washington entered and read a prepared address with visible emotion.   Recognizing the justice of their anxieties, he promised that he would make every proper effort to protect their interests and adjured them not to stain their record of patriotic devotion by a resort to lawless violence at the instigation of anonymous agitators.   With an appeal which his loyal comrades of Valley Forge and Morristown could not resist, he challenged them to yet another act of faith in the country and government for which they had endured so much that posterity might say, "Had this day been wanting, the world had never seen the last stage of perfection to which human nature is capable of attaining."   After he withdrew, the officers, led by Henry Knox and Rufus Putnam, adopted strong resolutions declaring their confidence in and affection for their commander and reaffirming their loyalty to the Congress of the United States. Three days later Washington addressed to the President of Congress one of the strongest letters ever to come from his pen, urging that prompt and full justice be done to these faithful leaders of the army.[37]

In mid-April Washington invited all officers to attend levees to be held in the Temple daily at noon.   On the 19th, the anniversary of Lexington and Concord, the cessation of hostilities was proclaimed from the Temple door.   Prayer was offered by Chaplain Gano, and the anthem entitled *Independence* was presented by vocal and instrumental music.   In the evening there were elaborate fireworks on a form built of more than 1,700 feet of 7-inch timber.   On 10 May, at the suggestion of General Knox, the officers met in the Temple and took the first steps in organizing the Society of Cincinnati.   During a violent hailstorm on the afternoon of 11 June, the building was struck by lightning.   The last troops left the camp on the 23d.   On 26 August the quartermaster announced that The Temple, the huts lately occupied by the troops, and the wood and timber lying about the camp would be sold at public auction on 2 September.   The only mediums of exchange which would be accepted were cash, bank notes, Mr. Morris's notes, Mr. Hillegas's notes, or debts contracted in the Quartermaster's Department since 1 January 1782.   Unfortunately the records of this sale do not seem to have been preserved.   A recent work

---

[36] Corning, *op. cit.*, p. 120; Louis Clinton Hatch—*The Administration of the American Revolutionary Army*, p. 146; Boynton, *op. cit.*, p. 59; *Writings*, XXIV, 272–73; XXVI, 222–32.
[37] Same as No. 36.

states that The Temple was burned soon after the departure of the troops.[38]

The Temple was designed to accommodate one brigade at religious services. The claim, especially urged in 1776, that one chaplain could not serve a brigade was based chiefly upon the current distribution of forces, which often separated by long distances the regiments of some brigades. In June of that year, New York undertook to raise 5 battalions of 750 men each. One chaplain was assigned to the battalion ordered to Canada, but only 2 were provided for the 4 which were to reinforce the army at New York. When Washington's army of about 6,000 men was reorganized in the late summer of 1782, his 22 regiments were grouped in 2 wings, 4 divisions, and 8 brigades. Eighteen regiments constituted the 6 New England brigades; the remaining 4 made up those of New York and New Jersey. Apparently each chaplain would serve about 750 to 800 men.[39]

Little seems to have been done to provide the men with chaplains of their own faith beyond Washington's argument that regimental assignments would go far toward accomplishing this because regiments were raised locally and most of the men would belong to the same religious group. With minor exceptions this principle was observed in early assignments, but later in the war it seems to have been considered less important. The Virginia convention directed in 1775 that dissenting ministers be allowed to preach to the troops at intervals for the benefit of those who might not care to attend the services conducted by the chaplains of the established church. Probably this action resulted from a petition in which the Baptists of the State declared their support of the Revolution and asked that four of their number whom they had chosen be permitted to minister to the soldiers with the same freedom as regular chaplains.[40]

It has been said that the chaplains were governed by two objectives—to save souls and to defend American liberties. There are many indications that the latter was not considered wholly subordinate in value. On the second Sunday after Lexington and Concord, Amos Farnsworth commented upon his chaplain's sermon with a delightful freedom in composition: "An Excelent Sermon, he incoridged us to go And fite for our Land and Country: Saying we Did not do our

---

[38] Boyton, *op. cit.*, pp. 65–66; Corning, *op. cit.*, pp. 115–16, 121–22; Heath, *op. cit.*, pp. 341, 352–53; *The Magazine of American History*, Vol. I, No. 1, p. 77; Fred L. Holmes—*George Washington Traveled This Way*, p. 160.

[39] *Archives of New York: The Revolution*, I; Boynton, *op. cit.*, pp. 46–47.

[40] *Writings*, VIII, 203; Clarke and Force—*American Archives*, 4 Ser., III, Col. 383; Headley, *op. cit.*, pp. 250–51.

Duty if we did not Stand up now." Such exhortations were common until the last regiment was discharged. Some chaplains were active in recruiting, some induced men whose term of service had expired to remain, all vindicated the justice of the revolutionary movement in a way to convince the doubtful that righteousness and opportunity for the years to come depended upon an American triumph.[41]

The impact of such moral imperatives upon the minds of the soldiery, confronted by stern military duties in the midst of unparalleled privations, is incalculable. It has been pointed out that this morale-building force had no effective counterpart in the British Army, where several regiments had no chaplains and others were served by men of limited zeal. Chaplain Brudenell, who came to America as a volunteer and went through the Burgoyne campaign, was a worthy representative of his church. In the familiar painting of the burial of General Frazer he is shown calmly reading the service despite the cannonade from the American guns beyond the Hudson. An early writer states that this changed to the firing of minute guns as a tribute to a gallant foe as soon as the Americans realized the nature of the gathering on the opposite hill. This seems very doubtful because neither Burgoyne nor the Baroness Riedesel mentions it in the detailed accounts of the burial which they wrote soon afterward and of which both were eye witnesses. Both of them emphasized American kindness after the surrender, and they certainly would have recorded so marked a courtesy. The Baroness wrote that Gates declared that he would not have permitted the firing if he had known that a funeral was going on.[42]

During the battle of 7 October, Major John Acland was wounded and carried a prisoner into the American camp. Lady Harriet, his wife, was greatly distressed but accompanied the army during the miserable retreat through rain and mud on the 9th. Already on this expedition she had nursed her husband through a severe illness in Canada and after he had been wounded at Hubbardton. Encouraged by the resolute little Baroness, she resolved to go to him. Burgoyne gave her a note of introduction to Gates, and she started down the river in an open boat, escorted through rain and darkness by Chaplain Brudenell. She was treated with kindness by the American officers and cared for her husband in the little house which still stands on Bemis Heights until he was able to go to Albany. Several writers state that

[41] French, *op. cit.*, pp. 175–78.

[42] Edward E. Curtis—*The Organization of the British Army in the American Revolution*, pp. 10–14; *Memoirs of Madame Riedesel*, p. 122; Lossing, *op. cit.*, I, 65–68.

she married the chaplain after her husband's death, but this is contradicted by what seems convincing authority.[43]

Frederick V. Melsheimer, a chaplain of the Brunswick dragoons,
has been described as one of the "legitimate spoils of war." Wounded
and captured at Bennington, he determined after a time to throw in
his lot with the new country and served as a Lutheran pastor in
Pennsylvania the rest of his life. Educated at the University of Helm-
stedt, he made a lifelong study of insect life and was known as the father
of entomology in America. It is said that he sometimes let his congregation wait while he satisfied his scientific interest in a handsome
butterfly which chanced to flit through the open windows of his
church.[44]

Naturally little could be done officially to help discharged chaplains in their readjustment to civil life. Washington anticipated such
a problem as early as the spring of 1776. Writing to the congregation
at Woodstock, Conn., he praised in highest terms the work being done
by Chaplain Abiel Leonard, their minister, and urged that they allow
him to continue so valuable a service. He closed with the hope and
expectation that they would welcome the chaplain back to his pulpit
after the struggle for liberty should be won. Unhappily, more than
the goodwill of the congregation was necessary to this end. This
accomplished and devoted clergyman served through that year as the
chaplain of Knox's artillery but became insane in 1777 and died the
following year.[45]

Like the surgeons, the chaplains were not commissioned officers
but served under contracts for periods of 6 or 12 months. In general
they were men of education. Considering how many were reared in
New England, it is not surprising to find that a large majority of those
for whom records are available were graduates of Harvard or Yale. A
considerable group were Princeton men, and several more were graduates of other American or European colleges. Besides conspicuous
leadership in public and church affairs, several of these men in later
years served the various colleges of their time as administrators or
teachers, building on a broad foundation the cultural institutions of a
free people.[46]

The chaplains of the Revolution established a group of precedents
which never have been lost. Their influence in the support of disci-

[43] *Ibid.;* William P. Courtney in *The Dictionary of National Biography,* I, 59–60.
[44] Dixon Ryan Fox—*Ideas in Motion,* p. 75.
[45] *Writings,* IV, 163; Heitman, *op. cit.*
[46] *Yale Biographies; Catalogus Senatus Academici, Universitate Harvardiana; et al.*

454841 O—58——6

pline and morale was so valuable that chaplains have been considered an essential part of the military organization in all emergencies. Serving without military rank, they gained a place in the confidence of officers and men which no commission could have conferred or maintained. When rank was conferred in later years, those who were true to the tradition of the office were accorded a deference out of proportion to their grade. The spirit of interfaith comity, of mutual respect and cooperation, has persevered and grown; and the comradeship which chaplains have discovered in camp and on the battlefield has been a potent factor in moderating prejudice and rivalry among sincere people of all faiths.

CHAPTER V

From Washington to Lincoln

With the end of the Revolution in sight, Congress began the serious consideration of the kind of army to be maintained in the coming years of peace. As a basis for their further action the committee having the matter in charge asked the detailed recommendations of the Commander-in-Chief. Before preparing his reply, Washington asked the recommendations of his principal officers. Ten of them submitted their proposals within a few days, Timothy Pickering writing 32 pages on the subject. These documents are among the Washington papers in the Library of Congress. They all felt that a standing army was needed chiefly to guard the frontiers. Four believed that it should be a Continental force independent of the States. Seven urged that 1 or more military academies be established, and 3 named West Point as a desirable location. Steuben thought that the skilled artisans among the German prisoners would be glad to remain in America and work in a government ordnance plant. George Clinton proposed a reserve corps of officers and recommended that State colleges give a degree in military science. Heath quoted the Chevalier Folard as saying that the art of war is "a trade for the ignorant, a science for men of genius," and urged that military academies teach both the technical and the sublime parts of war.

Rufus Putnam was the only one to mention chaplains. He recommended that 3 regiments of infantry and 1 of artillery be maintained and that each have its chaplain. The same provision was included in his plan for the organization of the militia. This would have assigned 1 chaplain to a group of 1,175 officers and men. He made the further proposal that the pay scale then in force be continued except for chaplains, surgeons, and mates, who were receiving at least 25 percent too much. At that time chaplains were paid the same as colonels.

Washington sent his recommendations to Congress on 2 May 1783. He proposed a force of 2,631 officers and men under Continental control. Four regiments of infantry numbering 477 each were to be formed, and the remaining 723 were to constitute a regiment of artillery.   Each regiment was to have its chaplain.   One was to be stationed at a post near the north end of Lake Champlain, one at Niagara, another on the portage between the Scioto and Sandusky, and one on the Carolina-Georgia frontier.   Presumably the headquarters of the artillery chaplain would have been at West Point.   The general called attention to the fact that he was advising the assignment of chaplains to regiments rather than to brigades and stated his belief that the pay of chaplains, surgeons, and mates was too high.[1] In several particulars he followed the suggestions of Rufus Putnam, though he proposed a much smaller regiment.   In specific points he adopted the recommendations of Steuben, Knox, and others, and several seem to have been wholly his own.

This plan was presented to Congress on 11 June and referred to the committee, which consisted of Hamilton, Madison, Ellsworth, Wilson, and Holten.   After further consultation with the general, they submitted a detailed report on 23 October.   With some important variations, it paralleled Washington's recommendations.   The committee proposed 4 regiments of infantry and 1 of artillery, the latter to include a corps of engineers.   In the former, as a means of attracting superior men, colonels, majors, and captains were to receive respectively $100, $70, and $50 a month, with allowances, though Washington considered these rates to be needlessly high.   In the artillery they were to be higher still.   Four professors were to have been paid $100 a month, but this was reduced to $75, the amount allowed to the drawing master.   Plans for a regiment of dragoons were dropped.[2]

A chaplain was to have been assigned to each regiment.   Like the surgeon, he was to receive $40 a month, 1 ration, and forage for 1 horse.   As the money value of the ration was fixed at six-ninetieths of a dollar and forage was worth double that amount, the chaplain's pay and allowances would amount to $553 a year.   The nearest comparison is with the captains of infantry, who would have received $624.33.   Congress gave an indefinite approval to the plan, but in 1785 it voted to raise 700 troops.   Line officers were to receive less than recommended by the committee, surgeons and mates somewhat more, but no reference was made to chaplains.   Two years later the same number of troops were voted, and the pay scale remained unchanged.[3]

As Secretary at War of the Confederation, Henry Knox submitted to Congress on 18 March 1786 "A plan for the general arrangement

---

[1] *The Writings of George Washington*, Bicentennial Ed., XXVI, 315–16, 374–84.
[2] *Ibid.*, p. 480n; *Journals of the Continental Congress*, XXIV, 492, 494, 501, XXV, 549–51, 722–45.
[3] *Ibid.*, XXVIII, 248, XXXIII, 604.

of the militia of the United States." This had been requested in order that it might be submitted to the several States, but no steps seem to have been taken at that time to put the plan in operation. The Constitution gave Congress a general power over the organization and training of the militia; and Knox, now Secretary of War, submitted his plan to the President on 18 January 1790. Three days later Washington forwarded the document to Congress. Though the plan was not adopted, it was not forgotten. In 1819 a committee of the House made it a part of a report on pending legislation. Knox proposed to organize the troops into self-sufficient units called legions to consist of 153 officers and 2,880 men. A major general, two aids, an inspector, and a chaplain constituted the staff of each legion. As a part of his training program Knox offered a suggestion of more than ordinary interest in view of the large place given to chaplains in promoting good citizenship since World War II:

> Every legion must have a chaplain, of respectable talents and character, who, besides his religious functions, should impress on the minds of the youth, at stated periods, in concise discourses, the eminent advantages of free governments to the happiness of society, and that such governments can only be supported by the knowledge, spirit, and virtuous conduct of the youth—to be illustrated by the most conspicuous examples in history.[4]

The first legislation under the Constitution continued the pay scale of 1785, but the Act of 30 April 1790 allowed an increase to lieutenant colonels commandant, though reducing subordinate line officers, surgeons, and mates by amounts varying from 10 to 33 percent. These rates remained in effect when the Act of 3 March 1791 authorized the President to appoint a chaplain, whose pay of $50 a month was to include all allowances.[5] As the value of the ration had become a variable item, an exact comparison cannot be made, but it is estimated that the chaplain received slightly more than the surgeon and from $6 to $9 more than the monthly pay of captains.

A law of 1792 placed the chaplain in the General Staff without changing his pay status, but in 1795 he was allowed two rations and forage, which were valued at $6 a month. Chaplains were not mentioned in the succeeding military legislation until the Act of 16 July 1798 directed that 12 regiments of infantry and 1 of dragoons be raised and authorized the appointment of 4 chaplains with the pay

---

[4] *Proceedings of the Massachusetts Historical Society,* Ser. I, VI, 381–94; *American State Papers,* I, 6–10, 824.

[5] 1 *Stat.* 95, 119, 223.

and emoluments of a major.[6]   The fortunate termination of the troubles with France made it possible to discharge these emergency troops early in the summer of 1800.   Possibly a chaplain, appointed to the General Staff under the law of 1792, was stationed at West Point during this period.   The fact that the Corps of Engineers at that post was constituted a military academy in 1802 makes this conjecture seem more plausible.[7]

In 1808, foreign perils brought a law which ordered the raising of eight additional regiments and the assignment of a chaplain to each brigade, with the pay and emoluments of a major of infantry.   Early in 1812, with the country on the verge of war, Congress ordered 13 regiments to be raised at once.   They were to be very large, numbering in the infantry more than 2,000 officers and men and nearly that many in the artillery.   Nevertheless, only one chaplain was provided for each brigade.   The next year 20 more regiments were authorized, and the same provision was made for chaplains.[8]   Some of the militia regiments called into the Federal service had their own chaplains, and Congress did not attempt to substitute the brigade chaplaincy of the national forces, but a law of 18 April 1814 gave these men only the pay and rations of a captain of infantry, with the addition of forage for one horse.[9]

Because of lost records, the number of chaplains who served with Federal troops is uncertain.   Seven were listed in 1814, and many years later Dix remembered that number having been appointed by the President.   Thompson states that the surviving records give the names of ten.   One of these was the venerable David Jones, who served from 2 April 1813 till 15 June 1815, being then in his 80th year. James J. Wilmer of Maryland is the only one known to have died in service.[10]   Still more uncertain is the number who may have served with State troops, some for very short periods.   Unfortunately the meagre records tell very little about the experiences of these chaplains and their methods of work.

A law of 1815 which fixed the pay of officers at the same rates as in 1802 did not mention chaplains, but the Act of 24 April 1816 authorized one to each brigade, with the pay and emoluments of a major.   It further authorized a monthly allowance of $8 a horse when

---

[6] 1 *Stat.* 241, 430, 483, 558, 604.
[7] 2 *Stat.* 85, 132.
[8] 2 *Stat.* 481, 671–74, 794–96.
[9] 3 *Stat.* 134.
[10] Donald A. Thompson—*American Army Chaplaincy,* p. 11; *Congressional Globe,* 1847, p. 220.

forage was not drawn in kind, but specified that neither money nor forage be given except for horses actually in use.   Two years later the characteristic post-war spirit of economy led to the repeal of those parts of this law which concerned brigade chaplains, judge advocates, hospital surgeons, and mates.   A further provision of the Act of 24 April 1816 directed that a chaplain be stationed at the Military Academy and serve as professor of geography, history, and ethics, with the same pay and emoluments as the professor of mathematics.   The reorganization of the peace establishment in 1821 made no other provision for chaplains.[11]

For many years the army posts had no chaplains except those chosen informally and paid by voluntary contributions.[12]   The Secretary of War, Lewis Cass, in a report dated 21 November 1831, declared intemperance the prevailing vice of the army.   Recommending that ardent spirits be not continued as a part of the ration, he asserted that the habits and morals of the men would have been much better if the $22,132 spent for 72,537 gallons of issue whiskey in 1830 had been spent for tea, coffee, and sugar.   Though the American soldier was well fed and clothed, he said his moral culture was wholly neglected, and added, "As he becomes a better man he will become a better soldier."   For the good of the service as well as of the men he recommended the appointment of chaplains at army posts.[13]

Five years later Benjamin F. Butler, the New York statesman temporarily holding two cabinet posts, made these proposals more specific.   He said that the constitutional prohibition against an establishment of religion did not lessen the obligation of Congress to provide military personnel with an opportunity for worship.   This, with the aid of a judicious and devoted chaplain, would be a great help in promoting discipline.   He thought the councils of administration of the various posts would be able to select chaplains more satisfactory to the local garrison than those who might be chosen by the national authorities and recommended legislation empowering them to do so.   The same plan, he suggested, might be extended to regiments in the field.[14]

Early in 1838 the Senate passed a bill to authorize such an arrangement at any post.   If approved by the Secretary of War, a chaplain should receive four rations, quarters, and an agreed sum not greater than $40 a month.   In the House it was stipulated that he should act

[11] 3 *Stat.* 224, 297–99, 426, 615.

[12] *The Military and Naval Magazine of the United States,* April 1833, p. 107.

[13] *American State Papers,* IV, 709.

[14] *Ibid.,* VI, 812.

as schoolmaster, and with this addition the bill was enacted.   During the debate one congressman opposed the measure because it introduced a new principle, a connection between government and the clergy, and insisted that choice by the regiments would be much better.   Apparently his objection was to the power of the Secretary to disapprove local selections.   When the probable cost was asked, it was stated that it would amount to $1,000 a man and that about 70 posts would employ chaplains.   This seems to have been considered too great an expense, for 2 days later a supplementary act limited the operation of this law to the 20 posts which the Secretary should consider most destitute of instruction.   Later references to this law seem to indicate that its sponsors attached major importance to the chaplains' duties as schoolmasters.[15]   Soon after this enactment, chaplains were employed at posts in Virginia, New York, and Maine and at forts in Michigan, Wisconsin, Minnesota, Iowa, Kansas, Indian Territory, Arkansas, and Louisiana.   The advance of the frontier soon placed a number in Texas and on the Pacific coast.[16]

The provision that certain courses at the Military Academy be taught by the chaplain was not wholly without precedent.   On 1 July 1816, the Secretary of War approved the course of study prepared by the faculty.   The studies of the last year included a review of the Latin and Greek classics usually taught in academies.   Secretary Crawford specified that this should be required only of those who had previously studied these languages.   He expected that this instruction could be given by the chaplain and remarked that he hoped the performance of these duties would induce Congress to make the appointment permanent.   The subjects assigned to the chaplain by the law of 1816 were likewise scheduled for the fourth year, and he seems to have been the only professor giving other than review instruction during the last year of the course.[17]   Thomas Picton was the first professor appointed under the provisions of this law.   He was a Presbyterian, but the 2 predecessors of whom records have been found and 5 of his 6 successors before 1861 were Episcopalians.   One of these men was a graduate of the Academy, and the others had experience in educational work or other special qualifications for the post.[18]

When the Mexican War broke out, several regiments were sent to the theater of operations without chaplains.   Supporting a motion

---

[15] 5 *Stat.* 259, 308; *Globe*, 1838, pp. 134, 487–88, 496, 1847, pp. 221, 346.
[16] Thompson, *op. cit.*, pp. 16–17.
[17] *American State Papers*, XII, 838.
[18] Files, OCCh.

for their appointment to all regiments, Senator Hannegan declared that if chaplains had been provided for those which had gone into Mexico, the crimes and disorders of which so much had been heard would have been as 1 to 100, because no power on earth was so well calculated to maintain order, propriety, and decency in camp as the chaplains.   He urged that they receive the pay and emoluments of a major of dragoons, which was said to amount to $2,182.82 a year. Several felt this to be too much, but the senator pointed out that chaplains would not need horses, forage, or servants and would actually draw only about $1,100.   One senator favored regimental chaplains but would pay no more than $1,000.   Another would pay $500 and allow only one to a brigade.   A third suggested that the Government provide rations but leave it to the churches to select and support the chaplains.   Sevier said that there were so many religious men in the Army that it was not necessary to have chaplains who would feel that they must conduct morning and evening prayers every day and preach every Sunday.   Saying that the battle of New Orleans was fought on Sunday, he tried to imagine the situation when Jackson's men were taking post for the battle if they had been stopped by chaplains to hear them preach.   The ministers of his church preached and prayed all year for $200, and he offered to supply the whole army from his State at that rate.   In more serious vein he proposed that chaplains receive $500 a year and two rations, but his amendment was defeated by one vote.   Webster proposed $1,000, and this figure was accepted by the Senate.   The House reduced the amount to $500, but the conference committees recommended a compromise, and the Act of 11 February 1847 gave chaplains $750, 1 ration, and forage for 1 horse.[19]

Other important provisions were included in this law.   Hannegan urged that every regiment have its chaplain, stating that the components of a brigade often would be stationed so far apart that a chaplain could not serve more than one regiment.   Moreover, he expected him to do much more than conduct services of worship.   He should be a companion to the soldier in times of distress and minister to the sick and dying.   These views were endorsed by Cameron and others, and Commodore Perry was quoted as saying that the chaplain did more than any other officer to maintain order in the Navy.   It was pointed out that there would be 52 regiments to be supplied, but the Senate voted 39 to 3 that each regiment should have its chaplain.   The House would agree only to a brigade chaplaincy, so the Senate yielded

---

[19] *Globe,* 1847, pp. 216–17, 220–23, 303, 346, 349, 352, 377; 9 *Stat.* 124.

this point.   Assuming the figures given during the debate to be correct, it will be seen that the Senate was willing to give more than
$50,000, plus allowances, to have chaplains in the army; the House
would not pay as much as $9,000; and the matter was compromised
at less than 13.   At first the senators expected the appointments to be
made by the President, but the proposal that chaplains be elected by
the regiments was advanced, primarily to avoid forcing upon any group
a clergyman of a faith different from that of the majority.   Westcott
said he was ready to give a Bible, psalm book, and hymn book to every
man but felt that chaplains should not be assigned to particular units.
He urged that a sufficient number be selected from all the important
religious bodies and serve the troops wherever their activities would be
most acceptable.   Simmons remarked that in his experience truly
pious people did not object to preaching by men of other groups but
those with no piety were most sensitive to the rights of conscience.
Butler deprecated the canvass for votes which he expected whenever
a number of candidates desired election, but the majority voted that
each volunteer regiment should choose its own chaplain.   When the
House changed the bill to allow only one chaplain to a brigade, it provided that he be chosen by the councils of administration of the component regiments, and the Senate accepted this method of selection.[20]

Another provision of this bill authorized the Secretary of War to
order a post chaplain to join the army in Mexico whenever a majority
of the men at his station had left for service in the field and provided
that his compensation should stop and his office be deemed vacant if
he should refuse to comply with such an order.   At first the House
intended that all regular chaplains should go to the field, but the Senate conferees stressed the remoteness of some chaplain posts and the
importance of the chaplain's work as schoolmaster, so it was agreed to
leave this matter to the discretion of the Secretary.   In the discussion
it was stated that only 12 men were involved, as 2 chaplaincies had
been vacant for some time and 6 had been discontinued since the with-
drawal of the troops from those posts.[21]

More than once during this debate the senators referred to the
claim being spread widely in Mexico that the war was one of religious
propaganda, a Protestant crusade for the overthrow of Catholicism in
that country.[22]   The ignorant and illiterate were not the only Mexicans to hold this belief.   Supporting a proposal to raise funds for de-

---

[20] *Ibid.; Globe, loc. cit.*
[21] *Ibid.,* p. 346.
[22] *Ibid.,* pp. 220, 222.

fense by taxing church property, a member of the Mexican Congress asked, "If the Yankee triumphs, what ecclesiastical property or what religion will be left us?"   At the time of Scott's attack upon Vera Cruz, Tornel ordered the clergy to preach a crusade against the heretical invaders, and tales of American atrocities were circulated vigorously.   A pamphlet called *Clamor de las Ovejas* declared that some Vera Cruz churches were to be sold by the Americans to Protestants, others to Mohammedans, others to worshippers of Venus, and some would be used to house pigs.   To counteract the fanaticism being roused on religious grounds, Scott ordered that American soldiers salute the Mexican priests as well as the magistrates.   The general and his principal officers attended mass, and complied when they were invited to march in the procession.   The churches of the country were respected except for one or two found to be the rendezvous of guerilla bands, and priests were not molested unless they were actively hostile in such ways as by inducing American soldiers to desert.[23]

President Polk felt that Mexican resistance to the American forces would be desperate unless the priests could be satisfied that their churches and religion would be secure.   A proclamation in Spanish promising religious freedom and kind treatment was sent to Taylor for distribution among the Mexicans, and several bishops were asked to select priests who could accompany the army as chaplains and reassure the Mexican clergy.   It has been stated that the President's object in arranging for these chaplains was to check desertions among the Irish soldiers,[24] but we have his own statement in the account of his interview with the Bishop of New York on 19 May 1846:

> Bishop Hughes had come to Washington upon an invitation given by Mr. Buchanan upon consultation with me some days ago. Our object was to procure his aid in disabusing the minds of the Catholic priests and people of Mexico in regard to what they most erroneously supposed to be the hostile designs of the government and people of the United States upon the religion and church property of Mexico.[25]

The President explained the misconceptions which were being cultivated as an aid to the war spirit among the Mexican people and asked if some Spanish-speaking priests could accompany the troops as chaplains while others preceded the army into Mexico to assure the clergy that their religion and church property were secure under the

---

[23] Justin H. Smith—*The War with Mexico*, II, 10, 142, 346, 221, 458–59.

[24] Eugene Irving McCormac—*James K. Polk: A Political Biography*, p. 421; Thompson, *op. cit.*, p. 22.

[25] Allen Nevins, Ed.—*Polk: The Diary of a President, 1845-1849*, p. 97.

American constitution and would be protected by the army.   The
Bishop said that he knew the Archbishop of Mexico and would be glad
to visit the country and confer with him or to cooperate in other ways.[26]

Necessary arrangements soon were made, and within 6 weeks
Father John McElroy, pastor in Georgetown, and Father Anthony Rey,
professor at Georgetown College, reported to General Taylor on the
Rio Grande.   As they were not chosen by the method prescribed by
law, their appointment was unofficial, but they were received cordially
by Taylor, and it was arranged that McElroy should remain at the
base hospital while Rey accompanied the expedition against Monterey.
Father McElroy's first task was to find a place to live, and he felt that
the cruelties of war had not been exaggerated when he was compelled
to pay $10 a week for a small room containing little besides an old cot
with no mattress at a boarding house run by an American.   At one
time there were 800 sick and wounded to whom the chaplain ministered, but he found time to conduct a school for the children, teaching
the three R's and geography 4 hours a day.   The tragic irony of
Father Rey's experience could scarcely be surpassed.   After several
months with Taylor's army he was killed by Mexican guerillas in January 1847.   The people who feared an American attack upon the
Catholic Church killed the priest sent into their country as a messenger of good will.[27]

After the war the Army reverted to the system of post chaplain,
and a law of 2 March 1849 increased the authorized number from 20
to 30.[28]   During these years there arose a considerable opposition to
government chaplaincies, whether in the Army, Navy, or Congress.
Certain groups felt that public support of religious ministrations compromised the principle of complete separation between state and church.
Some other factors tended to discredit the system: Several members of
Congress deprecated the poor taste of clergymen electioneering for the
chaplaincy of either house.   The law did not specify the qualifications
of post chaplains, and sometimes men who were not clergymen were
chosen.   It was said that retired sergeants or cooks were known to have
been appointed and that chaplains sometimes held civilian positions,
giving very little time or effort to their military duties.[29]

Early in 1856 the House of Representatives debated at length the
question whether to elect a chaplain or continue an arrangement un-

---

[26] *Ibid.*

[27] Thompson, *op. cit.,* p. 22; Terence King—"The First Catholic Chaplains," *The Army and Navy Chaplain,* July–August 1942, pp. 20–22.

[28] 9 *Stat.* 351.

[29] Thompson, *op. cit.,* p. 18.

der which the daily sessions were being opened with prayer by the local clergymen in rotation.   Some felt that this plan would satisfy many critics of an official paid chaplaincy.   Others considered it an imposition to ask gratuitous services from the clergy.   Numerous candidates were proposed and supported by various members, one of them on the ground that his prayers would be short.   One nominee was Miss Antoinette Brown of New York.   It was stated that she was regularly ordained, but the byplay of debate failed to decide whether this made her a clergyman or clergywoman.   This momentous question remained unanswered at the following session though she had become Mrs. Blackwell in the interval.   Finally the House chose for its chaplain Daniel Waldo, a revolutionary veteran then in his 95th year.[30]

During this debate a representative from Tennessee presented a petition from 149 of his constituents, which is a good summary of the contemporary arguments against the employment of chaplains supported by public funds.   Of the 7 propositions advanced by the petitioners, 3 rested on constitutional grounds: Powers not delegated to the United States were reserved to the States or to the people—but the power to employ clergymen never had been so delegated; Congress could make no establishment of religion—but chaplains chosen and paid by Federal authorities actually were in some degree such an establishment; religious tests for public office were forbidden—but the qualifications demanded of chaplains constituted a religious test.   The petitioners were concerned about the immense increase in the number of chaplains, saying that the Army had 30, the Navy 24, and Congress 2, at a total cost of about a quarter of a million dollars.   It was stated that there was no more reason for chaplains in regiments or ships than in towns or counties, and such a group would tend to become an aristocracy, serving for hire.   The petitioners denounced compulsory attendance at religious services, citing the case of a soldier alleged to have been fined and imprisoned for his failure to attend.   Finally, they declared that the support of religion should be voluntary and that maintenance by the Government would lead to corruption.   Similar questions arose when the House was organized for the next session.   One member said he wished to nominate an excellent minister as a compliment though he knew he would decline the office if elected because he believed public support of chaplains to be wrong.   Another declared in support of his candidate that he was a "regular Hard Shell Ironside Baptist, . . . a very pious man; and though not of eminent ability, he has enough talent to pray for such a crowd as this."   Notwithstanding

---

[30] *Globe,* 1856, pp. 178, 478–86.

this unimpeachable indorsement, the House reelected its aged chaplain.[31]

Two sections of the Act of 3 March 1855 were of interest to chaplains. One stated that they should share in the extra pay authorized by a law of 28 September 1850 for the officers and men who served in California before 1 March 1852. This bonus for officers was at the rate of $2 a day. The other specifically included them in a grant of 160 acres of land to every officer or man who had served honorably in any war since 1790.[32] This provision was an amendment sponsored by Senator Shields. In support of his motion he declared: "I can testify from my own knowledge that some of those chaplains hazarded their lives as much as any soldier in the army. . . . They are as meritorious as any class to whom the benefits of the bill are to be extended." So many confusing amendments were added to various parts of the bill that the Senate swept them all away by adopting a concise substitute, but the indomitable Shields insisted that his provision for the chaplains be reinstated. He said they should share in the bounty though they were noncombatants and took no part in the fighting. Douglas said he was mistaken in the latter point, adding: "I know some who did as much fighting as praying. Some of them were the most efficient men in the army—particularly in the western wars." Thus supported, Shields' amendment was enacted into law.[33]

Two years later the pay of officers was increased $20 a month, and the Secretary of War was authorized to allow this additional pay to chaplains on recommendation of the councils of administration. At the same time the commutation value of the ration was raised from 20 to 30 cents.[34] This gave the post chaplain a compensation valued at $1,159, in addition to quarters and fuel, for a normal year.

The earliest specification of a uniform for chaplains which has been found is in the Army Regulations of 1816. They were to wear that of the General Staff without the gold epaulets, which indicated military rank. The coat was blue, single breasted, with 10 yellow gilt buttons. The standing collar was "not to rise higher than the tip of the ear, and always as high in front as the chin will permit in turning the head." Pantaloons or knee breeches were optional, but high military boots were to be worn only in time of war. The regulations of 1821 stated that chaplains and certain others had no uniform, which

---

[31] *Ibid.*
[32] 9 *Stat.* 504; 10 *Stat.* 639, 701.
[33] *Globe,* 1855, pp. 313, 361, 364, 566, 1032.
[34] 11 *Stat.* 163.

implies civilian dress.   On 11 June 1832, Order No. 50 of the Adjutant General directed chaplains to wear "citizen's dress with buttons of the Corps of Engineers, round hat and black cockade with gold eagle," and the suit was to be black.   General Order No. 36 of 1839 added a dress sword, an optional frock coat of blue, the forage cap of the engineers, and a blue cloak.   The next year General Order No. 7 directed that chaplains' uniform should be the dress usually worn by the clergy.

The long period between two great wars drew to a close with religious ministrations provided by the Government for less than one-third of the army posts.   Critics were saying that some chaplains were incompetent and that improper motives often dictated assignments.[35] Most chaplains were stationed far from the chief centers of population, and neither the religious leaders nor the public paid much attention to the circumstances of army life.   Critical observation and friendly encouragement might have contributed greatly to the effectiveness of these chaplains.

---

[35] *Globe,* 1857, p. 724; Thompson, *op. cit.,* pp. 18–19.

CHAPTER VI

The Trumpet That Shall Never Call Retreat

Three million Americans came under the influence of army chaplains during our 4 tragic years of civil strife. Though such relations sometimes were indirect, great numbers of young men experienced religious earnestness and moral purpose more vividly through their army associations than ever before. A marked revival of religious interest began in Lee's army after the great battles of 1862 and continued until the end of the war. William Jones believed that more than 15,000 men in that army professed conversion and that similar movements occurred in all the Southern armies.[1] Charles Quintard said that the proportion of true and active Christian men in the Confederate army was greater than in any other since that of Cromwell.[2]

In the more numerous Union army a greater number of chaplains were carrying on their work with the same evangelical vigor. Their writings make numerous references to periods of exceptional religious interest and dedication, but no reliable statistics can be given.[3] Less tangible influences for good were constantly at work in both armies, and the ideals of the chaplains were projected through the life of the nation for many years. The more capable among the soldiers became leaders in the political and business life of all localities, and many of the chaplains later held public offices or positions of influence in education or in the church. For the span of a generation social and political reforms and forward movements in religion and education of utmost importance in the expanding life of the reunited nation were rooted back in the hopes and fears and resolutions of the tense years of war.

Few chaplains preached a religious message so abstract that they did not try to apply it to the moral issues of the contest as they saw

---

[1] J. William Jones—*Christ in the Camp*, p. 390.

[2] Rev. Arthur Howard Noll, Ed.—*Doctor Quintard: Chaplain, C. S. A.*, p. 2.

[3] Frank Milton Bristol—*The Life of Chaplain McCabe*, p. 77; *Memorial and Letters of Rev. John Adams, D. D.*, p. 87; Rev. J. J. Marks, D. D.—*The Peninsula Campaign in Virginia*, p. 60; D. P. Conyngham—*The Soldier of the Cross, passim.*

them.   These were the concrete principles of right which they urged the soldiers to uphold if necessary with their lives.   All but universally these men saw justice and obligation as they were conceived by the dominant group of their neighborhood and section.   Few penetrated the faulty perspective of 1861 nor questioned the fevered avowals of the local press and orators.   Thus, the cause in which they were enlisted was sacred and demanded their unqualified support.

Those Confederate chaplains who have left a statement of their political views in 1861 accepted unanimously the Southern contention and urged the support of the war as a moral and religious duty.   Secession was considered an inherent right of any State.   Slavery was a local matter, hypocritically attacked by the North from motives of economic rivalry.   They blamed Northern preachers for starting the war by their attacks upon slavery and charged them with corrupting the gospel.   The operations of Union troops were denounced as invasion and aggressive war, and the men were exhorted to defend rights as sacred as those of 1776.

Confederate victories before Gettysburg were interpreted as evidence of the divine favor.   On Thanksgiving Day following the election of Lincoln, Dr. Quintard, afterward Bishop of Tennessee, preached a strong sermon in support of the Union to his regiment and a large company of civilians in Nashville.   By the next summer he was ready to take the field with the soldiers of the Confederacy.   Repeatedly during the war he preached his "war sermon", exhorting the people to do their utmost because "not only the rights of our people and the glory of our nation, but the Church of God was imperilled."   Joseph Cross agreed with this view and hoped the war would free the South from the skeptical philosophy which had poisoned Northern Christianity.[4]

Several Union chaplains have left accounts of their military experiences which show that they entertained no doubts of the justice of the Federal position.   Those writing many years after the war expressed their opinions less violently than contemporaries but with no less certainty of their fairness.   Holding that citizenship and allegiance were national, they looked upon States' rights as a dead issue, brought to life again to support indefensible political and economic claims.   This led them to denounce all secessionists as rebels and traitors.   Chaplain Pepper called on General Lee in Richmond after the sur-

---

[4] Noll, *op. cit.*, pp. 10, 44; The Rev. Jos. Cross, D. D.—*Camp and Field: Papers from the Portfolio of an Army Chaplain,* Books Three and Four, pp. 251, 376.

454841 O—58——7

render and was impressed by his greatness and goodness of heart, except for the "one dark spot on his fame, treason." [5]

Slavery was branded as an intrinsic evil, denounced as such by statesmen of North and South and in process of gradual extinction before the growing demand for cotton buried moral and humanitarian considerations under a wave of greed.   Though shamed before the world by the existence of slavery, the North had made concessions and compromises, hoping to appease the insatiable demands of the South. When agreements like the Missouri Compromise were swept aside, it showed that the pledged faith of the South could not be trusted.   For years Southern leaders had been preparing the minds of the people for war, declaring that the alleged tyranny of the Northern majority could be resisted in no other way.   Finally, when it appeared that a limit might be set to this sacrifice of national honor to the arrogance and cupidity of a section, they did not hesitate to plunge the country into war and assail the government which guaranteed to protect all their legitimate rights.   The attack upon Sumter convinced those who still clung to hope that further appeasement would be futile and that the only alternatives were anarchy or war. [6]

Even before bloodshed had embittered sectional feeling, some clergymen were declaring their convictions in strong terms.   W. G. Brownlow was a fiery parson and editor in Knoxville, Tennessee. Without attacking slavery, he tried ardently to keep his State from leaving the Union.   After secession he was imprisoned for a time but later was allowed to pass through the Union lines and is listed as chaplain of an Ohio regiment for 1 day.   After the war he served as governor and senator.   Replying to the invitation of General Gideon Pillow to serve as chaplain of his brigade, he wrote on 22 April 1861: "I return for an answer that when I shall have made up my mind to go to hell, I will cut my throat and go direct and not travel by way of the Southern Confederacy." [7]

Some chaplains describe episodes which reveal the development of these convictions with the progress of the war.   Chaplain Marks, captured during the Seven Days, tells of a discussion with Major Ker, the Confederate officer having him in charge.   Frankly stating the Northern claim that the war was due to Southern aggression, he drew

---

[5] Marks, *op. cit.*, p. 241; Rev. J. B. Rogers—*War Pictures*, pp. 25, 98; Capt. George W. Pepper—*Personal Recollections of Sherman's Campaigns in Georgia and the Carolinas*, p. 455.

[6] Richard F. Fuller—*Chaplain Fuller: Being a Life Sketch of a New England Clergyman and Army Chaplain*, p. 326; cf. Marks, *op. cit.*, p. 434; Rogers, *op. cit*, p. 98; Pepper, *op. cit.*, p. 160; Adams, *op. cit.*, p. 18; H. Clay Trumbull—*War Memories of a Chaplain*, p. 369; *et al.*

[7] Quoted by Jacob Payton, 17 Mar. 1941, Files, OCCh.; John Beatty—*Memoirs of a Volunteer, 1861-1865*, pp. 279-80.

from the Major a sharp denunciation of the attack upon the South, ending in the vow that his strongest wish was for revenge.   Prominent men among the bystanders agreed, saying that they wished to see no more prisoners taken and that peace would be considered only if the United States restored or paid for their slaves, paid all the war debt, gave the South half of the territories, and allowed Maryland, Kentucky, and Missouri to join the Confederacy.   The chaplain declared that he would be considered a lunatic to go home and advocate peace on such terms and rebuked his hearers for expressions of malice such as he never had heard in the North.   When violence threatened, a North Carolina colonel pushed through the crowd to protect him, and Major Ker quieted the assailants by insisting that a prisoner must not be treated so ungenerously.[8]

Caleb Pillsbury, chaplain of the 22d Wisconsin Infantry, and George Bradley, his successor in that unit, tell with warm approval how the regiment dealt with fugitive slaves in Kentucky.   On 13 March 1862, an article of war forbidding military personnel to return fugitive slaves to their masters was approved.   During the debate in Congress proposals to exempt Delaware, Maryland, Kentucky, and Missouri from its operation and to provide that it should not apply to the slaves of loyal masters were defeated.[9]   Nevertheless, it was considered good policy to bid for the support of Kentucky slaveholders by helping them recover the slaves who came into the Union camps. Accordingly General Gillmore directed the regimental commanders to send to headquarters a number of Negroes who had taken refuge with the various units.   This order Colonel Utley of the 22d positively refused to obey on the ground that it concerned a matter outside the sphere of military authority.   He declared that the regiment was from a State where slavery could not exist and never should be degraded into a group of slave-catchers.   Feeling was strong in other regiments, and the general did not press the matter.   Judge Robertson, whose son was in the Confederate army, demanded the surrender of a slave boy whom he had hired out for years and who had fled from the cruelty of his employer.   The colonel permitted him to talk with the boy and ask him to go voluntarily but would allow no compulsion. In the end he sent the judge away with a stinging rebuke for his failure to protect his slaves from abuse by others.[10]

About this time a superior Negro girl was bought in Lexington

---

[8] Marks, *op. cit.*, pp. 434–36.

[9] Henry Wilson—*Military Measures of the United States Congress, 1861-1865*, pp. 22–24.

[10] Rev. George S. Bradley—*The Star Corps*, pp. 62–80.

for $1,700 by a man who hoped to reap a profit by placing her in a house of prostitution. She escaped and sought refuge in the 22d. Two officers conducted her in disguise to a distant city where friends sent her on to Wisconsin and freedom.[11]   When the army passed through Georgetown, 40 armed men rushed upon a Michigan regiment and seized the Negroes who were with it.   Colonel Utley sent word to the citizens that the 22d would march through their town the next morning with fixed bayonets and loaded guns.   If any interference was intended, all women and children should be removed at once. At Louisville a crowd was determined that no Negroes should leave with the 22d.   Pillsbury marched far in advance of the regiment and warned the citizens that any attempt to seize them would cause trouble.   When the regiment passed, one man sprang between the ranks and laid hands upon a Negro but an instant later retreated to the sidewalk at the points of several bayonets.   The steamboat captain refused to take Negroes out of the State but was told that he had no choice but must take everyone whom the colonel ordered on board. Thus the 22d Wisconsin left Kentucky with the chaplain rejoicing that none who had claimed their protection had been dragged back to slavery.[12]

Some chaplains were perplexed by repeated Confederate victories and the religious quickening in the Southern army, for they could not conceive of ultimate providential favor toward the cause which rested upon slavery.   They interpreted floods which hampered the Union forces and the further defeats that followed as a rebuke to their pride and punishment for temporizing when moral principles were at stake.   Emancipation was hailed as the end of compromise, making moral purposes and military ends to coincide.   No longer were they striving only to preserve the American democratic ideal; now they were leaders in a divine crusade against the cruelties of slavery.   What Moses had done in one century and Washington in another, they felt that they were doing on a grander scale with the supreme compulsion of patriotic fervor sustained by divine inspiration.   This enthusiasm spread among the soldiers and showed itself in many camps during the second winter of the war.   Few doubted that they were fighting God's battle for a better world and that He expected them to persevere.   Thousands were lifted to a new loyalty as they voiced their faith in the key line of Mrs. Howe's great Battle Hymn:

He has sounded forth the trumpet that shall never call retreat.[13]

[11] Rogers, *op. cit.*, pp. 127–30.
[12] Bradley, *loc. cit.*
[13] Adams, *op. cit.*, pp. 90, 93–97; Bristol, *op. cit.*, pp. 136, 191–203.

Another matter which gained an ever-increasing place in the thought and feeling of Union chaplains with the progress of the war was the suffering of the captives in Confederate prisons. Early in 1862, Secretary Stanton sent Bishop Ames and Hamilton Fish to Fort Monroe to ask permission from the Confederate government to visit Southern prisons and give medical supplies, food, clothing, and comforts to the inmates, offering to give corresponding privileges in Union prisons. Darbey Ball, a former chaplain of the First Virginia Cavalry, warned President Davis against the Bishop as an uncompromising antislavery man who was disguising sinister purposes under the specious pleas of humanity. Secretary Benjamin reported to Mr. Davis that he had tried to divine Stanton's purpose, feeling certain that he did not expect his proposal to be taken seriously. Concluding that he wanted but would not ask for a general exchange of prisoners, he had named commissioners to negotiate with Ames and Fish to that end. When the latter replied that they had no authority except for the original project, he attributed their attitude to the changed situation since the captures at Fort Donelson had placed a large surplus of prisoners in Federal hands. In December 1864 the Christian Commission named Horatio G. Jones and Bishops Janes and Lee to visit Union prisoners in Southern prisons and distribute food, clothing, medicines, and religious literature. The War Department and General Grant approved, but the Confederate authorities refused to permit the plan to be carried out.[14]

The death rate of more than 100 a day at Andersonville and its causes moved several chaplains to strong words. Marks said that the Confederate government had "thrown itself out of the pale of Christian civilization." Bradley would hang the responsible officials without mercy.[15]

On the other hand, Charles McCabe believed that in the summer of 1863 when he was confined at Libby, General Winder did the best he could for his prisoners with what resources he had. He told of bearing a message from the prisoners to President Lincoln at the time of his release, urging the President to make no concessions out of consideration for them, and of Lincoln's assurance that he would not.[16]

Charles Humphreys was among the Union officers whom General Jones confined under the fire of the Union siege guns at Charleston. At that time Secretary Stanton had induced the President to stop the

---

[14] *Official Records*, Ser. II, Vol. III, pp. 213-99; 783-87; 821-23.

[15] *Ibid.*, VII, 696; William W. Sweet—*The Methodist Episcopal Church and the Civil War*, p. 149; Marks, *op. cit.*, p. 389; Bradley, *op. cit.*, pp. 59, 224.

[16] Bristol, *op. cit.*, pp. 90, 201.

exchange of prisoners on the ground that it gave General Lee an immediate reenforcement in exchange for an equal number of Union men so weak from illness and starvation that they would not be able to serve for months. When the prisoners in Charleston were given the opportunity to send a delegate to Washington to urge their release by exchange and had the chaplain in mind for this mission, he assured them that they were serving the Union better where they were, and the group refused to name a delegate. Telling this story many years later, he quoted from Colonel Chandler's incisive report to President Davis, recommending the appointment of someone with some feeling of humanity to command Confederate prisons and the abandonment of a policy intended to relieve their crowded condition through the death of their inmates.[17]

The destruction of public and private property as a military measure led to violent recrimination in later years. A few chaplains have recorded their contemporary opinions on the subject. While deprecating forms of destruction in Georgia which had little military importance and were contrary to Sherman's orders, Bradley pointed out that burning supplies and tearing up the railroads on which they could be moved would weaken fortified places like Richmond and Charleston and hasten the defeat of the Confederacy. He declared that Sherman avoided battle when he could on the famous march and summed up the philosophy of the campaign in the words, "It is much better to conquer by destroying property than life."[18] Half a century later an echo of this debate was heard in the Chaplain School. A clergyman from South Carolina spoke bitterly of Sherman's men who killed his grandmother's pig. A New Hampshire colleague pointed out that Sherman's rule was to accomplish his purpose by killing the pig instead of the grandfather whenever possible.

The foregoing summary of the arguments of those persons of the North and South who tried to interpret sectional differences in terms of right and wrong is necessarily an oversimplification. Specific points were seen in varying perspective by those who advanced them, and the opposing positions on major issues sometimes did not rise above diametrical contradiction. From this confusion emerge a few significant facts. The South felt it was defending itself. Where the leaders strove to maintain the new political institutions, the common soldier was sure he was protecting his wife and children from outrage and op-

---

[17] Charles A. Humphreys—*Field, Camp, Hospital, and Prison in the Civil War,* pp. 130–39.
[18] Bradley, *op. cit.,* pp. 204, 224; cf. Rogers, *op. cit.,* p. 253.

pression. The maintenance of slavery became less important than the right to regulate it in their own way, especially to those who owned no slaves; and prominent officials early in the war proposed gradual emancipation as the price of the foreign recognition which they felt would insure victory.[19] Southern independence seemed as inherently right as that of the original States; Lee was reenacting the role of Washington; and the Spirit of '76 soon became that of '61.

Conversely the people of the North saw the Union as the embodiment of their most cherished rights. The development of the years had made every citizen the heir to vested interests, social and cultural as well as political, and national in scope. These were being attacked by the people of the South, stampeded into bloody strife by an unscrupulous minority who did not hesitate to ruin what they could not rule. To crush the Confederacy was to save for coming generations this priceless heritage of South and North alike. Slavery, tolerated for a time while fair controls were being sought, was none the less a national disgrace. Southern aggression showed that the slave interests would respect no compromise and submit to no restraint. Human bondage must be destroyed, partly to help suppress an iniquitous rebellion, but still more to destroy a cruel wrong which robbed a whole people of the simplest rights of respectable living.

Many years after the war a Union chaplain summarized the spirit of the two armies as he saw them at that time. He said that, in general, Union soldiers were animated by principle, not passion; by patriotism, not party zeal; by loyalty to the Republic, not to a theory; and by regard for the rights of all and the life of the nation, not by revenge or retaliation. The Confederates, he believed, were influenced less by great principles and more by party spirit and passion. They hated the views of the North, hugged State sovereignty and slavery, were brave and zealous but often harsh and cruel to prisoners, and fought for themselves but not for humanity.[20] This statement contains an interesting echo of a remark by President Davis. Arguing with a senator in support of the plan to arm the slaves, he said, "If the Confederacy falls, there should be written on its tombstone, 'Died of a theory.'"[21]

Holding such firm convictions of the righteousness of their cause, it was inevitable that many chaplains should feel that active support of

---

[19] Noll, *op. cit.*, p. 127.
[20] Rev. Frederic Denison—*A Chaplain's Experience in the Union Army*, p. 44.
[21] Jefferson Davis—*The Rise and Fall of the Confederacy*, I, 518.

combat was a part of their duties. Frederic Denison of the First
Rhode Island Cavalry insisted that it was as legitimate for a chaplain
to fight as to exhort the men to do so. He wore a captain's uniform
and told with gusto how he captured six of Jackson's men who took
him for a "real captain" with a strong following at hand.[22] General
Smith commended Chaplain Bennett of the 32d Ohio Infantry for
fighting in the ranks all day with a musket at Atlanta, which was "his
custom on all such occasions," and Lorenzo Barber of the Second
Sharpshooters was praised by General Berdan for using his skill as a
marksman with the skirmishers at Chancellorsville.[23] Milton L.
Haney of the 55th Illinois Infantry was awarded the Medal of Honor
for conspicuous gallantry in helping retake the Federal intrenchments
near Atlanta after the fall of General McPherson.[24] When his regiment was hard pressed at Resaca, John M. Springer of the Third Wisconsin Infantry seized a musket and fought for 4 fours before he fell
with a mortal wound.[25] Arthur Fuller of the 16th Massachusetts Infantry was slain while firing on the Confederates at Fredericksburg,
and Nathan Baker fired repeatedly at men in the works at Vicksburg.[26]

Several chaplains tell of encouraging the men in battle or of check-
ing them in retreat.[27] A number served as aide-de-camp or assistant
surgeon without relinquishing their chaplaincies.[28] Others were placed
in charge of refugee camps, hospitals, or ambulance trains.[29] In emergencies they took temporary command of various groups. When one
of Sherman's supply trains could not start because no officer was available to take charge of the guard, Christy buckled on a sword, offered
his services, and took the train through. When asked what he would
have done had he been attacked, he said, "Why, I would have told the
boys to pitch in." At Hope Church his regiment found itself nearly
out of ammunition. The chaplain begged all he could carry in his
handkerchief and pockets from reserve units in the rear and distributed
it along the line.[30]

---

[22] Denison, *op. cit.*, pp. 10, 22.

[23] Lt. Col. Wm. F. Fox—*Regimental Losses in the American Civil War,* p. 43.

[24] *The Medal of Honor of the United States Army,* p. 165; cf. *The Army and Navy Chaplain,* Oct.–Nov. 1943, p. 18.

[25] Fox, *loc. cit.*

[26] *Ibid.;* Fuller, *op. cit.,* p. 302; Ms. copy of Baker's diary at Hq. Vicksburg Military Park.

[27] Humphreys, *op. cit.,* p. 19; Adams, *op. cit.,* p. 63; A. D. Betts—*Experience of a Confederate Chaplain,* p. 8; Conyngham, *op. cit.,* p. 29; *et al.*

[28] Denison, *op. cit.,* p. 16; Noll, *op. cit.,* p. 41; Humphreys, *op. cit.,* p. 94.

[29] Rogers, *op. cit.,* p. 211; *Personal Memoirs of U. S. Grant,* I, 425; Conyngham, *op. cit.,* p. 179; Marks, *op. cit.,* p. 240.

[30] Conyngham, *op. cit.,* pp. 88, 126.

These episodes show that the status of chaplains as non-combatants and the corresponding obligation to refrain from hostile activity were not fully recognized at the time. Chaplain John F. Mines of the Second Maine Infantry remained to aid the wounded after first Bull Run, confident that he would not be held a prisoner. Sent to Richmond by Beauregard, he stayed for a few days with the rector of St. James' Church on parole. Then he was arrested and confined on recommendation of the Confederate commissioner, James Lyons. In the discussion which followed, Lyons justified this action on the ground that Mines had defended the policy of the Federal Government in conversation with him, showing himself "impenitent and vindictive." As these sentiments were expressed among the wounded prisoners and repressed "any tendency to penitence in them," he considered the chaplain a bad person to be at liberty.

Mines wrote several piteous letters, begging for his release. He claimed that he had long been a proslavery Democrat, friendly to the South, had been deceived into accepting the chaplaincy of a Maine regiment by the claim that a large Union party in the South was calling for deliverance from an oppressive majority but had learned his mistake since coming to Richmond, and that he had repented deeply and been severely punished for his sin. These appeals he reinforced by citing his youth and inexperience, illness and other trouble in his family, and his desire to go home and work for the peaceful separation of the southern States from the Union. Though he replied rather severely to the chaplain, Lyons recommended his release, pressing the matter upon Secretary Walker and later upon Secretary Benjamin and President Davis. In December, Mines was paroled, and soon afterward he was exchanged for the Confederate Chaplain North.[31] Later he served as colonel of a Union regiment, and after the war he published several books under the name of "Felix Oldboy."[32]

In June 1862, General Bragg proposed to General Halleck a continuing policy by which medical officers and chaplains who might be captured by their respective armies should be released without unnecessary delay. On 1 July the Confederate War Department issued General Orders No. 46, which included the following provision:

> III. All chaplains taken prisoners of war by the armies of the Confederate States while in the discharge of their proper duties will be immediately and unconditionally released.[33]

---

[31] *Official Records,* Ser. II, Vol. II, pp. 1497, 1515, III, 177, 756.
[32] Noll, *op. cit.,* pp. 15–16.
[33] *Official Records,* Ser. II, Vol. IV, pp. 27–28, 795.

On 26 July the Union authorities reciprocated with the following paragraph in General Orders No. 90:

> I. The principle being recognized that chaplains should not be held as prisoners of war, it is hereby ordered that all chaplains so held by the United States shall be immediately and unconditionally discharged.[34]

Instructions for the government of the armies of the United States, prepared by Francis Lieber and revised by a board of officers, were published in General Orders No. 100 on 24 April 1863. Paragraph 53 directed that chaplains and medical officers who might fall into the hands of United States forces should not be treated as prisoners of war unless the commander had reason to retain them or they were allowed to remain with their companions by their own desire. This policy seems to have been carried out generally until the end of the war, though it was suspended for about 3 months in the summer and early autumn of 1863 because of a dispute about the exchange of other prisoners.[35]

It is true that these regulations of the two governments did not expressly forbid chaplains to bear arms and participate in combat, but such an obligation seems to be implied by the immunities extended to them. However, the matter was not seen in this light by all military authorities. The combat exploits of Chaplains Haney, Bennett, Barber, and Springer already mentioned took place after the issue of these instructions, but all were commended by higher authority, in the case of Haney the highest in the land. A similar confusion existed among the chaplains of the Confederacy. On 25 April 1863, the chaplains of the Second and Third Corps, Army of Northern Virginia, discussed this question. Some defended their custom of using a musket with the soldiers of the line, but the majority felt that this would be wrong in ordinary battle situations. After the opinions of many prominent officers were presented and considered, it was agreed that no absolute rule could be stated but that the chaplain's primary duties would normally place him in charge of the ambulances, at the point where the litter bearers met the ambulances, or at the field infirmaries.[36]

Commissioner Lyons was not alone in his fear of chaplains' influence upon the political opinions of the men of his own or the opposing army. In July the commander of Fort Delaware sent two Confederate

---

[34] *Ibid.*, p. 288.

[35] *Ibid.*, V, 67–74, VI, 112, 158, 165, 281, 283, 337, 762.

[36] Jones, *op. cit.*, p. 522.

chaplains to Johnson's Island for tampering with his men and trying to induce them to desert.   Two months later Colonel Hoffman, the Union Commissary General of Prisoners, wrote to a New York minister who had forwarded the request of a Confederate chaplain for permission to attend the prisoners of war at a hospital on David's Island:

> It is not thought advisable to associate officers and enlisted men, prisoners of war, together, owing to the bad effect of their influence and example, and there is probably no class of officers whose influence is more powerful to keep up the spirits of the rebels than their chaplain.   If they would confine themselves to their proper calling there would not be the least objection to their presence among the sick and wounded, but as this is not possible it would be very injurious policy to admit them in the hospitals, where they would scarcely preach that our cause is righteous or that they have engaged in the rebellion without a cause.[37]

A few days later Colonel Hoffman received a frank proposal from the United States Christian Commission that full advantage be taken of such an opportunity by sending a judicious minister to work among the prisoners at Point Lookout, Md.

> Hundreds of this class at Gettysburg to whom our commission has brought the Gospel of Christian kindness and sympathy, have been, as we believe, fully won.   Instead of enemies they are our friends.   Prejudiced against us by designing men, they have been surprised to find us neither infidels nor heathen, and when released they will go to their homes all through the South to tell of the sad delusion which has possessed them.[38]

A month later the colonel wrote to the Commanding General at Point Lookout that there was no objection to visits among the prisoners by clergymen at stated times, but there must be no doubt of their loyalty, and the visits must be for religious purposes and not for political discussion.[39]

The spirit of the time is indicated by the number of clergymen who served as combat soldiers.   Ninety-seven Union chaplains are known to have been appointed after prior service, 23 of that number having been officers.   A large number of other clergymen served as line officers throughout the war.[40]   Two Methodist ministers of the North Indiana Conference raised a regiment, one serving as colonel, the other as lieutenant colonel.   Three members of the Conference

---

[37] *Official Records*, Ser. II, Vol. VII, pp. 156, 249.
[38] *Ibid.*, p. 284.
[39] *Ibid.*, p. 363.
[40] Reports of the adjutant generals of various states.

were company officers in the same regiment.[41]   Incomplete records
show 208 ministers of the southern Methodist Church serving as Confederate chaplains, besides 12 in the Union Army and 141 as officers
or men in other branches.[42]   Probably the proportions in other religious bodies were not dissimilar.   Jones mentioned a Georgia regiment
that enrolled 14 ministers, 13 of them Baptists.[43]

Equally significant is the appointment of a number of chaplains to
other branches, in several cases to the command of Negro troops.   A
number became assistant surgeons, and one a hospital steward.
Others served as regimental adjutant or quartermaster.   Edward D.
Neill of the First Minnesota was appointed private secretary to the
President.   Several commanded regiments, and five became general
officers.   Among these was Eliphalet Whittlesay, chaplain of the 19th
Maine Infantry in 1862, who later served as assistant adjutant and
judge advocate and was advanced to the grade of brigadier general.[44]
Another was William A. Pile, chaplain of a Missouri regiment in 1861,
commander of a light battery the next year and of a regiment of infantry soon afterward, brigadier general late in 1863, and brevet major
general in 1865.   Later he represented his State in Congress and
served as governor of New Mexico and minister to Venezuela.[45]

James C. Beecher, brother of Chaplain Thomas Beecher and of
the other distinguished children of Lyman Beecher, returned from mission work in China to become chaplain of the 67th New York Infantry,
After a year he was appointed lieutenant colonel of the regiment and
the following summer was put in command of a regiment of Negro
troops.   He left the service in 1866 as a brigadier general by brevet.
At intervals during the following years he served churches in New
York, but an unbalanced mind caused him to end his life by suicide
in 1886.[46]   In the autumn of 1862 Samuel Fallows became chaplain
of the 32d Wisconsin, but resigned the following summer.   In 1864
he helped recruit the 40th Infantry and served as lieutenant colonel
until he was put in command of the 49th Regiment early in 1865.   In
October he was brevetted brigadier general for meritorious service.
During the next 10 years he was pastor of Methodist churches in Mil-

---

[41] Rev. H. N. Herrick, D. D., and William Warren Sweet—*A History of the North Indiana Conference of the Methodist Episcopal Church*, p. 73.
[42] Sweet, *Methodist Church and Civil War*, Appendix E.
[43] Jones, *op. cit.*, p. 24.
[44] Reports of adjutant generals; Francis B. Heitman—*Historical Register and Dictionary of the
United States*, passim.
[45] *The Cyclopedia of American Biography*, V, n. p.
[46] *National Cyclopedia*, III, 131.

waukee, state superintendent of public instruction, and president of
Illinois Wesleyan University.   Becoming a clergyman of the Reformed
Episcopal Church, he spent the remaining 47 years of his life as a rec-
tor or bishop in Chicago.[47]

John Eaton seems to have been the one chaplain whose advancement to brigadier rank was a direct outgrowth of his service as a chaplain.   A Dartmouth graduate, he had been a school principal in
Cleveland and superintendent of schools in Toledo before his ordination and appointment to the 27th Ohio in 1861.   Late in the next
year he was chosen by General Grant to arrange for the care and employment of the large number of Negroes who had attached themselves to the army.   He organized them in camps, provided for their
physical needs and education, and employed them at fair wages to
pick cotton on the abandoned plantations and cut wood for Government boats.   The next year he was placed in charge of these matters
in the whole Department of the Tennessee.   Grant sent him to the
President with a personal report of his work, and Lincoln questioned
him in great detail on this and later occasions about the problems and
possibilities of the enterprise.   When the Freedman's Bureau was organized, many of his plans and methods were adopted and he was
made an assistant commissioner.   Grant had urged him to accept an
appointment as colonel of one of the Negro regiments being organized
in the area, but Eaton felt that this would complicate his status and
prevent his return to normal chaplain duties.   After a year's experience he felt that the military rank would help in his work and was
appointed to the Ninth Louisiana Infantry, a regiment guarding various localities in his district.   In 1865 he became a brigadier general
by brevet.[48]

During the Federal occupation of Memphis, local feeling against
Union soldiers, especially those connected with schools and other enterprises for the freedman, was intense.   One night a man was shot
near Eaton's home.   As the victim resembled him closely, the chaplain always believed that he himself was the man the murderer had
intended to kill.   After he became president, Grant appointed Eaton
Commissioner of Education.   Later he served as president of Mari-
etta and Sheldon Jackson colleges and began the organization of a
public school system in Puerto Rico after its acquisition by the United
States.   Eaton told the familiar anecdote about Lincoln's wish to
know the brand of whiskey used by Grant so that he could send some

---

[47] *Dictionary of American Biography*, VI, 261; cf. Alice Fallows—*Everybody's Bishop; passim.*

[48] Grant, *op. cit.*, I, 425; *Dictionary of American Biography*, V, 609; John Eaton—*Grant, Lincoln and the Freedman, passim.*

to his other generals, saying that he got the story direct from the President a few days after the event.   Though he enjoyed this joke, he was emphatic in his denial of the prevalent reports of Grant's intemperance, declaring that he never saw him under the influence of liquor during a long acquaintance and remembered numerous banquets in later years when Grant's glass remained untouched throughout the evening.[49]

Eaton had one experience which illustrated the far-reaching consequences which may result from even the simplest activities of an army chaplain.   As he needed to consult General Grant, he went to the headquarters near Vicksburg a few days before the surrender.   He carried letters from a brother to Captain James Shirley, whose home stood between the opposing lines.   The Shirleys had come from New Hampshire a dozen years before and were ardently attached to the Union.   When the Confederates retreated into the defenses of Vicksburg, they destroyed many buildings outside the lines which might afford shelter to their enemies.   Though the barns were burned, Mrs. Shirley refused to leave her home.   This delayed for a moment the man sent to burn the house, and the Union advance was so rapid that he was slain before he could throw his torch to the roof.   Except for one or two trifling changes, the house still stands exactly as it appears in a photograph taken during the siege.   Eaton found that Grant had sent the Shirleys to a place of safety several miles away, and here he delivered the letters.   Apparently he did not fully discharge his mission at his first call.   The Shirleys had a vivacious and accomplished daughter who was as strongly attached to the Union as her parents.   Admiration for the steadfast loyalty of the family through these trying years seems to have prepared the chaplain's mind for other forms of admiration, and some time later he and Miss Shirley were married.[50]

Many chaplains felt it a primary duty to promote the morale of the troops in order that they might be better fighters, as well as for its other values.   Trumbull tells of the time when his regiment was comfortably situated in Florida after a hard campaign and the rumor spread that they were to be sent to Virginia for what promised to be the hardest fighting of the war.   As there was much complaining that they had done their share already, the chaplain preached on the text: "Shall your brethren go to war, and shall you sit here?"—Numbers 32:6.   The next morning the surgeon greeted him with the question: "Chaplain, what did you preach about yesterday?   I was kept up

---

[49] *Ibid.*
[50] *Ibid.*

until midnight making out discharges for officers who wanted to go back to their commands." The colonel had this sermon printed under the title, "Desirableness of Active Service." Months later during a night march near Petersburg so violent a storm came on that the men were halted and lay in the mud till dawn. As the chaplain passed along the line, a soldier delighted his comrades by drawling, "I suppose, chaplain, this is what you would call the 'desirableness of active service.'" It is not surprising that a line officer said of him, "We count our chaplain as good as a hundred men in a fight, because the men fight so much better when he's with them."[51]

General Pendleton, himself a clergyman, addressing the chaplains of Lee's army in April 1863, declared that the two objectives coincide when he said, "The better Christian a man is, the better soldier he is." Jones tells of a brigade composed of 5 regiments, in 3 of which there had been a marked revival of religion. In a hard battle soon afterward these three held the field when the others broke and fled. Stating that one company was the only exception of which he knew, he cited an average casualty rate of more than 40 percent among church members but less than 17 in the case of other soldiers.[52]

According full importance to the support of morale and loyalty to duty, most chaplains would have agreed that the chief purpose of their efforts was to lead men to begin the religious life or to intensify their devotion to its ideals. The recognized indices of success in these endeavors varied greatly. To some it was important that the men follow a course of instruction and continue to participate in the recognized sacraments and other forms of worship. To others a transforming emotional experience was basic, followed as it should be by a faithful use of the aids to spiritual growth. Others discounted emotion but held that a definite commitment and perseverance in righteous living were essential. Declaring that success cannot be measured by the number of conversions, Humphreys said that he aimed to elevate rather than convert, to induce more reverence, more kindness, faith, truthfulness, honesty, loyalty in all he met. Fuller seems to have seen his task in a similar light. A contemporary wrote that the army recognized him as "a man going about doing good" and added, "It matters not how poor or how degraded a man is who comes in contact with Mr. Fuller, he withdraws from that contact a better man."[53]

---

[51] Trumbull, *op. cit.*, pp. 82–86, 107.

[52] Jones, *op. cit.*, pp. 281, 510, 518.

[53] Humphreys, *op. cit.*, p. 17; Fuller, *op. cit.*, p. 275.

CHAPTER VII

Of Laws and Men

Thirty post chaplains, several of them stationed in southern States, were all that were authorized by Federal law in the spring of 1861. Militia regiments which responded to the President's proclamation of 15 April were organized by State authority, and many had their own chaplains. Clearly neither system could meet the needs of the large army which it was apparent must be raised by the national government.

On 3 May, additional troops were called both to augment the Regular Army and for volunteer service. The following day the War Department issued General Orders Number 15 and 16, the former for the organization of the volunteer regiments, the latter making similar provision for the new units of the Regular Army. Both orders authorized a regimental commander to appoint a chaplain on the vote of field officers and company commanders. Men so appointed must be regularly ordained Christian ministers, and they were to receive the pay and allowances of a captain of cavalry. The fact that these orders were issued without clear legislative authority may explain the refusal of some paymasters to pay chaplains in the 90-day regiments until the Secretary of War specifically ordered that they be paid the same as other chaplains.[1] During the debate on the bill which became law on 17 July 1862, an attempt was made in the Senate to allow only one chaplain to a brigade as a measure of economy, but the proposal was rejected.[2] The assignment of one chaplain to a regiment seems to have been considered the normal arrangement throughout the war.

Experience soon showed the value of religious ministrations to the sick and wounded, though hospital chaplains were not authorized by law. Later it was held that the appointive power conferred upon the

---

[1] *The War of the Rebellion: A Compilation of the Official Records of the Union and Confederate Armies* (hereafter cited as *Official Records*), Series III, Vol. I, pp. 151–57, 368, 375.

[2] Henry Wilson—*Military Measures of the United States Congress, 1861-1865,* p. 37; *Congressional Globe* (hereafter cited as *Globe*), 1862, p. 1079.

President by Article II, Section II, paragraph 2, of the Constitution is plenary in the absence of a statute, but President Lincoln at that time believed that he had no authority to appoint chaplains for this duty. He wrote to several clergymen, inviting them to serve in various hospitals and promising that he would ask Congress to pay them the same as chaplains in the army.   This promise he fulfilled in his annual message of 3 December 1861.   Five months later Congress authorized the appointment of hospital chaplains and approved the President's action in naming several on his own authority.[3]

Congress met in special session early in July of 1861, and on the 22d a law established the same provisions for chaplains of volunteers that the War Department had ordered in May.   Similar legislation for the new regiments of the Regular Army was enacted on 3 August.   It specified the same qualifications but authorized appointment as the President should direct.[4]   The law of 17 July 1862, amending that of 22 July of the previous year, contained the following significant provisions:

> No person shall be appointed a chaplain in the United States army who is not a regularly ordained minister of some religious denomination, and who does not present testimonials of his good standing as such minister with a recommendation for his appointment as an army Chaplain from some authorized ecclesiastical body, or not less than five accredited ministers belonging to said denomination.[5]

None of this legislation established minimum educational qualifications.   Those which satisfied the authorities of the various churches were all that the law required.   Nor was an age limit specified. McCabe referred to a Chaplain Brown, one of his associates in Libby Prison, being nearly 80 years old.   John Pierpont served over a month with the 22d Massachusetts at the age of 76.   Jones mentioned the zeal and energy of Dr. Joseph Stiles, a Confederate chaplain of 70 years.[6]

The problem of a conscientious objector was linked to the appointment of chaplains in a peculiar way.   When the Senate was debating the draft bill of 1863, Sumner attempted to exclude clergymen from its provisions.   McDougall and Howard thought this a mistake because

---

[3] *The Military Laws of the United States,* 4th edition, p. 477, note; *Official Records,* Ser. III, Vol. I, pp. 709, 712, 721; *The Public Statutes at Large of the United States of America,* XII, 403 (hereafter cited in the form: 12 *Stat.* 403).

[4] 12 *Stat.* 270, 288.

[5] 12 *Stat.* 594.

[6] Frank Milton Bristol—*The Life of Chaplain McCabe,* p. 137; *Massachusetts Soldiers, Sailors, and Marines in the Civil War;* J. William Jones—*Christ in the Camp,* p. 226.

the loyal clergy were the most fighting group among the people.   Harris and Clark tried to exempt all conscientious objectors, but the attempt failed.   Early in the next year Wilson sponsored a measure by which clergymen and members of pacifistic bodies would have been assigned to noncombatant duties.   Dixon wished to specify that drafted clergymen be employed as chaplains or in hospitals.   In the end all reference to ministers was stricken out, and the Act of 24 February 1864 allowed persons declaring on oath or affirmation that they were conscientiously opposed to bearing arms and were prohibited from doing so by the rules of the religious bodies of which they were members to be employed in hospitals or in the care of freedmen or to be excused on payment of $300 for the benefit of the sick and wounded.[7]

The Confederate government worked out a slightly different answer to this question.   Petitions from the Society of Friends and other groups brought the matter before Congress in 1862.   An attempt to exempt professors and students at theological seminaries from compulsory military service was defeated, but the Act of 1 May 1863 excused all regularly licensed ministers and persons who had been members of Quaker, Dunker, Nazarine and Mennonist societies since 16 April 1862, provided that each person so exempted furnish a substitute or pay a tax of $500.[8]

As the Federal statute of 17 July 1862 dropped the proviso that chaplain's must be of the Christian faith, it made possible the appointment of Jewish chaplains.   This change had been under consideration for at least a year.   When the bill for the organization of volunteer troops was pending in July 1861, Congressman Vallandigham proposed an amendment by which a "regularly ordained minister of some religious society" would be eligible for appointment as a chaplain instead of the office being limited to those of the Christian faith. Though he called attention to the large number of Jews in the army and stressed the piety and learning of the rabbis, his proposal was rejected.[9]

About the time this law was passed, the officers of the Fifth Pennsylvania Cavalry, ignorant of its provisions and those of the War Department order of 4 May or ignoring them, elected Michael M.

---

    [7] Wilson, *op. cit.*, pp. 46–47, 56–58; 13 *Stat.* 9.
    [8] *Journal of the Congress of the Confederate States of America* (hereafter cited as *Journal, C. S. A.*), II, 320, 379, 431, 450, 460, 490, III, 306, 370, 421.
    [9] Wilson, *op. cit.*, pp. 1–4; *Globe*, 1861, p. 100; Rabbi Bertram W. Korn—"Jewish Chaplains during the Civil War," *American Jewish Archives*, Vol. I, No. 1, p. 7.

Allen, a Jewish soldier, to be regimental chaplain. Though he was
not a rabbi, he was well educated and widely experienced in synagogue activities.   For 2 months he performed the many and varied
duties of a chaplain, conducting informal services like those common
in the nonliturgical churches and preaching on the great themes common to Christians and Jews.   Numerous complaints about chaplains
who did not meet the prescribed requirements brought an order from
the Assistant Adjutant General that all such must be discharged.   This
order applied to Chaplain Allen only as it did to a considerable number of others, but he avoided possible embarrassment by resigning on
26 September.[10]   Though he lacked two of the qualifications required
by law, it seems fair to describe him as the first Jewish Chaplain in the
Army of the United States, for he was appointed by the authority
designated by law and performed the duties of his office creditably for
a considerable time.

The officers of the Fifth Pennsylvania made another attempt to
obtain a Jewish chaplain, nominating Rabbi Arnold Fischel. Whether
they hoped that the term "Christian" would be interpreted with un-
precedented breadth or be ignored or thought that their action might
call attention to what they considered unjust discrimination is uncertain.   Only the latter purpose was served in any degree, for Secretary
Cameron, in whose honor the regiment was often called "Cameron's
Dragoons," felt compelled by the law to disapprove the nomination.
An active agitation followed, and, on recommendation of the President,
the law of 17 July 1862 removed this limitation.[11]

In September the Board of Ministers of the Hebrew Congregations of Philadelphia, at the invitation of the President, recommended
Reverend Jacob Frankel for hospital chaplain in that locality.   He
was appointed at once and served until 1 July 1865.   Warmly indorsed for the hospital chaplaincy by the Jews and Christians of Louisville, Rabbi Bernhard H. Gotthelf was appointed on 6 May 1863 and
served for 28 months.   Providing libraries of German books for the
large number of German-speaking soldiers in the hospitals of the Ohio
Valley was one of his notable achievements.   Reverend Ferdinand L.
Sarner, a graduate of two German universities, was chosen chaplain of
the 54th New York Infantry in April 1863 and served until October of
the next year.   As the regiment was composed largely of German immigrants but contained very few Jews, it is probable that Dr. Sarner

---

[10] *Ibid.*, pp. 8–11.
[11] *Ibid.*, pp. 11–12; 12 *Stat.* 594; Carl Sandburg—*Abraham Lincoln: The War Years*, II, 44.

was chosen primarily because of his knowledge of the German language and culture. He was wounded at Gettysburg and finally discharged for disability. After years as an editor and teacher, he became the rabbi of a congregation in Memphis, where he died during the yellow fever epidemic of 1878, the same which took the life of Rabbi Gotthelf at Vicksburg. Though not barred by specific legislation, no Jewish chaplains are known to have served in the Confederate army.[12]

Another amendment designed to provide the distinctive forms of worship of their faith for a minority group was offered by Congressman McClernard when the volunteer bill was under consideration in July 1861. He proposed that brigade commanders be empowered to appoint a Roman Catholic chaplain for the brigade when none was assigned to any subordinate unit, but his motion was rejected. A few days later the Secretary of War called upon Senator Wilson and urged him to support this proposal. He pointed out that it was important because few regiments had Catholic chaplains and suggested that one might serve two brigades. The Senator urged these considerations in the Senate the next day, but the recommendation was rejected in the interest of economy. Some general officers, among them Rosecrans and Stanley, accomplished the purpose of this proposal by attaching Catholic chaplains to their headquarters. The president arranged for the inclusion of Catholic priests among his early appointments of hospital chaplains. Some regiments were composed largely of Catholic men, and it was possible in most instances for them to obtain Catholic chaplains. One of the most distinguished of these was Father John Ireland, chaplain of the Fifth Minnesota Infantry from June 1862 until the following April and later the Archbishop of St. Paul.[13]

Further provisions of the Act of 17 July 1862 grew out of conditions which reflected a measure of discredit upon the chaplains as a group. Some who had been appointed early in the war had been drawn to the military service by a spirit of adventure. Others were deficient in education or lacked a deep and enduring devotion to their task. Some who were capable leaders in civil life were not adaptable to the conditions of the military service. When a group of clergymen stated these facts to the President, he said that little could be done

[12] Korn, *loc. cit.*, pp, 6, 12–22.

[13] Wilson, *op. cit.*, p. 3; *Globe,* 1861, pp. 100, 179; D. P. Conyngham—*The Soldier of the Cross,* pp. 30, 46; Sandburg, *op. cit.*, II, 44; *Dictionary of American Biography,* IX, 494–97.

about it while most of the chaplains were chosen by the regiments they were to serve.[14]

Late in 1861 Benjamin F. Larned, Paymaster General, was asked by Senator Henry Wilson to suggest ways of reducing military expenses. His reply, dated 5 December, contained a significant reference to the chaplains then in the service. After making several recommendations, one being that five million dollars be saved by abolishing regimental bands and another that less cavalry regiments be organized because they cost more and were worth less than infantry, he stated that many chaplains were utterly unworthy of their positions. Without vouching for its truth, he cited the report that one regiment maintained a French cook by mustering him as their chaplain. He urged that clergymen be appointed only with the recommendation of their highest ecclesiastical authority.[15]

These proposals had a conspicuous influence upon the bill sponsored by the Senator. Brigade bands of 16 men were substituted for those of 24 then authorized to each regiment, and several other economies were adopted substantially as proposed by the paymaster. His suggestion that appointments to the chaplaincy be limited to men specifically recommended for the post was followed, and the appropriate commanders were required within 30 days "to inquire into the fitness, efficiency and qualifications of the chaplains of hospitals or regiments, and to muster out of service such chaplains as were not appointed in conformity with the requirements of this act, and who have not faithfully discharged the duties of chaplains during the time they have been engaged as such." The latter clause left such wide discretion in the application of the former that this part of the law was widely disregarded. General Orders No. 152, 6 October 1862, called the attention of post, district, and brigade commanders to it and directed that it should be complied with at once. A month earlier the War Department ordered that chaplains must present a copy of documents showing the fulfillment of the legal requirements before being mustered and that these papers be filed with the Adjutant General.[16]

An important law became effective on 9 April 1864. It recognized the "rank of chaplain without command" in the regular and volunteer service and made several provisions tending to place chaplains on the same footing as other officers. The quarterly report to

---

[14] Sandburg, *op. cit.*, III, 326.
[15] *Official Records*, Ser. III, Vol. I, p. 728.
[16] *Ibid.*, II, 278, 519, 651; 12 *Stat.* 594.

the regimental commander required by the 1861 law was changed to a monthly report to the Adjutant General, and the chaplain's duties at funerals and Sabbath services were stated. The cryptic phrase "rank of chaplain" proved to be rather confusing. Some held that it implied a new grade between those of captain and major. To clarify this matter, the Adjutant General, on 31 October 1864, proposed that the law be amended so "that the chaplains' rank shall be, as it formerly was in reference to pay and allowances, assimilated to that of captain, and that their names shall appear on the rolls and returns next after those of the medical officers." Four months passed before Secretary Stanton submitted this suggestion to the President, and the war ended without action by Congress.[17]

William Corby enjoyed for many years the temporary rank conferred upon him in the field. Riding between two surgeons at the head of a group of horsemen one night, he was approached by an excited lieutenant who called him "General" and asked where he should direct the ambulances. Knowing that it would be correct, he replied, "Have them driven to Fairfax." After a night out of doors the chaplain and his companions stopped at a sutler's tent for supplies, and the surgeons entered. A soldier rode up, tossed his reins to the chaplain, and told him to hold his horse. Just then one surgeon came out, saluted, and said, "General, I have a good supply for today." They rode away, though not so rapidly as the soldier, the chaplain lamenting the transitory nature of greatness: "Last night I was a general; now a private offers me a dime to hold his horse."[18]

This incident suggests more important reasons for chaplains wearing a uniform by which they could be recognized easily. General Order Number 102 of 1861 prescribed: "The uniform for chaplains of the army will be plain black frock coat, with standing collar, and one row of nine black buttons; plain black pantaloons; black felt hat, or army forage cap, without ornament. On occasions of ceremony, a plain chapeau de bras may be worn." In 1864 General Order Number 247 prescribed black braid around the buttonholes and a gold embroidered wreath on the hat. Some chaplains seem to have been unaware of these directives. As the law gave them captain's pay, they wore the uniform and insignia of that grade, including sword and pistol, and sometimes were mistaken for officers of the line.

Reports were no more popular in those days than in later times. Stonewall Jackson, said to live by the New Testament and fight by

---

[17] 13 *Stat.* 46; *Official Records,* Ser. III, Vol. IV, pp. 809, 1207.
[18] Very Rev. W. Corby, C. S. C.—*Memoirs of Chaplain Life,* pp. 204–05.

the Old, maintained that the Bible gave a rule for everything. Asked by an officer what was the scriptural authority for military reports, he recommended a study of Joshua's report of the battle with the Amalekites.[19]

Highly practical, if less idealistic than other matters, were the provisions for the pay and allowances of chaplains. The total compensation of post chaplains was valued at $1,100 when War Department orders of 4 May 1861 promised chaplains of volunteers the pay and allowances of captains of cavalry. The bill authorizing the employment of volunteers introduced in the Senate on 6 July contained the same provision. It was stated during the debate that this amounted to $145.50 a month, or $1,746 a year. The chairman said that the Committee on Military Affairs had been under great pressure to recommend the pay and allowances of a major of cavalry. The bill was passed with an amendment authorizing only the pay and allowances of Regular chaplains, but it was recalled from the House for reconsideration, and the higher amount was restored. It was argued that chaplains in the Regular Army had a permanent status while the volunteers had undertaked an uncertain service at heavy cost and should be paid accordingly. However, the deciding factor among the senators seems to have been the feeling that they must keep faith with those already on duty who had been promised the pay of captains of cavalry by the President. In the House one member thought the pay of a second lieutenant of infantry would be enough, for most chaplains would be single men with light duties. Another proposed that of a captain of infantry, though he mentioned clergymen of his acquaintance who had relinquished salaries of $1,800 to enter the chaplaincy. Another urged that chaplains would have to maintain a horse and should have the allowances of a cavalry officer. This point seems to have carried some weight, for the bill passed with the original provision concerning pay and became a law on 22 July 1861.[20]

The status of hospital chaplains led to an instructive senatorial debate. On 3 December 1861, President Lincoln asked Congress to comply with his promise to those clergymen who had been serving in military hospitals at his invitation and pay them at the same rate as army chaplains. During the debate some held that the President had done all he had promised in recommending payment, but Congress

----

[19] Douglass Southall Freeman—*Lee's Lieutenants*, I, XIII, Jones, *op. cit.*, pp. 99–100.
[20] 5 *Stat.* 259; 11 *Stat.* 163; 12 *Stat.* 270; *Official Records*, Ser. III, Vol. I, p. 154; *Globe*, 1861, pp. 50–54, 100; Wilson, *op. cit.*, pp. 1–2.

was under no obligation to take any action.   Others said that these
chaplains should be paid, but the lower rate allowed to post chaplains
was sufficient.   The majority felt that volunteer chaplains were so
much more numerous than those of the Regular Army that the men
serving the hospitals reasonably expected the pay of captains of cavalry.   It was soon agreed that the higher rate should be paid for prior
service, but no commitment for the future was recognized.   The Committee on Military Affairs thought the pay of regular chaplains was
enough.   Harlan believed that arrangements could be made for the
clergymen living near a hospital to serve the inmates in rotation or for
one of them to do so in addition to his parish duties for a comparatively small salary.   Foster did not want chaplains who would walk
through the hospital occasionally and make a prayer but the type who
would be devoted and constantly active.   He asserted that hospital
work was more exacting than service in the field because the chaplain
who had been on duty all day was often called out again at night and
was constantly exposed to infectious diseases and burdened with the
cares and sufferings of many sick and wounded men.   Insisting that
hospital chaplains rendered 10 times the service of those assigned to
regiments, he carried his point, and their pay was made the same as
that of volunteer chaplains by the Act of 20 May 1862.[21]

This discussion inevitably called in question the justice of the pay
of regimental chaplains.   Many senators felt no obligation to continue
any specified rate into the second year.   Some thought regulars and
volunteers should be on the same footing, others that the latter could
not be reduced fairly except by decreasing the pay of captains of
cavalry.   As many felt this rate, now reckoned at $1,758 a year, was
needlessly high and that economy was imperative, it was voted to pay
all chaplains $100 a month.   Scant attention seems to have been paid
to the objection that this would give an unfair advantage to post chaplains who were stationed in safe places and were given quarters worth
an additional $25 a month.   Several felt that chaplains with families
could not provide for them at the new rate of pay and supported an
amendment to allow one ration a day, valued at $116.80 a year.   One
senator wished to specify that it be drawn in kind, but Grimes, the
mover, did "not want to compel them to take it in salt pork and junk."
This section, changed to allow two rations while on duty, was included
in the Act of 17 July 1862.   This meant a reduction of slightly more
than 18 percent for regimental and hospital chaplains instead of the

---

[21] John G. Nicolay and John Hay, eds.—*Complete Works of Abraham Lincoln,* VII, 60; *Globe,*
1863, pp. 1078–82; 12 *Stat.* 403.

32 first voted by the senators and a saving of about $325 a year where the advocates of economy had hoped for $600 or $700.[22]

This law, providing that the pay of all chaplains should be "one hundred dollars per month and two rations a day when on duty," was interpreted in a way never contemplated by those who enacted it. Apparently the phrase "while on duty" was felt to limit the monthly pay as well as the daily rations, for all compensation to chaplains was withheld not only while they were on leave but when sick, wounded, prisoners, or absent on special duty.   Denison believed this policy was prompted by hostility to the chaplains, but it may have reflected the caution of finance officers who feared being held responsible for over-payments under a statute of doubtful meaning.   Quoting this law in relation to another problem, the Attorney General inserted a comma after *month,* showing that he had no doubt of its meaning; but for want of this comma many chaplains were left wholly without pay for vary-ing periods during the next 2 years.[23]

This matter was brought up in both houses of Congress early in 1864.   Senator Foster presented the facts, allowing himself an ironical reference to those whose privilege it was to construe the law. He cited the case of Chaplain Barber who had been shot while aiding the wounded and was then lying without funds in a boarding house in Washington kept by a chaplain's widow for whom no provision had been made although her husband had been killed in line of duty.   He mentioned another chaplain who had been ordered to assist two wounded officers to their homes but had lost his pay for the period of his absence.   The Act of 9 April 1864 specified in terms which could not be misunderstood that chaplains absent from duty should suffer no loss of pay and allowances different from that of other officers in the same situation, and this provision was made retroactive.   Under the law of 3 March 1863, officers could receive only half their pay and allowances for the time they were absent with leave except when this was due to sickness or wounds.   On 20 June 1864, this was changed so that absences not exceeding 30 days in any year could be author-ized for other reasons without loss of pay.[24]

These transactions may have resulted in part from an understand-ing by some chaplains that they were not bound as strictly as other officers by the usual rules of absence.   After nearly 3 years of service

---

[22] *Globe,* 1862, pp. 1078–88; 12 *Stat.* 594–95.

[23] Rev. Frederic Denison, A. M.—*A. Chaplain's Experiences in the Union Army,* p. 41; *Globe,* 1864, p. 1165; *Official Opinions of the Attorneys General of the United States,* XI, 41.

[24] *Globe,* 1864, pp. 1163–64; 13 *Stat.* 46; 12 *Stat.* 736; 13 *Stat.* 145.

Chaplain Henry N. Hudson wrote to General Butler, "You know . . . that in the matter of voluntary absence custom and usage allow a somewhat wider margin to chaplains than to other officers." This he justified, not because of the exceptional duties they had to perform, but on the ground that their pay was small, with no chance of promotion, and that their office was not as closely related to the efficiency of an army as that of other officers.[25] The circumstances which elicited this statement were as dramatic as they were unusual.

The chaplain was about 44 years of age in 1864 and had some reputation as a reader and critic of Shakespeare. During his years in the army he wrote occasional letters on military affairs to the New York *Evening Post*. Soon after his transfer to the Army of the James, commanded by Benjamin F. Butler, that officer made his ill-starred attack upon Petersburg. In a private letter to the editor of the *Evening Post* and basing his opinion upon statements by his regimental commander and other officers, the chaplain told how Generals Smith and Gillmore gained advantageous positions within the Confederate lines but were forbidden to intrench by Butler because the movement was offensive. When the Confederates counterattacked, Smith's forces were driven back, but Gillmore took steps to turn this defeat into a victory until he was peremptorily ordered to retreat by Butler. The chaplain characterized these orders as an act of presumption followed by one of timidity. His letter was published anonymously, the editor remarking that several advantages seemed to have been lost through Butler's errors.[26]

A few days later Hudson was ordered to New York on special duty by Gillmore, with permission to visit his home. Within a week his son had died and his wife was ill. Later he had a serious illness himself. When an order to rejoin his command came from Butler, he reported to his colonel, who was then in New York, but got no further orders. Later he submitted his resignation, which was approved and forwarded by the colonel. This brought an order from the general that he give his parole to return at once or be sent under guard. When he reported, Butler questioned and rebuked him harshly and ordered him confined. After more than 50 days of confinement under conditions which he considered purposely cruel, the chaplain demanded trial or release according to law and was returned to his regiment but not allowed to leave it. Friends laid the matter before General Grant,

---

[25] (Henry N. Hudson)—*A Chaplain's Campaign with General Butler, passim.*
[26] New York *Evening Post,* 17 Feb. and 24 May 1864.

who investigated the case and gave him leave of absence for the short period until the end of his term of service.[27]

After his discharge and Butler's relief from the command of troops, the chaplain published a pamphlet of 64 pages in the form of a letter to the general.   He charged that Butler used his absence as an excuse for punishment without trial but that his harshness was partly in revenge for criticisms in the anonymous letter but chiefly because Hudson would not make statements which could be used in an attack upon Gillmore, as Butler was trying to throw the blame for his own blunders upon that worthy officer.   Butler replied in a pamphlet of 48 pages over the signature of the officer who had confined the chaplain.   It bore the title *Official Documents Relating to a "Chaplain's Campaign (not) with General Butler", but in New York.*   He called the chaplain a scoundrel before his appointment and a hypocrite afterward, justified the long imprisonment without trial on the ground that any court the general could have convened would have been prejudiced against the chaplain, and that he had confessed his guilt anyway.   Gillmore's orders and leave of absence were declared to be invalid, ostensibly sending Hudson to New York on business which was merely pretended to be in the public service but really to get him away in order that he and Gillmore might escape the consequences of the critical letter sent to the newspaper. By inuendo he hinted that Grant's order for the chaplain's release was the result of improper or doubtful influences.   Fortunately it is unnecessary to ravel this tangled skein of charge and recrimination.   The chaplain's defense of his prolonged absence was rather feeble.   If the stenographic record of his interview by Butler was correctly transcribed, he was not always frank in his answers to questions designed to implicate Gillmore in the published criticisms. On the other hand, had he been as unscrupulous as his opponents charged, he would have made out a better case.   Butler's language during their conversation and his later course lend some color to the chaplain's claim that his absence was unimportant but the general hoped to use him to injure General Gillmore.[28]

The law of 1862 had allowed chaplains to draw forage for only one horse, for one of the complaints mentioned by Paymaster Larned was that even chaplains, from whom he expected something better, considered the forage allowance an emolument and drew commutation for three horses when they had only one.   In 1864 Congress

---

[27] Hudson, *op. cit., passim.*
[28] *Ibid.*

authorized forage for two horses, for it had been stated in the Senate that chaplains in the field were not allowed to transport baggage in Army wagons and needed a second horse for this purpose.   Quarters and fuel, without the privilege of commutation, were authorized for those assigned to hospitals, posts, or forts under the limitations then applicable to surgeons.   This was said to have a money value of $72 a month in Washington and half that amount in other places.   The same law entitled chaplains and their dependents to a pension of $20 a month in case of disability or death incurred since 4 March 1861.[29]

Another legal question concerned the pay of chaplains.   The organization of Negro troops led to the selection of colored ministers as chaplains of some of the regiments.   Records which may not be complete show 139 chaplains assigned to some of the 158 Negro regiments.   Only a few of these are known to have been Negroes, though others well may have been.   Among them were Henry M. Turner, William Hunter, James Underdue, and William Warring, of the First, Fourth, 39th and 102d United States colored troops respectively, and Samuel Harrison of the 54th and William Jackson and John R. Bowles of the 55th Massachusetts Infantry.   The Act of 17 July 1862, among other provisions, authorized the employment of persons of African descent for labor on fortifications and for similar tasks at a monthly wage of $10.   The army paymaster interpreted this to limit the pay of all Negroes to that amount.[30]

Chaplain Harrison was chosen in the usual manner and commissioned by the Governor of Massachusetts.   Outfitting himself at a cost of $300, he joined his regiment in South Carolina, but was allowed only $10 a month by the paymaster.   He appealed to Governor Andrew, who forwarded the papers to the President, and he asked a ruling from the Attorney General.   On 23 April 1864, Mr. Bates replied that no law prohibited the appointment of Negro soldiers or officers, Harrison had been commissioned and mustered the same as other chaplains and was entitled to the same pay, the wage limitation of $10 a month applied only to the type of laborers specified in the law and employed under its provisions, and be believed the President should order the pay department to conform to this decision.   Sumner read this opinion to the Senate in support of legislation to define the rights of Negro troops.   When the conference committees had adjusted the disagreements between the houses, he thought the enactment had

---

[29] 12 *Stat.* 594; 13 *Stat.* 46; *Official Records,* Ser. III, Vol. IV, p. 728; *Globe,* 1864, pp. 1163–64.
[30] *Official Opinions, loc. cit.; Globe,* 1864, pp. 1164, 2879.

"dwindled down to the little end of nothing." Apparently the ruling of the Attorney General was considered to have settled the question as it concerned chaplains, for some thought it unnecessary when Wilson offered an amendment to the pay bill of 1864 stating explicitly that colored chaplains should receive the same as others, and he withdrew his motion.[31]

The experience of the Confederate government in providing religious ministrations for the Southern army was strikingly parallel to that of the government at Washington, with some significant variations. As early as 27 April 1861, L. P. Walker, Secretary of War, wrote to President Davis:

> I cannot more appropriately conclude this report than by urging upon Congress the passage of a law empowering this Department to appoint chaplains for the service. Military experience demonstrates the importance of religious habitudes to the morality, good order, and general discipline of an army in the camp or in the field. If we expect God to bless us in our struggle in defense of our rights—to terminate, in all probability, only after a protracted and bloody war—we must recognize Him in our actions.[32]

Six days later an act of the Confederate Congress empowered the President to appoint for the duration of the war such number of chaplains as he might deem expedient and to assign them to regiments, brigades, or posts. The same law fixed their pay at $85 a month, with no other allowances. Within 2 weeks one senator proposed to reduce this to $40, another to $25 and rations; but after some debate it was set at $50 a month by the law of 16 May. This was half the pay of a first lieutenant of cavalry as established by the Act of 6 March 1861. It seems probable that this drastic reduction was made less from the desire for economy than to discourage men with less than the highest devotion from entering the chaplaincy. In August an attempt to increase chaplains' pay failed, but rations were allowed at that time. The proposal that military rank be conferred upon chaplains was rejected. The next spring a friendly senator tried to give them the grade of captain but found less support in his own branch than in the House. Early in 1863 the proposal was revived at the request of two chaplains but without success. One of these chaplains had been in the army for about 8 months, the other slightly more than a year.[33]

In December 1861, the Senate entertained a resolution to in-

---

[31] *Ibid.*

[32] *Official Records,* Ser. IV, Vol. I, p. 252.

[33] *Ibid.,* pp. 129, 275, 327, 595; *Journal, C. S. A.,* I, 99, 124, 174, 226, 361, 450, 462, 608, II, 171, V, 119, VI, 57.

crease the pay of chaplains, and a bill for this purpose was reported favorably late in January.   A resolution of the Georgia Conference of the Methodist Church called attention to this matter in March, and a bill fixing the amount at $80 a month, with rations, was taken up. Senator Baker failed to increase the pay to $100 a month "with the rank of captain," and the bill became a law on 19 April, being supported in the House by a petition from a group of Richmond ladies. The next year a proposed change, though favored by a majority, failed in the House for want of a quorum.   The money value of rations was fixed at $1 a day in January 1864, and chaplains were authorized to commute them at that price or draw them in kind.[34]

Early in the war chaplains who wished to ride not only provided but maintained their own horses.   McGill lost his at a time when the price of a good one amounted to his entire pay for 8 or 10 months, but his regiment made up the sum and presented him with a fine horse. General Jackson believed that chaplains would be more useful if mounted and that this should be encouraged by an allowance of forage.   Three months before his death the matter was proposed in the House of Representatives.   After a delay of nearly a year, on the recommendation of General Hardee and others, chaplains in actual service in the field were authorized on 22 January 1864 to draw forage for one horse, *"Provided,* The Chaplain has a horse in his use"*, Betts said that before this provision was made, his horse was fed because his colonel regularly drew forage for one more horse than he had.   Various proposals to allow forage, fuel, and quarters to post chaplains were defeated shortly before the end of the war.   On the last day of May 1864, the President was authorized to appoint chaplains to battalions and general hospitals, with the pay and allowances then provided for regimental and post chaplains.[35]

A comparison of this legislation shows that Union chaplains of volunteers in the spring of 1861 received pay and allowances valued at $1,746 a year.   Their Southern counterparts began at $1,020 and were reduced immediately to $600.   The next year this was increased to $960 and rations.   A few weeks later the Union men were reduced to $1,433.60 and forage for one horse.   In 1864 they were allowed food for a second horse.   At that time the Confederate chaplain who commuted his rations was entitled to $1,325 a year and forage for one

[34] *Ibid.,* I, 534, 709, II, 79, 92, 99, 124, 160, 211, V, 190, 279; *Official Records,* Ser. IV, Vol. I, p. 1076, III, 53, 163, VI, 479, 481.

[35] Jones, *op. cit.,* p. 300; A. D. Betts—*Experience of a Confederate Chaplain, 1861-1865,* p. 33; *Journal, C. S. A.,* IV, 446, 616, 619, VI, 51, 75, 311, 543, 569, 613, 641, 683, VII, 453, 666, 718; *Official Records,* Ser. IV, Vol. III, pp. 194, 496.

horse.   The depreciation of Confederate currency toward the end of the war made the disparity between the pay of chaplains in the two armies greater than these figures seem to imply.

Like the Federal service, the Confederate army suffered during the early months of the war from an influx of preachers who lacked some of the qualifications which the competent chaplain must possess. Some were illiterate or narrowly sectarian, others were mercenary or lacked devotion.   While the proportion of such men among the chaplains was small, these inconsistencies made them conspicuous and tended to reflect upon their sincere and capable associates.   An English officer in the Confederate army referred to them in caustic terms:

> Another class who patriotically rushed to Richmond and obtained salaries to which they were unaccustomed, was a race of long-jawed, loud-mouthed ranters, termed for courtesy's sake ministers of the Gospel.   With profound respect for a class "called of heaven" for the administration of holy offices, I may be allowed to observe that, taken as a whole, these long-bodied individuals who were saddled on our regiments simply considered themselves "called" to receive one hundred and twenty dollars per month, with the rank of captain, and the privilege of eating good dinners wherever chance or Providence provided—to be terribly valiant in words, and offensively loquacious upon every topic of life, save men's salvation.   Where they all came from none knew or cared to know, especially as but little was seen or heard of them, save when some fortunate "mess" had turkey or chicken, and *then,* of course, the minister was sure to put in his appearance, and fuss about until invited to dine.   Most of these gentlemen were particularly condescending in their small talk, could wink at "trifles" after a few weeks' residence, and sometimes betrayed alarming proficiency in handling cards at a social game of poker.[36]

He added a number of quotations from sermons by these chaplains to which he had listened with amazement as much for their moral and theological implication as because of their historic and scientific content.   Most of these "bores and drones" resigned, he wrote, when the salary was reduced to $80 a month and rations, leaving the field to the true men of character and intelligence whose ruling purpose was to do good in every way that conditions would permit.   Though this writer exaggerated many things beside the compensation of Confederate chaplains, he was right in the opinion that the marked reduction in pay made the office less attractive to men whose motives did

---

[36] An English Combatant—*Battlefields of the South*, p. 194.

not rise above those of self-interest.   The Union authorities hoped to obtain similar results by appointing only those men who were specifically recommended for this work by the religious organizations to which they belonged.   When the pay of Union chaplains of volunteers was reduced in July 1862, it seems to have been wholly for reasons of economy.[37]

The names of slightly more than 2,300 Union chaplains are known.   An exact count is impossible because some served more than one unit at different times and a few names are in such form that they may represent two men or only one.   For example, John Smith and J. C. Smith may be indistinguishable, though no such confusion seems to have been occasioned by the name of Orange V. Lemon, an Indiana chaplain.   It is not strange that the populous State of New York furnished 385 of these men and that Illinois, Pennsylvania, Ohio, and Indiana supplied an additional 955.   The published records of no other State name as many as 100, though Wisconsin, Massachusetts, Iowa, and Kentucky approached that number.   Fifteen chaplains from Tennessee are listed in what seems to be the only official roster of Union troops issued by any of the seceded States.   The records of some States name only the chaplains first appointed to certain units, though other sources show that some of them resigned and had successors.   A few chaplains commissioned by their governors but not mustered into the Federal service are known to have served their regiments for several months and been paid by the State.[38]   Some soldiers acted as chaplains without any official status.   Neither they nor the clergymen employed by the Christian Commission are called chaplains in the Government records, but this confusion does appear in some private publications.   Comparing available military records with church statistics and other sources which cover parts of the field, it is estimated that about 3,000 chaplains were appointed to the Union forces by governors, regimental or post officers, or the Federal authorities.

Assuming this number to be substantially correct and accepting two million as the approximate number of individuals at some time in the Union service when allowance is made for duplications, we find a general average of one chaplain for something like 670 men.   Though this ratio may approximate the facts for the period of the war as a whole, several factors would make it a false index of specific situations.

---

[37] *Ibid.; Globe,* 1862, 1078ff.

[38] Orville J. Nave—*Nave's Handbook of the Army Chaplaincy,* p. 8; Ms. records, N. H. Chaplains' Association.

Many regiments took the field with more than 1,000 men but retained their chaplains after the strength had fallen to 400 or 300. Others had none for long periods. Some chaplains saw 3,000 to 4,000 men on the rolls while they were assigned to a regiment. Others resigned after short periods of service. In 2 or 3 States more than half the chaplains resigned, and in several others the proportion was surprisingly large. In most instances these men were serving units enlisted for 3 years, for most of those appointed to 12-, 9-, or 3-month regiments were mustered out with the men. Partial computations seem to indicate that the average chaplain served between 12 and 15 months. When considered by themselves, those who resigned seem to have averaged about 2 months less. It is probable that the Iowa chaplain who resigned after 5 days and declined reappointment the next year and his Ohio colleague who served 1 day hold the record for brevity of service. Several were on duty for more than 3 years, and a few for more than 4.[39]

A reliable estimate of the number of chaplains who served at any time in the Confederate Army is all but impossible, as many of the military records have been lost. Among those which have survived are lists of about 400 men nominated to Congress early in the war by President Davis. Among them were 42 North Carolina men, but only 11 of them are included among the 60 chaplains of North Carolina troops mentioned in the State records. Though some may have been assigned to regiments from other States, it seems probable that several of those nominated by the President did not serve. Others were commissioned by a State but not by the Confederacy. A list of chaplains in Lee's army prepared by a staff officer, probably in 1863, names about 130 and shows an equal number of units with none. Jackson was unable to get chaplains for more than half his regiments, and other corps and armies seem to have been no better supplied. Early in 1864 there were 86 in the corps of Ewell and Hill, consisting of 36 Methodists, 20 Baptists, 20 Presbyterians, 6 Episcopalians, 3 Catholics, and 1 Lutheran. At the time it was remarked that the Baptist group was disproportionately small. One estimate places the probable number of Episcopal chaplains in the Southern armies at 100, and a list of Methodists believed to be about 90 percent complete contains 210 names. Although the Georgia Baptist Convention took the ground that government chaplaincies were wrong, the church

_____

[39] Reports of the Adjutant Generals of various states.

454841 O—58——9

as a whole had a large number of chaplains in service; and the Presbyterian Church sent a large quota.[40]

Secondary sources are confused by the fact that many clergymen, sent to the Confederate armies as missionaries or evangelists under the auspices of their churches, were called chaplains by some writers.   A leading biographer of Woodrow Wilson refers to his father as a Confederate chaplain, but a history of the First Presbyterian Church of Augusta, Ga., clarifies the matter by calling him a chaplain under the mission board.   After the battle of Chickamauga the church was used as a hopsital, and Dr. Wilson ministered to the wounded there and elsewhere, but there seems no evidence that he ever was an army chaplain.   A few Confederate chaplains in their writings mention fellow workers who otherwise would be unknown, but frequently they use terms as indefinite as "Brother Smith" and leave the reader in doubt whether they refer to chaplains or civilian clergymen.   One modern student of this subject believes that the actual chaplains in the Confederate army did not exceed 600.   Another has lists of more than that number and thinks the total was close to 1,000.   With all relevant facts in view, it seems probable that the latter is more nearly correct.[41]

Sixty-six Union chaplains are known to have died in service, not to mention those who succumbed to the hardships of camp and field soon after their discharge.   Fourteen of these were killed under varying circumstances, some of them quite exceptional.

There is unusual interest in the story of Arthur B. Fuller, chaplain of the 16th Massachusetts Infantry.   The son of a prominent citizen and brother of Margaret Fuller, he was widely known in New England.   Sixteen months of service with his regiment left him so ill that further duty in the field was impossible.   Accordingly he resigned with the promise of an immediate appointment as chaplain of a hospital. Before he could leave the camp, his regiment was asked for volunteers to cross the river and drive the sharpshooters out of Fredericksburg. Fuller offered himself and was among the first to cross, though he was warned that he could not hope to be exchanged if captured with his discharge papers and that his family would not be allowed a pension if he were killed.   Some months later his brother said that he believed

---

[40] *Journals, C. S. A., passim;* Dabney Ms., Union Theological Seminary, Richmond, Va.; Betts, *op. cit.,* p. 29; Jones, *op. cit.,* pp. 230, 233, 358, 382, 490; William W. Sweet—*The Methodist Episcopal Church and the Civil War,* Appendix.

[41] Ray Stannard Baker—*Woodrow Wilson: Life and Letters,* I, 51; *Memorial of the Centennial Anniversary of the First Presbyterian Church, Augusta, Georgia,* p. 178; Herman Norton to Author, 11 April 1955; Sidney J. Romero to Author, 20 April 1955.

the chaplain's action was prompted by the hope of contributing to army morale, feeling that confidence in the new commander was of supreme importance after the general dissatisfaction resulting from the removal of McClellan.   Possibly the few shots fired by him before he was killed may have mitigated in some small way the disaster of the following day, but his patriotic example had a wide and helpful influence.   Governor Andrew, General Andrews, and Chief Justice Bigelow were in the great company who attended his funeral in Boston to honor the way he had lived and died.   Recommending that his widow receive a pension, a committee of Congress reported that, though he was technically out of the service for a few hours before his death, they felt that he really was killed in line of duty.[42]

John M. Springer of the 3d Wisconsin Infantry, who had served in the ranks before appointment as a chaplain, died 2 weeks after he received his death wound at Resaca while fighting bravely to sustain his hard-pressed regiment.   General Reno reported that Orlando N. Benton of the 51st New York Infantry was killed at New Bern "while nobly encouraging the men to do their duty."   More in keeping with the normal functions of a chaplain was the death of Francis E. Butler of the 25th New Jersey, who fell during the siege of Suffolk while carrying water to the wounded.   Horatio S. Howell, 19th Pennsylvania, was shot during the retreat through Gettysburg on the afternoon of the first day and died on the steps of a church.   George W. Bartlett of the famous 1st Maine Cavalry was struck by a shell and blown to pieces at Cold Harbor.   Two weeks after leaving home John W. Eddy of the 72d Indiana was slain by a cannon ball at Hoover's Gap near Chattanooga.   Of Thomas L. Ambrose, killed in the trenches before Petersburg, the historian of the 12th New Hampshire wrote, "a braver man never lived; a truer man never wore the garb of Christianity".   Unfortunately, little is known about the death of John L. Walther, 43d Illinois, at Shiloh, of Levi W. Sanders, 125th Illinois, at Caldwell's Ferry, or of George W. Densmore, 1st Wisconsin Cavalry, at L'Anguille Ferry.[43]

Three other chaplains who were killed while in military service should be associated with this group.   George Knox, who served at different times in the 1st, 10th, and 29th Maine Infantry, was killed at Ceder Creek when his horse reared and fell upon him.   Daniel Fos-

---

[42] Richard T. Fuller—*Chaplain Fuller: Being a Life Sketch of a New England Clergyman and Army Chaplain*, pp. 291–333.

[43] Lt. Col. Wm. F. Fox—*Regimental Losses in the American Civil War*, p. 43; Capt. George W. Pepper—*Personal Recollections of Sherman's Campaigns in Georgia and the Carolinas*, p. 200.

ter, chaplain of the 33d Massachusetts for 15 months, resigned late in 1863 to become captain of a Negro company and was killed at Chapin, Va., the following year.   Half a century after the event Captain Harrison Trow, one of Quantrill's guerilla leaders, told of the death of U. P. Gardner, chaplain of the 13th Kansas.   On 22 November 1864, a clash took place between the guerillas and a Union force near Cane Hill in the Cherokee country.   The latter were worsted and fled after a sharp action in which Trow said that the chaplain stood his ground and fought with the best of them.   In the pursuit Jesse James, afterward a notorious outlaw, killed the Union commander and overtook the chaplain, telling him to turn so that he would not be shot in the back.   Gardner said who he was and asked to be spared, but James, then a boy of 17, grimly shot him down.   Kansas State records give the name as Ozem B. Gardner, 25 November as the date, and call the locality Timber Hill, C. N.[44]

Of the 52 other chaplains recorded as having died in service, one was a suicide and one died in an institution for the insane.   "Missing" is the only record for four who might be added to these lists if all the facts were known.   Eleven chaplains were dismissed, one for falsehood, one for disloyal correspondence, another for absence without leave, and two "for the good of the service."   The 11 Illinois chaplains who lost their lives were the greatest number given by any State. The Medal of Honor was awarded to three chaplains: Milton L. Haney of the 55th Illinois for fighting bravely to help retake the intrenchments near Atlanta from which his regiment had been driven, John M. Whitehead of the 15th Indiana for carrying the wounded to the rear under very heavy fire at Murfreesboro, and Francis B. Hall of the 16th New York for the same type of service at Salem Church.[45]

Fox tells of the gray-haired Confederate chaplain and his two sons who lay dead in front of the 27th Indiana at Resaca.   Apparently the 3d Wisconsin was in the same part of the line, for a soldier of that regiment wrote a few days later that when they were attacked by the 18th Alabama, a lieutenant of that unit was killed at the first fire; but his father, a gray-headed chaplain, took his son's sword and led the advance until he also was slain.   There seems no doubt that

---

[44] *Memorial and Letters of Rev. John Adams, D. D.*, p. 171; *Massachusetts Soldiers, Sailors, and Marines in the Civil War;* John P. Burch—*Charles W. Quantrell: A True History of his Guerrilla Warfare on the Missouri and Kansas Border,* as told by Captain Harrison Trow, p. 226; Adj. Gen. M. R. McLean to C. of Ch., 16 March 1950.

[45] Reports of the adjutant generals of various states; *The Medal of Honor of the United States Army,* pp. 165, 122, 126; Fox *op. cit.*, p. 44.

he was J. P. McMullen, an aged missionary of Baker's Brigade but shown to have been a chaplain at some time by the records of his church. By a striking coincidence Chaplain Springer of the 3d Wisconsin fell while fighting valiantly to repel this attack.[46]

The names of 25 men who died in the Confederate service have been compiled from various sources with a reasonable presumption that they were chaplains. Five are known by their last names only. Thirteen were killed in battle, one of them after accepting a commission as a line officer. How or where some of them met their death probably will never be known. One or two may not have been commissioned chaplains. Apparently the civilian clergymen played a larger part in the religious life of the Southern army than did their Union counterparts, and it would not be strange if some of them died in camp or even on the firing line.

In proportion to the population of the United States, the terrible struggle of the 60's remains the greatest and most deadly contest in which the American people ever have been involved. Nearly one-tenth of the population were in uniform at some time, and few of the older people could not count at least one son or nephew who never came home or who returned maimed or broken in health. Ratios of chaplains to the population are equally striking. One entered the service for something like each 8,000 of the people, and three were lost for every million. The proportions of chaplains enrolled and of those who lost their lives have never been equalled since the Revolution, even if the Union forces alone are compared to the population of the whole country. It is not strange that such a concentration of strong feeling, of resolute purpose and disappointment, of enmity and comradeship, and of tragic suffering should be the focal point of the nation's history for three generations. For many years there were few communities of any size in North or South which did not have a religious leader whose sense of public duty was intensified by vivid memories of what plain and honest men will endure for what they believe to be right.

---

[46] *Ibid.;* Wm. Wallace to his wife, 22 June 1864, ms. in private possession, cited by Bell I. Wiley to Author, 17 March 1955; *Official Records*, Ser. I, Vol. 38, pt. 3, p. 845; *Ministerial Directory of the Presbyterian Church, U. S., 1861-1941,* compiled by Eugene C. Scott.

CHAPTER VIII

From Sumter to Appomattox

"The Lord's will be done" was Secretary Cameron's answer when General McClellan asked permission to use government lumber for the construction of chapels at Camp Dennison. Jones told of a chaplain at Yorktown who did not preach for 3 months because there was no suitable place. After Gettysburg a deepened seriousness made difficulties of this nature seem less formidable. Once when Jones was announced to preach to a Mississippi brigade, he felt that the heavy rain would prevent the service, as there was no place to meet in shelter. As he heard singing, he went out and found a congregation. No one stirred when he told them they need not stay in the rain, so he preached for 40 minutes. On a similar occasion he felt that a heavy fall of snow would keep the men away, but he counted 14 barefoot listeners in the crowd. The men said that they performed military duties in all kinds of weather and saw no reason for making an exception of religious services.[1]

Some chaplains were provided with assembly tents by friends, by benevolent organizations, by the army, or by the men of the regiment.[2] In January 1862, Marks had a great service of dedication in his new tent. This started a quickening of religious interest which continued for many months. At Winchester, McCabe had a tent belonging to the government. During the night retreat he met the commissary, who asked him what he had done with it. He replied, "I folded it up and—" "Bang!" went the Confederate cannon, and they ran in opposite directions. He next saw the commissary in Iowa 2 years later. Running up to him in pretended breathlessness, he finished his sentence. Many chapels were made of such materials as could be found. In summer they might be rustic bowers affording shade and seats.

---

[1] *The War of the Rebellion* (hereafter cited as *Official Records*), Ser. I, Vol. II, pt. I, p. 388; J. William Jones—*Christ in the Camp*, pp. 214, 248–49, 260.

[2] Richard F. Fuller—*Chaplain Fuller: Being a Life Sketch of a New England Clergyman and Army Chaplain*, p. 181; H. Clay Trumbull—*War Memories of a Chaplain*, p. 16; *Memorial and Letters of Rev. John Adams, D. D.*, p. 141; Frank Milton Bristol—*The Life of Chaplain McCabe*, p. 123; D. P. Conyngham—*The Soldier of the Cross* (Ms., Notre Dame Library), p. 96.

These structures were more substantial when it seemed probable that either army would remain in camp for any considerable period.   Jones mentioned 40 chapels built by Lee's men along the Rapidan late in 1863 and 60 on the Petersburg line in the next year.   In December 1863, Adams began the construction of a log chapel, which was to be a reading room as well as a place of worship.   It was 30 by 18 feet, had a fireplace, and was covered with canvas.   It was finished in time to be used on the first Sunday of February.   Five days later the troops left the camp.[3]

Naturally the need for field and camp equipment varied according to the usages of the churches to which the chaplains belonged and in some degree with the preferences of the individuals.   Most chaplains had transportation by furnishing their own horses.   Alexander Betts tells of a fund being raised among the officers to buy a horse for another chaplain during the time when Confederate chaplains were being paid only $50 a month.   Being without a horse brought compensations in his case.   He was very anxious to be at home during a domestic emergency.   His request for a leave was approved at every step till it reached corps headquarters, and General Lee concurred in Jackson's disapproval.   Remembering that Stonewall never had seen his own little daughter, he tried to be content with the restrictions made necessary by army service.   During these days of disappointment he was able to lead a fine young man into the Christian life and reflected that he might have missed this opportunity had he gone home.   This seemed still more important 6 months later when his friend died in his arms.   When the chaplain's leave was disallowed, the colonel suggested that he ask for time to go to North Carolina and buy a horse. This request was approved, and he was able to be at home during the time of greatest anxiety and to ride back to Virginia on a fine animal.[4]

Father Paul Gillen served informally in the Army of the Potomac for many months before accepting an appointment as chaplain. Being attached to no regiment, he could go from place to place and minister to the Catholics in many organizations.   As he was receiving no pay, McClellan provided him with a horse and two-wheeled ambulance.   He named the horse "Sarsfield," a famous name in Irish military history, but soon bought a rockaway to replace the ambulance.   Removing the front seat, he packed some blankets and provi-

---

[3] Rev. J. J. Marks, D. D.—*The Peninsula Campaign in Virginia*, p. 60; Bristol, *op. cit.*, p. 123; Jones, *op. cit.*, p. 250; Adams, *op. cit.*, pp. 138–41, 198.
[4] A. D. Betts—*Experience of a Confederate Chaplain, 1861–1865*, pp. 32, 47.

sions, a chapel tent, and a folding altar of his own invention in this space.   Dr. John Dwyer remarked, "Father Paul's horse and carriage was a combination of a Plimpton bedstead, a cathedral, and a restaurant all combined."   Once he was captured by Mosby's men, but when they learned his identity and examined his equipage, they released both him and Sarsfield.   About this time a general order excluding civilians was issued to free the army from a variety of obnoxious persons and practices.   Though he was held in high esteem by Hancock and great numbers of soldiers besides those of his own faith, Father Gillen had to leave the Army of the Potomac.   Some time later he was appointed to a regimental chaplaincy in the Corcoran Legion.[5]

Among the difficulties which chaplains encountered in the performance of their duties, actual physical danger was not the least. Humphreys tells of crossing a river on a night so dark that the column missed the ford.   Trying to clamber up the steep bank, the colonel's horse fell backward and knocked the chaplain into the water.   Here he lay with his head above water part of the time but unable to move while the horses scrambled over him.   He saw visions of his body floating away and his military record ending in the single word, "Missing."   After an interval which he never could estimate, he succeeded in dragging himself out of the horses' path.   Christy was away on one occasion when a part of his regiment was sent across the Tennessee on a dangerous mission.   Feeling that he should go with them, he followed and was in time to see them land on the opposite bank. Though he never had handled any boat, he tried to cross in a dugout. A moment more and he was floundering in the water while the canoe floated away.   Though he could not swim, he managed to touch bottom and soon was able to wade ashore.[6]

During the march to Manassas, Jones had what seemed a solid acre of men at service.   While they were singing, a shell fell in their midst but did not burst.   They moved to a safer spot for the sermon, and within a short time a score of shells exploded in the area they had left.   At Chickamauga three bullets passed through the cape of Trecy's greatcoat, and his hat was blown off by a shell.   His vestments were captured but were retaken the next day.   On one occasion an officer going into action asked him to take care of his purse.

---

[5] Very Rev. W. Corby, C. S. C.—*Memoirs of Chaplain Life;* pp. 307–10; Conyngham, *op. cit.,* pp. 121–27.

[6] Charles Humphreys—*Field, Camp, Hospital, and Prison in the Civil War,* pp. 216–18; Conyngham, *op. cit.,* p. 79.

Later he found the chaplain ministering to the wounded in an exposed part of the front line and demanded:

> "What brings you here, Father?"
> "My duty, of course, Captain."
> "Then, by Jupiter, hand me out my purse, for it is much safer
>   with me than with you." [7]

Some felt that chaplains were hampered by the lack of a definite status and that regulations should have defined their place and duties more fully.   Marks felt this so strongly that he said the appointment of chaplains was only a concession to the religious sentiment of the country and declared it better that they be abolished than continued with existing limitations.   He admitted that some chaplains were not young and adapted themselves to new situations with difficulty but said those who incurred the dislike of the officers were persecuted and thwarted in their work   Rogers felt that chaplains suffered many rebuffs because the officers regarded them as sinecurists.   He thought many unnecessary activities interfered with Sabbath services and sometimes were intended to do so.   Bradley stated the chief drawbacks to religion and morals in the army as he saw them: most officers were irreligious, there was no Sabbath, and many soldiers had left home thinking that living by Christian principles would be impossible in the army and had not tried. [8]

Quite different were the implications of the story McCabe enjoyed telling at his own expense after he was reminded of the incident by his former colonel more than 40 years after it happened.   Soon after joining his regiment, he conducted a series of special meetings afternoons and evenings in the rustic chapel the men had built.   One day at the hour for dress parade the call was sounded, but virtually no men appeared.   The adjutant reported that the chaplain had them all in church and would not let them out.   The colonel sent a message, directing him to dismiss the meeting, but he replied that he could not do so because the service was going so well he felt it would not be right.   Then the colonel sent a guard who brought the chaplain to headquarters.   Here he listened to a rather severe rebuke for disrupting camp discipline.   For 2 or 3 days this rankled, then he went to the commander's tent and said, "Colonel, you were right and I was wrong; henceforth I will obey orders." [9]

---

[7] Jones, *op. cit.*, p. 253; Conyngham, *op. cit.*, pp. 45, 19.

[8] Rev. Frederic Denison, A. M.—*A Chaplain's Experience in the Union Army*, pp. 15, 45; Marks, *op. cit.*, pp. 46–47; Rev. J. B. Rogers—*War Pictures*, pp. 14, 18, 255; Rev. George S. Bradley—*The Star Corps*, p. 286.

[9] Bristol, *op. cit.*, pp. 77–78.

Some chaplains reported very happy relations with the line officers. Jones said the most of them gave the faithful chaplain every courtesy and assistance.   He mentioned a general who was notoriously cross and profane but who welcomed a colporter, entertained him while in camp, and urged him to do all the good he could.   Leaders of strong religious faith like Gordon, Jackson, and Lee lent powerful support to the chaplains by example as well as through the exercise of military authority.   General Gordon held "family worship" at his quarters every night, and across the lines in the Union camp General Howard and staff began the day with morning prayers.   Eaton mentioned repeatedly the intelligent and never-failing support of General Grant in his perplexing task of caring for the Negro refugees in the Department of the Tennessee.   On one occasion the provost marshal stopped him when he was directing a group of new arrivals to the place where they could be quartered.   Saying that there appeared to be a conflict of orders, the chaplain suggested that they consult the general.   The colonel stated his complaint, but before Eaton could say a word Grant replied, "Chaplain Eaton is carrying out my orders, Colonel, and they must be obeyed."[10]

On 6 September 1861, McClellan issued a general order enjoining greater respect for the Sabbath, forbidding unnecessary work or movements on that day, and requiring officers to maintain decorum and to allow the men to attend services.   A more stringent order of 27 November directed that morning inspections on Sunday be ended before church time and warned officers not to hinder attendance by the men.[11] President Lincoln lent powerful support to this endeavor through an executive order published on 15 November:

> The President, commander-in-chief of the army and navy, desires and enjoins the orderly observance of the Sabbath by the officers and men in the military and naval service.   The importance for men and beast of the prescribed weekly rest, the sacred rights of Christian soldiers and sailors, a becoming deference to the best sentiment of a Christian people, and a due regard for the Divine will, demand that Sunday labor in the army and navy be reduced to the measure of strict necessity.   The discipline and character of the national force should not suffer, nor the cause they defend be imperiled, by the profanation of the day or name of the Most High.   "At this time of public distress"—adopting the words of Washington in 1776— "men may find enough to do in the service of God and their coun-

---

    [10] Jones, *op. cit.*, pp. 215, 229, 348, 362, 491; Adams, *op. cit.*, p. 92; John Eaton, Ph. D., LL. D.—*Grant, Lincoln and the Freedman*, p. 28.
    [11] Rev. J. Pinkney Hammond—*The Army Chaplain's Manual*, p. 34.

try without abandoning themselves to vice and immorality." The first general order issued by the Father of his Country after the Declaration of Independence indicates the spirit in which our institutions were founded and should ever be defended. "The general hopes and trusts that every officer and man will endeavor to live and act as becomes a Christian soldier, defending the dearest rights and liberties of his country."[12]

Barnes told of being thwarted by the commander of the 17th New Hampshire who persistently ordered so much unnecessary work on Sundays that there was no time for services. Though he cited regulations and the President's order, he received no cooperation from the colonel until he threatened to report the matter to the Adjutant General.[13]

As a low churchman General Lee saw nothing distasteful in the emotional evangelism which many chaplains considered their most rewarding form of service. He frequently attended prayer meetings and preaching services and treated chaplains of all faiths with unfailing courtesy. During the winter of 1863–64 when discerning leaders of the Confederacy began to recognize the stern fact that ultimate victory was by no means certain, the religious spirit in the army did much to maintain its morale. A less famous order had been issued in 1862, but Lee's general orders No. 15 were published on 7 February 1864:

> I. The attention of the army has already been called to the obligation of a proper observance of the Sabbath, but a sense of its importance, not only as a moral and religious duty, but as contributing to the personal health and well-being of the troops, induces the commanding general to repeat the orders on that subject. He has learned with great pleasure that in many brigades convenient houses of worship have been erected, and earnestly desires that every facility consistent with the requirements of discipline shall be afforded the men to assemble themselves together for the purpose of devotion.
>
> II. To this end he directs that none but duties strictly necessary shall be required to be performed on Sunday, and that all labor, both of men and animals, which it is practicable to anticipate or postpone, or the immediate performance of which is not essential to the safety, health, or comfort of the army, shall be suspended on that day.
>
> III. Commanding officers will require the usual inspections on Sunday to be held at such time as not to interfere with the attendance of the men on divine service at the customary hour in the morning. They also will give their attention to the maintenance of

---

[12] John C. Nicolay and John Hay, Eds.—*Complete Works of Abraham Lincoln,* VIII, 76–77.
[13] Ms. records, New Hampshire Chaplains' Association.

order and quiet around the places of worship, and prohibit anything that may tend to disturb or interrupt religious exercises.[14]

On 14 November 1864, the Confederate House of Representatives adopted resolutions commending those officers who had exerted
themselves to have the Sabbath observed in their commands and
urging the fullest cooperation with chaplains and missionaries in the
performance of their religious duties.[15]

Sectarian differences of belief and practice occasionally hampered
a chaplain in his work or embarrassed him in other ways. Significant
changes had occurred since the Revolution, when the clergy of the
large religious bodies, each dominant in a considerable part of the
country, demonstrated not only that they were separated by no insuperable barriers but that they could tolerate the few minority groups
which had chaplains in the service. The phenomenal spread of the
Methodist movement until its members had become the most numerous group in many States, paralleled by a marked growth among the
Baptist and allied organizations, resulted in a large proportion of
soldiers and chaplains being accustomed to think of an emotional
evangelism as the primary function of the church. Naturally this
caused some distrust of the adequacy of practices in which sacraments
and ritual were conspicuous. It was equally natural that others should
deprecate those religious activities which seemed to belittle such observances. Both appeared deficient to those who considered religious
nurture the chief continuing task of the church. Corby felt that ceremonies without sacraments were inadequate but that a proper combination of the two make a solemn impression. This, he believed, was
the reason why Catholic soldiers treated their chaplains with respect
and obedience while others showed discourtesy and indifference to
theirs. Quintard, who seems to have combined the best qualities of
the high churchman and of the evangelist, quotes his jovial reply to
the man who was arguing against the use of forms: "You know that
when the earth was without form, it was void; and that is the way
with many Christians." [16]

Recent immigration had brought into the country certain elements which affected the relations and work of chaplains. Large
groups had come from northwestern Europe, many of them locating
in the North Central States. Several of their standards of propriety,

---

[14] Douglas Southall Freeman—*R. E. Lee: A Biography*, II, 496, III, 241; *Official Records*, Ser. I,
Vol. 33, p. 1150.

[15] *Journal of the Congress of the Confederate States of America*, VII, 272.

[16] Conyngham, *op. cit.*, p. 146; Rev. Arthur Howard Noll, Ed.—*Doctor Quintard: Chaplain,
C. S. A.*, p. 156.

especially in relation to drinking and Sabbath observance, differed
from those which had gained a wide acceptance among religious people in America.   Naturally these men were perplexed when they
entered the army and came under the ministrations of chaplains who
made moral issues of matters which they never had viewed in such a
light.   Two factors kept this problem from becoming serious: these
immigrant groups soon organized independent churches along national
and linguistic lines and were able to provide a considerable number
of chaplains for their own soldiers; and they tended generally to conform to the prevailing mores of the communities where they lived.[17]

The growth of the Roman Catholic population in the United
States brought about a different relationship.   Many Americans who
were of English or Scottish origin had inherited from the controversies
of the Tudor and Stuart periods a deep distrust of Catholicism.
Many of them believed it to be an organization habitually active in
politics and subservient to a foreign ecclesiastical authority which
claimed an allegiance transcending that owed by citizens to the state
and a prior obedience in case of disagreement with the civil authorities.   These were abstract opinions to most Americans, because Catholics had never been numerous in more than a few localities.   The
large migration of the midcentury, especially that originating in Ireland, changed this situation in many American communities.   Naturally most of those who sought a home in the new world to escape
starvation during the famine years brought with them no wealth and
little culture.   Americans might be willing to hire them at small
wages to perform menial tasks but expected them to remain in Shanty-
town on the other side of the tracks.   When intemperance led to
quarrels and violence, it was assumed that both were characteristic of
the Irish temperament.   Participation in politics and a bid for a
larger place in the economic field were resented as an intrusion by
many of the older inhabitants.   Unhappily, sentiments of this nature
were linked in many people's minds with the fact that nearly all of
the Irish immigrants were of the Catholic faith, and this led to a widespread prejudice against all Catholics.[18]

Prejudices of this nature appeared frequently among the soldiers
and sometimes were manifest also by the chaplains.   Ouellet mentioned the hostile literature distributed by sectarian agencies.   A Confederate soldier told Chaplain Gache that he thought the Catholics were
the worst people on earth, as he never had heard anything good about

---

[17] Marcus Lee Hansen—*The Immigrant in American History,* pp. 97–128.
[18] *Ibid.*

them, but said he would like to join the church of the Sisters who had
been caring for him.   When he learned that the Sisters were Catholics, their kindness outweighed this preconception, and he still felt that
he would like to belong to their church.   Captured by South Carolina
troops at Malvern Hill, Scully heard the confession of a sergeant standing in the attitude of conversation so that neither of them would be
molested.[19]

An anecdote which Major Conyngham told at the expense of his
Protestant friends is equally good as an illustration or as a joke.   A
wounded man in the hospital at Charleston was greatly surprised to
learn that his nurses were Catholics, for he knew the latter were very
bad people.   Asked to cite the instances of Catholic wickedness he himself had seen, he was unable to state any except that the Catholic in
the next bed swore terribly.   This brought a quick protest from his
neighbor: "Now, you shut up!   I'm not a Catholic but a North of Ireland Presbyterian."   Naturally prejudices of this nature engendered
their counterpart among those toward whom the distrust was directed.
Conyngham himself was surprised when a Protestant writer made an
honest statement about the work of the Sisters and praised a number
of Catholic chaplains.   Scully attributed the abuse he suffered from
the Confederate officer who had captured him to the fact that his cap-
tor was descended from the Huguenots, "that fiercely bigoted race,"
and believed the brigade commander treated him kindly because his
sister had been converted to Catholicism.   When Denison invited a
priest of St. Augustine to spend several days at the fort where he was
stationed and minister to the Catholic men, he was criticized by some
of the Protestant chaplains of the department, but the priest was pleased
as much as surprised by his liberality.[20]

The close association of men who marched and fought together
did much to remove prejudices, whatever their cause.   Christy mentioned the Protestants in his regiment who attended mass and said that
a few years in the army would do more to allay bigotry than half a
century in civil life.   Trumbull told of the cordial support given him
by Catholic generals, such as Foster, Gillmore, and Gibbon, and of the
Catholic men who often attended his services and welcomed his prayers when they were sick.   Fuller said that he invariably preached on
the great themes in a spirit in which all could join and that Catholics
and Protestants of various sects attended his services.   Trecy told with

---

[19] Conyngham, *op. cit.,* pp. 99, 111, 159.

[20] *Ibid.,* pp. 14, 99, 217, 220, *et passim;* Denison, *op. cit.,* p. 32.

appreciation of the Protestant chaplain who went through his regiment urging the Catholic men to attend mass. Trumbull mentions being on a transport with a Catholic chaplain and arranging a joint service. He conducted a simple but dignified worship with no sectarian characteristics, and his colleague gave an inspiring and helpful address. This expression of cordiality between the chaplains did much to promote a like spirit among the men. Sheeran tells of the Confederate captain who had been a Protestant preacher but received him cordially, provided him with a tent and other conveniences for hearing confessions, and attended mass the next morning. Another Confederate chaplain at his request baptized the brother of a Baptist preacher into the Catholic faith, the brother being present and manifesting a sincere good will.[21] Such incidents show the mutual respect which was taking the place of distrust as the adherents of the various faiths came to understand and appreciate in some degree the motives and ideals of other groups.

The conduct of public worship is the most conspicuous function of a chaplain, and securing the attendance of the largest number who will benefit from the services is a primary consideration. Few civil war chaplains seem to have favored compulsory attendance. Trumbull and Humphreys specifically requested that the men be not ordered to attend, though the latter suggested that the presence of the officers would have a good effect. After 2 years of experience Marks believed that all should be ordered to church once on Sunday and that the chaplain should preach on subjects which would find a response in every mind. Rogers held similar views and described a hospital service where the patients were ordered to attend by the surgeon in charge, but his method of gathering a congregation at a convalescent hospital where he was stationed at a later time was to take his stand under a tree or in some other appropriate spot and begin singing.[22]

General Burk told how Ouellet discouraged absence from mass after the retreat to Harrison's landing. The men were tired, and breakfast had just been served, when they were called to church. Several placed their food on the ground in front of their shelter tents but crawled inside to escape notice. Observing this, the energetic priest went swiftly through the company streets kicking over the containers of coffee, then returned to the chapel and assured the worshipers that he knew who had been the trustworthy men during the cam-

---

[21] Conyngham, *op. cit.*, pp. 28, 80, 161, 199; Trumbull, *op. cit.*, pp. 23–24, 27–28; Fuller, *op. cit.*, p. 179.

[22] Trumbull, *op. cit.*, p. 19; Humphreys, *op. cit.*, p. 389; Marks, *op. cit.*, p. 45; Rogers, *op. cit.*, pp. 18, 30, 80.

paign and who the "coffee-coolers" and "skedaddlers." These terms, coined in this dramatic manner, were long prominent in the distinctive vocabulary of the army. Denison told of a Catholic soldier who protested having to attend services conducted by a Protestant. The colonel would not excuse him, saying that he also was a Catholic but attended the chaplain's services, which would not harm either of them. When legislation to provide chaplains for the volunteer forces was pending, Congressman Sherman moved the proviso that no soldiers be compelled to attend regimental or other services in violation of any religious scruples they might have. In support of his motion he cited the case of a soldier confined in the guardhouse because, in loyalty to the teachings of his childhood, he had refused to attend a service conducted by a Protestant chaplain, but his amendment was lost.[23]

Trumbull believed that careful preparation made sermons attractive, so usually wrote his in full. One day a soldier looked into the chapel tent, saw that he was speaking without notes, and walked away saying, "Pshaw! he is only talking; I thought he was preaching." Rogers made the interesting remark that camp sermons must be short and direct but men in hospitals will listen with interest to longer discourses. Pepper, whose long service as a correspondent enabled him to hear many other chaplains, said that their sermons should be "redolent of gospel," not dealing in scholastic philosophy nor in the efficacy of "what men call the sacraments" nor in "the icicle beauty of mere morality." Trumbull tells how he met the situation when his regiment was on picket duty. By going from post to post and quoting an appropriate text with brief remarks at each, he was able to bring a religious message to the entire unit.[24]

Several chaplains described services or other events of special interest. Corby arranged a military mass in which the customary forms of courtesy were used as expressions of religious devotion. The troops presented arms during the more solemn parts of the mass, bands played at appropriate intervals, and cannon were fired at the consecration. Fuller found an informal prayer and conference meeting both popular and helpful. The men met in front of his tent in the early evening. For a few minutes he gave them a summary of the latest news, especially anything from home, and invited them to

---

[23] New York *Tablet*, quoted by Corby, *op. cit.*, p. 302; Denison, *op. cit.*, p. 18; *Congressional Globe*, 1861, p. 101.

[24] Trumbull, *op. cit.*, pp. 77, 98; Rogers, *op. cit.*, p. 83; Capt. George W. Pepper—*Personal Recollections of Sherman's Campaigns in Georgia and the Carolinas*, p. 204.

comment or ask questions. This was followed by prayer, religious discussion, and the singing of hymns. Jones had the Christian men of his regiment take turns in leading informal prayer meetings every evening. He told of a Union officer who had been captured and was conversing with his guard about the better clothing and equipment of the Federal soldier when the Confederate remarked, "I am sure you do not have as good prayer-meetings as we have." [25]

Adams and Humphreys regularly offered prayer at dress parade. Trumbull felt that this practice was totally different from compulsory attendance at preaching services and described its observance in the Tenth Connecticut Infantry. At the command, "Take your places, gentlemen, for prayers," the two right and two left companies faced inward, forming a hollow square, and hats were removed during the prayer. A Catholic soldier objected to the removal of his hat during prayers by a Protestant chaplain, saying that it was a matter of conscience, but the colonel satisfied him that this was part of a military ceremony rising above all sectarian considerations and would in no way compromise his faith. During a delay on the railroad, Hoge preached to the men on the train. After the battle of Franklin, Quintard officiated at the burial of 5 Confederate generals, 3 of whom he picked up on the field and buried with the aid of a single Negro. At Antietam, Corby galloped in front of the Irish Brigade as they were rushing into battle, told the men to make an act of contrition, and gave a hasty absolution. Within a few minutes 506 of them had fallen. At Gettysburg he gave general absolution to Hancock's corps a moment before they joined in deadly strife near the spot where his statue now stands. [26]

Sacraments and religious ceremonies were frequently observed according to the practices of the various faiths. Marks told of improvising sacramental wine from grape jelly and water. Trumbull described a communion service in a New Bern church with three chaplains participating, enlisted men distributing the elements, and a soldier at the organ. In emergencies when a priest could not come, Catholic Sisters sometimes baptized the very sick and prepared them for death. One patient had his nurse call a clergyman to prepare him. The minister offered to read from the Bible and pray with him, but the soldier said anyone could do that. He asked if there was something on his mind that troubled him, but he said there was not.

---

[25] Corby, *op. cit.*, pp. 99, 140; Fuller, *op. cit.*, p. 181; Jones, *op. cit.*, pp. 471, 513.

[26] Adams, *op. cit.*, p. 76; Humphreys, *op. cit.*, p. 382; Trumbull, *op. cit.*, pp. 20–22; Jones, *op. cit.*, p. 525; Noll, *op. cit.*, pp. 112–16; Corby, *op. cit.*, pp. 112, 181ff.

The sick man was satisfied only with the more tangible rites of the Catholic faith.[27]

Jones mentioned frequent baptisms in the Rapidan. Though they were in full view and easy range of the Union pickets and the tall form of General Gordon was usually conspicuous among the spectators, they never were disturbed. In 1 year he preached 161 sermons, baptized 222 persons, and secured 12 chaplains. He referred to a Georgia chaplain who preached from 4 to 6 times daily, baptized 238 men, and saw 500 profess conversion in 1862. He described a solemn service beside the Antietam during the march to Gettysburg when a chaplain baptized 14 veterans of the battle of the preceding year. After a lecture by Chaplain Lacy on the character of Stonewall Jackson, given on Washington's birthday, Jones went to a millpond where an opening had been cut in the ice and immersed 14 men. Two days later he baptized nine in the Rapidan. Sometimes he performed baptisms 2, 3, or even 4 times without changing clothes. The fact that he had no others was a sufficient reason, though not the only one.[28]

Quintard tells of a wedding, hampered but not prevented by the exigencies of war. Invitations were out for the marriage of General Brown to a lady of Griffin, Ga., at nine in the evening, and the groom and staff arrived on the preceding day. The next morning brought an order from General Johnston for them to report immediately at Rome, far away across the State. The chaplain was hastily summoned from the hospital and read the service. Two weeks later the couple were able to take a short wedding journey. Fiske officiated at an unusual marriage while assigned to duty with Negro refugees. Many of them felt that they should be regularly married, now that they were to be free. Accordingly the chaplain performed the ceremony for 119 couples within an hour.[29]

Some chaplains found visiting from tent to tent very profitable. Jones contrasted two remarks overheard among the men: "We don't like Mr. _____; he smokes his pipe and enjoys himself with the officers, preaches sometimes and hardly ever comes among us." "Our chaplain is a good man; he often comes round to see us, is always at work and has done a great deal of good; we all like him." Trumbull emphasized the difficulty of taking a friendly interest in the complaints of the men without encouraging insubordination. He once saw, peer-

[27] Marks, *op. cit.,* p. 65; Trumbull, *op. cit.,* pp. 254, 256; Conyngham, *op. cit.,* pp. 254, 256.
[28] Jones, *op. cit.,* pp. 248, 254, 306, 354, 364, 498.
[29] Noll, *op. cit.,* p. 133; Eaton, *op. cit.,* p. 31.

ing from the barred door of Castle San Marco, St. Augustine, what he thought the most repulsive face he ever had seen—coarse, stupid, and marked by low cunning.   Speaking kindly to the man, he learned that he belonged to his regiment and had been confined almost continuously for insubordination.   Several times later the chaplain saw him and never failed to greet him pleasantly.   When the regiment went north for active operations, this man approached Trumbull and told him the story of his life as they leaned over the transport rail in semiprivacy.   He had never known his parents and had grown up on the streets of New Orleans.   The chaplain was the first person who ever spoke to him kindly.   He had listened to the prayer meetings from outside the old chapel in the fort and wanted to go right and to do his duty in the fight that was coming.   When the battle came, Lino did so well that the captain whom he had tormented so long called him out before the company and commended him for bravery and good service.   The chaplain hastened to congratulate him; and Lino said: "Yes, they called me coward, but I tried to do my duty.   'Taint always the frisky ox that's at the far end of the yoke." [30]

Two incidents are striking examples of the variety of evangelistic methods used by the chaplains.   Feeling irresistably impelled to speak to him about his personal religious life, Quintard went to headquarters and asked General Bragg to send out his secretaries so that they could be alone.   Although embarrassed by the general's sternness, he talked earnestly of the obligations of the Christian life and of the influence of the commander's example upon an army.   With tears in his eyes Bragg thanked him, saying that he had waited for 20 years for someone to talk to him in that way.   After a period of instruction the chaplain was privileged to present the general to the bishop of Georgia for confirmation.   In another camp it was feared that a theater near one of the chapels would hamper the revival movement that was starting, but the preaching of Andrew Broaddus attracted the larger crowds.   Soon the owners of the theater and some actors were converted, and the chaplain was invited to transfer his services to the larger building. [31]

Few duties were more exacting or more rewarding than ministering to dying men.   Though methods differed widely, the chaplains sought to meet them where they were and, with full recognition of their limitations or antecedents, to lead them into a sustaining faith

---

[30] Adams, *op. cit.*, p. 214; Marks, *op. cit.*, p. 60; Jones, *op. cit.*, p. 489; Trumbull, *op. cit.*, pp. 110, 112–15.

[31] Noll, *op. cit.*, pp. 78–79; Bell I. Wiley—*The Life of Johnny Reb*, p. 181.

and courage.   Seeking to comfort a captain who had but a few hours to live, Humphreys repeated some of the penitential psalms, then asked if he was willing to die for his country.   The captain replied that he was but said he had been a bad man and asked the chaplain to administer the sacrament.   Sensing his spiritual possibilities, the chaplain said that no sacrament was necessary because "The sacrifices of God are a broken spirit."   The dying man happily finished the text, "a broken and a contrite heart, O God, thou wilt not despise."   Soon he passed into the shadows, confident that all was well with one who willingly died for his country with a contrite heart.[32]

Corby tells of a deserter who was to be shot and was being aided by a minister of limited experience.   Believing that faith was a first consideration and that it consisted of an attitude of mind, he was trying to lead the man to a declaration of belief, but with little success. Seeing the need for a more tangible and voluntary expression of purpose, the chaplain induced the soldier to accept baptism, exhorted him to offer his life to God, and saw him go to his death with confidence. Denison tells of a man who had enlisted three times to get the bounty and had deserted twice.   After a long interview he was convinced that the culprit was truly penitent and obtained a pardon.   Ever afterward the man was true to his pledge and loyal to the service.   Several other chaplains left records of their ministrations to condemned men.   Sometimes they discovered extenuating circumstances and obtained a pardon, even at the moment of execution; but always they strove to bring the convict to repentance for the wrong he had done and to prepare him to meet his death on a high moral and spiritual plane.[33]

These four personal episodes illustrate much more than the normal methods of a Congregational, Episcopal, Unitarian, or Catholic chaplain in ministering to individuals and of the grounds on which they could make a spiritual appeal to the moron, the general, the dying hero, and the convict.   They show them, each true to his own convictions and the usages of his church, adapting their message to the needs and their methods to the spiritual capacity and status of those whom they would serve.   The chaplain, like the apostle, had learned to become all things to all men.   In the debate on a proposal to save money by reducing the number of chaplains, Senator Clark of New Hampshire showed how their counseling activities were conceived by a layman:

---

[32] Humphreys, *op. cit.*, pp. 248–50.

[33] Corby, *op. cit.*, pp. 122–27, 312, 347; Denison, *op. cit.*, p. 21; Conyngham, *op. cit.*, pp. 41, 113, 133; Noll, *op. cit.*, p. 83; *et al.*

> I think a good chaplain is the most effective man in the regiment, and I can now point to men who are doing more good as chaplains than almost any man in the regiment. Though they do not fight, they do a great deal towards keeping the regiment ready to fight; they are with the sick, they are with the suffering, they do a great deal to keep your army such as it ought to be. In my judgment, you had better not take away from the regiment the man to whom the soldier goes in his time of suffering, or when he needs advice. You had better let him be with the men, and let the men be close to him, and about him, and let them see him every hour of the day, and let them come to him readily and ask his advice, and let him be a friend to them, and a close friend, and about them all the time.[34]

Religious literature was a very important aid in the chaplain's work. Bibles, Testaments, and Scripture portions were provided by societies or individuals for distribution in both armies. Practically all publishers of Bibles were in the North. This made it more difficult for the Confederate chaplains to supply their men than for those of the Union army. A Nashville printer brought out an edition in 1861, but the supply was limited. The next year Moses D. Hoge escaped through the blockade and brought back from England a cargo of 10,000 Bibles, 50,000 Testaments, and 250,000 miscellaneous publications. (His English contacts may have been one reason why he was selected by the Virginia legislature in 1875 to deliver the oration at the unveiling of the statute of Stonewall Jackson given by English admirers.) The British and Foreign Bible Society gave unlimited credit to the Confederate Bible Society and provided many thousand Bibles or portions. Not only did the American Bible Society contribute to the needs of the Union army, but several large shipments were sent into the Confederacy. Usually these were distributed through local organizations. Marks gave out Testaments in English, German, French, and Italian; and Denison returned from leave with 300 Douay Testaments for the Catholic men of his regiment.[35]

The "Silent Comforter" had a page for each day of the month with an appropriate text in large print. Trumbull hung copies on the walls of hospital wards, guardhouses, and similar places, arranging to have the pages turned at such a time that the men would be greeted with a new message each morning. Some found tracts useful in beginning a conversation or to give it more lasting effect. Occasion-

---

[34] *Congressional Globe,* 1862, p. 1082.

[35] Jones, *op. cit.,* pp. 148–55; Henry Kyd Douglas—*I Rode with Stonewall,* editor's note, p. 366; Marks, *op. cit.,* p. 45; Denison, *op. cit.,* p. 26.

ally they were put on a string and hung from a tree so that passing troops could pull them off and read on the march.   Quintard prepared a devotional booklet primarily to give comfort to the sick and wounded.   General Polk was greatly pleased with it and addressed copies to Generals Johnston, Hardee, and Hood, with his compliments. They were in his pocket a few hours later when he was killed by a cannon shot.   Stained with his blood, they were forwarded to the friends for whom they were intended.[36]

Several chaplains maintained libraries for the use of the men. Humphries received a large shipment of books from King's Chapel, Boston, and had a log house built to contain them.   Two days later the regiment moved, and he had to send the books to a hospital.   A Mississippi regiment received 160 periodicals for its library.   Fuller was one of the editors of *Army Melodies,* a song book widely used in services and for less formal singing.   A selection from this book was sung at his funeral.   Denison wrote about a dozen "army hymns." They were printed by Rhode Island friends in a convenient size for pasting in the men's pocket Bibles.   When he was transferred to the heavy artillery, he revised them to suit his new assignment.[37]

McCabe demonstrated the effectiveness of song in a manner almost unique.   During the weary months in Libby Prison when all other diversions failed, his associates often turned to him and said, "McCabe, sing for us!"   He had memorized the "Battle Hymn of the Republic" when it was published in the *Atlantic Monthly,* and led his comrades in singing it to the popular marching tune which has been associated with it ever since.   At a meeting in the Capitol on 2 February 1864 with the President in the audience, he was called upon and sang the stanzas, the great throng joining in the familiar chorus.   Mr. Lincoln asked that they sing it again, and this time the band joined with thrilling effect.   The next year the chaplain was asked to sing it at a memorial service for the President in Chicago. In recognition of his share in popularizing the hymn, Mrs. Howe sent him an autographed copy in 1904.   Two years later the hymn was sung over his body as it lay under his country's flag.[38]

Practically all chaplains saw a great value in active membership in a church, but the usages of the various bodies differed so widely that no uniform procedure was practicable.   Several times Quintard arranged for the confirmation of groups ranging from privates to gen-

---

[36] Trumbull, *op. cit.,* p. 30; Jones, *op. cit.,* pp. 483, 490; Noll, *op. cit.,* p. 97.

[37] Humphreys, *op. cit.,* pp. 5, 424; Jones, *op. cit.,* pp. 207, 508; Fuller, *op. cit.,* pp. 175, 180, 309; Denison, *op. cit.,* pp. 11, 26.

[38] Bristol, *op. cit., passim.*

erals when the Bishop of Georgia visited the camp.   Chaplains co-
operated in examining candidates for membership in various churches,
and it usually was possible for them to be received according to the
usages and by a clergyman of the church they were joining.   Membership was then certified to the home church.   Alexander Betts, who
was a Methodist, mentioned receiving a young man into the Missionary Baptist Church.   Sometimes regimental or camp churches were
organized on broad platforms of doctrine and practice, and many
were admitted who never had been associated with any church.
Christian associations were formed in many regiments and brigades,
requiring only good character and earnest purpose for membership.
Their devotional and conference meetings did much to build character and religious knowledge.[39]

The importance of organization among themselves was not overlooked by the chaplains.   Scully described a meeting of chaplains in
Washington early in the war which he would not have attended had
he realized that the chief purpose of the gathering was to plan how
they might gain for themselves the rank and pay of the military grades
from lieutenant to brigadier and the corresponding uniform and
insignia.   At a time when there were 44 chaplains in his corps, Betts
was chosen to preach to them at their next meeting, which would be
in 2 weeks.   In Lee's army, chaplains' associations met every Tuesday
and seem to have been organized by corps.   They discussed practical
questions, such as the best place for chaplains during combat and
whether they should bear arms, and they sent circular letters to their
churches urging cooperation in their work.   Jackson urged the chaplains of his corps to plan their work with as much system as was expected in other branches.   Some felt that the promotion of fraternal
relations among them through these meetings was even more
important.[40]

Stonewall Jackson had the highest confidence in his fellow
Presbyterian, Beverley T. Lacy, and appointed him general chaplain
of his command.   He supervised the work of all chaplains, exerted
himself to obtain others for regiments needing them, served as a channel of intercourse between the army and the various churches, and
gave the unity and vigor of an ecclesiastical organization to the work
of chaplains and civilian ministers in the army.   His leadership is
given credit for a large share in bringing the revival of religion which

---

[39] Noll, *op. cit.*, pp. 73, 92–94, 96; Jones, *op. cit.*, pp. 226, 520; Betts, *op. cit.*, pp. 30, 47; Adams, *op. cit.*, p. 187; Fuller, *op. cit.*, p. 184.
[40] Conyngham, *op. cit.*, p. 95; Betts, *op. cit.*, pp. 29, 31; Jones, *op. cit.*, pp. 94, 230, 325, 336, 522–25.

swept through the army in the winter of 1862–63.   A Union chaplain referred casually to John C. Granbery as Chief of Chaplains of Lee's army, but he may have been confused by the fact that Dr. Granbery seems to have supervised the work of missionaries sent to the army by his church.   A relative who knew him intimately doubts that he ever directed the work of other chaplains.[41]

Chaplains of all faiths fought the prevalent vices with a unanimity which transcended all sectarian lines, though they might differ about their comparative seriousness.   Rogers considered profanity and sabbath-breaking the outstanding evils in the army.   Remarking that Negroes almost never swore, he said it was a relief to get away from white troops when he was put in charge of a refugee camp.   When Adams heard a man swear, he would tap him on the shoulder and say, "I hope God will not hear that prayer of yours."   Trumbull told the men that the colonel had detailed him to do all the necessary swearing and that they might send for him if some had to be done.   They usually took it as a joke and rebuked each other for meddling with the chaplain's work, but the general effect was good.   He declared that less profanity was heard in the army than on the streets of most northern towns and quoted the remark often heard in camp after some especially violent cursing, "You swear like a new recruit."[42]

Humphreys rationalized his opposition to profanity, saying that it destroyed a man's sense of reverence and thus undermined his respect for authority.   Jones reflected the seriousness attached to this vice by others than chaplains in an anecdote of a Confederate soldier who had been cared for by a profane but kind Union nurse called Billy.   When he was dying he threw his arms around him and said, "Billy, you have been very kind to me; Billy, you must quit swearing; you are too good to go to hell; quit swearing, Billy."[43]

Others saw intemperance and gambling as the most pernicious evils.   Jones deplored the drinking among Confederate officers after Bull Run, saying that the surgeons often outdid the others.   He mentioned a general who fell from his horse at a review and lay drunk in quarters most of the time for weeks without losing command.   What he saw about him led him to exclaim, "While Lincoln may slay his thousands, the liquor maker at home will slay his tens of thousands." The captain of a dispatch boat thought Denison lacking in essential qualities of an officer because he declined to drink with him.   At a

---

[41] Douglas, *op. cit.*, editor's note, p. 373; J. H. Granbery to author, 28 Dec. 1955.
[42] Adams, *op. cit.*, p. 31; Trumbull, *op. cit.*, p. 106; Rogers, *op. cit.*, pp. 217, 228.
[43] Humphreys, *op. cit.*, p. 385; Jones, *op. cit.*

complimentary dinner for their commander his fellow officers went beyond the limits of courtesy in urging Fuller to drink the pledges to their guest, but the colonel rapped on the table and called for three cheers for the chaplain, "a man whom we all honor the more because, in public or private, uniformly consistent with his principles."[44]

Several chaplains formed temperance societies and urged the men to promise abstinence.   Cooney believed that more men would take the pledge and a greater proportion would keep it if he did not ask too much at one time, so asked them to promise not to drink for 6 months or a year.   Dillon's campaign which gave the 63d New York the name of the "Temperance Regiment" was one of the best known of these efforts.   He induced several prominent officers to hold the offices in their society and had special medals cast to remind the members of the obligations they had assumed.   In the Chickahominy swamps the water was so bad that whiskey was issued by the commissary.   Others appropriated the share the temperance men would not touch.   For reasons that were not recorded, Sergeant Quinn and Private Rutledge both claimed the portion of Sergeant Dwyer.   Insisting that the matter be settled by the time-honored rules of the arena, their comrades formed a ring.   In a moment the doughty little private stretched the big sergeant flat on the ground, and it was held that he had fairly won Dwyer's share for as long as the issue should continue.[45]

Scully and Sheeran told of seizing gamblers' money in the midst of a game.   One used it for the benefit of the church; the other gave it to an orphanage.   Late one night Denison saw a light in a tent and approached, thinking that someone was sick.   He realized his mistake when he heard an excited voice saying, "Who will go it?"   Laying a Testament on the cards, he said, "I've got it, boys," and left.   He never reported the incident, but the men gave away the story themselves.   It was told in their camp paper and did much to end gambling in the regiment for a long time.[46]

One incident well illustrates the problems which result from differences of opinion about the propriety of various practices.   Damasio Taladrid was chaplain of a New Mexico regiment composed largely of men of Mexican ancestry.   He joined in one of their popular games and placed his bet with the others.   Because of the stringent regulations about gambling the commander felt that he must prefer charges,

---

[44] Jones, *op. cit.*, pp. 268–69; Denison, *op. cit.*, p. 41; Fuller, *op. cit.*, p. 194.

[45] Fuller, *op. cit.*, p. 193; Adams, *op. cit.*, p. 143; Conyngham, *op. cit.*, p. 134; Corby, *op. cit.*, pp. 291–94.

[46] Conyngham, *op. cit.*, pp. 101, 179; Denison, *op. cit.*, pp. 37–38.

but he stated his belief that the chaplain was not aware of this regulation and recommended that the charges be dismissed.   This view was accepted by higher authority, and the matter went no further.[47]

Many chaplains forwarded the soldiers' money to their families for them.   One day Scully was walking to town with $22,000 he was to send home for the men when he saw three burly ruffians closing in on him.   Drawing his revolver, he convinced them that he could not be molested without serious consequences.   Cooney often took care of the men's money till they needed it.   When his regiment was reorganized and paid a bounty, Ouellet was on hand with a supply of envelopes and induced many to send the money to their families.   Denison was made assistant allotment commissioner for Rhode Island and soon discovered and exposed the tricks and frauds of the county brokers. This saved thousands of dollars both for the soldiers and for the State.[48]

Quintard helped to draft the constitution of the Order of the Southern Cross.   This was to have been an agency for the relief of distressed soldiers or their families, but active military operations defeated the movement.   Chaplains encouraged benevolent giving and services as acts of worship as well as for their humanitarian value.   Sheeran took a Christmas gift of more than $1,200 from a Louisiana regiment to an orphanage in Richmond, and Corby sent about the same amount to the Archbishop of New York as a donation of the Irish regiments for the poor in Ireland.   During a time of distress in Fredericksburg some of the Virginia troops contributed several hundred dollars for civilian relief.   A Mississippi brigade agreed to go without their rations one day in ten, and one day a week at another time, and send the food to the poor of Richmond.   After the armies had moved away from Savage's Station and the wounded were on the verge of starvation, Marks organized those able to walk into groups to pick berries in the surrounding forest for their helpless comrades and believed that many lives were saved in this way.[49]

Education had its place in the chaplains' program.   Betts had a writing school in the chapel, and Fuller arranged for five instructors to teach the common branches, mostly to soldiers of foreign birth. Marks organized a debating society and classes in Latin, German, and arithmetic when the gloomy fall days began.   Jones told of chaplains having classes ranging from the most elementary subjects to higher

[47] *The Army Chaplain*, Apr. 1932, pp. 6–8.

[48] Conyngham, *op. cit.*, pp. 100, 110, 134; Denison, *op. cit.*, pp. 35–36.

[49] Noll, *op. cit.*, pp. 92–94; Conyngham, *op. cit.*, p. 181; Corby, *op. cit.*, pp. 146–47; Jones, *op. cit.*, 368, 398, 469; Marks, *op. cit.*, pp. 359–60.

mathematics and the classic languages.   He mentioned a middle-aged
man who learned to read in the army and committed to memory most
of the New Testament and the Book of Job.   Patients in the hospitals
sometimes made remarkable progress, even learning to read within a
few days after being given a spelling book or reader.   Egan interested
a group of officers in a school of logic, and this mental exercise became
very popular.[50]

Among prisoners of war, those with intellectual ambitions had at
least one advantage, they were free from most forms of competing activity.   The "University of Libby Prison" was one of the most famous
of these prison schools.   There were native teachers for at least four
modern languages and competent instructors in the classics, mathematics, rhetoric, and some of the sciences.   McCabe gained a substantial introduction to the French language during his months in Libby.
The students made a rule that no one could have anything to eat until
he could ask for it in French.   The chaplain said that *Voulez-vous* this
and *Avez-vous* that often flew around their table when there was nothing but bean soup upon it, adding that there was much more of the
Voulez than of the *Avez*.[51]

Bradley encouraged wood carving as a beneficial hobby and urged
the people at home to take an interest in what their men were doing.
Several chaplains wrote for the papers, telling of army life and urging
people to write often to their soldiers.   In such an article Trumbull
told of a soldier who had received 2 letters in 2 years.   He received a
bundle of friendly letters for him to address to men who were receiving no mail.   They were written by a Vermont lady who had lost a
brother in the service.   Though her hands were so crippled that it was
very hard for her to write, she kept up this service till the end of the
war.   Many chaplains acted as regimental postmasters.   Several times
members of Congress urged that they be authorized to frank the soldiers' mail.[52]

Humphreys distributed many cavalry mittens made by the ladies
of his home town.   Denison kept a journal, which later was accepted
as establishing the right of several widows to pensions.   Adams was
appointed commissioner for his regiment with power to administer
oaths and execute legal papers.   After several great battles he was able

---

[50] Betts, *op. cit.*, p. 56; Fuller, *op. cit.*, p. 187; Marks, *op. cit.*, p. 57; Jones, *op. cit.*, pp. 211, 217–
18, 363; Conyngham, *op. cit.*, p. 113.
   [51] Bristol, *op. cit.*, pp. 103, 133.
   [52] Bradley, *op. cit.*, p. 86; Trumbull, *op. cit.*, pp. 143; Humphreys, *op. cit.*, p. 423; *Congressional
Globe*, 1861, pp. 50, 101.

to send the reassuring message to his neighbors in Maine: "None of our Gorham boys have fallen." The home folks saw more than a soldier's joke in his description of the guideboard set up where his regiment had been repairing Virginia roads: "Gorham, Maine, 672 miles; Richmond, 20 miles." [53]

George Pepper believed that chaplains should have been given the rank of major or colonel, but most of his colleagues felt that the respect of officers and men depended more upon sharing their dangers and trying to be of service to them. Even those who scoffed at his theology admired the character and devotion of the faithful chaplain. After dark but while the firing was still heavy at Malvern Hill, Ouellet went into the front lines with a lantern to minister to any Catholics he could find. One man said he was not a Catholic but would like to die in the faith of any man who would come to see him in a place like that. [54]

Those chaplains who could combine spiritual ministrations with skill in bandaging wounds and relieving suffering gained an especially large place in the affections of the men. Quintard, who was a doctor of medicine, saved many a limb and life by his knowledge and skill. His brother officers were not above a joke at his expense. He rode an unusually good horse and was in the habit of hanging a canteen of whiskey on his saddle when an especially hard day's march was expected so that he could give some stimulant to men who might become exhausted. One day the colonel drew up beside him, said that his horse was very rough, and asked if the chaplain would change for a little while. Eager to accommodate, he dismounted at once. The colonel and other field officers rode a short distance to the front, gave the chaplain an exaggerated salute, waved the canteen, then sampled its contents liberally. The chaplain recovered his horse and lent him to General Johnston for a grand review a few days later, but the next time he saw his canteen it was empty. [55]

The hope of every chaplain who took the longer view was admirably stated by Adams: "I want this regiment, bold and daring as it is in the country's cause, to be eminent for moral and religious influences, and to be welcomed at home as good citizens, made wiser and better by the discipline of army life." It is reasonable to ask how far such hopes were realized. Though many chaplains counted their converts and baptisms by the hundreds, no statistics can measure the value of

---

[53] Humphreys, *op. cit.*, p. 5; Denison, *op. cit.*, p. 14; Adams, *op. cit.*, pp. 53, 147.

[54] Pepper, *op. cit.*, p. 197; Trumbull, *op. cit.*, p. 8; Adams, *op. cit.*, p. 240; Fuller, *op. cit.*, p. 315; Corby, *op. cit.*, p. 306.

[55] Noll, *op. cit.*, pp. 64–69.

their work.   Many felt that army discipline and the stark realities of
war gave the men a deeper sense of responsibility and greater self-
control.[56]

Another fair question concerns the permanence of the decisions
for the better life reached under the shadows of the battlefield or in the
weakness of the hospital.   Jones cited a Virginia pastor who said that,
of 27 members of his church who returned, all but 2 were more earnest
Christians than when they went to war.   The chaplain hoped that the
scarred veteran would not experience a religious chill on returning to
the home church.   After diligent inquiry he could learn of only 3 of
the 410 men he had baptized who had abandoned their religious profession.   He cited a brother chaplain who did not know that even one
of his 400 converts had proved unfaithful.   He added that nine tenths
of the candidates for the ministry immediately after the war had decided upon this life work while in the army.   Among them were General Evans and three members of his staff.   Many of the brilliant class
enrolled at the University of Virginia in 1865 had been prepared for
advanced study in army chapels.   There was admiration as well as
humor in the remark of a Richmond editor that a certain State already
had 12 universities and according to latest reports the people were cutting poles for another.   The aged Dr. Stiles remarked, "The way to
convert a nation is to convert its army." [57]

Stonewall Jackson believed that sectarian distinctions and preaching were out of place in the army and would ask of a chaplain only
that he preach the gospel.   Lacy thought they would learn to be better preachers in the army, being short and sharp and cutting many
useless appendages from their sermons.   Jones said that enduring privation would make them efficient and hard-working, men who would
stick to their posts.   Field service, in his opinion, would improve the
health of many delicate men.[58]   Taylor discussed the same question
from a slightly different point of view:

> I think, among the many evils of war, we should not forget
> such a benefit as this, that it corrects the growing tendency to effem-
> inacy.   How desirable, if many of our young preachers in this
> school shall learn to "endure hardness."   Then they can preach as
> the pioneers did, and not be concerned what they shall eat, or

---

[56] Adams, *op. cit.*, p. 144; Denison, *op. cit.*, p. 7; Trumbull, *op. cit.*, p. 100; Noll, *op. cit.*, p. 3;
Conyngham, *op. cit.*, *passim.*

[57] Jones, *op cit.*, pp. 262, 326, 396, 463, 494; William W. Bennett—*A Narrative of the Great
Revival which Prevailed in the Southern Armies during the Late Civil War between the States of the Federal
Union*, p. 402.

[58] Jones, *op. cit.*, pp. 94, 229–30, 519.

where they shall sleep; nor need to be coddled by the mothers in Israel, or have eggs and brandy mixed for their throats by the pretty daughters in Israel.[59]

The record of the chaplains, both North and South, is a legacy richer than was ever realized by those who made it. Catholic and Methodist chaplains were conspicuous leaders in the temperance cause. Episcopalians, Unitarians, and Catholics were truly evangelistic. Presbyterians and Baptists joined with others in prayer for wisdom and strength. Chaplains from New York and New Orleans brought the consolations of a common religion to the wounded and suffering of both armies. Those who could understand, recognized and carried to their homes an appreciation of the worth of a faith which strengthened character and sustained a life of righteousness, though its usages and symbols might differ widely from their own.

The same consciousness of transcendent values revealed the spiritual achievements in both armies as a common moral victory, certain to bear fruit in the years to come. Grant's courtesy to a gallant foe at Appomattox found many parallels among the superior chaplains. Marks paid a tribute to the character of Stonewall Jackson, and Quintard was distressed by news of Lincoln's death. In the spring of 1865 he was welcomed to Nashville by the provost marshal and worked among the sick until he said he had virtually been transformed into a Union chaplain. The Union officers gave him a purse of gold in appreciation of his services when he left for New York. Betts wept when he saw Union soldiers marching to prison and singing, "We're going home to die no more," and realized that many of them would die before they could regain their freedom. Years afterward Trumbull sought out and thanked the hotel keeper who had sent him the best meal his house could serve and refused payment when he was very sick in the prison camp at Columbia.[60]

For a third of a century Quintard's ministry was a continual expression of the spirit symbolized at the funeral of his old commander, General Loring, when 3 Confederate and 3 Union veterans served as pallbearers. More than 40 years were given to McCabe, secretary and bishop, but called "chaplain" to the day of his death. During that time he went up and down the country performing many important duties but constantly giving his brilliant lecture on "The Bright Side of Life in Libby Prison." Meeting the nation's resentment at one

---

[59] *Ibid.*, p. 228.

[60] Marks, *op. cit.*, p. 363; Noll, *op. cit.*, pp. 137, 147; Betts, *op. cit.*, p. 65; Trumbull, *op. cit.*, p. 288.

of its sorest spots, he did not fail to describe the admirable characteristics and kind acts of honorable foemen in terms which did much to
bury the hatred of the past under the charity and patriotism of the
present and high confidence for the years to come.[61]

---

[61] Noll, *op. cit.*, p. 53; Bristol, *op. cit.*, p. 118ff.

CHAPTER IX

From Grant to Pershing

Most volunteer chaplains were discharged during 1865, but some were still on duty in the following year. By the Act of 28 July 1866 rank, pay, and allowances as established in 1864 were continued, and chaplains were authorized the same transportation as other officers when ordered from one field of duty to another. The President was empowered, with senatorial approval, to name 1 chaplain for each of 4 regiments of colored troops, and the chaplains so appointed were to teach the common school branches to the enlisted men. Except for this provision, the chaplaincy reverted to the 30 post chaplains authorized in 1849. This provided about 1 chaplain for 10 military stations. Thirty years later the number of posts had decreased, but Charles Pierce remarked with some disdain that 34 chaplains at 80 posts were all that 60 million people could afford.[1]

Further enactments on 2 March 1867 directed that all chaplains be commissioned by the President and gave them the same status as other officers in relation to tenure, retirement, allowances, and pensions. The law contained a slightly cryptic reference to "the grade of chaplain, which is hereby established, to rank as captain of infantry." This punctuation and the fact that the "rank of chaplain" had been recognized in 1864 make this statement rather ambiguous, but it seems to have been intended only to specify that chaplains should rank with captains of infantry.[2]

The appropriation bill of 1870 included several provisions of importance to chaplains. When it was under consideration on 9 July, Senator Corbett moved that chaplains' pay be increased from the proposed $1,400 to $1,600, saying that they always had received captain's pay, but this amendment was defeated. The House passed this item without change, but the amount was increased to $1,500 by the con-

---

[1] 14 *Stat.* 337; Theophilus Gould Steward—*Active Service, or Religious Work among U. S. Soldiers,* p. 75.

[2] 13 *Stat.* 46; 14 *Stat.* 423.

ference committee, and this became a law on 15 July. This gave chaplains the same pay as first lieutenants, not mounted. Another provision of the law specifically included chaplains and others having assimilated rank among the officers entitled to an increase of 10 percent of their current yearly pay for each 5 years of service. Moreover, it increased from 80 to 160 acres the amount of public land among the reserved sections along railroads which veterans who had served for 3 months and remained loyal were allowed to claim under the terms of the Homestead Act. A minority in the House opposed this provision on the ground that it was unfair to other settlers.[3]

Some line officers resented the law which gave chaplains the rank of captain immediately on appointment, while they sometimes served 15 years or longer as lieutenants without promotion. This feeling was more understandable in those cases when a few years of service would make the chaplain eligible for retirement. To this attitude was attributed a measure of the coldness toward chaplains shown by some officers. Others were antagonized by the chaplain's resistance to vices which had attached themselves to some recreations of the soldiers and had been tolerated at remote and lonely posts.[4]

The Geneva Convention of 22 August 1864 provided that chaplains, as well as medical personnel and others employed in the care of the sick and wounded, should participate in the benefits of neutrality. This authorized them to continue their service even after occupation by the enemy and to rejoin their own forces after the wounded were properly cared for. The United States concurred in this convention on 16 May 1882 and gave its provisions the force of law.[5] It has been contended that the authority for medical personnel to be armed when necessary for the protection of the sick and wounded from marauders applies to chaplains by implication, and a number of chaplains have felt that it was proper for them to carry weapons for their own defense during operations against uncivilized tribes or an enemy who refused to respect noncombatant rights. Such considerations were apt to be forgotten if a chaplain found himself in the midst of a Sioux or Apache ambuscade in the '70's or '80's.

Colonel Baker told of a chaplain whose name had escaped him but whose action he remembered with admiration. Noted for his quiet dignity about the post, he went with a party of soldiers and civil-

---

[3] 16 Stat. 320; Congressional Globe, 1870, pp. 5405, 5457, 5460, 5586, 5614.

[4] David H. Stratton—"The Army and the Gospel in the West," Western Humanities Review, summer, 1954, p. 251.

[5] 22 Stat. 940, 943.

454841 O—58——11

ians on a journey which made it necessary for them to camp for the night in an exposed location. Hostile Indians attempted to rush the camp at dawn but were repulsed. Joined by other parties, they surrounded the group and kept up a sharp fire all day. After several of the party had been killed or wounded, the women and civilians became alarmed and began to pray loudly. Declaring that there is a time to fight as well as a time to pray, the chaplain set the women to loading the rifles which he and the other men fired. At night he crept through the line of besiegers and brought help from Fort Reno. In a similar situation another chaplain is said to have prayed internally without slackening his efforts to repel the enemy.[6]

Various chaplains found opportunities to elevate the life of friendly Indians near their stations. On Sunday afternoons Charles C. Pierce conducted services 4 miles from the post, and the older Indians often came in and filled the room. One day an old Indian stopped him in the service and said, "You are telling us about God's Book and you have shown it to us. Why, we never heard of it before. Now tell us everything you know." Later he said to the chaplain, "Indians know nothing of God's Book. I never saw it before. I guess the white men have had God's Book all this time and have tried to keep the Indians from getting it. But today I see all these boys and girls have books, and it may be that the Indians are going to get God's Book." Though the books which the old man saw in the hands of the boys and girls were songbooks, the chaplain was careful not to dampen the confidence nor to mar the gladness with which he saw evidence of a better day dawning for the children of his people.[7]

Orville J. Nave, a veteran of the Civil War and a chaplain from 1882 to 1905, expressed himself vigorously on the status of chaplains during this period. He felt that their uniform should be military instead of the virtual civilian clothing which they wore during much of this time. He was indignant because they were deprived of their seats on the councils of administration, saying that this was done because one chaplain voted against authorizing the sale of beer in the post exchange. The law which had the effect of limiting the chaplaincy at West Point to civilian clergymen impressed him as an affront. When he published a manual on the chaplaincy in 1917, he was confident that the status of chaplains and their opportunities for usefulness had

---

[6] John F. Finerty—*War-Path and Bivouac, or the Conquest of the Sioux*, pp. 405–6; Stratton—*op. cit.*, p. 253.

[7] Steward—*op cit.*, p. 76.

improved over what they had been prior to 1898; but he quoted a letter written on 26 July 1882 by General Sherman, then commander-
in-chief, and seemed to concur in the general's gloomy view of conditions at that time.[8]   With characteristic force and frankness Sherman
wrote:

> My dear Sir—Yours of July 24th is received, and if your
> brother, the Rev. _____, of Illinois, will make his application to
> the Secretary of War for a Chaplaincy in the Army, and send me
> his papers, I will endorse and lay them before the Secretary for the
> Action of the President, who alone always makes these appoint-
> ments.
>
> I never give original letters to the President or Secretary of
> War because it would be wrong for me to do so, as they might refer
> several applicants to me for selection, and I would seem to be com-
> mitted to the one holding my letter.   I think there are several hun-
> dred applicants now, each one of whom is stronger in the Faith than
> St. Paul, and most of whom before appointment, are anxious to be
> martyrs; but once appointed and confirmed they object to our fron-
> tier posts because they are ill adapted for raising a large family of
> small children.
>
> Of course the whole system is now a farce and meant to be so.
> If Congress wanted the Army to have the influence of Religion, it
> would allow the Commanding Officer of each post remote from
> civilization to hire and pay for a minister while employed, like Sur-
> geons.   Of such posts there are nearly a hundred, whereas the
> Chaplains are limited to thirty—say half of whom are sick, or don't
> like the isolation of Texas, Arizona, etc.   Of course there are no
> vacancies now, and they are gobbled up as soon as the telegraph
> announces a death—there are no resignations—and so greedy are
> the applicants that they will not even wait for the funeral.
>
> If your brother wants to join in this scramble to become a
> martyr, let him send me his papers, and I will see they are filed;
> and then let him have some Senator or member of Congress to rush
> to the President the moment he learns a Chaplain is "in extremis."
>   Very truly yours,
>   W. T. SHERMAN, General [9]

On 17 September 1875 General Custer wrote concerning a missionary who had been detained at the fort for some time on his way to
the tribes: "If our large posts on the remote frontier, which are situated far from church and Christian influences, had chaplains who were
as faithful Christians as I believe Mr. Marchett to be, and who, like

---

[8] In Steward—*op. cit.*, pp. 42–43; Orville J. Nave—*Nave's Handbook on the Army Chaplaincy,*
passim; Harper's Weekly, 10 Aug. 1895.
[9] Steward—*op. cit.*, p. 43.

him, are willing to labor faithfully among the enlisted men, the moral standard, now necessarily so low among that neglected class, would be elevated far above its present level, and great results would follow." Other writers believed that the Government provided a limited number of chaplains only to satisfy a public demand and that many soldiers would have preferred to have none, but several chaplains and other officers contradicted this opinion.   In 1896 Pierce was the only chaplain among the five posts in Arizona.   He rode 125 miles in 2 days to visit Fort Grant, a post understood to be totally devoid of religious interest.   Within 2 hours of his arrival he conducted a service in which a good company joined heartily.   The response of this isolated group convinced him that most soldiers and their families wanted Sunday services and a Sunday school for their children.[10]

Funerals were conducted by officers when no chaplain could be obtained.   Bibles, hymnbooks, and religious literature were furnished by several civilian agencies.   At many posts where chaplains seldom appeared, officers' wives frequently opened their homes to those who cared to meet and sing hymns on Sunday evenings.   On several occasions when a passing missionary stopped at the fort, General and Mrs. Custer invited him to hold services in their parlor.   One who was induced to remain for some time was given the use of a vacant barracks for a chapel, and every night hundreds of soldiers joined in the singing of hymns.   On 25 June 1876 a group of women met in the Custer home in deep anxiety for their husbands, who had marched against the warlike Sioux.   As they sought comfort in the great hymns of faith, it was well that they could not see the distant slopes of the Little Big Horn.   Ten days later a boat came down the river with the news that told 26 of them that they were widows.[11]

Chaplains found many ways to help in the civilian communities as the country was settled.   Often one would supply a neighboring church until a pastor could be obtained.   Other worthy institutions were given friendly support by the military communities.   A hospital was established at Prescott, Ariz., by the Catholic Sisters of Charity. Officers and ladies of Fort Whipple gave a play for its benefit.   One officer, whose talents were not in the dramatic field, pledged a share of his winnings at poker.   Some time later his wife visited the hospital and was asked, "What has become of the colonel?   We have not seen

---

[10] Elizabeth B. Custer—*"Boots and Saddles" or Life in Dakota with General Custer,* p. 249; Stratton—*op. cit.,* p. 252.
    [11] Custer—*op. cit.,* pp. 247–8, 267–8.

him for a long time." The reply was: "Ah, well, then, Mother, he can't have been winning."[12]

In addition to their other duties, chaplains were superintendents of post school until a regulation of 1895 left this to the discretion of commanding officers. Though they might do no teaching themselves, this frequently involved responsibility for a day school for children and one for the men at night. On the last day of 1877 the Secretary of War convened a board to consider the establishment of schools at military posts. This board recommended that Chaplain George G. Mullins have general charge of education in the Army. He held this position for several years, making annual reports to the Secretary of War.[13]

The uniform which offended Nave when he went on duty in 1882 was the plain black of the Civil War, with braid excluded from overcoat sleeves by General Order No. 92 of 1872. The shepherd's crook of frosted silver on a shoulder strap of black velvet was authorized in 1880 by General Order No. 10. A marked change came in 1884 when Circular No. 1 prescribed that chaplains should wear the uniform called "undress for officers" but should not wear the full dress chapeau of staff officers. In 1897, regulations made this uniform optional with a frock coat with falling collar and authorized the wearing of vestments while conducting services.

A regulation of 1 May 1899 substituted a silver Latin cross for the shepherd's crook on shoulder straps. General Order No. 169 of 1907 gave chaplains a black frock coat as their full dress uniform, but they were to wear the same dress, service, and white coats as other officers. On the olive drab and khaki coats a bronze cross was to be worn in place of insignia of rank, and a silver cross on the white coat. A black hat was prescribed with the dress and full dress uniforms, but chaplains wore the same caps or hats as other officers with the white and service coats. On 15 August 1917 Special Regulations 41 and 42 made the silver cross the badge of the chaplaincy for all uniforms and placed it on the coat collar where other officers wore insignia of branch. This implied that chaplains should wear insignia of rank in the same manner as other officers.

The intense feeling with which Americans supported the war with Spain was the swift culmination of a prolonged growth. Sympathy with any group of colonials seeking independence from an imperial overlord was spontaneous. Some knew that reforms promised

---

[12] Stratton—*op. cit.*, p. 258.
[13] Steward—*op. cit.*, p. 42; G. G. Mullins—*My Life is an Open Book*, title page.

to the Cubans after the war of 1868–78 had not been carried out, and others remembered the *Virginius* affair and other humiliations of the United States at Spanish hands.   When the revolution began in 1895, most Americans hoped that it might succeed; but the humane manner in which it was opposed by Captain General Campos made it easy for most citizens to acquiesce in President Cleveland's policy of neutrality.

All this was changed when Weyler, the new governor, initiated the cruel reconcentration policy.   Soon American papers were describing conditions which doomed great numbers of civilians to starvation and disease.   A group of congressmen visited the stockades in Cuba and reported that conditions were worse than they had been pictured by the press, and relief agencies began to distribute food and other necessities.   Early in 1896, Congress adopted a resolution urging the recognition of the insurgents, and Cleveland's last message intimated that intervention might become necessary.   Few Americans coveted Spanish territory or hoped for other forms of gain, but a mounting public opinion demanded that this intolerable situation so near our coast should be ended.   The destruction of the *Maine,* quite generally believed to have been an act of Spanish treachery, reinforced with an intensified indignation, and the growing conviction that the establishment of Cuban independence by force of arms was a duty to humanity.[14]

Viewing the war as an unselfish effort to liberate the oppressed, many devout people saw the hand of Providence in the incidents of battle.   The Spanish fleet at Manila, backed by the guns of the forts, was considered equal in power to Dewey's force, but the trifling damage to the American ships seemed supernatural.   The same disparity in losses appeared at Santiago in the naval battle and on land.   Of the advance through the jungle George Van Dewater wrote: "Reverent men entered on this campaign believing in the righteousness of their cause and that God would prosper it.   Few came out of this campaign, we venture to believe, without firm conviction that had not God been on our side, the enemy would have swallowed us."   Describing the concentrated fire of the Spaniards when the Americans were huddled in front of San Juan Hill, he added, "It cannot be recalled by anyone there without a thought of the marvelous mercy of God." [15]

These views were shared by many of the church leaders of the

------

[14] *Congressional Record* (hereafter cited as *Record*), *passim;* John Spencer Bassett—*A Short History of the United States,* pp. 782–90; Archibald Karraker—*The American Churches and the Spanish American War,* pp. 277–83.

[15] George R. Van Dewater—*New York and the War with Spain,* pp. 226, 231; Karraker—*op. cit.,* p. 279.

country.   They raised funds to provide assembly tents and similar
equipment for the chaplains and to support the work of the Young
Men's Christian Association in the camps.   They attacked the Army
canteen for selling liquor, urged charity toward Alger, Shafter, Samp-
son, and Schley when they were subjected to severe criticism, and
praised Cervera as a gallant enemy.   The unforeseen acquisition of
the Philippines seemed to some a providential missionary opening, but
others shrank from taking up "the white man's burden" with all its
implications.   Cooperation with the natives to free the islands from
Spanish tyranny met with general approval, but strong opposition to
military pacification appeared when Aguinaldo realized that American policy would not bring early independence and arrayed his troops
against the American forces.   Many felt that American tyranny was
being substituted for that of Spain.   Bills to increase the Army elicited
scathing attacks upon the administration from both houses of Congress, and the new imperialism was denounced in the secular and religious press.   There is no doubt that the influence of religious
organizations and leaders was a powerful support to the chaplains
during the struggle with Spain and that they modified foreign policy
during the peace negotiations and afterward by direct contacts with
the President and other officials.[16]

The war found the United States with a Regular Army little
changed from that authorized in 1869.   During the years of peace the
regiments often consisted of about 500 men.   The law provided for
25 units of infantry, 10 of cavalry, and 5 of artillery.   Four of these
were Negro regiments, each of which had its own chaplain, and the
old law which authorized 30 post chaplains was still in effect.   Regular units soon were recruited more nearly to full strength, and a bill
to increase the number of chaplains was introduced into Congress but
was not reported.   Most of the volunteer regiments raised by the various States had chaplains appointed by the governors.   A law of 28
June 1898 gave them the pay and allowances of mounted captains.
This was computed to equal $2,000 a year, while post chaplains re-
ceived only $1,500.   In the debate it was pointed out that the latter
had the free use of a house and other advantages and lived in greater
ease and safety than a chaplain in the field.[17]

Intensive training of volunteers and recruits at many posts and
camps marked the early summer of 1898, and this entailed many and

---

[16] *Ibid.*, pp. 280–83; *Record, passim;* Karl Irving Faust—*Campaigning in the Philippines,* pp.
18–21.

[17] Steward—*op. cit.,* p. 87; *Record,* XXXI, 2449, 6444; 30 *Stat.* 729.

varied duties for the chaplains.   One of the first necessities was a shelter for assemblies and a place where the men could read or write and carry on varied recreations.   William Biederwolf obtained donations from the home towns of the men of his regiment and bought a tent 50 by 80 feet.   Frequently from 600 to 700 letters were written in a day in these facilities.   Nave went into Atlanta and got enough money in one day to pay for a 40 by 60 tent.   On another occasion he rented and equipped a tent on his personal credit but induced the quartermaster to pay the bill, though he remarked that such conveniences were apt to be appreciated more fully when the men paid the costs themselves.   He declared that the chaplain who could not get an assembly tent when it was not provided by the Government should resign, but during the summer he held services in a grove where seats for 1,200 people had been arranged.[18]

Several chaplains mentioned the comradeship among soldiers of different sections and races.   At Chickamauga, white and Negro regiments of the Regular Army were brigaded together with complete harmony and good will.   Steward recorded an incident which was typical of this spirit.   A Negro corporal, tired and thirsty, approached a spring and lay down to drink, though the water near the edge was roiled.   Seeing this, a white soldier called to him, "Hold on, bunkie; here's my cup." [19]

During the fighting near Santiago the Negro troops earned the admiration of the whole army, though the newspapers described some of their exploits in extravagant terms.   One of their chaplains told of an American editor's florid account of the charge of the Negro Regulars to rescue the Rough Riders.   Comparing their advance to the charge of the Light Brigade, he described the confusion in the American lines under heavy fire which threatened disaster until the colored troops advanced with the steadiness of parade and drove the Spaniards from their position.   Theophilus Steward said he was proud of the way his regiment did its duty in the lines that day, but there was no charge like that described in the papers and no rescue of the Rough Riders.[20] A short time later the 24th Infantry performed a service which Hilary Costen thought a better index of the capabilities of his race than spectacular daring on the firing line.   Yellow fever and malaria were rampant in the hospital at Siboney, and nurses for the sick were needed.

---

[18] William Edward Biederwolf—*History of the 161st Regiment, Indiana Volunteer Infantry*, p. 227; Nave—*op. cit.*, pp. 34, 48.

[19] Steward—*op. cit.*, p. 97.

[20] *Ibid.*, pp. 206, 132.

The men of the 24th were warned of the danger, but every man stepped forward when volunteers were asked.   Sixty were chosen, but within 2 days 42 were down with the epidemic.   Again there was a call for volunteers, and again every man offered.[21]

George Van Dewater was appointed "caterer" to the officers' mess of his regiment but found the business relations of the task burdensome.   As he was writing the regimental history and performing other special duties, he soon asked relief from the latest assignment. He told of a service on the eve of battle in Cuba.   In the twilight he could not see to read but recited the Episcopal service from memory, led the singing of several hymns, then preached in the dark.   He described the warm appreciation with which a wounded Cuban grasped his hand when he knelt by his side and recited the Lord's Prayer in Latin.   When the chaplain's picture was published in a New York paper among those killed at El Caney, he was able to see it as a joke.[22]

Nave recorded some of his tangible achievements during the encampment at Chickamauga.   The names of 115 men were certified to their home pastors as wishing to join the church, 800 took the total abstinence pledge, and 1,000 promised not to gamble.   Then, as always, the line officers relished a good-natured joke at the expense of the chaplain.   The train on which Biederwolf and a part of his regiment were riding was delayed for some hours.   The colonel, on a preceding train, wired the officer in charge, "Report condition of your command, including chaplain."   The reply went back, "Making best possible time, three couplings broke; all sober except chaplain." [23]

Nave described a project through which he tried to meet a very real need of the men returning from Cuba.   Many of them were convalescent from the tropical fevers but needed special diets which the hospitals were ill equipped to provide.   Mrs. Nave and her daughter began serving attractive light meals to those who needed them most. In a short time "Mrs. Nave's Kitchen" had become very popular, and it was arranged that the chaplain should have charge of the special diets for the four hospitals.   A vacant building was set apart for this use, and the surgeons gave tickets to men they thought should have this special food.   Ladies from Atlanta and the families of other officers helped, and soon from 250 to 350 meals were being served each day.   For 3 months the project operated on the personal credit of the

[21] W. Hilary Costen—*The Spanish War Volunteer*, p. 10.

[22] George W. Van Dewater—*History of the 71st Regiment, New York Volunteers*, pp. 209, 221, 228, 281.

[23] Nave, *op. cit.*, p. 49; Biederwolf, *op. cit.*, p. 52.

chaplain, but early in August a Red Cross agent visited the camp and was so favorably impressed that he offered to finance the enterprise and supply other needs.   The capacity was doubled and the project, rechristened "Mrs. Nave's Red Cross Kitchen," continued to perform an invaluable service until the middle of September.   The chaplain accounted for all contributions received by him.   Soldiers gave donations ranging from 25 cents to as many dollars.   A church sent him $47.75, and various amounts were received from the Grand Army of the Republic in Atlanta and from other organizations.   The Red Cross paid $835.   Total operating costs were $1,456.27; receipts from all sources amounted to $1,309.25; and the deficit of $147.02 was paid by the chaplain.[24]

Though Generals Shafter and Wheeler and a few of the other senior officers remembered the grim harvests of the 60's, the majority never had seen actual warfare, and to them the death of a dozen comrades seemed a major tragedy.   Several writers mention the deep solemnity with which the dead were buried, the chaplains reciting the service of committal and the men singing a hymn of faith over the remains of their fallen comrades.[25]

There was some criticism of the failure of the Army to provide all of the desirable features which are customary at civilian funerals. One writer was outraged by the manner in which cemetery workers handled the dead at a camp near New York.   He found that it was the custom to have a service at four in the afternoon for all who had been interred during the day and was indignant when he found one chaplain arranging to get four carloads of watermelons for the men instead of being at the cemetery.   When the hour arrived, a Protestant chaplain and a Catholic priest were there, but they waited a long time for some bodies which were to have been sent from the morgue.   An orderly brought an inquiry from the general, asking when the chaplain could leave with the body of a deceased captain.   As there was no sign of the party for whom they were waiting, the chaplain said he could leave at once and his Catholic associate could read the service. The journalist remarked sarcastically that 1 captain was worth more than 80 privates.   At a later time he was mollified in some degree by the reverence of a party of soldiers and the dignity with which the burial service was read.[26]   Most chaplains were able to identify and bury the dead with fitting decorum.   In the Philippines, Pierce offici-

---

[24] Nave, *op. cit.*, pp. 53–61.
[25] Theodore Roosevelt—*The Rough Riders*, Statesman Ed., p. 107; Edward Marshall—*The Story of the Rough Riders*, p. 162.
[26] Cleveland Moffett in *Leslie's Weekly*, 22 Sept. and 27 Oct. 1898, pp. 229, 326.

ated at the interment of 217 American soldiers within 80 days, using the full service of the church and making sure that none failed to receive all military honors.[27]

In several respects the war in the Philippines differed from the contest in Cuba. Cooperation with the natives was more difficult, and they were less capable of self-government. Though Manila lay helpless under Dewey's guns after the destruction of the Spanish fleet, he deferred the attack upon the city until the arrival of an adequate land force 3 months later. Among the troops were the First California Infantry and its chaplain, Father William D. McKinnon. On the voyage the transports were convoyed by the *Charleston* and lay in the offing when the cruiser bombarded the fortifications of Guam until the Spanish commander sent word that he was sorry not to return the salute but had no powder. It is doubtful whether this oft-told tale reflects more severely upon Spanish perspicasity or American gunnery. It may have encouraged the chaplain a short time afterward when the attack upon Manila was pending, for he entered the city, notwithstanding a painful wound, and negotiated with the archbishop and the Spanish chief of staff for a surrender which would avoid further bloodshed.[28]

Some details of this episode are not clear. The Belgian consul and others had been trying to effect an understanding which would prevent the bombardment of the city. The Spanish military code would not allow a surrender until all means of defense had been used. As early as 23 April the governor general had published a warning that a fleet manned by foreigners without instruction or discipline was coming "with the wild purpose of taking away from you all that implies life, honor, and liberty." Declaring that the Americans would substitute the Protestant for the Catholic religion and would rob them, he exhorted the people to defend the tombs of their fathers, the sanctity of their homes, and their possessions. The archbishop joined in this pronouncement against a "heterodox people, possessed by the blackest rancor and all the abject passions that heresy engenders," who would raze their temples, profane their altars, rob them of their religion, and treat them as slaves. After the naval battle he urged the natives to aid the Spaniards against the invaders by warnings even more lurid.[29]

Notwithstanding this abundance of superlatives, the armed insurgents in the suburbs were feared more than the Americans, and it was

---

[27] Faust, *op. cit.,* p. 313.
[28] James A. Le Roy—*The Americans in the Philippines,* I, 154, 232–50.
[29] *Ibid.*

insisted that they must be kept out of the city in case of a surrender. A Catholic priest, even though an American, would have distinct advantages over others in the attempt to penetrate such a maze of misunderstanding and pretense.   It is impossible to determine Chaplain McKinnon's share in satisfying the fearful that church and private property would be protected and in effecting the understanding that the city would be surrendered after enough resistance to satisfy Spanish honor and protect the principal officers from trial by court-martial. There seems no doubt that such an arrangement existed and that it saved many lives in both armies; but the Belgian consul, to whom we owe much of what we know about this transaction, was liberal in apportioning credit to himself.[30]

McKinnon was given the task of reorganizing the primary schools of Manila, and he supervised their operation for about a year.   He was credited with convincing President McKinley, through the medium of four public lectures, that the monastic orders must remain in the Islands, but the evidence for this statement is doubtful.   He served in the Philippines for several years, gaining the respect of all who knew him by his devotion to duty and his tender ministrations to the sick and dying.   Our information about him comes chiefly from Peter McQueen, a Congregational minister serving as a correspondent, who held him in high esteem.[31]

McQueen wrote vivid accounts of the work of several other chaplains but seems to have been most closely associated with Father Fitzgerald.   On one occasion an expedition was misled by a faithless guide and became hopelessly lost.   A native priest offered to tell about the roads and trails but knew so little Spanish that the Americans could not understand him.   When Fitzgerald arrived he was able to get the needed information by the use of Latin.   McQueen told of arriving at his destination late at night, sick and exhausted after a tramp of 35 miles.   The best place he could find for rest was beside a cart to which a bull was tied.   As he was about to lie down, Fitzgerald emerged from a pile of hay between the shafts and insisted that he take his place, while the chaplain lay on a board.   Notwithstanding the rain, McQueen lay in comparative comfort until the bull grew hungry and ate up his "unusual counterpane."   He told of Chaplain Hart overcoming the distrust of the natives by donning his vestments and saying Mass, and declared that a group of American priests imbued with

---

[30] *Ibid.*
[31] *Ibid.*, II, 72, 297; Faust, *op. cit.*, p. 309.

democratic ideals could pacify the Philippines much sooner than an army.[32]

The prolonged struggle to establish peace and order among the island tribesmen involved many of the most trying features of guerrilla warfare. There were long marches along jungle trails with the constant danger of falling into an ambush and the inconclusive combats with an enemy who would snipe from the forest or rush small parties or isolated stations but would not stand and fight in any numbers. It was said of Dr. Schliemann, chaplain of a Kansas regiment, that he was too reserved and too religious for Funston's fighting men, but he gained a lasting place in their esteem on the night of the fight at Caloocan when they saw him stalking through the woods with a rifle and bringing down the sharpshooters who had been keeping up a deadly fire.[33]

In 1936 the Chief of Chaplains asked his associates to give him an account of their most thrilling experience. Although on his deathbed and suffering great pain, George D. Rice wrote his reply on 20 November. Additional facts were supplied by General Patterson before the story was published. The chaplain was present at the capture of Fort Bacolod, Mindanao, in April 1903. While fighting was still going on, Surgeon Robert U. Patterson and some hospital corpsmen crossed a deep trench on logs to aid the wounded. With his Bible and notebook, the chaplain crossed with them. Suddenly, as the surgeon was kneeling beside a wounded man, a Moro darted around a corner and rushed at the chaplain with his weapon raised to strike. Patterson sprang to his feet in time to plant a heavy fist on the passing Moro and knock him into the trench.[34]

Two chaplains of this period have left estimates of how military service affects the moral and spiritual life of the soldier. Biederwolf had some months of service, chiefly in southern training camps. He declared that army life was not a moulder of character but that the drift was antimoral and antireligious. His subsequent career as an evangelist suggests the criteria on which this judgment may have been based. Gilbert questioned the captains and sergeants of his regiment. They were all but unanimous in the opinion that, except in the use of profanity, the men had improved since coming to the Philippines.[35]

The war in Cuba and the Philippines called the attention of the

---

[32] *Ibid.,* pp. 310, 312.

[33] *Ibid.,* p. 313.

[34] *The Army Chaplain,* July 1937, p. 73.

[35] Biederwolf, *op. cit.,* p. 226; Faust, *op. cit.,* p. 313.

American people to various features of army life which they had scarcely noticed during the years of peace.   Among these, the so-called canteen was an institution of special concern to the chaplains.   The substitution of post exchanges operated under military control for privately managed traders' stores began in 1880, and within a decade they were found at virtually all army posts.   While the private stores had sold liquor with comparatively little restraint, the exchanges were allowed to sell only light wines and beer, and these only when the commanding officer was convinced that the sale of these beverages in camp would keep many soldiers from seeking them in adjacent communities where they would find hard liquor and various forms of vice. So large a part of the profits of the exchanges was derived from the beverage trade that few commanders withheld permission at least for the sale of beer.   The advocates of temperance believed that the lightest liquors are habit-forming and demanded that the canteen be abolished.[36]

By 1900 the question had become a matter of serious debate in both houses of Congress.   The proponents of the sale of beer argued that the exchanges could not operate without it.   They introduced statements from numerous officers, including several chaplains, who believed that drunkenness and other vices would increase if the men who wanted beer had to go off the post to get it.   Convinced that this conclusion was correct but feeling the weight of an extensive counteropinion, one representative who knew his Hamlet declared, "It is the Woman's Christian Temperance Union which doth make cowards of us all."   The opposition sustained its case with equal conviction. Senator Gallinger presented the statements of several physicians that beer is intoxicating and warned that stronger liquors would be sold surreptitiously if beer were allowed.   He introduced a long letter by Chaplain Nave telling what he had seen of beer in the post exchanges. The chaplain declared that he never had seen a canteen properly regulated but several that were centers of drunkenness and boisterous disturbance.   He cited the case of an exchange officer who instead of regulating was drunk nearly all the time and mentioned a soldier who got drunk at the canteen and killed a comrade.   The senator read letters from Generals Miles, Shafter, and Wheeler and from several other prominent officers stating the belief that beer should not be sold at the exchanges.   The law, enacted by more than a two-thirds vote in both houses, was approved on 2 February 1901.   It forbade the sale of beer, wine, or any intoxicating liquor in exchanges or trans-

---

[36] Karraker, *op. cit.,* p. 280.

ports or on any military premises and made the Secretary of War responsible for the enforcement of the law.[37]

Postwar legislation concerning chaplains began with the Act of 2 March 1899, which authorized 42 regiments in the combat arms. Thirty chaplains were to be assigned to regiments or posts at the discretion of the Secretary of War, with the proviso that Negro regiments be not deprived of their chaplains. Two years later the office of post chaplain was abolished by the Act of 2 February 1901. Thirty regiments of infantry and 15 of cavalry were established by this law, and the President was authorized to appoint a chaplain to each of these and 12 to the Corps of Artillery with the rank, pay, and allowances of a captain of infantry. Appointments were limited to persons under 40 who satisfied the established requirements, and transportation was provided for chaplains in the field. A month later it was enacted that chaplains of volunteers who had served during the war could be appointed to original vacancies if they had been less than 42 years of age when first appointed. On 12 June 1906 an additional chaplain was authorized for the Corps of Engineers, and on the 25th of the following January the President was empowered to appoint 2 additional chaplains for the coast artillery and 1 for each field artillery regiment.[38]

A special interest attaches to the Act of 21 April 1904 because it established distinctions in grade and pay among chaplains as a continuing policy in time of peace. On 8 February, Senator Scott stated that chaplains had always been regarded as mounted officers but had not been paid as such. A bill he was supporting would give them this additional pay and would permit the promotion of about one-third of them to the grade of major after a long period of distinguished service. The House made important changes. A member stated that the provision for promotion, though less than had been authorized in the Navy, was enough to attract good men. It had been recommended by the churches of the country, and he considered this a proper concession to a demand from the best people.[39]

As finally enacted, the law directed that chaplains to be appointed in the future should have the grade, pay, and allowances of a mounted captain after serving for 7 years in the corresponding status of a first lieutenant. The President was authorized from time to time to promote to the grade of major a total never to exceed 15 of those chaplains who had served 10 years as captains and expected to remain on

---

[37] *Record*, XXXIV, 113–21, 510, 531, 675–703, 773; 31 *Stat.* 758.

[38] 30 *Stat.* 977; 31 *Stat.* 748, 895; 34 *Stat.* 256, 861.

[39] *Record*, XXXVIII, 1712, 5003.

duty. It was specified that all should be addressed officially as "Chaplain" regardless of grade. This law reduced the base pay of new appointees during the first 7 years of their service from $1,800 to $1,600. It increased their base pay after that period to $2,000, with the possibility of advancement to $2,500 after another 10 years.[40]

Although the Act of 25 April 1914 to provide for raising volunteer forces in actual or threatened war was passed months before the outbreak of the contest in Europe, it is probable that the lawmakers of the nation were conscious of the ominous world situation. Among the arrangements for a swift expansion of the Army in case of need they included authority for the appointment of one chaplain to each regiment with the same rank and pay as regular chaplains. By the summer of 1916 the danger of American involvement in the conflict was acute. On 3 June it was enacted that the Regular Army include 64 regiments of infantry, 25 of cavalry, and 21 of field artillery. A chaplain was appointed to each regiment of these arms and of the engineers and 1 for each 1,200 officers and men in the coast artillery. A proviso gave priority to qualified veterans under 41 years of age.[41]

During the half century after the Civil War a number of significant steps in the evolution of the chaplaincy took place. Articles 52 and 53 were dropped when the Articles of War were revised in 1916. These provisions had been reenacted from time to time with little change since they were established by the Provisional Congress of Massachusetts early in April 1775, and their roots can be traced to still earlier times. The first of these enjoined regular attendance at services and imposed a penalty for misbehavior. The other directed that those guilty of profane swearing should be fined, officers $1 and soldiers one-sixth of that amount for each offense. Bateman said that he did not know of a single instance in which such a fine had been paid and remarked that an incalculable welfare fund would have been provided had the rule been enforced.[42] The failure to reenact these articles, which had been ignored for more than a century, does not imply a diminution of respect for the values they were intended to preserve.

Nave told of including a protest against drunkenness and disorder at the post exchange in his official report, only to have it returned with a peremptory order to delete this comment. At the funeral of a man

---

[40] 33 *Stat.* 226; *Army Register for 1907*, p. 582–83.

[41] 38 *Stat.* 348; 39 *Stat.* 166, 176.

[42] Chaplain Cephas C. Bateman—"Evolution of the Army Chaplains' Corps," *Army and Navy Register*, 26 June 1920, p. 805.

who had been hanged for killing a comrade while drunk, he spoke of the dangers of intemperance and urged abstinence and sobriety. As soon as the tenor of his remarks were recognized, the officer in charge interrupted, saying that it was time for the service to close. Being a vigorous person, Nave asserted his control over the religious exercises and proceeded.[43] By the end of this period few officers would have interfered with a chaplain's freedom either in conducting a service or in making an official report. The law of 1904 was a long step toward placing chaplains on a parity with other staff officers. Insistence upon higher qualifications and ecclesiastical indorsement had replaced the old post chaplains with superior men. The Spanish War had brought the chaplaincy to the attention of the religious leaders of the country and left a closer relation between the churches and their chaplains. Moreover, a new generation of church leaders had learned ways of cooperation in a national emergency which would prove of great value in the years to come.

---

[43] *Congressional Globe*, XXXIV, 682.

CHAPTER X

How Chaplains Were Made in 1918

The great war was 32 months old when the United States entered the struggle in April 1917. Preparation for American participation had been more psychological than material. The traditions of 1776 had given many American schoolboys a presupposition that Britain was a tyrannical power, and the deference accorded to German culture sustained a widespread prejudice in favor of its homeland. Many considered isolation from European contests to be a sacred American principle. These sentiments yielded slowly to the cumulative weight of the indefensible diplomatic and military policies of the Central Powers. Celestine Bittle describes his farewell from his aged mother. She still loved the old home but had enjoyed many privileges in the new and charged him to be a faithful American chaplain. She added: "I do not like to see Germany lose, but I want to see America win." [1]

The Act of 12 May 1917 continued the authority for the allotment of 1 chaplain to each regiment and for each 1,200 in the coast artillery.[2] This made no provision for large numbers of service troops nor for the fact that the new plan of organization put 3,600 in a regiment. On 27 September 1917, representatives of the Roman Catholic Church and of 30 Protestant bodies acting through the General Committee on Army and Navy Chaplains of the Federal Council of Churches called attention to these facts and asked that a chaplain be provided for each 1,200 persons in the Army.[3] General Pershing recommended three chaplains for each regiment, emphasizing that "Men selected should be of the highest character with reputations well established as sensible, practical, active ministers or workers, accustomed to

---

[1] Celestine N. Bittle—*Soldiering for Cross and Flag*, p. 9.
[2] 40 *Stat.* 72.
[3] Hearing on S. 2917, "Increasing the Number of Chaplains in the Army."

dealing with young men." These proposals were carried out by the Act of 25 May 1918.[4]

The obligation to provide religious ministrations for minority groups was recognized early in the planning for the wartime army. On 17 May 1917 Senator Sheppard introduced a bill to authorize specifically the appointment of Jewish chaplains. This measure never was reported, but the situation was met with fair adequacy by the Act of 6 October 1917 which authorized the President to appoint 20 chaplains at large from groups having no apportionment under the existing quotas. The Act of 25 May 1918 had the effect of removing this limitation. Of about 400 English-speaking rabbis in America, 149 applied for the chaplaincy, 34 were recommended by the Jewish Chaplains' Committee, and 25 were in service when the Armistice stopped further appointments.[5]

The task of the Catholic Church was somewhat different. At the declaration of war there were 16 Catholic chaplains in the Regular Army and 9 in the National Guard. This was slightly more than 17 percent of the total. Those in the Regular Army nearly equalled the authorized quota of 24 percent. At the time of the Armistice 1,023 priests were serving in the Army or Navy or under the auspices of the Knights of Columbus, and 500 applicants were awaiting appointment.[6]

At the declaration of war there were 74 chaplains in the Regular Army and 72 in the National Guard. During the period of hostilities 2,217 others were commissioned in some component of the Army. In general the inquiry by church officials into the fitness of candidates for this type of service was less exacting than it became in later years. In some degree this was because few of them had any background in military experience and considered chiefly those qualifications which would affect a clergyman's efficiency in the civilian ministry. Equally significant was the fact that the Army had no agency except temporary boards of officers for the examination of applicants in those intangible elements of fitness which cannot be evaluated by formal tests. This became an important function of the Chaplain School as soon as it was established. Of the 2,217 chaplains appointed during the war, 1,042 received the approval as well as the training of the School.[7]

---

[4] John J. Pershing—*My Experiences in the World War*, I, 284; 40 *Stat.* 561.

[5] *Congressional Record*, LV, 2428; 40 *Stat.* 394, 561; Lee J. Levinger—*A Jewish Chaplain in France*, Introduction and p. 93.

[6] George J. Waring—*United States Catholic Chaplains in the World War*, pp. xiv–xv.

[7] *The United States Army Chaplaincy*, W. D. Pamphlet 16–1, p. 16.

To obtain such a number of competent chaplains was no simple task.   The War Department made repeated appeals to the chaplaincy commissions or other officials of the churches.   They transmitted this call to the younger men, stressing service in the chaplaincy as a duty to the country and to the church.   Many educational and other private institutions helped the Government find qualified men.   One of these was Harvard.   War was declared on Friday.   On Monday morning the University was registering students for military service, and the application forms included the chaplaincy among the specialties for which they could apply.   Hundreds of men volunteered without prompting from any source, and their papers were processed before legislation established the positions to which they could be appointed. Despite all efforts, the Army never obtained close to a thousand of the chaplains authorized by law.[8]

Like all military training, that provided for chaplains is designed to prepare them for efficient service as part of the military organization. As they must have completed a normal professional education before appointment, their Army training is primarily to acquaint them with the structure and functioning of the military organization and with the methods of performing their professional duties most successfully. In times of peace this preparation can be broad and thorough, but the emergencies of war permit only a rapid survey of the essentials, for new units of a huge citizen army are formed more rapidly than chaplains can be provided.

Several chaplains have published books or pamphlets designed to help colleagues with meager experience.

The Army Chaplain's Manual, by J. Pinkney Hammond, appeared in 1863.   The same year William Young Brown published a small book entitled *The Army Chaplain: His Office, Duties, and Responsibilities.*   He was one of the hospital chaplains appointed by President Lincoln in 1861, and his book is filled with helpful information and suggestions. In 1893 a pamphlet called *Manual for U. S. Army Chaplains* was published by G. W. Simpson.   It was written by himself and Chaplains T. W. Berry and C. C. Pierce, with a section by General O. O. Howard. Though it is brief, it contains much of practical value.   Very informative was the symposium on chaplains' work by 14 chaplains and some others compiled by Theophilus Steward about 1898 under the title *Active Service: or Religious Work Among U. S. Soldiers.*

---

[8] Cephas C. Bateman—"Evolution of the Army Chaplain Corps," *Army and Navy Register,* 26 June 1920.

The War Department in 1912 issued a pamphlet by George J. Waring with the title *Chaplain's Duties and How Best to Accomplish his Work.* The manuscript had been submitted as part of his examination for promotion and was distributed for the information of other chaplains. Besides its many practical suggestions, it is interesting because of several specific recommendations advanced by the author. His proposals about chapel building, secular duties of chaplains, payment of civilian clergymen, and a chaplain's flag have all been adopted; but governmental action has been contrary to what he advocated in the matter of chaplains' rank and uniform and of the establishment of a Chief of Chaplains. In 1914, Joseph Clemens submitted to the War Department a manuscript under the title *Duties and Privileges of Chaplains.* The Adjutant General authorized him to circulate it privately, and it was published in pamphlet form. It is interesting to note that his recommendations about the rank and uniform of chaplains are the opposite of those made by Chaplain Waring.

Orville J. Nave, a Civil War veteran, who had been a chaplain for many years, published *Nave's Handbook on the Army Chaplaincy* in 1917. From this long experience he drew a wealth of helpful advice. A manuscript called *Suggestions for Newly Appointed Chaplains* was offered to the War Department in 1918 by Alva J. Brasted, later Chief of Chaplains. This, with copies of the handbooks of Clemens, Waring, and Nave, was sent to the Chaplain School with instructions that a manual be prepared by the faculty for publication and distribution. Apparently the change of faculty personnel and the end of the war soon after this action prevented the completion of the project at that time.

The most important agencies for the training of chaplains in 1918 were the schools operated for that purpose by the War Department. With few exceptions the many chaplains to be appointed from civil life were unfamiliar with military organization and usages, and some introduction to Army life was necessary if they were to avoid embarrassing blunders. Still more vital was the fact that the chaplaincy demands the highest devotion from men who must be ready to do their duty at any cost. These needs were recognized by civilian religious leaders as soon as by the military authorities. A plan for the training of chaplains was formulated jointly by the Harvard and Episcopal theological schools at Cambridge, Mass.; and the Andover, Newton, and Boston University divinity schools were soon associated in the project. Under this plan the spiritual preparation of the chaplain, as well as his military training, would have been stressed. It was submitted to the War Department in February 1918,[9] but plans for a school wholly under military auspices were being developed by that time, and this project was carried no further.

On 22 June 1917, the General Committee on Army and Navy Chaplains of the Federal Council of Churches of Christ in America voted to ask the Secretary of War for authority to organize a school for chaplains. The contemplated school was to have been held 1–15 August and to have been repeated for the chaplains of subsequent mobilization groups. The War Department was not in a position to approve this plan at that time, but the General Committee continued to study the project and invited Chaplain Aldred A. Pruden of Fort Monroe, Va., to discuss the subject at the meeting of the Committee on 31 January 1918. This the chaplain did at some length, explaining the need for such a school, suggesting a curriculum and daily schedule, and stressing the advantages of Fort Monroe as a location.[10] He had prepared this plan by direction of The Adjutant General, and his detailed memorandum on the subject was submitted to the Secretary of War on 8 February 1918 and approved the following day.[11] In all these negotiations there seems to have been close cooperation between the General Committee, representing many Protestant Churches, and the Roman Catholic Chaplaincy Bureau. A few weeks later they acted together in opposition to the projected transfer of the school to Fort Screven, Ga., recommending that it go to Fort Hamilton, N. Y., if it could no longer be accommodated at Fort Monroe, and ultimately acquiescing in the movement to Camp Taylor, Ky.[12]

Chaplain Pruden's plan for the school, with only minor changes, was established by *Special Regulation No. 496,* published by the War Department on 23 May 1918. It was provided that the student body should consist of 40 approved chaplain candidates and an equal number of newly appointed Regular, National Guard, and National Army Chaplains until such time as all of the latter group in this country should have attended the school. Chaplain candidates were to receive the pay and allowances of privates, first class, but should be on a parity with commissioned students in all matters concerning the internal operation of the school. Candidates manifesting unfitness for the chaplaincy could be eliminated at any time on recommendation of the school commander. Others should be approved for appointment in

[9] Arthur C. Piepkorn—*A Chronicle of the Training School for Newly-Appointed Chaplains and Chaplain Candidates during the First World War,* Ms. n. d. (hereafter cited as *Chronicle*) pp. 4–5.
[10] Virginia H. Boswell to Arthur C. Piepkorn, 20 Dec. 1943, File 314.7, OCCh.
[11] The Adjutant General to Secretary of War, 8 Feb. 1918. *Ibid.*
[12] Boswell, *loc. cit.;* D. W. Ketcham to Chief of Staff, 8 Apr. 1918, *Ibid.*

the grade of first lieutenant on the successful completion of the course. A normal day was to begin with setting-up exercises. One hour of drill and 3 of classes filled the forenoon, and 1 of equitation and 3 of lectures or conferences made up the afternoon program. Two hours of study were required in the evening. The course lasted for 5 weeks, and the chief subjects for intensive study were Military Law, International Law, Army Regulations, Organization, Insignia and Customs, and Military Hygiene and First Aid. With some modifications, this program was followed until the close of the school.

Instruction began at Fort Monroe on 1 March 1918. Of the 71 students on the roll on 10 March, 40 were commissioned chaplains. Of these, 7 held appointments in the Regular Army, 14 in the National Guard, and 19 in the National Army.[13] This ratio of chaplains to candidates in the student body was not maintained in later sessions, as few of these already commissioned could be spared from their duties in the field. A photograph taken near the end of the June session shows only 11 commissioned men in a body of 152 students. The school was moved to Camp Zachary Taylor, near Louisville, before the opening of the second term on 20 April. Six sessions were held in the new location, the last one beginning a few days after the Armistice. Intervals of at least a week occurred between classes.

Graduates of the 7 sessions numbered 66, 73, 129, 193, 237, 217, and 127, respectively, a total of 1,042. In all, 1,696 clergymen were authorized to attend the school. Of these, 1,315 reported, 915 were graduated and assigned to duty, and 127 finished too late for active service. All but four of the latter group accepted appointment in the Officers' Reserve Corps.[14] This shows that 273 entered the school but failed to graduate. More than 100 of these were in the last class and were allowed to leave when the cessation of hostilities had deprived them of the prospect of active duty. The first session with its majority of commissioned students was no more representative. The other 5 classes show 1,014 enrolled and 849 graduated, a loss of 165, or slightly more than 16 percent.[15] Some of these failed to complete the course because of illness or other emergencies, others on account of academic failure, but a large proportion were eliminated when the faculty became convinced that they lacked qualities of personality or the adaptability necessary to success.

The Armistice came when many students already were on their way to the school for the seventh session. It had scarcely begun when

---

[13] M. V. Oggel, 10 Mar. 1918, cited by Piepkorn, *Chronicle*, p. 11.

[14] Report of TAG to Sec. of W., 1919, p. 19.

[15] Piepkorn, *Chronicle*, p. 29.

orders were received from the Secretary of War that no more should
be admitted.   Chaplains in the school were to complete the course
and proceed to their units.   Candidates might choose between immediate discharge and the completion of the course with appointment in
the Officers' Reserve Corps in an inactive status.[16]   Those who remained were graduated at the end of 4 weeks, and the school was deactivated about the middle of January 1919.[17]

Several graduates of the school later held prominent positions as
college presidents, church leaders, or in other fields.   Among these
was John W. Bricker, afterward governor of Ohio and United States
Senator.   John M. Thomas had been president of Middlebury College for a decade before he attended the school.   One of the instructors afterward remarked: "We had a hack driver, a butcher, and a
pugilist come to that school to be trained as chaplains.   You can imagine how that college president stood out in the class." [18]   Presumably
these men had an ecclesiastical status not implied by their current oc-
cupations.   Chaplain Charles W. Baldwin secured a leave of absence
from the New York State Guard and attended the July class, apparently with no expectation of entering the Federal service.[19]

The following description of life in the school in June 1918 was
furnished by a student at that time who calls himself Chaplain Blank:

My introduction to the Army and to the School for Chaplains
and Approved Chaplain Candidates, to give the name in full, came
late on the afternoon of Saturday, 1 June 1918, too late for anything that day but paper work, inoculations, and chow.   On Monday we were grouped alphabetically in platoons of about thirty men
and arranged within the platoon by height.   The fourth man in the
front rank of each squad acted as corporal.   Fortunately our corporal, a genial Negro from Georgia named Jefferson, knew more
about marching than most of us.   The first afternoon we had drill
for three hours and learned to perform the simpler individual and
squad movements after a fashion.   Classes began the next day; so
did equitation.   The first hour in the "Bull Ring" saw us trotting
around the circle without benefit of reins or stirrups, encouraged
by Lieutenant Brinkley's assurance that "The only man who never
fell off a horse is the man who never got on one."

The regular staff and faculty consisted of the commandant, who
administered the school and gave some lectures, three chaplains
who taught the basic textbook courses, and a Coast Artillery lieutenant who had charge of calisthenics, drill, equitation, mess, supply,

[16] Director of Operations to TAG, 15 Nov. 1918, File 314.7, OCCh.
[17] Piepkorn, *Chronicle*, p. 30.
[18] William R. Arnold, statement to the author, 1947.
[19] Guy E. Shipler, Ed.—*War Work in the Diocese of New York*, p. 17.

and similar matters. A medical officer was detailed to teach us sanitation and first aid, but after a week or two he was thrown from his horse and injured so seriously that the course had to be discontinued. By that time we were struggling with the *Manual for Courts Martial* and regarded the poor surgeon's mishap as a special providence. Each of the three basic instructors taught three parallel sections during the first two weeks. Then enough men for two more platoons arrived, and the staff were told to graduate them with us. Twenty-five hours of teaching, besides special lectures and other duties, made rather a heavy week's work for these chaplains.

Military Law was an important subject in those days when chaplains frequently served as defense counsel in courts martial, and we studied it primarily with that end in view. Our instructor, Chaplain Fleming, was reputed to have defended more soldiers than any other officer in the history of the Army. He tried to teach us discipline and the customs of the service, saying by way of encouragement, "I don't care what you think of me today but care a great deal what you are going to think in six months." With this admirable intention he left the impression that the typical line officer is a more overbearing martinet than I have met in many years of service. At the end of six months I thought him a victim of a very faulty perspective.

The rules of land warfare, called International Law, we studied from a special text. The personal kindness and understanding of Chaplain Chenoweth, the instructor, helped us more than the facts he taught. Army regulations were assigned, one hundred a day, from the old blue volume with its 1,573 enactments. Chaplain Fealy, who taught this formidable material, felt that it would benefit from a sprinkling of spice. One day he called on me:

"Blank, stand up!" I rose.

"What is the practical significance of rank?"

I gave him a truly blank look, but one of the men near me said, "Pay."

"Hear the mercenary man talk about pay! The practical significance of rank is *nothing*. Say 'nothing'."

I said, "Nothing," and sat down.

We had several visitors during that session of the school. Chaplains from the western front gave us a vivid picture of trench warfare. British officers told us about chemicals and gas masks. Still more vividly I remember the inspection by Third Assistant Secretary of War Frederick P. Keppel on 3 July, because a group of us had planned a trip to Mammoth Cave on the holiday but were not allowed to leave camp. In the evening those who could get horses accompanied the Secretary and faculty on a brisk ride through the back roads of the camp. Immediately afterward we were invited to a reception. As I shook hands with Mr. Keppel, he smiled and said, "I can tell the men who went on the ride by the dust on their neckties."

In the School we were taught to indicate our military status in the form "First Lieutenant and Chaplain" and to wear the silver bars like other lieutenants. We did not know that the removal of insignia of rank from chaplains' uniforms had been ordered already. The Commandant spoke of the matter being under discussion, telling an amusing incident under earlier regulations when a harrassed regimental commander mistook the cross on his shoulder for the star of a brigadier. I was assigned to a Regular division in this country. Apparently the order about chaplains' insignia was not published in that division, for my associates still were wearing their bars when I was discharged in February 1919.[20]

This incident was the most dramatic in a debate which had continued for many years. The social barriers which have long existed between officers and enlisted men have been deemed necessary to discipline. Because of these practices, many have felt that chaplains should not have military rank lest it repel enlisted men who wished to consult them. Others believed that this impediment would be greatly reduced if the chaplain did not wear the insignia of his grade. On 30 March 1918, General Pershing cabled to the Secretary of War:

Believe work of chaplains would be facilitated if they were not given military rank. I have personally held this view for a long time. Many of our principal ministers believe that their relations would be closer if they did not have military titles and did not wear insignia. They should be given assimilated rank and pay. The above view is held by Bishop Brent, Bishop McCormick, and many others whom I have consulted. Recommend that the matter be given consideration again. Bill now pending before Congress.[21]

To carry out this recommendation, Special Regulations 42 and 41 were changed on 7 and 22 May, directing that chaplains wear the silver cross on shoulder loops and the sleeves of overcoats. This change was observed generally in Europe, but many chaplains in America knew nothing about it. Further changes in October directed that small crosses be worn on both sides of the coat collar, but these were removed the following May.[22] This made that part of the uniform the same as that of general officers, and the cross on the shoulder at a short distance resembled a star. If chaplains were not mistaken for brigadiers, it was easy to confuse them with field clerks; and recruits frequently were uncertain that they were officers.

Many felt that the removal of the evidence of rank degraded the chaplaincy in the estimation of the soldier. Bishop Brent was said to

---

[20] Anonymous manuscript, OCCh.
[21] D. W. Ketcham to CofS, 11 Apr. 1918; Cf. par. 2, Cable No. 508, File 314.7, OCCh.
[22] Change SR 42.

have changed his mind after seeing the new system in operation.   The change was opposed in the Chaplain School with such vigor that Chaplains Pruden, Fleming, and Fealy were relieved in the autumn of 1918 for "inciting the student body of chaplains to acts of insubordination in protesting against the removal of the insignia of rank from chaplains' uniform."   General Shanks declared his belief that the change did much harm and no good.   The first Chief of Chaplains shared this view and urged the restoration of these insignia, and on 19 March 1926 this was done.[23]

General Pershing had declared that the successful chaplain depends upon personality rather than rank.   This was reinterpreted to mean that no insignia will repel men who wish to consult a friendly chaplain.   Before the war, Chaplain Smith had asserted his right to entertain enlisted men in his quarters, and others followed his example.   Some eminent clergymen entered the chaplaincy but were impatient of distinctions which hampered their contacts with the men they came to serve.   The custom of addressing them as "Chaplain" rather than by rank has tended to emphasize the office rather than the grade.[24]

One other change of regulations concerned the insignia of chaplains.   When the Latin cross was substituted for the shepherd's crook as the chaplain's insigne, it was gratifying to many who considered it a sacred symbol where the other was merely a means of identification. This matter gained a new importance when the war brought a number of Jewish chaplains into the service.   To them the cross was the distinctive emblem of a different faith, and they protested against the regulation which made it a part of their uniform.   The Secretary of War authorized them to leave off the insignia of branch, but this negative remedy was no solution, and they asked for a distinctive badge which would represent their faith as the cross did that of their Christian colleagues.   The Secretary disliked distinctions among religions, and in June 1918 he authorized all chaplains to substitute the shepherd's crook for the cross.   This action was opposed so vigorously that the order was suspended.   Finally it was agreed that Jewish chaplains should wear a representation of the Tables of the Law surmounted by the Star of David and all other chaplains the cross, and this was ordered by Change 6 in S. R. 42, 15 October 1918.[25]

---

[23] File 314.7, OCCh.; David S. Shanks—*As They Passed Through the Port;* W. D. Cir. No. 19, 19 Mar. 1926.

[24] George F. Rixey *et al.;* AR 60–5.

[25] Memo. for CofS, 20 Aug. 1918, File 314.7, OCCh.; James M. Lawler to A. C. Piepkorn, 25 Jan. 1944, *Ibid.*

Several prominent representatives of the religious organizations of the country participated with Mr. Keppel in the inspection of the Chaplain School on 3 July 1918.   Their report recommended that the course should include information about agencies of governmental and civic relief and the work of welfare organizations; that a handbook about these agencies, including brief statements of the primary tenets of various religious bodies, be prepared for the guidance of chaplains; that clinical and experimental work be included in the curriculum; that a more spiritual note be introduced into the training; and that time be provided each day for private devotions and a full day near the end of the course for a spiritual retreat.   Secretary Keppel's report concurred in these proposals and recommended that an instructor with experience in social camp activities be added to the faculty.[26]

Graduates of the school differ in their evaluation of the course. Many of those with no military experience said that it introduced them to the essential usages of the Army more quickly than they could have learned them in any other way.   A few felt that much of what they learned would have been helpful in a training camp or in time of peace but had limited application to conditions in the European theater and pointed out that few of the instructors were experienced in trench warfare.   Some emphasized the value of intimate association with clergymen of all faiths.[27]

During the period of hostilities 2,363 chaplains held commissions under some component of the Army.   Of these, 146 had been appointed before the war.[28]   If none of the latter had attended the school, there would remain 1,179 commissioned from civil life who did not receive this training.   Actually some of the 146 were sent to the school.   To give some instruction to those who arrived in France with no training, a school was set up in an old chateau at Neuilly-sur-Suize, near Chaumont, in midsummer of 1918, and it was ordered that unassigned chaplains arriving in France should be sent there for instruction.   At first the course consisted of one week of lectures by such chaplains as might be available, but in late August Chaplain John A. Randolph was appointed commandant and established the following 10-day course:

Course	Hours
First Aid	6
Gas Defense Drill	6
Map Reading	1

---

[26] Piepkorn, *Chronicle*, p. 21.
[27] *Ibid.*, p. 30.
[28] *The United States Army Chaplaincy*, p. 39.

Course	Hours
Official correspondence	1
Equipment	1
Customs of the Service	1
The Chaplain at the Front	1
Identification and Burial of the Dead	2
Esprit de Corps	3
Lectures by Representatives of Welfare Agencies	4
French History	3
Censorship	1
French Language	10
Physical Exercise	15
Devotional Exercise	10

In addition to these 65 hours there were lectures by a number of visiting officers or clergymen. Later this program was revised so that a normal day included 2½ hours of drill and athletics and 4 of instruction.[29]

This program reflects the experience of the battlefield and contrasts with that of the school in the United States in several significant particulars. Not only was the course shorter, but the training day began later in the morning and followed a more leisurely schedule of activity. More than half of the actual instruction dealt with problems of the battlefront, matters receiving limited treatment at Camp Taylor. As the school served also as a replacement depot, many chaplains came there from hospitals for a period of recuperation before returning to their units. Thus the building of health and morale was one of its main purposes. In this particular the school seems to have been patterned after that operated by the British Army in which the physical and spiritual restoration of chaplains was a primary objective.[30]

By October 1918, the school had outgrown its quarters and was transferred to the Chateau d'Aux at Louplande, near LaMans. The size of classes seems to have varied widely, for some are said to have numbered from 100 to 150. About 600 chaplains took the course in the 6 months the school operated before it was closed at the end of January 1919. Some considered that it had little value for those without war experience. Others who had gone through the school in America stressed the importance of being taught by men who were acquainted with trench warfare. Some believed it the most valuable training of their whole military career.[31]

Several practical lessons about the training of civilians to serve

---

[29] Piepkorn—*The U. S. Chaplain School in France, 1918-1919,* Ms. n. d., *passim.*

[30] *Ibid.*

[31] *Ibid.*

as chaplains in an emergency were taught by the experiences of the schools of 1918 in the United States and France.   Those qualifications normally indicated by ordination and experience as clergymen proved to be an insufficient index of the fitness of candidates, and several had to be separated from the service on recommendation of the faculty. Equally important was the necessity of coordinating the objectives of military and religious authorities in the training of chaplains.   Early plans of church leaders stressed spiritual preparation, and this was reemphasized in the school in France and by those who inspected the school at Camp Taylor in July.   This recognized the fact that the parish clergyman enjoyed a variety of sustaining and stimulating influences which he may not find in the army and that the deficiency might be serious, especially in the case of younger men.

On the other hand, the urgent need for chaplains demanded that the course should be short, and the risk of sectarian differences forbade instruction in theology.   It was assumed that the professional education of candidates was adequate and that the purpose of the school was to adapt them to military life and service.   Experience in 1918 demonstrated the practical value of parts of the instruction being given by officers familiar with the type of combat into which the students would be sent. Similary it was shown that an economical use of teaching personnel can be made by having each instructor conduct a number of parallel sections in the same course.   Another apparent advantage was the grouping of some distinct but related short topics into a continuing course without change of instructor or schedule.

CHAPTER XI

Cantonment and Trench

The chaplain's task in 1917 had changed only in details from that of the 1860's. The stern agony of trench warfare as some had learned it at Vicksburg and Petersburg had become the rule. The constant use of artillery hastened the nervous condition known as "shell shock," and the stealthy onset of poison gas added an unpredictable element of horror. This produced many psychological cases to challenge the resourcefulness of both the surgeon and the chaplain.

Changes in religious emphasis, though not drastic, were significant. Evangelism in the narrower meaning of the term was less exclusively the method and purpose of the majority of chaplains. The growth of the liturgical churches had demonstrated the value of religious nurture. Many formed Bible classes and discussion groups where their grandfathers would have held prayer meetings between more formal worship services. A New England chaplain on duty at a training camp in the Ohio Valley remarked to a Y. M. C. A. secretary that he was no evangelist. The next Sunday he preached an earnest sermon on the rewards and obligations of the Christian life. When he invited those who would to dedicate themselves publicly to the higher life, quite a number responded. Later the secretary remarked, "I thought you said you were no evangelist."

A New Hampshire chaplain on duty with troops from the Carolinas and Tennessee said that his northern exegesis did not fit their southern conventional views, but he did not try to make liberals of them but to strengthen the great fundamentals which are sacred to liberal and conservative alike. He felt that his main task was not to raise morale by magnifying the faults of the enemy and rousing hatred but to clear the path between the human soul and the All Father.[1] A colleague saw a survival of medievalism in the notion advanced by some critics that chaplains were in the army to bless the weapons and military enterprises but felt that they really were harbingers of a dawning humanitarianism because they were there not to kill but to save.[2]

---

[1] Captain Carlyle Summerbell—*A Preacher Goes to War*, pp. 26, 28.
[2] Rabbi Lee J. Levinger—*A Jewish Chaplain in France*, p. 1.

Another factor very important to the chaplains was the presence in training camps and overseas of the representatives of welfare agencies, some of whom were definitely expected to carry on religious work. The largest number of recreation buildings were operated by the Young Men's Christian Association, but the Knights of Columbus, Jewish Welfare Board, Red Cross, Salvation Army, and some other groups carried on an important work. Many of the field agents of these organizations were clergymen; and religious services, whether conducted by a secretary or a chaplain, had a prominent place in the regular program of these installations.

In rare cases difficulties grew out of this overlapping of functions, but cordial cooperation was the rule. Chaplains were given office space and facilities for private interviews or large assemblies in the buildings of these organizations whenever possible and were helped in many important ways by members of the staff. Such cooperation often ignored sectarian lines. Mass and Jewish services frequently were held in Y. M. C. A. buildings. We are told of the Protestant secretary who walked 5 miles in the winter rain and borrowed a rosary to comfort a dying Catholic, of a French priest who confessed a dying soldier with a Protestant secretary as interpreter, and of a Baptist minister who played the organ for midnight mass.[3] After a considerable experience in France the chaplains were made coordinators of welfare work in the various units and areas. This brought a notable increase of efficiency.[4]

About 2,200 chaplains were on duty at the time of the Armistice when the greatest number of men were enrolled in the Army, an average of one chaplain to serve about 1,690 men. This shows why many regiments entitled to 3 chaplains had only 2 while some small units had none. When practicable, 1 Catholic and 2 Protestant chaplains were assigned to the large infantry regiments, but frequently only 1 of each faith could be provided. There were not enough Catholic chaplains in service to maintain such an arrangement everywhere, and a priority was given to the units overseas, where there was less opportunity to supplement the chaplain's efforts from civilian sources.

In the British service a Jewish chaplain was assigned to the headquarters of each army. The American practice was to attach them

[3] *Ibid.* p. 18; Summerbell, *op. cit.*, p. 40; William L. Stidger—*Soldier Silhouettes on Our Front,* p. 159.

[4] Alexander C. Zabriskie—*Bishop Brent, Crusader for Christian Unity,* p. 129.

to lower echelons but with the expectation that they should minister to their coreligionists in other units as circumstances might permit. The result was that they were everyone's chaplains as truly as their Catholic or Protestant associates except in relation to the distinctive observances of their faith. At one time there were 6 chaplains and 4 rabbis of the Jewish Welfare Board to minister to more than 50,000 Jewish men in the American Expeditionary Forces. Of the 25 Jewish chaplains appointed, 12 saw foreign service. One of these declared that he could not have served half so effectively without the friendship and help of his Catholic and Protestant colleagues.[5]

Chaplains were entitled to such articles of field equipment as were authorized for issue to all officers, but virtually no items of a professional nature were furnished by the Government. The Chaplain's flag was authorized but was seldom available during the emergency. Assembly tents were equally scarce. Most of the large churches had an agency for the help of chaplains. They provided such articles as Mass kits, communion sets, portable typewriters, and religious literature and supplies. One chaplain had an 8-page leaflet of prayers and hymns printed for use in his services. So many of the men sent them to the folks at home that his supply was soon depleted. The Y. M. C. A. furnished chaplains with a library of 52 carefully chosen volumes. Though the project was not undertaken until the month of the Armistice, 2,251 sets were distributed to chaplains at a time when they were much in need of help. Elzar Tetreau told of his many futile efforts to obtain flooring for a welfare building for the men after the other materials had been obtained by salvage. Not being for authorized construction, the requisition could not be filled. One day some lumber was delivered in the locality for a different purpose. Instantly the chaplain set the men at work nailing it down. Later the colonel congratulated him on getting his floor, and it dawned upon him that the project for which the lumber was drawn might have been a legal fiction.[6]

Usually chaplains on duty in the United States could be provided with horses, but they were seldom available in overseas areas. George McCarthy described the native horse assigned to him in France who showed an intelligence almost human and came to be more of a com-

---

[5] Levinger, *op. cit.*, pp. 8, 28, 82, 86, 132.

[6] Celestine N. Bittle—*Soldiering for Cross and Flag*, p. 97; Gustav Stearns—*From Army Camp and Battlefield*, p. 193; *Service with Fighting Men*, I, 608; Elzar Des Jardins Tetreau—*Pen Sketches and Diary of a Chaplain of Infantry*, p. 53; *et al.*

panion than a servant. On one occasion, in a forest recently occupied
by the enemy, he was attracted by a fine saddle which seemed to have
been abandoned on the roadside by some German officer and prepared to dismount, but his horse interposed a quick veto by snorting
and galloping furiously past. Later he realized that horse sense can
be a wholesome counterpoise to human curiosity, for the saddle probably was attached to a planted bomb. To say Mass for men in an
advanced position one Sunday morning, he found that he must cross
an open plain under heavy shell and sniper fire. Making sure that
his Mass kit and a bag of oats were secure, he rode into the open and
asked an unusual effort from the horse in his "native tongue," *"Allez!
Allez! Mon petit cheval!"* At top speed they passed through the bursting
shells and reached a protected area beyond. The horse rubbed his
nose against the chaplain with manifest pride in a worthy achievement
and received an extra portion of oats with evident approval. Where
the roads were badly damaged, horses would serve better than motor
vehicles, but chaplains were fortunate to have the use even of a motor-
cycle or car. Many had to walk wherever their duties called them or
catch rides on passing vehicles. After the Armistice the Jewish Welfare Board furnished Ford cars for the use of its chaplains who were
serving with occupation troops.[7]

The most conspicuous duty of the chaplains was the conduct of
public worship. If a liturgical form of devotion was usual in his
church, a chaplain often scheduled such a service at an early hour, to
be followed by one less formal for the men accustomed to simpler
usages. Several Catholic chaplains describe the hymns, sermons, and
prayers before the altars where they had said Mass at an earlier hour.
Many soldiers attended both services. A Jewish chaplain remarked
that men of other faiths who attended his services were always respect-
ful and interested.[8] We read of such meetings in recreation buildings
and mess halls, in various parts of ships, in an old French fort, a village church, a carpenter shop, a dugout, and a village square, under a
tree, at a gun implacement, and in the forest.[9]

One chaplain tells of an ordered attendance at his first service so
that the men could get to know him, and troops were marched to
church in a few units, but participation in any religious exercises was

---

[7] George T. McCarthy—*The Greater Love*, pp. 89, 91, 105; Levinger, *op. cit.*, p. 61.

[8] Bittle, *op. cit.*, p. 104; *The 120th Field Artillery Diary*, pp. 310, 401; Lee McCallum—*Our Sons at War*, p. 176; Levinger, *op. cit.*, p. 135.

[9] George Mozley—*Our Miracle Battery*, p. 60; Margaret Mayo—*Trouping for the Troops*, p. 99; Marian Gregory—*Memories of Service in France*, p. 59; L. F. Ranlitt—*Let's Go!*, p. 208; *et al.*

usually free from all compulsion.[10]   Many officers assisted the chaplains in other ways.   One general regularly served as acolyte with the
correctness of a seminarian, and a colonel played the organ for church
in his regiment.   McCarthy described a service during a bombardment so heavy that he felt it would be impossible to make himself heard
if he tried to preach.   Afterward the colonel told him that the din
seemed to subside after Mass began.   The chaplain remarked that he
now understood the regularity of the colonel's attendance, he wanted
to get into a quieter area.[11]

Anniversaries and special occasions gave the opportunity for service or other programs of unusual interest.   Gustav Stearns estimated
that 4,000 men were at his Thanksgiving service, singing from the hymn
leaflet he had published.   Easter Sunday found him on a troop train
in France.   Nothing daunted, he conducted services in twelve boxcars
while the train was in motion.   In one regiment 1,450 men joined in
a field communion service on the eve of embarkation.   Jews, Catholics, and Protestants participated, each giving the sanctity of his own
faith to the ceremony.   Carlyle Summerbell was invited by a French
priest to hold his Christmas service in the church after Mass.   To
avoid any chance of impropriety, he did not approach the altar but
stood near a lovely statue of the Virgin and preached to soldiers and
villagers from a passage of the "Magnificat."   At another time when
he expected many French people to attend his service as a courtesy,
he determined to read the Scripture in French.   Asking the village
schoolmaster to correct his pronunciation and emphasis, he was drilled
on the passage at great length and was able to read it to the satisfaction of his mentor.[12]

Another chaplain who had a better command of the language
preached in the village church, first in French to the civilians and then
in English for the soldiers in the congregation.   Invited to preach at
the observance of a Jewish holy day, a Methodist chaplain brought a
message of deep inspiration to his Jewish congregation.   Francis Duffy
said that, after Mass in a village church in Luxembourg on the Thanksgiving after the Armistice, he "unfrocked himself of his papistical
robes" and held a general service in the courtyard of a medieval castle, using a breach in the fortifications as a pulpit.   A month later he
celebrated the Christmas midnight Mass on the banks of the Rhine.

---

[10] Summerbell, *op. cit.,* p. 25; *History of the 101st U. S. Engineers,* p. 56; Captain Carroll J.
Swan—*My Company,* p. 41.

[11] Francis P. Duffy—*Father Duffy's Story,* p. 56; *Service with Fighting Men,* I, 615; McCarthy,
op. cit., p. 108.

[12] Stearns, *op. cit.,* pp. 224, 274; *The 139th Field Artillery,* p. 177; Summerbell, *op. cit.* pp. 70, 72.

The troops marched to church as the band played "Onward, Christian Soldiers" and "Adeste Fideles," and the German people in the congregation joined in their own language as they sang "Holy God, We Praise Thy Name." Memorial services and consecration of the colors are other occasions when chaplains were able to join with men of all creeds in exercises which were sacred to all.[13]

At one camp where the chaplain felt that more should be done for the military prisoners, he began a series of Sunday evening services with a band concert followed by an earnest sermon. A chaplain who spoke German arranged to say Mass for the prisoners of war confined in four stockades. The alter was placed so that the men in two inclosures could hear and see through the fence. Those who wished to attend from the other stockades were brought under guard. Two men sheltered the candles from the wind in their cupped hands. The chaplain closed with a brief sermon in English and in German. Another conducted services in German for the prisoners confined near his quarters. The Christmas eve program among the wounded was especially appreciated. This was followed by a communion service in Norwegian for a man who was very ill.[14]

A few comments on religious services in the army by men who conducted them deserve to be remembered. One declared it was never necessary to camouflage them with a lot of stunts. He announced them frankly, and the men came gladly. Another admitted that the attendance of men awaiting embarkation was abnormally large on the Sunday after the sinking of the *Tuscania*. One who usually ended his sermon with an invitation to make a public dedication to a life of righteousness said that he did not wish to frighten people with hell nor bribe them with heaven. Several stressed the importance of sermons being direct and practical. Topics such as "Loyalty," "Honesty," "Fear," and "Theft" were popular. Among the favorite hymns were "The Son of God Goes Forth to War," "Onward, Christian Soldiers," "Trust and Obey," "What a Friend We Have in Jesus," "Rock of Ages," "Nearer, My God, to Thee," and the "Battle Hymn of the Republic." Examples of the inappropriate are talks on "Courage" to supply men whose most dangerous task was handling cases of canned salmon and a moving talk about home and mother on the eve of battle.[15]

---

[13] Will Judy—*A Soldier's Diary*, p. 115; Levinger, *op. cit.*, p. 20; Russell G. Carter—*The 101st Field Artillery*, pp. 41, 260; *The Howitzer*, I, No. 14; Duffy, *op. cit.*, pp. 307, 315.

[14] *Sheridan Reveille*, No. 36, p. 3; Bittle, *op. cit.*, p. 101; Stearns, *op. cit.*, pp. 172, 236.

[15] Harold M. Kramer—*With Seeing Eyes*, pp. 338, 160; Stearns, *op. cit.*, p. 59; Summerbell, *op. cit.*, pp. 50, 57; *The Story of "E" Co., 101st Engineers*, p. 107; Levinger, *op. cit.*, pp. 162, 165.

More than one chaplain found that his standing with the men did not suffer as long as he could join in the laugh when some mischance put him in an amusing situation. Stearns tells of preaching from a pile of planks when he forgot himself and stepped off the edge into the arms of two officers who were expecting such a catastrophe. They insisted that no harm was done because he finished his interrupted sentence without the loss of a word and went on with his discourse. During the voyage to Europe he volunteered to conduct services for a Negro unit on the ship which had no chaplain. He was impressed by the singing of the spirituals, especially "Swing Low, Sweet Chariot." In the midst of one of his sermons the ship gave such a roll that he suddenly found himself in the middle of a pile of men on the deck. When they regained an upright posture, he finished his sermon with as much gravity as the situation would permit, but there was no more singing at that time, as all felt that the chariot was swinging low enough.[16]

Service to individuals has always been one of the chaplain's primary duties and privileges. A soldier's letter told of his chaplain spending much time at the Y. or K. C. hut playing the piano for the men but added a higher expression of appreciation: "One day he held a communion service just for me out here in the woods." Summerbell said he never pushed religion at the men and could go much farther when they raised the subject themselves. Celestine Bittle told of the soldier who asked his help to induce a comrade to come to confession and resume the religious observances he had been neglecting. After some negotiation it was arranged that they should meet the chaplain at a French chapel at a certain hour in the evening. Visiting many sick in the hospital earlier in the evening, the chaplain completely forgot this engagement until long after the time, when he was distressed at the thought of the men faithfully coming through the rain but failing to find him. When next he saw one of the soldiers, he tried to express his regret but soon realized that the man was apologizing also. Both soldiers had been ordered to guard duty that evening with no opportunity to inform him. At first he was tempted merely to tell them to think nothing more about it, but the humorous element was too good to be lost, and he told his part of the story. A good laugh all around made it doubly certain that all would keep their next appointment—and so they did.[17]

---

[16] Stearns, *op. cit.*, pp. 81, 228.

[17] Fullerton L. Waldo—*America at the Front*, p. 84; Summerbell, *op. cit.*, p. 10; Bittle, *op. cit.*, pp. 128, 198.

Another soldier attracted his special attention.   A member of a motor repair unit, he had gone to the front without leave, hoping to get into combat.   At his trial it was proved that he did not intend to go back to the shops, so he was sentenced to 10 years for desertion. The chaplain recognized an element of desperation in his attitude and finally induced him to confess that he had determined to bolt when taken out of the stockade so that the guard would have to shoot him. In this way he expected that his family would believe him killed in battle and would never learn of his disgrace.   The chaplain told him it would be more likely to have the opposite effect, as his family would be told that their son had been killed trying to escape after conviction of a serious crime.   He assured him that the fighting was over and prisoners in his situation would be pardoned in a short time, but nothing moved the boy from his resolution till the chaplain urged that he guard his mother from even a chance of learning that her son had been a suicide as well as a convict.   Not many months later he recognized this boy's name in the roll call of a body of troops at the Hoboken port. There he was in the front rank, restored to duty and beaming with gratitude and confidence as he met the chaplain's eye.[18]

One chaplain heard as many confessions as possible while the regiment was poised for an attack and gave a general absolution when they moved forward.   Another found the street corner of a French village the best place to hear confessions.   Sometimes as many as 500 men would come in a single afternoon, many of other faiths joining the line for a word of friendly counsel and encouragement.[19]

Performing marriages and counseling the young people were important functions, especially before troops went overseas, and occasionally these involved unusual features.   One couple arranged for a quiet wedding in a church just outside the camp, but the regimental band learned of it and insisted that there be a parade.   The chaplain estimated that 10,000 men marched to the church as the band played the wedding march.   Even the marital interests of prisoners were not neglected.   General Shanks told of seven men being marched under guard to the place where the chaplain and the prospective brides were waiting.   After the group ceremony, the bridegrooms were marched back to the stockade.[20]

The burial of the dead is always a duty for chaplains as import-

---

[18] *Ibid.*
[19] McCarthy, *op. cit.,* pp. 125, 136; Duffy, *op. cit.,* p. 109.
[20] *Ibid.,* p. 21; Major General David S. Shanks—*As They Passed Through the Port,* p. 129.

ant as it is melancholy.   The rule in the Expeditionary Forces was
that every soldier should be buried with military honors and the rites
of his faith unless there were insuperable obstacles and that the same
courtesies be shown to enemy dead.   Stearns described the solemnity
of a burial at sea when the ship's engines were stopped for the committal.   At his first funeral in France Bittle discovered that the dead
were being buried with very scanty clothing and obtained an order that
uniforms be provided for all future burials.   At his first burial of a
prisoner of war he followed the ritualistic service with a brief message
of comfort in German to the score of prisoners who had escorted their
comrade to his grave.   A German sergeant major followed with an
appropriate tribute.   As the guard had only service ammunition, the
volleys were fired into the pile of soil beside the grave.[21]

At a mass burial in the rain the Jewish, Catholic, and Protestant
chaplains in turn held their helmets over the prayerbook of a colleague
while the rituals of the three faiths were read.   Some chaplains were
made burial officers for entire divisions.   This involved the organization and supervision of many activities if the dead of the battlefield
were to be found and given proper burial and required daily reports
to the Graves Registration Service and monthly to General Headquarters.   Some chaplains were overwhelmed by the cumulative horror of these duties.   On the verge of insanity, one babbled of the
number of dead he had buried and of increasing his record.[22]

While the intimacies of the camp bred mutual respect among
men of all faiths, it was preeminently in the presence of death that sectarian considerations were forgotten.   Levinger read psalms for the
comfort of wounded Protestants, and a French Rabbi was killed at Verdun while he held a cross to soothe the last moments of a Catholic
soldier.   A warm friendship grew up between a Protestant chaplain
and a Catholic priest.   Bringing in a wounded Catholic soldier from
No Man's Land, the chaplain was killed.   At his funeral the priest
spoke a eulogy of notable tenderness and sorrow.   Such relations did
not suffer from the good-natured banter which sometimes made use of
theological terms.   A Catholic writer told with gusto of the Presbyterian and Catholic chaplains who served together and became fast
friends.   When the time came that they had to part, the former said:
"Well, goodbye, dear old partner.   We've had many sorrowful and
some happy experiences together.   After all, we both have the same

---

[21] McCarthy, *op. cit.*, pp. 61, 86, 110; Riley Strickland—*Adventures of the A. E. F. Soldier*, p.
183; Stearns, *op. cit.*, p. 67; Bittle, *op. cit.*, pp. 89, 105, 114.

[22] Levinger, *op. cit.*, pp. 51, 54; Thomas H. Barber—*Along the Road*, p. 90.

aims and ambitions.   Both of us wish to serve the Master—you in your way and I in His."[23]

Faint with hunger, McCarthy one day passed a Salvation Army hut and was invited by the worker to join him and his wife at dinner. He voiced the sentiment which was characteristic of all faiths when he prayed that the good God who had brought them together there would join them at some future day in his heavenly home above.   A Methodist chaplain was gratified as much as he was amused when two boys approached him and asked him to settle a bet.   They had wagered five francs, one that he was a Catholic, the other that he was an Episcopalian.   The chaplain's account of his effort to comfort a dying Catholic helps us to understand why he did not show any definite sectarian label.   The soldier asked for Father Wolfe, but the chaplain had to tell him that he was so far away that he could not be reached but offered to hear anything he might wish to say.   Feebly the boy voiced his regret for his neglect of duty and the wrongs he had done. Finding a small crucifix under his shirt, the chaplain held it to his lips, prayed that he might find forgiveness, and assured him of the infinite mercy of God.   A look of confidence spread over his face, and he was gone.[24]

Varied and unusual services were asked of the chaplain, sometimes because the men felt that he would not make light of anything important to them and would respect their confidence, at others because they felt he could be trusted to carry out difficult tasks with fidelity.   McCarthy told of the boy who asked him to help write a letter which would leave no doubt in the mind of a certain girl how much he loved her.   Asking how the soldier had acted when she came to see him off, the chaplain felt that this letter would be superfluous, but was ready to have a share in making assurance doubly sure.   The resulting composite masterpiece proved to be fully adequate to its primary purpose and helped pave the way to a postwar romance.   While waiting to begin an especially dangerous attack, a captain handed the chaplain a note to a man in the division who owed him $300, asking him to see that his family got the money if he should "get bumped." [25]

At the front he became much attached to a lieutenant in temporary command who was conspicuous for his care of his men and his devotion to duty.   When they were free, he often thrilled the chaplain

---

[23] Levinger, *op. cit.*, pp. 45, 137; Stidger, *op. cit.*, p. 161; Edward H. O'Hara—*World War at its Climax*, p. 255.

[24] McCarthy, *op. cit.*, p. 88; Tetreau, *op. cit.*, pp. 63, 21.

[25] McCarthy, *op. cit.*, pp. 42, 133, 97.

and other friends by playing great compositions on his violin. Growing confidential one evening, he told of the splendid girl in America who was to be his wife after the war and showed her picture with joy and pride. Shortly afterward he received a letter and opened it eagerly. A moment later, with a look of anguish on his face, he asked the chaplain to read it. She wrote that she admired him very highly but felt that she could not love him as a wife should and asked that their engagement be ended. Ten days passed, with the young officer making a brave attempt to be cheerful. Then a shell fragment laid him desperately wounded on the ground. Within 10 minutes the chaplain was kneeling by his side. With failing strength he asked him to read a letter he would find in his pocket and send it if he thought it all right. A moment later he was gone. The blood-stained letter told what his love for her had meant to the writer and always should. For this very reason he would not interfere but wished to do anything to increase her happiness. The chaplain forwarded the letter with a sublime pride in the manhood of a comrade whom tragedy could but lift to higher nobility.[26]

In 1917, the regulations designed to protect chaplains from the burden of secular duties were not very definite and assignments of this nature were quite common. Many were put in charge of the post exchange, a mess, the unit post office, special funds, bond sales, athletics, or the schools established after the cessation of hostilities. Some shrank from duty as defense counsel in courts-martial lest their lack of experience should deprive the accused of some right under the law. Perhaps the most onerous of these duties was the censoring of mail. Not only did the task demand sometimes half of a chaplain's working day, but his relations with the men were impaired if he found it necessary to cut important parts out of their letters or to refuse to forward them at all.[27]

Many chaplains participated in pistol practice without expecting actually to use weapons against an enemy; but one senior chaplain, formerly an enlisted man, is said to have helped man a gun and drive back the enemy during an emergency, and a colleague was cited for "caring for the wounded, encouraging the advancing troops, and throwing hand grenades without thought of personal safety." [28]

---

[26] *Ibid.*, p. 103.

[27] Stearns, *op. cit.*, p. 11; Summerbell, *op. cit.*, p. 45; Duffy, *op. cit.*, p. 318; Bittle, *op. cit.*, p. 259; Levinger, *op. cit.*, p. 183; Heywood Broun—*A. E. F.*, p. 116; Zabriskie, *op. cit.*, p. 124; *et al.*

[28] Stearns, *op. cit.*, p. 30; Summerbell, *op. cit.*, p. 100; file of John B. De Valles, OCCh.

The chaplains fought the habitual vices with the partial success of their predecessors of 1776 and 1861. During the trying months after the Armistice, gambling rose to serious proportions in some units. Wolfe once stumbled upon a game where the 100-franc notes were piled high. He quickly gathered up the money, saying, "It's for the mess fund, boys." Each payday Tetreau urged the men to think of their future needs and offered to send money home for them. The first time he forwarded more than 2,700 francs, and 2 weeks later it exceeded 5,500. One of the card sharks remarked, "Wait till next payday, I bet the chaplain will send away over 10,000 francs. He's the best poker player in the battalion."[29]

Occasionally a chaplain saw his ideals of abstract righteousness temporarily eclipsed by his sense of humor or of realistic justice. The chaplain of a certain signal battalion told of the clandestine payday games in hidden corners. These attracted little attention while the men took their gains and losses among themselves, but some card sharks from another unit decided that they would be an easy prey and developed the habit of getting into the game and carrying away most of the winnings. This practice, several times repeated, outraged the recognized code, and the signal men organized for defense. They found a man whose skill with cards made the invading experts seem like tyros. At the proper time he got into the next game, and the visiting infantrymen went home with empty pockets. To stimulate interest in sports for the entertainment of the men, Bittle frequently gave small money prizes to the winners. One boxer who had received a prize of 50 francs felt that the loser had done as much as he for the show and insisted that he take half of the prize. A few days later they met and the loser in this contest said: "You gave me 25 francs. I blew 10 on booze and shot craps with the other 15. I won 400, so here's your 200; 50–50, you know."[30]

Warmly supported by the officers, Summerbell tried to discourage profanity in his unit without defeating his plan by asking too much. Nearly two-thirds of the regiment signed pledges to *try* not to swear. Exclamations cast in classic mold, like "By Alcibiades!" or the more plebeian "What in Sam Hill!" often relieved strong feeling and caused a wholesome merriment. Duffy described a feast in France. He was in a company kitchen when two boys brought the cook a bag of German flour they had found in a dugout recently abandoned by the enemy. Immediate preparations were made for hotcakes for all, and

[29] Tetreau, *op. cit.*, p. 47.
[30] Bittle, *op. cit.*, p. 255.

the chaplain was invited to remain.   When the griddle was hot, the batter was mixed and poured.   The eager cook watched for the propitious moment and turned the first cake.   It fell with a crash.   The nonplussed cook investigated and found that his flour was plaster of paris.   Desperately he turned to the chaplain and said, "Oh, for Heavens sake, Father, go inside until I can let myself spill!" [31]

Several experienced chaplains have left their estimates of the effect of service upon the morals and faith of the soldiers.   One declared that the men were not brutalized, as many theorists expected.   Another said that they went into the trenches boys and came out men.   One with unusually wide contacts said that the soldiers in France were representative Americans living on a moral plane above that of civilian life at home.   Fair play, sincerity, courage, and loyalty were conspicuous in the code which often prompted them to heroic action.   Sex standards were about the same as in civil life with the added restraint of military discipline.   Property obligations as related to Government equipment and supplies were a different matter.   One chaplain's driver illustrates the attitude of thousands.   One night he had to drive 10 miles in the dark because the bulbs were stolen from their car.   The next day he "salvaged" a pair from another car.   When the chaplain demanded that he return them, he said he could not identify the car from which they had been taken and probably the other driver had got them in the same way.   When he found that these bulbs were burned out already, he felt that he had been cheated. [32]

"The religion of the trenches" was said to be neither more nor less than the religion of their boyhood in the old home.   A company commander said that many of his men attended church more than ever before, which made them better men and better soldiers.   Not all were as confident as this, especially after the cessation of hostilities withdrew the stimulus of danger.   One writer described a regiment so demoralized that there were 267 men in the guardhouse and 47 absent without leave and declared that the chaplain was their only support.   One regiment returned from France with so low a venereal rate that medical authorities doubted the figures.   An investigation showed that they were correct and that this fine record was attributed chiefly to the influence of Chaplain Ogilby. [33]

It may be asked how the war affected the chaplains themselves.

---

[31] Summerbell, *op. cit.,* p. 76; Duffy, *op. cit.,* p. 252.

[32] Levinger, *op. cit.,* pp. 195, 203; McCarthy, *op. cit.,* p. 82; Daniel A. Poling—*Huts in Hell,* pp. 156–63; Kramer, *op. cit.,* p. 338.

[33] Swan, *op. cit.,* p. 42; V. F. Sullivan—*With the Yanks in France,* p. 119; Zabriskie,*op. cit.,* p. 128.

Poling said that he saw a few who were disappointing and described one trying to smoke for the first time who "was doing his best to be a good fellow and succeeded only in being a fool." The great majority rose to higher standards of devotion and effectiveness when confronted by the challenge of war. He wished that every pastor in America might have at least 6 months of active service overseas, for he would never again be content with the ancient walls of ecclesiasticism and sectarian differences but would insist upon cooperation in advancing the vital things of life.[34]

Twenty-seven chaplains were wounded, 28 received American medals, and 57 the honor decorations of foreign nations.

Twenty-three died in service in 1918. They represented 8 great churches and were natives of 12 States and 2 foreign countries. Of the 11 battle casualties, 9 fell in the great advance that ended the war. Six died of disease far away from home. A special pathos surrounds the death of William F. Davitt. On the morning of 11 November, it was generally known that firing would cease an hour before noon. The chaplain arranged with the unit commander for a celebration and went to get the regimental colors. As he was returning, he was struck by one of the last German shells and died with his country's flag clasped in his arms. In the Chaplain's Plot of the Arlington National Cemetery stands a granite cenotaph and memorial tablet erected in 1926 by brother chaplains of all faiths to the memory and perpetual honor of these 23 faithful men.

One of the most colorful of this honored group was Colman E. O'Flaherty. Many years afterward his comrades were still laughing in enjoyment of his genial wit, while they held in lasting respect his courage and loyalty to duty. During an advance a tank driver became hopelessly lost. His attention was attracted by the chaplain rapping on the front of the vehicle with his walking stick. Offering to show the way, he strode across the field, reminding the observers of a trainer leading an elephant. At another point he advanced alone to see if any Germans remained in a piece of woods and suddenly came upon a group of 20. With the manner of a Prussian drill sergeant he lined them up and marched them into the American lines, saying that otherwise some one might have been hurt. On the first of October he went to the aid of some wounded men in an exposed position. As he knelt among them, a shell burst at that very spot. His commander

---

[34] Poling, *op. cit.*, p. 205.

said that the initial letters of his posthumous Distinguished Service Cross really should be interpreted: "Died in the Service of Christ." [35]

Duty with occupation troops after the Armistice challenged the resourcefulness of their chaplains. The problem of leisure and homesickness replaced the stimulation of danger. They promoted many forms of entertainment and a variety of educational projects. Some studied the history of the locality where they were stationed and visited places of interest. The work of Edmund Easterbrook, afterward Chief of Chaplains, is a good example of the initiative with which the complex problems of the situation were met. As senior chaplain of the American forces, he arranged a series of conferences among British, French, Belgian, and American chaplains which contributed to better relations among the allied forces. He organized a church, Sunday school, and Bible class in the royal palace at Coblenz, and the "Church of the Palace" was an important institution until the American forces were withdrawn in 1923. One of the most distinguished chaplains of the Regular Army wrote of the chaplains of the First World War: "I assert positively that no body of men of equal number and of equal rank have given a better account of their stewardship in any army, in any war, in any age." [36]

---

[35] *The Military Chaplain*, Winter, 1951, p. 24.
[36] Bateman, *loc. cit.*

CHAPTER XII

Between World Wars

The two decades following the Armistice were a period of great importance in the development of the armed forces. The natural revulsion from the destruction and suffering of war frequently was given an extreme expression. Economic conditions restricted expenditures for military purposes. Despite these and other impediments varied preparations were made for a possible emergency, and these proved to be vital to the life of the nation when the crisis came. This was equally true of the chaplaincy. It survived a variety of attacks, some sincere, others malevolent. It developed a system of organization and training which gave a professional supervision to chaplains' work and prepared a large number of men for usefulness in an emergency. During a part of this period more chaplains were on duty than ever before in peacetime. Their activities demonstrated the value of what they could do for the public welfare should the need arise.

Supervision of chaplains' activities by a chaplain was not wholly without precedent. In the Spanish army of the 16th century, companies numbered about 250 men, and each had its chaplain. The *tercio* was composed of from 6 to 12 companies and had a supervising chaplain at headquarters. Samuel Moody has been called the chief of chaplains of the Louisbourg expedition of 1745. Beverley T. Lacy supervised the work of both chaplains and missionaries in the army of Stonewall Jackson and acted for headquarters in the procurement of additional chaplains. When two or more chaplains were assigned to the large regiments of the First World War, it was natural that the senior should take the lead in coordinating their work within the unit. Supervising chaplains in divisions were designated in the spring of 1918 by order of General Pershing. Usually they were the senior chaplains of the group, but one instance is known in which a National Army chaplain with a short period of service as a first lieutenant was named division chaplain although there were Regulars with longer experience among his associates. When Francis Duffy was made division chaplain, he was not separated from his unit but continued as regimental chaplain.[1]

A part of Pershing's plan for the administration of chaplain affairs in 1918 was that there should be an administrative chaplain's office at the headquarters of the American Expeditionary Force. Early in that year he asked Bishop Charles Brent, who was in France as a special agent for the Young Men's Christian Association, to work out a plan of organization for the chaplains under his command. Bishop Gwynne, Deputy Chaplain General of the British forces, visited headquarters at this time and explained the administrative system used in the British Army. Several of its features were adopted for the American plan.[2]

The general favored an arrangement by which the chaplains would have formed a corps with Bishop Brent at its head, but the bishop convinced him that a better plan would be the appointment of a permanent executive committee of chaplains to study conditions and make recommendations direct to the general. It is significant that this committee included a Catholic chaplain, a clergyman of a Protestant church with the episcopal plan of organization, and one of a body which follows the congregational system. Among their duties were the assignment of chaplains to units and installations in the European Theater, visits to chaplains in the field, investigation of situations affecting the moral welfare of the troops, and supervision of the Chaplains' School in France.[3]

As chairman of this group, Brent was frequently called the Chief of Chaplains of the American Expeditionary Force. He used this title himself in 1924, and it is inscribed over his tomb at Lausanne. As he had no military status when he planned this organization and was asked to administer it, he was recommended for appointment in the grade of lieutenant colonel. Legal restrictions would not permit this, but he was commissioned a major in the Adjutant General's Department, though his personal record is in the usual form—"major and chaplain."[4]

A modification of this administrative system was continued among

---

[1] Sir Charles Oman—*A History of the Art of War in the Sixteenth Century*, pp. 59, 70; Fairfax Downey—"Yankee Gunners at Louisbourg," *American Heritage*, Feb. 1955, p. 54; Henry Kyd Douglas—*I Rode with Stonewall*, editor's note, p. 373.

[2] Lee J. Levinger—*A Jewish Chaplain in France*, p. 74; George T. McCarthy—*The Greater Love*, p. 75; Francis P. Duffy—*Father Duffy's Story*, p. 98.

[3] John J. Pershing—*My Experiences in the World War*, I, 283; Duffy, *op. cit.*, p. 254; Levinger, *op. cit.*, p. 141; Alexander C. Zabriskie—*Bishop Brent: Crusader for Christian Unity*, p. 127.

[4] *Ibid.*, pp. 124, 197; Personal file, OCCh.; Hearing on S. 853, 24 Mar. 1939, p. 5.

the occupation troops after the Armistice.   As senior chaplain of the American forces, Edmund Easterbrook coordinated the activities of American chaplains and maintained helpful cooperative relations with the chaplains of the British, French, and Belgian armies.[5]

So fully did the supervision of chaplains' work by chaplains demonstrate its value during the war that it was included with slight opposition in the reorganization that followed.   Chaplains with important administrative functions were placed in the headquarters of such territorial organizations as corps areas and military districts and of divisions and higher tactical units.   They had their place in the National Guard and organized reserves, and when the Civilian Conservation Corps was established, a measure of supervisory responsibility was placed upon the senior chaplain in each district.   Three chaplains with years of experience in that corps told very similar stories of their relations with a Regular chaplain who returned from an oversea assignment and became their superior.   He began by prescribing detailed rules for carrying on their work in situations he knew nothing about, insisting upon some methods which did nothing but limit their activities and leave them with a sense of irritation at being thwarted in their normal programs and treated without ordinary courtesy.   Fortunately, such bureaucracy among supervising chaplains seems to have been very rare.

Early in 1936, Army regulations governing efficiency reports forbade any chaplain except the Chief of Chaplains or the commandant of the Chaplain School making a report on another chaplain.[6]   Doubtless this rule grew out of the fear that a chaplain's judgment might be warped by sectarian prejudice.   It ignored the fact that a chaplain would be professionally capable of a more penetrating evaluation than would any other officer.   An old Army story tells of the chaplain who challenged a low efficiency rating with success on the ground that the rating officer was not competent as he never had come to hear him preach.   Few commanders have been as frank as the colonel who said, "Chaplain, I have given you a high efficiency rating because I suppose you have been performing your duties, though I have no idea what you are supposed to do."   Chaplains' judgment may be fallible, but it is seldom biassed along sectarian lines.   What a chaplain of a widely different faith said of one administrator might have been said of most others: "He leans over backward to avoid any favoritism to his own group."

---

[5] Reports, OCCh.
[6] W. D. Circular No. 1, 2 Jan. 1936; AR 600–185, 7g.

If the supervision of chaplains' activities by men of the same profession enhanced efficiency in lower echelons, it followed logically that a central administrator would benefit the chaplaincy as a whole.   This opinion was stated by William Y. Brown in 1863 but contradicted by George Waring in 1912.   The latter feared such an arrangement would hamper individuals and cause friction.   During the First World War a colonel in the office of the Adjutant General was in charge of chaplain procurement.   Though a courteous gentleman with a high respect for spiritual values, he made no pretense of a professional understanding of chaplains' problems.   By contrast, chaplains for the Navy were chosen and supervised by a chaplain with many years of experience.   A Senate bill which seems to have reflected the fear of sectarian bias would have established a commission of three, representing the major faiths for the administration of chaplain affairs.   This was changed in conference to provide for a single chief of chaplains and became a law on 4 June 1920.   He was to have the rank and pay of colonel during a 4-year term, and his chief duties were to investigate the qualifications of candidates for appointment and supervise the work of chaplains.[7]

The first Chief of Chaplains was appointed on 15 July 1920. Eight others have followed him.   Two were reappointed, and three were retired for age before the completion of the normal 4-year term. Their average age at appointment was about 57.   They were: John T. Axton, Congregationalist, 1920–28; Edmund P. Easterbrook, Methodist, 1928–29; Julian E. Yates, Baptist, 1929–33; Alva J. Brasted, Baptist, 1933–37; William R. Arnold, Catholic, 1937–45; Luther D. Miller, Episcopalian, 1945–49; Roy H. Parker, Baptist, 1949–52; Ivan L. Bennett, Baptist, 1952–54; Patrick J. Ryan, Catholic, 1954—.

A proposal that the chaplains be established as a corps was favored by General Pershing.   Advanced by the War Plans Division in 1917, it was approved by the Secretary of War, but Congress took no action at that time.[8]   A bill to establish such a corps passed the Senate in 1920, but this provision was voted out of what finally became the National Defense Act of that year.[9]   Subsequent legislation used the phrase "Corps of Chaplains," and this could be interpreted as establishing the corps by implication.   So could the Act of 21 November 1941 "To constitute an Army Chaplains' Corps with a brigadier gen-

---

[7] 41 *Stat.* 769.

[8] Zabriskie, *op. cit.*, pp. 125, 132; Hearing on bill "To Increase the Number of Chaplains in the Army," 16 Apr. 1924, pp. 36–38.

[9] Bill S. 3792; *Congressional Record*, 20 Apr. 1920, Vol. 159, pp. 5898, 7844, 7916; 41 *Stat.* 769.

eral as Chief" had not the specific provision for a corps been deleted from that part of the bill governed by the enacting clause.   The Officer Personnel Act of 1947 and the Army Organization Act of 1950 leave no doubt that the chaplains no longer constitute a corps, if they ever did.[10]   This question involved some practical considerations.   For years it was urged that an enlisted branch of the Chaplains' Corps should be established so that assistants might be especially trained for this service as an army career.

Few developments between the great wars were more important to the army as a whole or to the chaplaincy than that of the reserve components.   From earliest times militia chaplains were chosen locally, many of them for a single year, though some were reappointed.   The rule that only those Federally recognized could be called into Federal service tended to establish high standards for chaplains of the National Guard.   For years they were encouraged to apply for a parallel commission in the Officers Reserve Corps.   By 1933, nearly 94 percent of the National Guard chaplains held this dual status.   As this actually made an individual a part of two units which could be on duty simultaneously, it tended to confuse the organizational plan and was forbidden by AR 140–5, 16 June 1936.   To make them eligible for certain duties in time of peace, Federally recognized officers of the National Guard were authorized by AR 130–15, 1 November 1934, to apply for Federal commissions in the same arm and grade in the National Guard of the United States.   They could be appointed to a higher grade in this service only after a corresponding promotion in the National Guard.   In 1939, a change in this regulation provided that if a vacancy existed in the National Guard of the United States, those with proper qualifications might retain their commissions in that component after the termination of their National Guard status.

More than 100 candidates graduated from the Chaplain School after the Armistice and were commissioned in the Officers Reserve Corps.   Chaplains of the National Army discharged in the following months were invited to apply for appointment in the Regular Army or Reserve under requirements less exacting than if they had been without experience.   For several years, regulations specified that Reserve chaplains without previous service must be college and seminary graduates between 21 and 60 years of age.   In 1931, the upper limit was reduced to 35.   The Chief of Chaplains reported that procurement was hampered by this change.   At that time the list of Reserve chaplains showed 220 Methodists, 188 Presbyterians and an equal number

---

[10] 55 *Stat.* 779; 61 *Stat.* 884, 885, 912; 64 *Stat.* 267, 270.

of Episcopalians, 182 Catholics, and 154 Baptists.   These 5 groups
contributed 77 percent of the total, and the remainder was divided
among 15 other bodies, each of which furnished 75 or less.   The records of later years show minor changes in these proportions and the
inclusion of men sponsored by several other groups.[11]

The pacifist movement, which seems to have reached its height in
the early 30's, had an especial bearing upon the chaplaincy.   Impressed by the horrors and destructiveness of war, many clergymen felt
that they as individuals and the church as an institution must renounce
all connection with what was often called "the war system."   They
urged that a religious ministry to the armed forces should be provided
through civilian clergymen with no military status and supported from
private funds.   This propaganda led some Reserve chaplains to resign
their commissions and discouraged many young clergymen from applying for appointment.   Some churches announced that they would
sponsor no more chaplains, and others debated such a move.   By 1931
there were indications that an increasing number of thoughtful men
who saw the full implication of this movement were applying for Reserve commissions in an attempt to offset its dangerous tendencies.   In
December 1938, the Federal Council of Churches declared impracticable at that time the plan to replace chaplains with civilians and urged
the churches to keep in closer touch with their chaplains.[12]

Training plans for chaplains during the years between the great
wars had three major purposes.   One was to introduce the men appointed to the Regular service without previous experience to the organization and usages of the Army.   Another was to acquaint Reserve
chaplains with military institutions and policy so that they might be
ready for useful service in case of an emergency.   A further purpose
was to inform men of all components of changes in these matters and
to give them an opportunity to learn some of the newer techniques
which might be very useful in their work.   In times of peace it was
possible to consider all these subjects more thoroughly than under the
pressing necessities of war.

The old plan of placing new chaplains in the office of an experienced colleague for some months was narrowly limited and seldom
gave them a balanced introduction to their new duties.   In November
1919, a board of 5 chaplains, including 3 who had been active in training during the war, was convened in Washington to consider training
plans.   This group recommended the establishment of a permanent

---

[11] *The Army Chaplain,* Jan.–Feb. 1932, *et seq.*
[12] *Ibid.,* Jan.–Feb. 1932, p. 5, Jan.–Feb. 1939, pp. 86–88.

school to conduct a 5-month basic course twice each year and to develop an advanced course later. It was stated that such a school would help chaplains to serve men of other denominations, train them as Army officers so that they could mingle with others on an impartial level, save them from embarrassing blunders by teaching them Army regulations and customs, prepare them to serve as defense counsel through an acquaintance with military law, give them the benefits to be derived from the experience of older chaplains and the fellowship of men of different faiths, help to rid individuals of mannerisms and defects and to standardize activities on a high level, and give chaplains an appreciation of the military institution and its history.[13]

Orders for implementing the board's recommendations were issued on 28 January 1920, and the school opened at Camp Grant, Ill., on 15 May with a staff of 5 chaplains and 10 other officers and a student body of 15. All chaplains commissioned since 1 January 1913 except graduates of the wartime school were eligible. AR 350–150, 20 September 1920, outlined the course of study and provided that the commanding officer of the post should be commandant and a chaplain selected by the War Department would serve as director. Twenty-one subjects were named in the curriculum, a total of about 280 hours of instruction. Major emphasis was placed upon matters of general military importance, and the remainder was divided between those related directly to the chaplain's work and exercises valuable for physical conditioning.

Several proposals for modification of the curriculum were advanced from time to time. One officer urged that more time be allowed for subjects which chaplains would use in their everyday duties. Another advised more time for equitation and instruction in the Spanish language. A prominent chaplain advocated the inclusion of pedagogy, religious education, public speaking, and military history and strategy. Only minor changes resulted from these recommendations. The course was extended to 6 months in 1922, and 11 Regular chaplains studied Spanish in a class taught by another student. Later sessions were about 3 months long, and the last 2 did not exceed 6 weeks.[14]

The school remained at Camp Grant during four sessions but was moved to Camp Knox, Ky., in the summer of 1921. Two classes were

---

[13] Par. 40, SO 256–0, WD, 1 Nov. 1919; CofCh to Wait C. Johnson, 29 Dec. 1921 *et seq.*, File 352, OCCh.

[14] File 352, OCCh., 1921 *et seq.*

held at that post, but a transfer to Fort Wayne, Mich., was made in the early autumn of 1922.   After 3 sessions here the school was moved to Fort Leavenworth, Kans., where 5 were held.   So few chaplains could attend that the course was offered only once each year, and biennial classes were proposed.   Six students attended in 1926, 2 the next year, and only 1 was available for 1928.   Two chaplains and 20 officers of the Command and General Staff Schools gave the instruction at that time, and the commandant declared it a waste of energy for so many to "shadow box with one student."   The director recommended that the school be closed unless more students could be obtained. Earnest effort could produce only 1 Regular and 11 Reserve chaplains for a short term in 1928.   Though the chaplains stationed at Fort Leavenworth were considered the faculty of the school for years and worked on extension courses, instruction for resident students was not offered again.   Eleven sessions of the peacetime school were held, and a total of 189 students attended.   At least 20 of these were Reserve chaplains.[15]

Section 127a of the National Defense Act of 4 June 1920 authorizes the assignment of officers to civilian schools as students.   Acting under this provision, the Chief of Chaplains from time to time has selected men to attend prominent universities to supplement their professional education in some practical field or to qualify for important special assignments.   Such plans were hampered by the scarcity of funds, but the Chief of Chaplains was able to effect an arrangement with the University of Chicago and the Catholic University of America by which he could send men to these institutions for only $60 a year.   It was decided that four men be sent to a university each year, including all of those newly appointed to the Regular Army; but 4 years after this policy was announced by one chief, it was abandoned by his successor, who was convinced that greater benefit would be derived from this schooling after some years of service with troops.[16]

This plan included the establishment of initial training centers at Fort Sheridan, Ill., and Fort Meade, Md.   It was intended that newly appointed chaplains would be ordered to one of these posts at least 3 months before the opening of the term at the nearby university.   Here they would study an intensive program based on the correspondence course and gain practical experience under the direction of older chaplains.   It was expected that they would visit the fort and perform some

[15] *Ibid.*

[16] CofCh to TAG, 24 Nov. 1930, *Ibid.*, and to all chaplains who had attended civilian schools, 12 Mar. 1935, File 210.66, OCCh.

chaplain duties regularly during their year at the university. Three men new to the service were sent to Fort Sheridan in August 1931. They listened to informal lectures and visited military institutions for about 6 weeks before the opening of the university. During the year they regularly conducted services at Fort Sheridan. One chaplain arrived at that post in December 1932 and went to the university in two weeks. The next year one arrived in time to conduct services on four Sundays and visit many installations before entering the university. This seems to be all that ever came of this plan.[17]

Twenty-five chaplains studied in some civilian school during the 1923–41 period. All took a full program for 1 academic year except 4 who took less and continued their regular duties, 3 who attended part of the year, and 1 who took evening courses after a full year of study.[18] One Chief of Chaplains believed it very important that his colleagues should be versed in the newer psychological techniques but warned against a materialistic viewpoint and stressed the reality of human choice and divine inspiration and guidance. His successor said that he was disturbed because some schools had become so ultra-modern that graduates of conservative institutions attending them became confused and did not remain long enough to think their psychological and spiritual problems through to an intelligent conviction. He added that he saw few evidences of enhanced usefulness in the later records of men who had taken these advanced studies. On the other hand some chaplains of mature judgment declared that they were greatly benefited by this schooling and earnestly recommended that this policy be continued.[19]

Adequate training for Reserve chaplains was a very different problem. Among them were bishops, professors, secretaries, and pastors of large and small parishes. Many were veterans and graduates of the 1918 school. Others were appointed later and had no military experience. Most of them were very busy, and some found it all but impossible to be away from their regular duties for many days at a time. Some shared the high confidence of the early 20's that aggressive militarism had been so discredited that extensive preparations for defense were unnecessary. To them military training seemed a waste of time and effort.

For several years chaplains and other Reserve officers continued

---

[17] *Ibid.,* Feb.–May 1931; personal file of A. V. Simoni, 1931–32; reports of Elmer E. Tiedt, OCCh.

[18] CofCh to TAG, File 210.66, OCCh., *passim.*

[19] *Ibid.,* 1935, and to Harry C. Fraser, 11 Jan. 1933, personal file, OCCh.

in good standing and had expiring commissions renewed under very lenient conditions. However, it was soon realized that this would not develop and maintain a staff of efficient officers, and minimum training requirements were set up for those who would remain eligible for assignment and active duty. Some chaplains gained valuable experience through brief periods of active duty in summer training camps. The plan contemplated at least 2 weeks of such duty each summer, but funds were seldom available for all who wished to attend, and some volunteered to serve without pay. Many Regular chaplains conducted brief schools for Reserve chaplains near their stations, but the chief agency for the military education of chaplains of the civilian components was the correspondence course developed by the Chaplain School and administered by the corps areas and comparable units.[20]

This course as first announced in 1924 included Practical Duties of Chaplains, American Political Institutions, Military Sociology, and six common subcourses prepared by other branches. In 1929 a much more comprehensive course was divided between subjects appropriate for the study of first lieutenants and those intended for captains. For several years a list of books on psychology, government, and military history was recommended for the reading of chaplains of field grade, and one requirement for promotion to the grade of lieutenant colonel was a certificate that at least six of these works had been read. In 1941, a partial series of subcourses for majors was published.[21]

The announcement for 1931 is typical. Subcourses primarily for first lieutenants allotted 65 hours to Practical Duties of Chaplains, Office Organization and Administration, Welfare and Recreation, and Burials and Graves Registration, while 100 hours were given to military subjects such as Administration and Military Law. Captains were expected to devote 78 hours to Military Sociology and the Rules of Land Warfare and Military Government and 58 to common subcourses. Though other subcourses replaced some of these from time to time, the course retained this general character until extension course work was suspended early in 1942.

The perplexities inevitable in the preparation of lesson material in a rapidly developing field are vividly shown in the story of the subcourse called Military Sociology. These lessons carried 60 hours of credit and leaned heavily toward the psychological background of the subject. Forty books were listed for study or comparative reading, and

---

[20] File 352, OCCh., *passim.*
[21] *Ibid.,* 1924 *et seq.;* Tr. Cir. No. 25, WD, 5 Apr. 1941.

some lessons gave specific references to as many as seven of these. Some of these works dated from the beginning of the century and were not in agreement with more recent concepts and interpretations. To clarify the situation, the Adjutant General recommended that Munson's *Management of Men* be adopted as the sole text, but the Chief of Chaplains argued that psychology can never be an exact science and that chaplains are capable of studying different points of view and forming mature conclusions for themselves. The director of the school favored the proposed text, and this was approved after 4 years of experience with this subcourse.[22]

For 3 years nothing was done to carry out the new plan, then a later director undertook to revise the course. For the next 6 years he reported his progress annually or the reasons why none had been made, then a new director undertook the task. Selecting four recent books for study, he began work enthusiastically, only to be hospitalized with an inflamed and badly swollen foot. This untoward event delayed work on the lessons for some weeks but gave rise to the camp joke of the year when his jolly Catholic colleague remarked, "That Methodist chaplain with Episcopal leanings is in the hospital with a Catholic disease." The revised lessons were reviewed by a chaplain who had just completed an intensive study of psychology. He reported that several concepts accepted in this course had already been rejected by foremost students in that field. At first the Chief of Chaplains hoped that something could be salvaged from the wreck, but in 1939 he recommended that Military Sociology be dropped from the course.[23] Thus ended ignominiously this academic project which had embarrassed 4 Chiefs of Chaplains and perplexed 4 directors of the school.

Answers to some practical questions grew out of the experience of these years. Special texts were prepared for a number of subcourses for which no appropriate study material could be found. As long courses tend to discourage home study, it was ruled that subjects requiring more than 30 hours be divided, with 20 as the ideal. Lessons requiring 3 hours of work were substituted for shorter ones in the belief that this would be about the time that most students would devote to study in an evening. The best form of examination questions was debated for years. The true-false question was quite generally rejected as requiring very little thought and inviting trick questions.

---

[22] File 352, OCCh., 1926–28, *passim*.
[23] *Ibid.*, 1931–39.

The completion type was favored over the multiple-choice form as stimulating thought and expression, but the Chief of Chaplains argued that mature men should be allowed to express themselves fully through answers of any length.[24]

Another question puzzled many students and some instructors. It was required that solutions to all lessons and examinations bear the student's certificate that he had received no unauthorized assistance. In such a study as Military Law it would be necessary to refer to the *Manual for Courts Martial* for data on which to base a solution. Examinations in some other subjects referred to all texts previously used. This seemed to authorize the student to look up factual material after the examination was before him. No authoritative answer to this question was given till the revision of AR 350–3000 on 30 March 1946 which stated that students in this situation might refer to texts unless a contrary statement appears on the lesson or examination.

During the 18 years before extension work was interrupted in 1942, the enrollment of chaplains increased from 55 to 599. Total credit hours of subcourses completed during the year rose from 1,366 to 27,361. Averaged over several years, 85 percent of the men enrolled were commissioned in the Reserve, 14 in the National Guard, and four-tenths of one percent in the Regular Army. The remainder were civilians or enlisted men of one of these components.[25]

Fiscal Year 1931 stands about midway between the great wars. As some postwar movements were declining and the resurgent militarism of Europe was not yet conspicuous, it may be taken as fairly representative of the period. On 30 June of that year there were 120 chaplains in the Regular Army: 1 colonel, 3 lieutenant colonels, 32 majors, 70 captains, and 14 first lieutenants. These men represented the following religious groups: Baptist 14, Catholic 31, Christian 1, Congregational 8, Disciples of Christ and Episcopal 7 each, Evangelical 1, Lutheran 8, Methodist 26, Presbyterian 12, Reformed 12, Unitarian 1, Universalist 2. They were assigned 11 to Hawaii, 9 to the Philippines, 7 to Panama, 1 each to China and Puerto Rico, 3 to the office of the Chief of Chaplains, 2 to the Chaplain School, 1 to a civilian school, and 85 to posts or transports.[26]

The National Guard had 209 chaplains of whom 170 held Reserve appointments as well. The latter and 1,045 other Reserve chaplains

---

[24] *Ibid.*, 1927–40.
[25] Reports, *Ibid., passim.*
[26] Report of the CofCh, *The Army Chaplain,* Jan.–Feb. 1932, pp. 3–5.

were commissioned in these grades: lieutenant colonel 13, major 112, captain 537, first lieutenant 553.   Thus the total of all components equalled 1,374.   Though 225 of the reserve components had received active duty training during the year, 227 were ineligible for this or for assignment or promotion, 165 of them veterans of the First World War.[27]

No drastic change occurred in these statistics in the following years except in relation to the Civilian Conservation Corps.   Where Regular Army chaplains conducted 19,358 services for 1,943,176 persons in 1936 and civilians ministered to 223,550 in 3,809 religious meetings, Reserve chaplains on duty with the civilian organization reported 5,658,667 persons at 57,916 services conducted by them and 5,503,011 in attendance at 120,399 led by civilians.   During that fiscal year 284 Protestant, 52 Catholic, and 2 Jewish Reserve chaplains had been called to this duty, and 259 were still serving when this report was made.[27]

The Civilian Conservation Corps gave many chaplains their longest period of active duty.   The training value of this service for officers was stressed in early discussions of the project, but any military training for enrollees was meticulously avoided.   While the immediate purpose of the plan was to relieve unemployment during the depression, it was recognized as a promising opportunity to develop many immature boys into honorable and trustworthy citizens.   Education in its broadest sense was the key to the task, and the vital place of moral and spiritual values in the process was recognized from the first.

In a few instances chaplains were assigned to camps where a thousand or more men worked on some large project, but in most cases their duties took them to from 6 to 12 or more smaller camps spread over a large area.   One district 450 miles long had 26 companies and 3 chaplains.   Each drove his own car 2,000 miles a month and visited every camp.[28]   It was more common for each chaplain to serve a number of camps in one part of a district.   In a camp far from the boys' homes or from a town, a chaplain might get a large congregation in the evening or at any time on Sunday.   Others might be almost deserted at those times, thus plans must be adapted to situations.

One chaplain visited seven camps every Sunday.   Another reached four by driving 230 miles, but a colleague gave up the attempt to have any Sunday service before evening.

Concerts, lectures, plays, and many other wholesome programs were brought to camp by the chaplains.   Some gave or arranged

---

[27] *Ibid.*
[28] *Ibid.*, Jan.–Feb. 1937, p. 117, July–Aug. 1939, p. 37.

regular showings of motion pictures.   Before educational advisors were provided, many chaplains organized classes in various subjects, usually teaching some themselves.   One invited those interested to form a class in English composition.   At the first meeting he talked of the importance of such features as coherence and euphony in English prose.   Soon he realized that most men in the group were of foreign birth and wished to learn the simplest conversational English.   One chaplain organized a field meet where 1,500 men from various camps came together in a central city.   The townspeople were gratified by the good order and clean sport as participant and spectator sought to uphold the honor of his camp.   This spirit was carried over into a contest between camps for the highest attendance at religious services.[29]

Individual problems were many and varied.   One chaplain regularly took with him some boy who was homesick or poorly adjusted to his situation.   By the time he had distributed the hymn books and helped shovel through a few snowdrifts, his troubles were less acute. Jack was a veteran who had lost his right to practice law and been left by his family through drink.   One morning the chaplain found him on his bunk in a slovenly attitude refusing to go to work.   Asking if he had mastered his education and been admitted to the bar for nothing, he urged him to get back his self-respect and be a father of whom his family could be proud.   A new expression came into Jack's face.   He gave the military salute and said he would tell the skipper that he would go to work that afternoon.[30]

Unusual situations sometimes developed in this service.   One chaplain spent a month with 1,800 men on an island in Lake Superior fighting a stubborn forest fire.   His message was doubly welcome amid the clouds of smoke.   The Ohio flood of 1937 caught a chaplain with the companies who were building dikes in southern Illinois.   For 3 weeks he was busy incessantly helping civilians to safety, finding food and shelter for those who must remain, and relieving distress in many ways.   The men jammed a church for a service of thanksgiving when the danger was past.   A Vermont blizzard marooned one chaplain in a remote camp.   As miles of road must be shoveled before any vehicles could travel, he continued his rounds on snow shoes.[31]

On 5 April 1938, the Civilian Conservation Corps observed its fifth anniversary.   At that time it was providing almost 5 times as many religious services as the Regular Army and had nearly 4 times as

---

[29] *Ibid.*, Jan.–Feb. 1935.
[30] *Ibid.*, Apr.–May 1934, p. 7, July 1937, p. 62.
[31] *Ibid.*, July–Aug. 1936, p. 17, Jan.–Feb. 1937, pp. 90–96, July–Aug. 1934, p. 13.

many persons in attendance.   During those years, important work had been provided for 2,242,000 men, about 1,800,000 of them between 17 and 21 years of age.   Individuals remained in camp an average of 9 months.[32]   What this experience did for them in physical and mental development or in the growth of character is beyond computation by any human system of statistics.   What it did for the Reserve chaplains was equally intangible but very real.   They learned how to adapt themselves to an infinite variety of situations and to carry on their work without many aids which they would have considered indispensible in a civilian parish.   They came to know a body of young men who were more representative of the youth of the country than any group in any home church.   These factors may have outweighed even the formal training program of the Army when they were called to cope with the perplexing exigencies of war.   Paul D. Moody, a college president with experience as an administrative chaplain in time of war, recommended that theological students serve an internship as chaplains in the Army or Navy.[33]

Strenuous service like that of the chaplains who were on duty with the Civilian Conservation Corps inevitably brought its casualties. Who will say that those who suffered injuries, sickness, or death in line of duty merited less of honor than if this had occurred in time of war? John Marvin Dean, a veteran of the First World War and of prior service in the Philippines, died in November 1935 while on duty in Virginia and was buried in the Chaplains' Plot at Arlington.   Isaac F. Jones, injured in a motor accident while touring his camps, died on 21 December 1936.[34]

The Army Chaplains Association was a voluntary organization of present or former chaplains of all components formed on 25 April 1925 to strengthen faith, morality, and understanding within the Army, to uphold the Constitution, and to promote justice, peace, and goodwill.   In general its officers have been experienced men who were not on duty but who knew the chaplain's problems and needs.   In 1940, the Navy chaplains accepted an invitation to join the Association and support its objectives.   After the separation of the Air Force from the Army in 1948, the organization was renamed The Military Chaplains Association of the United States of America.   It was incorporated by act of Congress on 20 September 1950.   In many ways this group has exerted an intelligent and wholesome influence to im-

---

[32] *Ibid.*, Oct.–Nov. 1938, p. 72.
[33] *The Army and Navy Chaplain,* Jan.–Feb. 1941, p. 3.
[34] *The Army Chaplain,* Jan.–Feb. 1936, p. 15, Jan.–Feb. 1937, p. 17.

prove the status and equipment of chaplains and enhance the effectiveness of their work.[35]

American experience has been helpful to some allied and friendly powers in developing a chaplaincy similar to that of the Army of the United States. In 1936, President Quezon chose Edwin Ronan to organize and train a corps of chaplains in the army of the Philippine Commonwealth. He was a veteran of the First World War who had learned chaplain administration under Bishop Brent in France. The President explained to the Chief of Staff of the Philippine Army that he expected a proportionate number of chaplains to represent the Roman Catholic majority, the Independent Philippine Church, and the Mohammedan and Protestant groups and that complete religious freedom should be maintained. Four of these chaplains were reported missing in action in the desperate fighting early in 1942. Three were Catholics and one an Anglican.[36]

This interbellum period began in the enthusiasm of victory and the joyous confidence that free peoples would never again be forced to defend their possessions and institutions with arms. Gradually a shadow spread over these hopes with the rise of new tyrannies less scrupulous than the ancient royal houses. Many clergymen who had hoped for the best realized that they must be prepared for disappointment and be ready to do their part if another emergency should arise. Extreme concepts of independence were sacrificed to efficiency, and a system of administrative chaplains was established. Reserve components were developed and trained. Thousands of boys who were called when the crisis came had learned in the conservation camps that the chaplain was their friend. The religious bodies of the country had recognized that their chaplains were carrying on a vital part of the work of the church and deserved encouragement and support. The Reserve chaplains themselves could see that another great war, should it come, would mean both opportunity and responsibility for them. When the emergency did come, a substantial number of capable and dedicated men were ready to meet it.

---

[35] *The Military Chaplain,* Spring 1950, p. 2, June–July 1955, p. 24.
[36] *The Army Chaplain,* Jan.–Feb. 1937, p. 101; *The Army and Navy Chaplain,* Apr.–May 1942, p. 2.

CHAPTER XIII

Nine Thousand Men

When the United States was precipitated into war by the attack upon Pearl Harbor on 7 December 1941, the situation differed greatly from that of April 1917 when the country entered the first world struggle. On the earlier occasion, American involvement had not been anticipated by large numbers of people, and few preparations were made until after the declaration of war. The beginning of hostilities in 1941 found many training camps in operation and a large army well advanced in its basic training.

In the summer of 1940 there were 137 chaplains in the Regular Army. Of about 1,000 Reserve chaplains, 770 were eligible for active duty, and 145 of them were serving with the Army and about 100 with the Civilian Conservation Corps. Only half of the remainder were qualified for duty. During the next year many appointments were made in the Officers Reserve Corps, but a law of 22 September 1941 authorized temporary appointments in the Army of the United States. By the day of Pearl Harbor, 140 chaplains of the Regular Army, 298 of the National Guard, and 1,040 Reserve chaplains were on duty, a total of 1,478. A number of eminent and influential men who held Reserve commissions were discouraged from going on active duty in the belief that they were more useful in their civilian positions than they could be in the Army. When two chaplains were elected bishops, the Chief of Chaplains secured their release from military service to accept these positions with some difficulty. He disapproved for the same reason when another bishop requested active duty, adding, "What would the AG think if I went to him and reversed all the arguments I used to get those other men relieved?" [1]

In selecting clergymen for service as chaplains, the primary objective was to provide satisfactory services of worship and other religious observances for the greatest possible number of military personnel. Soon after the First World War a system of proportionate quotas

---

[1] 55 *Stat.* 728; Data supplied by CofCh.

had been established.   Based upon the religious census of 1916, these apportioned 98.2 percent of any authorized number of chaplains among 22 religious bodies.   The remainder could be allotted to smaller churches or distributed among the larger groups as circumstances might require.   Naturally the small number of chaplains of the Regular Army came from a few of the larger churches when selected on this basis, but appointments in the Reserve Corps were made without reference to quotas.   This left some bodies with less than a normal proportion of Reserve chaplains, in some instances because the strength of the pacifist movement in these groups had discouraged their ministers from accepting appointment.   The established quotas were the basis for requests to the various churches and for appointments during most of the war.

The 1936 religious census, published in 1939, showed important changes in the numerical strength of some churches, though the matter was complicated by the varying methods of computing membership used in different bodies. The revised system of quotas shown in the following table was authorized by the Secretary of War on 1 May 1945.[2]   It apportioned 7,887 men, who constituted 92.79 percent of the total, among 40 named groups.   These churches had 7,920 on duty on 2 September 1945, the large excess of chaplains over the quotas of a few of these bodies reflecting the greater numbers asked and authorized under the quota system in effect until a short time before this tabulation was made.[3]   Moreover, when it became evident that some churches never would be able to fill their quotas, authority was obtained to appoint as many as 135 percent of the quotas of such bodies as could provide qualified men.

Religious bodies	Quota Percentage	Quota Number	On duty 2 Sept. '45
Roman Catholic	30.46	2,589	2,278
Methodist	11.00	935	1,200
Baptist, South	8.89	756	947
Baptist, Colored	7.20	612	84
Jewish	3.70	315	243
Presbyterian, U. S. A.	3.65	310	426
Protestant Episcopal	2.92	248	298
Baptist, North	2.66	226	412
Disciples of Christ	2.34	199	387
Lutheran, Missouri Synod	2.20	187	215
United Lutheran	2.13	181 }	374
American Lutheran	2.11	179 }	

[2] File 320.2, OCCh.
[3] Statistical tables furnished by CofCh.

Religious bodies	Quota Percentage	Quota Number	On duty 2 Sept. '45
Congregational Christian	2.00	170	305
Evangelical and Reformed	1.37	116	69
Latter-Day Saints	1.07	91	34
African Methodist Episcopal	.90	77	73
Presbyterian, U. S.	.88	75	138
United Brethern	.73	62	60
African M. E. Zion	.73	62	18
Churches of Christ	.63	54	30
Christian Science	.57	48	24
Colored Methodist Episcopal	.46	39	10
Evangelical	.42	36	46
Reformed in America	.37	31	43
United Presbyterian	.35	30	51
Greek Orthodox	.30	25	3
Conservative Brethren	.30	25	1
Assemblies of God	.29	25	34
Seventh-Day Adventists	.27	23	2
Church of the Nazarene	.27	23	42
American Baptist	.24	20	*0
Latter-Day Saints, Reorganized	.19	16	1
Federated Churches	.18	15	0
Christian Reformed	.16	14	17
Free Will Baptist	.16	14	*0
Salvation Army	.15	13	28
Primitive Baptists	.14	12	1
Russian Orthodox	.14	12	0
Friends	.14	12	3
Unitarian	.12	10	23

*Included among other Baptists

The 7.21 percent not included in the foregoing table allowed 613 to be obtained from other sources. At the end of the war, 221 of these were on duty, representing the following religious bodies:

Religious bodies	On duty 2 Sept. '45
General Association of Regular Baptist Churches, North	14
Independent Fundamental Churches of America	15
Methodist, South	1
Bible Presbyterian	9
Norwegian and Danish Evangelical Free Church	1
Pentecostal Holiness	4
Brethren, General Conference	1
Brethren, Progressive	1
Brethren (Old Constitution)	1
Church of God (Indiana)	11
Church of God (Pennsylvania)	1
Foursquare	4
Reformed Episcopal	2
Cumberland Presbyterian	20

Religious bodies	On duty 2 Sept. '45
Orthodox Presbyterian	6
United Grace and T. E. A.	1
Universalists	10
Advent Christian	7
Baptist General Conference of North America	6
German Baptist	1
Seventh-Day Baptist	4
Swedish Baptist	9
Evangelical, Free	5
Christian and Missionary Alliance	28
Evangelical Missionary Covenant	23
Associated Reformed Presbyterian	9
Free Methodist	13
Wesleyan Methodist	7
Evengelical Congregational	3
Moravian	3
Presbyterian Church in Canada	1

These tables show a total of 8,141 on duty at the time of the Japanese surrender (Roman Catholic 2,278, Jewish 243, Protestant 5,620). This included 124 Chaplains of the Regular Army. At some time between the beginning of the emergency on 9 September 1939 and the surrender on 2 September 1945, a total of 9,117 chaplains had been in service, 8,896 of them during the period of actual war.[4] Counting a few who had not yet reported for duty, it was reckoned that the 8,171 in service or under orders in July of 1945 were the greatest number of chaplains who can be said to have served at any specific time during the war. As the Army then numbered about 8,200,000, the proportion of chaplains had almost reached the 1 to 1,000 ratio recommended by the Chief of Chaplains.[5]

The Acts of 3 June 1916 and 12 May 1917 had authorized 1 chaplain to each 1,200 personnel of the coast artillery, and this ratio was made general by the Act of 25 May 1918.[6] The Chief of Chaplains urged that 1 be provided for every 1,000 of the troops to be raised for the Second World War. From 1 September 1941 till the end of the war, the number of chaplains authorized increased from 2,000 to 9,000 in 1943, but decreased to 8,500 in 1945. The percent of the authorized number on duty or on orders varied, as the quota was changed several times, but it reached 97.83 on 30 June 1944, when only 7,750 were authorized, and was 95.78 at the end of the war.[7]

---

[4] Statistics furnished by CofCh, *Army and Navy Chaplain*, Oct.–Nov. 1945, and to the author, 30 Jan. 1956.

[5] Army strength given by Chief of Military History.

[6] 39 *Stat.* 176, 40 *Stat.* 72.

[7] Records, OCCh.

A comparison of these tables shows vividly a problem for the procurement agencies of the cooperating churches. The progress of the war brought changes in general military plans, including the size of the Army necessary for success. The number of chaplains needed by this force would vary correspondingly, and this would change the quotas of the religious groups. In 1943, when 9,000 chaplains were authorized, several churches put forth extreme efforts toward filling what seemed impossible quotas. Later decreases in the authorized total brought these goals nearer. When the new percentages were established in 1945, some bodies found themselves with a surplus already in service, but others saw their objectives farther away than ever.

The experience of the Military Ordinariate in trying to supply the number of Catholic chaplains asked by the War Department parallels that of several other accrediting agencies and illustrates the problems with which many had to deal. In 1942, the Chief of Chaplains stated that he never had enough Catholic chaplains to fill requisitions. To emphasize the need a few months later, the Ordinariate declared that half a million Catholic men did not have the services of a Catholic chaplain. Early in 1943 there were 1,284 on duty against a quota of 2,250. Within 8 months the total was increased to 1,884, which gave a temporary surplus of 9 over the new quota. At the end of the war 88 percent of the quota, or about 5.8 percent of the Catholic priests in the continental United States, were in the Army.[8]

Two problems of procurement grew out of the variant meanings given to the term "Catholic." Several churches or parties called Catholic are not affiliated with the Church of Rome. Among these are the Old Catholics, Anglo Catholics, Polish National Catholics, and the Eastern Orthodox bodies often called the Greek Catholic Church. Manifestly it would be inappropriate for the War Department to deal with the clergy of these groups through the Military Ordinariate of the Roman Catholic Church. This left them among the Protestant bodies whenever a classification did not go beyond a grouping according to three major faiths. Thus the term "Catholic" came to be restricted to the Roman Catholic Church, while all other Christians were sometimes referred to as "Protestant." The other question resulted from the fact that there are in this country a number of Roman Catholic congregations accustomed to worship by other than the usual Latin rites. When some priests of the Greek rites applied for appointment as chaplains, it was decided that it would be impossible for them

---

[8] File 080, Military Ordinariate, 1942–43, OCCh.

to minister to any number of men accustomed to this ritual, as the few in the Army would be widely scattered and must find their spiritual leadership in chaplains of the Latin rites.[9]

More than half of the Jewish rabbis in the United States offered their services, and 311 were appointed chaplains in the Armed Forces. About four-fifths of these were in the Army. The Jewish Welfare Board had a large part in making selections and assisted the chaplains' work in many ways. Though some rabbis questioned the adequacy with which the Board and the chaplains recommended by it represented all branches of American Judaism, these matters were adjusted without serious difficulty to the War Department. Very few regiments contained enough men of Jewish faith to warrant the assignment of Jewish chaplains, and the usual practice was to attach one to the headquarters of a division or comparable unit or installation. In this way they were able to provide the distinctive services of their faith for a fair proportion of Jewish soldiers, often with the assistance of civilian rabbis or chaplains of other faiths.[10]

Several problems are suggested by the names of the religious bodies listed in the preceding tables of quotas. Those which represent differing plans of Church administration have a bearing upon procurement methods but little relation to the practices and objectives of chaplains at work. Several emphasize a distinctive rite, and others are broadly liturgical in their worship. Chaplains of these groups have found no difficulty in providing both the special observances of their faith and more general forms of worship as the inclination of their men might require. Similarly the War Department did not find it necessary in the selection of chaplains to consider distinctions such as those implicit in terms like "liberal" and "fundamental." Among the reasons for this attitude are the fact that the respected and useful clergy of several of the largest churches differ in this type of belief from one extreme to the other and the conviction that these questions do not concern the usefulness of a chaplain in a way to make them proper bases for selection.

Further reference to the table of quotas will reveal a number of significant facts. One of these is the 790 chaplains authorized to Negro churches and the fact that only 174 were in service at the end of the war. While it must not be forgotten that other churches furnished

---

[9] *Ibid., passim.*
[10] File 080, Jewish Welfare Board, OCCh.

many Negro chaplains, the fact remains that these four groups filled only 22 percent of their combined quotas. This shows the impossibility of providing all Negro units with chaplains of their own race. In many instances white chaplains were assigned, some commanders insisting that this was preferable if the other officers were white. A chaplain was apt to be embarrassed if he found himself the only Negro in a group of officers, and it was believed that this fear deterred many qualified clergymen from entering the chaplaincy. Notwithstanding these considerations the Chief of Chaplains was convinced that normally a Negro chaplain could serve Negro troops more acceptably than any other and arranged for such assignments whenever possible. During the war he modified the educational requirement in such a way that many Negro ministers who had been barred by previous regulations were able to qualify. When the question of providing Negro Catholic chaplains arose, the Chief of Chaplains stated that it was not practicable because he did not know of a Negro regiment in which as much as 2 percent of the personnel were of the Catholic faith.[11]

A similar problem was presented by a number of churches to which proportionate quotas were accorded. Among these were the Christian Scientists, the Friends, and two branches of the Eastern Orthodox and of the Mormon churches. These organizations observe rites or emphasized principles so different from those to which the majority of Americans are accustomed that a serious question arose concerning their ability to minister effectively to persons not affiliated with their respective groups. This question was especially important because the comparatively few adherents of these churches were dispersed so widely in the Army that a chaplain of any of these faiths would find it impossible to bring together any considerable number of coreligionists at any time. It was argued, however, that all chaplains perform many important services which are totally independent of the faith they profess or that of the men they serve and that, whenever possible, every soldier should be able to consult a chaplain of his particular faith in situations of special importance. Although quotas were established for these groups, none of them filled more than a small fraction of the places authorized. The general practice throughout the Army was to attempt to provide the rites and worship of any faith group when a considerable number of men requested them. If this could not be done by obtaining the services of a chaplain of some other

---

[11] File 080, Negro Churches, OCCh.

unit or of a civilian clergyman, the men frequently were transported to churches outside the camp.

In 1942 the War Department organized an all-Greek battalion and authorized a Greek Orthodox chaplain. Although the Chief of Chaplains immediately asked Archbishop Athenagoras to select a suitable candidate and repeated the request several times, nearly a year passed before a man of proper age and physical condition with a sufficient knowledge of the English language could be found. A similar problem arose in 1943 when the 442d Infantry was organized. The Japanese Americans who composed this famous regiment were largely Buddhist in faith, and the Buddhist Mission of North America was asked to furnish a chaplain. After a considerable effort Bishop Matsukage found it necessary to report that he was unable to find a qualified candidate among the limited number of ministers connected with his mission. Later, two Christian chaplains of Japanese descent were assigned to this regiment and one to the Hawaiian Department.[12]

It early became evident that detailed quotas could not be proportioned to the demonstrable opportunity for chaplains to serve men of their particular faiths. This was true not only of the bodies just mentioned but of the Protestant groups in general. Naturally, this raised the question of the justification of the quota system when extended to a large number of the smaller churches. Virtually all Protestant chaplains regularly conducted services of worship so free from sectarian characteristics that the great majority of Protestant soldiers could participate without any sense of inadequacy. Many chaplains, especially those of the liturgical churches, supplemented these services with others in which their particular ritual was used.

The training and conviction of some chaplains led them to give a special emphasis to certain practices or doctrines. In some instances these were outstanding tenets which their churches had been organized to maintain, but many of the same beliefs or customs received a corresponding emphasis from chaplains of other groups. Manifestly it was impossible to arrange quotas that would give every doctrine of this nature its fair degree of emphasis and opportunity. Beyond such considerations lay the fact, more fully recognized than in the past, that religious ministration to military personnel is as much an obligation as a privilege of the religious organizations. Proportionate numerical quotas satisfied those who feared that their group might receive less

---

[12] File 080, Greek Orthodox, *passim*, Buddhist, 26 Mar. 1943, OCCh.; *Chaplains of the Fifth Army*, p. 81.

than its share of opportunity and stimulated those who were slow in assuming their due portion of responsibility. Viewed in this light, these quotas are justly proportioned to the size of the respective religious bodies in the total population rather than to the number credited to them in the Army.

Several important qualifications for appointment to the chaplaincy are prescribed by law. Those required of applicants for commissions in the Officers Reserve Corps, The National Guard, and the Army of the United States parallel but are less exacting in some particulars than those demanded of candidates for the Regular Army. This follows naturally from the expectation that the latter will serve the Army for many years under the conditions either of peace or of war, while the anticipated service of the others would be largely in a time of emergency when conditions would force into the background various matters which are considered important in normal times. In December 1941, AR 605–30 specified that an applicant for original appointment in the Regular Army must be—

a. A male citizen of the United States.
b. Between the ages of 23 and 34 years.
c. Regularly ordained, duly accredited by and in good standing with some religious denomination or organization which holds an apportionment of chaplain appointments in accordance with the needs of the service.
d. A graduate of both 4-year college and 3-year theological seminary courses.
e. Actively engaged in the ministry as the principal occupation in life and be credited with 3 years' experience therein.

Except for a few appointments early in the war, virtually all chaplains selected from civilian life during the period of hostilities were commissioned in the Army of the United States—the comprehensive term which included the Regular Army, the National Guard, the Officers Reserve Corps, and much besides.

Unless terminated sooner, these appointments were to continue until 6 months after the end of the emergency. Some received temporary promotions in the Army of the United States without vacating their prior permanent grades in the Regular Army or some other component. In some instances these were possible because requirements were less exacting than in the case of other appointments. These requirements were modified in some particulars as the exigencies of

war made this necessary.   They can be understood best when compared with the qualifications demanded of applicants for appointment
in the Regular Army.

The rule that chaplains must be male citizens of the United States
was challenged in two particulars.   When the Women's Army Auxiliary Corps was established, it was urged by an organization of women
ministers and by individuals that the training schools for these women
and any large units in which they might be organized be served by
female chaplains.   It was contended that they would be able to understand more fully the particular problems which would confront
this group of military personnel.   In opposition, it was pointed out
that the possible assignments for female chaplains would be extremely
limited and apt to be temporary.   When an informal inquiry at their
training camps showed that very few of the young women desired
female chaplains, the matter was carried no further.   When the need
for chaplains became acute, the citizenship rule was modified and the
appointment in the Army of the United States of citizens of cobellig-
erent and friendly powers was authorized.[13]

Where the applicants for appointment in the Regular Army in
1941 had to be between the ages of 23 and 34, the corresponding limits
in the Officers Reserve Corps were 24 and 42.   Though the disparity
in these minimums might be interpreted to imply that holding a commission in the Reserve Corps requires greater maturity than service in
the Regular Army, it is believed to be a survival from the time when
most newly appointed chaplains of the latter component were sent to
a university for a year of specialized instruction.   The Act of 4 June
1920 permitted the appointment to the Regular Service of men under
the age of 58 who had served as chaplains during the First World War,
and the act of 3 April 1939 placed the upper limit at 45.[14]   As this
statute was permissive, it did not bar the War Department from placing the upper limit at 34 by executive authority.   Appointments in the
Officers Reserve Corps were suspended early in 1942, but those made
subsequently in the Army of the United States were subject at first to
the same age limits.   The maximum was raised several times during
the war until it reached the age of 55, but only a few men over 50 were
appointed.

The rule that chaplains must be regularly ordained caused little

---

[13] File 210.4, OCCh.; TM 16–205, 1944, p. 11.
[14] 41 *Stat.* 769; 53 *Stat.* 557.

difficulty in normal times, as the churches entitled to quotas for the Regular Army all observe this rite in dedicating their men to the clerical office.   In the case of churches which ordain to higher and lower orders, it was invariably interpreted to mean the major or holy orders which in the usages of the specific church would qualify a man to discharge the full pastoral office.   When the need for chaplains during the war opened the door for their appointment from many of the smaller church bodies, some were included which follow the practice of ordaining their ministers only after they have demonstrated their pastoral ability and have been called to a parish.   This would bar from the chaplaincy some young men who might be as well educated and experienced as men in other churches who already had qualified for ordination.   On 12 August 1941 the Chief of Chaplains stated that he felt the licenses of such men were practically the equivalent of ordination and that they should be considered eligible for part-time service with the Civilian Conservation Corps as contract clergymen.[15] However, this judgment could not be applied to the qualifications of applicants for the chaplaincy, which were specifically fixed by law, and ordination according to the usages of a responsible religious body continued among the positive requirements.

At the first glance, being accredited by and being in good standing with some religious organization seem different ways of stating the same qualification.   However, the former has been interpreted to include much more than a certification of the latter, and in some instances chaplains have functioned for considerable periods under an indorsement from a church in which they were no longer in good standing, possibly having transferred their membership to another organization.   The first legislation prescribing such indorsement is the Act of 17 July 1862, which requires testimonials of good standing and a recommendation for appointment from some authorized ecclesiastical body.   This implies certain qualifications at the time of initial appointment but is silent about any review of these matters at a later time.   The Act of 3 April 1939 required no more.[16]

AR 140–25 in 1941 directed that the accreditation of Reserve chaplains be recertified annually, that those changing their religious affiliation obtain a new indorsement from the church of their present membership, and that those failing to maintain accreditation be reported to The Adjutant General for appropriate action.   As a matter

---

[15] File 080, OCCh.

[16] 12 *Stat.* 594; 53 *Stat.* 557.

of policy indorsements were accepted only when a candidate or chaplain had been a member of the accrediting church for a year. Periodic recertification could not be required of the chaplains of the Regular Army, but the quotas of various churches were so small that if a chaplain were to change his church affiliation he might bar further appointments from his new church for a considerable time. On 28 June 1941 the Chief of Chaplains stated his conviction "that a reasonable compliance with moral obligations would require that, if a Regular Army chaplain desires to change his religious affiliation and does so, he should resign his Regular Army commission and compete for reappointment . . . with other candidates representing the church of his new allegiance." [17]

As it was necessary for thousands of clergymen with no previous military experience to be selected for the chaplaincy during the war, their initial indorsement was a very important step in the process of procurement. The agencies through which the various religious bodies gave this certification were still more important, for they often served as the link between the government and the churches in dealing with other vital matters. The Military Ordinariate of the Roman Catholic church, headed by Archbishop Spellman of New York with Bishop O'Hara as auxiliary, was the indorsing agency for that church. Recognizing well in advance the magnitude of its task and aided by experience during the First World War and later, when it had been ably directed by Archbishop Hayes and Chaplain Waring, it not only made discriminating selections among candidates but was able to induce many priests to apply. Under the leadership of Dr. Cyrus Adler until his death, and afterward of Dr. David de Sola Pool, the Jewish Welfare Board obtained the applications of many able rabbis of the various branches of American Judaism and accrediated a group of well-qualified chaplains.

A similar agency acting for the many branches of Protestantism would have been a strong unifying factor among them and a great help to the Government. The General Committee on Army and Navy Chaplains, which had continued since its establishment early in the First World War by the Federal Council of the Churches of Christ in America, attempted to meet this need as far as circumstances would permit. On 11 June 1940 it held a meeting to which were invited the representatives of all organizations concerned with the indorsement of chaplains for the Army or Navy. The response was so en-

---

[17] File 080, General Commission, OCCh.

couraging that the body was reconstituted as the independent General Commission on Army and Navy Chaplains. During the war years the successive chairmen were Dr. Weaver, Bishop Leonard, Dr. Pugh, and Bishop Sherrill. The directors were Dr. Moody, Dr. Devan, and Bishop Lee. Of these gentlemen, Bishops Sherrill and Lee and Drs. Moody, Pugh, and Devan had been chaplains in the First World War. The Commission was the primary liaison between the Government and about 40 churches. These included all but one or two of the Protestant bodies numbering more than a million members and represented the vast majority of American Protestants.

While the Commission acted as the accrediting agency for some of its constituent bodies, this function of necessity involved a large measure of cooperation by some agency in most of the member churches. Several preferred to deal directly with the War Department, though they continued to support the Commission as a very useful agency in other matters and as a splendid example of interchurch comity. Eleven of the smaller churches had their own accrediting agencies, and others indorsed through the commissions of some larger cognate bodies. Thus the Northern Baptist Convention acted in this way for five groups, the American Council of Christian Churches for four, the National Association of Evangelicals, the Congregational Christian church, and the Methodist Church for two each, while the Presbyterian church in the United States, the Evangelical and Reformed Church, the United Brethren, and the Presbyterian Church in the United States of America each performed this service for one other body. All members of the Synodical Lutheran Conference of North America accredited their chaplains through the Missouri Synod.

Notwithstanding the apparent definiteness with which the educational requirement for chaplains was stated in Army Regulations, it left a number of practical questions unanswered. Graduation normally implies the awarding of academic degrees, and for the convenience of brevity it was frequently said that candidates must hold the A. B. and B. D. degrees or their equivalents. Little difficulty resulted from the fact that some reputable colleges awarded the B. S. or Ph. B. degrees for programs of study emphasizing science and mathematics or modern languages instead of the classics traditionally associated with the A. B., while other schools gave the latter degree for study in any of these fields. A different problem appeared when an applicant's primary degree was definitely in some professional field, such as education or law, and represented a combination of cultural and professional courses.   If his transcript of credits showed a serious deficiency in any of the subjects considered essential to every liberal education, the examining board was authorized to require him to pass written examinations in these fields.[18]   The fact that some institutions give diplomas but not degrees emphasized the necessity of dependence upon actual transcripts of credits.

More serious was the problem of men educated in foreign countries where cultural attainments were hard to measure by American standards.   In 1940, the Chief of Chaplains stated that the education of Catholic priests is sufficiently standardized in all countries so that the fact of their ordination would be considered evidence of the educational equivalent of the A. B. and Th. B. degrees.   The Jewish Welfare Board early took the position that it would not indorse candidates who proposed to take examinations in lieu of presenting credits.   This brought a protest from the Federation of Orthodox Rabbis of America on the ground that the vast majority of the rabbis of that body could not meet the requirement of the Bachelor's degree or its equivalent, because they never had attended secular schools, though they had studied for the rabbinate all their lives.   It was stated that leading universities recognize this as the equivalent of any college education. However, the Jewish Welfare Board maintained its position that all Jewish chaplains should meet all the requirements set for chaplains in general.   This may have deprived some capable rabbis of the opportunity to serve as chaplains, but it made certain that the representatives of American Judaism as a whole were a group of chaplains well educated by the standards familiar to Americans.[19]

A related question concerned the length of a course of study as an index of its adequacy.   Explaining the usual education of the priests of his church, the Russian Orthodox representative suggested that 6 years of training at a theological seminary after high school should be considered the equivalent of the A. B. and Th. B. degrees. The Chief of Chaplains declined to accept this as a general rule, saying that each applicant must be judged individually.[20]   A Lutheran college and seminary submitted detailed statements of curricula under which students could earn both the academic and the theological degrees in 6 years.   After careful study in the Office of the Chief of Chaplains it was reported that these programs seemed the quantitative equivalent of 7 years of study in many institutions because the aca-

---

[18] AR 605–30, 16 Dec. 1941.
[19] File 080, Military Ordinariate, 8 Apr. 1940, Jewish Welfare Board, 17 Feb. and 3 Mar. 1941.
[20] File 080, Russian Orthodox, 8 and 14 Feb. 1941.

demic year was longer and the curriculum more intensive.   In general, institutions were recognized or otherwise according to their classification in the *Federal Security Bulletin* or the *Christian Higher Education Bulletin*.   Doubtful cases were determined after a careful review of all relevant facts.

Early in the war it could be seen that some churches could not supply their share of chaplains if the high educational standard were to remain unchanged.   As formal education is only one of the necessary qualifications, though a very important one, it was recognized that other abilities might offset deficiencies in this field.   Accordingly the educational and experience requirements were modified together in such a way that either might compensate in some degree where the other was lacking.   Thus revised, the circular of information stated that to be eligible for appointment in the Army of the United States a candidate must be a graduate of a 4-year college and 3-year seminary course with at least 1 year of ministerial experience, of the college with such theological training as his church may require for ordination and 2 years of experience, or of the seminary alone with 3 years of ministerial service.   Because the need for Negro chaplains was especially acute, it was ordered that those who had demonstrated their ability by 3 years of successful ministerial experience should be considered eligible if they could present credits for 60 semester hours of study at a recognized institution.

Some questions grew out the application of the phrase, "actively engaged in the ministry as the principal occupation in life."   Few doubted that it should include ordained men who were professors or administrators of church colleges, but did it include teachers in secular institutions or public schools?   The same uncertainty existed about those employed by benevolent or welfare agencies having little or no church connection.   Most situations of this nature could be met by the rule that these men should be considered to come within the meaning of the law if assigned to these duties by the regular appointing authority of their churches.   When this rule could not be applied, each case had to be judged in the light of the work performed. Student supply pastors whose studies required them to be absent from their churches for several days of the week were credited with half time, but during much of this period 1 year of full-time work was required of all.

In procuring chaplains for the Second World War, the Army had some advantages which were lacking in 1917–18.   About one-eighth of those needed were available in the Reserve Corps and already had some training and military experience.   Most of the churches of the country had standing agencies to deal with matters concerning chaplains.   Not only were these boards or committees of great help in recruiting and screening applicants, but they encouraged and guided their chaplains in important ways after they were in service.   The Army seems to have recognized more fully than in the past the value of capable chaplains.   The church saw its obligation to send its best men where they were needed most.   To the young clergymen of the country the situation clearly meant great opportunity and the imperative of duty.

CHAPTER XIV

Administrative Problems

The most striking change in the organization of American military forces in recent years has been the emergence of the Air Force, first as an autonomous division of the Army, then as a primary defense force on a parity with Army and Navy. What seems to have been the first step in American military aviation, the proposal to bombard Vera Cruz from balloons a century ago, did not get beyond the planning stage. Balloons used during the Civil War were for observation only, and little progress had been made when one was raised over the jungles of Cuba in 1898. The rapid development of the dirigible and of the machines heavier than air gave both a considerable combat importance during the First World War, but the idea that they were useful primarily for observation and belonged in the Signal Corps was slow in yielding to broader concepts.

Before 1941, the importance of air support of ground and sea forces was fully demonstrated, though experience in the European armies had given new vigor to the discussion of the merits of independent administration and unified command. By the Act of 18 December 1941 the President was authorized to redistribute certain government agencies for the more efficient prosecution of the war; and on 28 February 1942 he ordered the reorganization of the Army into the Ground Forces, the Air Forces, and the Services of Supply. This arrangement was to be effective on 9 March and continue until 6 months after the end of the war.[1]

Several problems arose in the adaptation of the chaplaincy to the new organization. A few hints can be drawn from earlier experience with cavalry and artillery units which frequently operated in detached sections. Many Civil War chaplains rode with small parties of cavalry on dangerous missions, often carrying the medical supplies and substituting for the surgeon as well as performing their own services for the wounded. The nature of air combat quickly demonstrated the impossibility of chaplains flying with their men, and it was agreed

---

[1] 55 *Stat.* 838; Executive Order 9082.

that their normal place of duty was at the base.   In this way they could minister to the crews of many planes before departure in a time of active combat and to the wounded at their return.   The Chief of Chaplains discouraged the training of chaplains as pilots, believing that it would divert time and interest from their primary duties.   Instruction in parachute jumping was a different matter.   At times it involved not only the personal safety of the chaplain but his ability to accompany his men in an attack.   Some of the first to land in Italy and France arrived in this way.[2]

Another reason for a separate air force supplied the basis for a parallel argument in favor of an independent chaplaincy.   This was the distinctive psychology of the service.   Like the cavalry of earlier times but to a greater degree, service in the air involved sudden dangers, swift action, instant decisions, dash, and daring.   The unpredictable factors bred fatalism in some and recklessness in others. To meet them on a ground of common understanding, a chaplain must be able to recognize these facts and their implications.   It was considered important that those chosen for duty with airmen should be young, alert, and resourceful.   Equal importance was seen in administration by a succession of supervising chaplains well versed in the characteristics of air service.

To accomplish this, staff chaplains were authorized in the headquarters of all higher echelons of the organization worked out for the Air Forces.   At the head was the Air Chaplain, with important administrative functions.   Charles I. Carpenter assumed these duties on 28 July 1942 and performed them for nearly 3 years.   He was succeeded by Gynther A. Storaasli, who had been director of the school for Air Force chaplains and their assistants.   On 6 April 1942 an Air Force liaison officer was established in the office of the Chief of Chaplains.   During the war he performed the important duties implied by his title.   It was urged with some plausibility that there should be a single administrative chaplain for the Ground Forces and one for the Services of Supply, corresponding to the Air Chaplain.   However, experience showed that the older arms and services presented less complex problems than those resulting from the tremendous growth of the Air Forces, and an intervening link between the headquarters of higher echelons in these branches and the Chief of Chaplains was deemed unnecessary, though he did find it advantageous to designate a member of his staff as Ground Forces liaison officer.[3]

---

[2] File 201.4, OCCh., *passim.*
[3] *Ibid.;* File 029.11, 27 Mar. 1943.

Individual chaplains have always been free to refer their problems directly to the Chief of Chaplains since the establishment of that office.   Many perplexities have been clarified and some faulty situations corrected in that way.   The monthly report, forwarded to the War Department since 1864, has given every chaplain an official channel through which he could transmit information or make specific recommendations to a central authority.   At intervals through the years the report form, long known as Form 3, has been enlarged and made more specific.   Besides classified statistics of his activities, it requires the chaplain to give definite information about such matters as secular duties or deficient equipment and invites comment on other situations relevant to the moral status of the command.   As it passed through the intervening headquarters on its way to the Adjutant General before and to the Chief of Chaplains since 1920, it gave the commanders in each echelon the opportunity to state by indorsement what had been done or to comment otherwise on situations mentioned by the chaplain.

In the normal processing of reports at the various headquarters, they passed under the scrutiny of the supervisory chaplains, who were familiar with chaplains' needs and with the applicable directives.   If a report indicating the need for corrective action reached the Chief of Chaplains without prior indorsements showing that such action had been taken, an inquiry was addressed to the proper headquarters.   In most instances this brought the necessary action or information. Some reports contained statements of facts which the originating chaplains did not intend as complaints.   These might be a lack of equipment which the chaplain considered unimportant or some duty of a secular nature which he was eager to perform and which he felt would not interfere with his primary responsibilities.   In such cases the Chief of Chaplains seldom felt it necessary to press the matter, though he sometimes pointed out that laxity in maintaining a principle by some might react to the disadvantage of others.[4]

Inclosures with a few reports which reached the Chief of Chaplains show that the persons who processed them in lower headquarters had aimed at perfection with more zeal than judgment.   Though his report was not returned for correction, one chaplain was rebuked because he had used ciphers instead of the word "none."   Others were told that they had entered the record of unusual gatherings in the wrong section.   One report was returned for correction because it was dated one day late, as the regulation specified that chaplains should

---

[4] *History of Chaplains' Activities in the Pacific,* p. 105.

report on the last day of the month.   A junior chaplain in a high-level office made a collection of excerpts from various reports, attached a critical comment or question to each, and distributed the list among the chaplains.   No doubt the intent was to promote efficiency, but the men who recognized items which they had written felt that their efforts were being held up to ridicule in ignorance of the actual situations.   Though such transactions were rare, they attracted attention out of proportion to their actual importance.[5]

A Form 3 for December 1945 illustrates several limitations upon the monthly report as a means of gaining prompt action on matters which unit chaplains believe should be corrected.   The originating chaplain recommended more drastic restrictions on the distribution of liquor, stating that 97 percent of the guardhouse trouble was caused by drinking.   Ten weeks after this was written, it was returned for comment by an intermediate headquarters.   Five weeks later the unit commander replied, outlining the methods used to prevent drunkenness, stating that 22, not 97, percent of the offenses which had brought men before courts-martial during 9 months had been committed after drinking, and adding that the chaplain would be reminded of his duty to advise the commander in such matters.   Nine months and a few days after this report was written it was processed in the office of the Chief of Chaplains.[6]

At least three details in this episode are revealing: the chaplain's generality that 97 percent of disciplinary cases were the result of drink, the colonel's rejoinder which implied that 22 was the real figure but ignored the many cases of lesser offenses which did not reach a court-martial, and the statement in the 12th indorsement that the originating chaplain was no longer a member of the unit.   The reason for his transfer is not stated, but it occurred within a few days of the time when the unit commander wrote his defensive indorsement.   Undoubtedly it was wise, as the basis for mutual understanding and cooperation seems to have been destroyed.[7]

A few chaplains seem to have expected a lack of sympathy and cooperation from their commanders.   Their attitude revealed itself at times in an insistence upon their rights regardless of the situation in such matters as equipment or unusual work.   The same men usually felt that the only way to improve conditions bearing upon any form of vice was to force action through the intervention of higher

---

[5] Files, OCCh.

[6] Robert M. Small, Form 3, December 1945.

[7] *Ibid.*

authority.   To insert a real criticism of the unit commander in an official report and insist that it go forward would almost certainly result in hard feeling.   A few chaplains were browbeaten into rewriting a report in which they had made such statements, and others state that they were afraid to make important recommendations lest they precipitate trouble.   In some cases of this nature commanders have investigated the basis for complaints by the chaplain, made such corrections as seemed proper, and forwarded the report with an indorsement showing what action had been taken.   Frequently, supervising chaplains have advised their juniors to inform them unofficially of such situations, and corrective measures have been instituted without embarrassment.   Many more chaplains have found unit commanders ready to meet them more than half way in matters affecting the real welfare of the men and to give friendly consideration even to those proposals with which they might find it necessary to disagree.[8]

Early in the war the officials of several churches asked that their chaplains be allowed to report their activities direct to church headquarters.   While the chief purpose was statistical, these reports gave an opportunity for the chaplain to state his need for supplies which the church might furnish or to complain about policies or conditions which would be of concern to church officials.   At first many chaplains sent an extra copy of Form 3 to their church offices.   It soon became apparent, however, that many of these reports would contain restricted information, and the various churches were invited to prepare their own forms on which their chaplains could report any desired facts which were not classified.   These informal channels proved to be of value to the religious organizations and in many instances brought substantial help to the chaplains.[9]

The reorganization of the Army into the Ground and Air Forces and the Services of Supply and its detailed application to service commands, posts, and similar installations placed the activities of the chaplain and a group of related interests under the personnel officer. This caused serious concern to a number of chaplains who felt that the chaplaincy was being degraded from its coordinate status with other services.   The Chief of Chaplains assured them that their status as staff officers and their right of direct approach to their commanders stated in AR 60–5 remained unchanged.   The new organization was understood to substitute the personnel officer for the adjutant as the

[8] Homer E. Blough, Form 3, Aug. 1946; Hal D. Bennett—"How to Keep a Chaplain," *The Military Chaplain,* Apr. 1951, p. 17; *History of Chaplains' Activities in the Pacific,* p. 106.
[9] TM 16–205 (1941), 73–b; File 080, Military Ordinariate, OCCh., 28 Aug. 1942.

normal channel of approach to the commanding officer, and it was pointed out that this was logical in headquarters like those of service commands where the chaplains were concerned so largely with personnel matters. The ill effects feared by these chaplains do not seem to have materialized.[10]

In a few instances chaplains suffered momentary embarrassment because of confusion about spheres of jurisdiction, either among themselves or in relation to other services. One post chaplain made a direct request to a local volunteer motor corps for transportation for a recreational enterprise but was informed by the camp Red Cross that all such applications must be channeled through that office. Another post chaplain assumed that his office had a measure of control over all chaplains in the camp although two full divisions were stationed there. He was promptly undeceived by one of the division chaplains. The hospital chaplain at the same post, vigorously supported by the senior medical officer, made repeated efforts to obtain a library for the hospital. The post commander, a colonel, was sympathetic but powerless. He had no funds for a purchase of books, and the generals commanding the two divisions in the camp insisted that the libraries in their division areas pertained only to the divisions. This barred personnel of the station complement from the use of the libraries except by courtesy of the divisions and prevented the transfer of any books to the hospital. Then the divisions marched out for extended maneuvers. The colonel sent for the chaplain, told him that the generals were away and the libraries as well as the rest of the camp were under his command, and told him to take the books.

The wide dispersal of antiaircraft troops in the Pacific led to the assignment of chaplains to battalions. Those best acquainted with the situation deemed it a distinct improvement over assignment to regiments. An inspecting officer who studied this situation felt that distances were so great that the administrative chaplains of various commands could not perform their duties adequately and that there should be a supervising chaplain in each brigade.[11]

Another important question concerned the assignment of chaplains to serve those minority groups which differ widely in belief and practice from the large religious bodies. Early in the war there was a serious deficiency of Jewish chaplains. Those available were attached to camps, corps, and similar units more comprehensive than divisions

---

[10] TC No. 9, OCCh., p. 4.
[11] *History of Chaplains' Activities in the Pacific*, p. 110.

to serve all Jewish men as they were able. The appointment of many Jewish chaplains later made possible less difficult assignments. It was urged that chaplains of the Latter Day Saints be assigned to divisions or corps so that they might minister to the men of their faith scattered through these larger units. Some chaplains of the Christian Science faith were assigned to such major organizations in an at-large status to serve primarily the men of that faith. At headquarters where three or more administrative chaplains were authorized, such as those of important theaters of operations, the usual practice was to assign one Catholic and one Jewish chaplain, in addition to one or more Protestants, with the expectation that each would handle matters of special concern to his faith group as well as his share of general business. At those headquarters where only two were authorized, the usual arrangement was for one to be a Catholic and the other a Protestant. Though this did not give a strictly proportional representation in these positions, it was the only feasible plan for providing a sympathetic understanding of the distinctive interest of the major groups at these important administrative centers.[12]

While the procurement of chaplains was the most conspicuous field of cooperation between the administrators of the chaplaincy and the civilian religious organization, it was not their only important relationship.

Early in 1943, plans were made for visits to the principal theaters of operations by representatives of the chief religious groups. The purpose of this project was twofold. Much value was seen in the encouragement which soldiers and chaplains far from home would derive from the messages of friendship and confidence to be brought by these religious leaders. It was further recognized that they would bring back to the religious people of America reliable information about moral conditions in the Army and what was being done for the spiritual welfare of their sons. At first when facilities for transport and accommodation were severely burdened, it was planned to send only representatives of the three major faiths and of the Negro churches. Later it was possible to adopt a more liberal policy.

The first of these extended tours was made by Archbishop, afterward Cardinal, Francis J. Spellman, Military Vicar of the Roman Catholic Church. Already he had visited many chaplains in the home country and in Canada, Alaska, and the Aleutians. Early in 1943 he began a journey which covered 46,000 miles and lasted for

---

[12] *Ibid.*, p. 404ff; Howard G. Badger, Form 3, July 1946; *Story of Christian Science Welfare Activities*, p. 179.

24 weeks, visiting the British Isles, North Africa, Egypt, Persia, Madagascar, and South Africa.   Later he made a similar visit to the Pacific Area.   Wherever he went he was greeted with enthusiasm as a messenger from home and addressed large groups of soldiers.   In conferences with chaplains and commanding officers he was able to clarify a number of practical questions involving the relations of the Army and the church.   His account of his experiences, published soon after his return, was widely read and made a valuable contribution to public information and opinion.[13]

Though Archbishop Spellman had declined the services of a military aid, some of the other clergyman who made such visits were glad to accept this form of help.   In April 1943 Bishop Adna W. Leonard, Chairman of the General Commission on Chaplains, went to Great Britain as a first step in the visitation of the camps and battle fronts. He was accompanied by Chaplain Frank L. Miller, head of the Planning and Training Division in the Office of the Chief of Chaplains. After visiting a number of installations in Great Britain, they flew to Iceland with General Andrews.   Attempting a landing in the fog, the plane crashed into a rocky hill, and all members of the party except one enlisted man were killed.   Chaplain Miller was held in a very high esteem by all who knew him for his sterling character and unfailing kindness, as well as for his executive ability and devotion to duty.

Dr. William Barrow Pugh, a chaplain of the First World War, was chosen to succeed Bishop Leonard as chairman of the General Commission.   In a short time arrangements were made for him to complete the tour of visitation begun by Bishop Leonard.   His military aid was Deputy Chief of Chaplains George F. Rixey.   Rabbis Barnett R. Brickner and Phillip S. Bernstein, successive chairmen of the committee on Army and Navy activities of the Jewish Welfare Board, made similar visits to the chief areas of military operations with Chaplain Aryeh Lev of the Office of the Chief of Chaplains as military aid.   Several other prominent churchmen visited the troops overseas during or soon after the end of hostilities.

The visits of Bishop John Andrew Gregg, representing the Fraternal Council of Negro Churches of America, elicited unusual interest, and he and his message of encouragement and inspiration were welcomed heartily by Negro and white troops alike.   With Chaplain John A. De Veaux as military aid, he made an extended trip through Australia and the Pacific and later toured military installations in Europe, Asia, and Africa.   He published a delightful narrative of his

[13] Francis J. Spellman—*Action this Day, passim; History of Chaplains' Activities in the Pacific,* p. 502.

journey, spiced with humor and brightened with an unfailing goodwill toward all he met.   In North Africa a piece of his baggage containing his travelers checks and toilet articles was stolen.   He exclaimed, "Well, I declare!" but found other means of getting along.   He was deeply gratified by the fairness with which he saw Negro soldiers treated wherever he went.   The color line was first encountered in Natal, where the law would not permit his accommodation at a hotel. Local authorities were perplexed by the necessity of complying with the law and of showing proper courtesy to a representative of the American President.   Finally it was arranged that he should go to a missionary hospital maintained by American Congregationalists, where he was welcomed cordially.   He delighted his host by remarking that it was very appropriate that he should go to a hospital because, after traveling around the world, he had discovered that he was suffering from "an incurable case of malignant pigmentation." [14]

One relationship of great importance between the chaplains and the civilian churches grew out of their interaction in the development among the men of organizations which were branches of those already existing within the churches or were sponsored to a considerable extent by them.   Several of the large churches had young people's societies pertaining exclusively to one body.   Though the objectives and methods of all were much the same, none of these would have been appropriate for general organization among young men with such varied religious affiliations.   So far as they concerned work among Protestant men, the alternatives were to form local units of a society already operating in various churches and independent of sectarian lines or to organize a new movement primarily for service personnel which would be equally inclusive.   Both plans were followed to some extent and with a good measure of success.

The Catholic problem was simpler.   The Holy Name Society offered a helpful means of mutual encouragement in moral and spiritual growth to men of that faith.   This movement began in 1274 when Gregory X directed the Dominican Order to preach greater respect for the holy names as a means of improving the low standards of faith and morals of the period.   Introduced into America more than a century ago, it had demonstrated its social as well as its spiritual values.   Its specific demands of its members were that they abstain from profane speech, observe Sunday and days of obligation, and take communion together once a month.   This emphasis upon the outward forms of reverence inevitably reacted to deepen its inner

[14] John A. Gregg—*Of Men and Arms, passim.*

sources, and the organization readily adapted itself to other forms of wholesome activity.   The formation of units of the society by Catholic chaplains was actively encouraged by the Military Ordinariate. Early in 1942 there were 125 at various military stations and more than 50 were being organized.   Two years later the good accomplished by the spread and activities of this movement was widely recognized.[15]

Early in the war while the bulk of the Army was still in the training camps, a movement named the Guardians of America was launched by Chaplain Cohee and others.   It was not narrowly religious in the sectarian sense but was designed to unite all men in a common fellowship and deepen their appreciation of and devotion to the cause in which they were enlisted.   As character building was the supreme purpose, the program sought to capture interest wherever it might be found and direct it toward higher things, using to this end a variety of hobbies such as archery, wood carving, radio, or debating.   This movement served a useful purpose, especially during the training period.[16]

The Society of Christian Endeavor had several advantages for work among the armed forces.   It had been carrying on these activities to some extent for half a century, and it had no affiliation with any particular church.   This freed it from narrow sectarian commitments but did not impair the vital idealism of its purposes and methods.   As its units had been functioning for years in many local churches of several of the large religious bodies, it would be easy for soldiers from those churches to unite in such a society in camp.

Leaders of the organization were not slow in recognizing the opportunity.   Devotional and other literature was provided, including a handbook for chaplains wishing to form local societies, and soldiers who had belonged to chapters in home churches were urged to help their chaplains organize units in camp.   Chaplain Alva J. Brasted, former Chief of Chaplains, consented to act as Army representative of the Society.   Before the end of 1942 more than 400 units had been organized in the armed forces.   The Society of Christian Endeavor was rapidly gaining a place in the esteem of service personnel which would make it the outstanding organization of its kind in the postwar church.[17]

Splendid as were the aims and principles of this great organization, a number of religious leaders saw limitations which would keep it from performing the fullest possible measure of service and proposed an or-

---

[15] John T. Tracy—"The Holy Name Society," *Army and Navy Chaplain*, July–Aug. 1942, p. 8; Cf. *Ibid.*, July–Aug. 1944, p. 6.

[16] *Ibid.*, July–Aug. 1942, pp. 1–2, 10.

[17] *Ibid.*, Apr.–May 1942, p. 13, July–Aug., p. 6, Oct.–Nov. p. 9, Jan.–Feb. 1943, p. 3.

ganization wholly of service personnel and adapted to the conditions under which they live. During the Civil War the Young Men's Christian Association organized the United States Christian Commission, the chief civilian agency for religious work. In the War with Spain an attempt was made to revive this commission, but the name soon gave place to that of the parent organization. The "Y" had continued to function as one of the welfare agencies, but its religious activities sometimes were overshadowed by its social program. Moreover, these organizations did things for the soldiers. The recognized need was for some form of association of soldiers who would do things for themselves and for others.

During July and August 1942, representatives of the General Commission on Army and Navy Chaplains, the Federal Council of Churches, and the International Council of Religious Education worked out plans for the Service Men's Christian League. Bishop Adna W. Leonard, Chairman of the General Commission, had a major part in this work and has been called the father of the League. At this point occurred a splendid act of magnanimity. Dr. Daniel A. Poling, president of the World Christian Endeavor Union, became convinced that the greatest ultimate good would be accomplished through unanimous support and threw the full weight of his great society behind the new organization. He declared that the Christian Endeavor welcomed the coming of the Service Men's Christian League and would serve with the new organization, the Holy Name Society, and the agencies of every faith as they ministered to the men who were battling to save America. The new organization was announced on Armistice Day, Dr. Poling himself making the address in which its program and objectives were described. It was estimated that the sponsoring agencies represented 90 percent of the Protestants of the country.[18]

From its earliest inception it was emphasized that the League was to be a subordinate agency to help the chaplains in their work. The founders adopted the following statement of purpose:

1. To offer to the chaplains of the armed forces a program for men on active duty, which may be used at their discretion.

2. To provide a means of Christian fellowship, devotion, evangelism, and education for the purpose of fortifying the serviceman's Christian life.

3. To assist the man in service in maintaining his church

---

[18] *Ibid.; Military History of the Second World War: The Corps of Chaplains*, p. 140.

affiliation and to prepare him for Christian citizenship in his community, nation, and world when he returns to civil life.

4. To provide for the chaplains and the men in the armed services such helps—devotional, evangelistic, educational, and organizational—as may be required to enable the Service Men's Christian League to fulfill its ministry for Christ.[19]

In planning the qualifications to be required of members, the organizers of the League found themselves in a dilemma. A statement so general that it could include the "liberal" groups would seem meaningless to some of the stricter bodies. On the other hand a definite evangelical emphasis with its usual implications would have seemed a perpetuation of errors and mistaken values to many. A compromise statement would have satisfied the extremes neither of right nor left, and many chaplains and civilian leaders would have felt that the League did not stand for enough to merit vigorous support. In this situation it was agreed that an auxiliary membership should be offered to those who were unwilling to sign a statement including a personal acceptance of Christ.[20]

One of the first projects undertaken by the League was the publication of *The Link,* a monthly periodical for members and other service men. It combined religious and instructive material with other forms of literature to make a broad cultural appeal to the young men in uniform. Later a chaplain's bulletin was undertaken. This was named *The Chaplain* and was published monthly with the cooperation of the General Commission. Besides the four interfaith groups which sponsored the League in the beginning, the National Council of the Young Men's Christian Association, the United Council of Church Women, and about 40 church bodies gave financial or other help to these enterprises.[21]

A few chaplains felt that the League program in their regiments demanded too much of their time and effort, but the great majority looked upon the organization as a great help in accomplishing their work. In some places local units of the society kept religious interest active during periods when the installation had no chaplain. One told of a sunset vesper beside a lake when three young men came forward and dedicated themselves to the ministry. Another described the vital interest which drew a large company to the League tent

---

[19] *Ibid.,* pp. 141–42.
[20] *Ibid.,* p. 143.
[21] *Ibid.*

every night in the week for sociability, games, and a devotional service before "Taps." [22]

These are a few of the more conspicuous ways in which the interaction of the administrative leaders of church and army has operated to help the chaplains and their work.

The Chief of Chaplains never has been content to limit his administrative functions to such material considerations as personnel assignments, supplies, equipment, and funds but has recognized that spiritual needs in some situations may be more imperative than any of these. For years the periodic Circular Letter gave information about directives and policies but always found space for some message of friendly encouragement and frequently referred to other sources of inspiration. During the war years many publications designed to be helpful to chaplains were offered by private agencies for inclosure with the Circular letter.   These varied from poems on a single card to bound volumes. So many inclosures went with 1 month's letter that the whole of letters and inclosures weighed several tons.

During the gloomy days of 1942, morning devotions were instituted in the office of the Chief of Chaplains.   Those members of the staff who chose to do so joined in 5 minutes of reverent supplication for the strengthening of their own spirits and for the welfare of all chaplains.   Men on the distant battle lines knew the hour at which they were being especially remembered with confidence and affection among the immediate associates of their chief.   This practice won the warm approval of the Secretary of War.   The time was changed to noon and extended to 15 minutes, and workers in adjacent offices were invited to join.   A considerable number regularly used a part of their noon hour in this way, and many hundreds participated year by year in special services for such occasions as Christmas and Lent.

One Sunday in December 1944, General Stoner, Chief of Army Communications, called the chaplain on duty in the office of the Chief of Chaplains and offered to transmit messages of encouragement to chaplains in all parts of the world if the Chief of Chaplains would prepare them.   This was at the moment when the Battle of the Bulge was causing keen anxiety to the Western Allies.   The offer was gladly accepted, and for many weeks carefully written messages called Chaplaingrams were flashed around the world on Fridays.   Many a chaplain's Sabbath sermon reflected the confidence and echoed the thought of his chief in faraway Washington.

---

[22] *Ibid.,* p. 142; Hal H. Martin, Form 3, July 1947; *The Army and Navy Chaplain,* Oct.–Nov. 1947, p. 1.

CHAPTER XV

Training for the Great War

About one-sixth of the chaplains who served at some time during the Second World War already were on duty on 7 December 1941. Ten percent of them held appointments in the Regular Army, 20 in the National Guard, and the remainder in the Officers Reserve Corps. Some of the Regulars were comparatively new to their duties. So were a number of the chaplains of the National Guard, while the prior experience of others was limited to brief periods at summer encampments of their units. Among the Reserve chaplains were veterans of the First World War and many who had served with the Civilian Conservation Corps, but a large number had been appointed recently with no prior service. Though some had been studying the Extension Course for years, others had scarcely begun. Moreover, it was evident that many new appointments must be made to meet the needs of the expanding Army. Basic training for the majority and further instruction for others would enhance materially the value of their work.

On 25 September 1940 the Chief of Chaplains recommended the reactivation of the resident school for chaplains, and a detailed plan was submitted the next year. It was decided that the best available place was at Fort Benjamin Harrison, Ind., and the school was activated at that post as of 2 February 1942. Curiously the order read "Fort Benjamin Franklin," but there seems to have been no doubt of its intent.[1] Scarcely was the school in operation before revised plans for the expansion of the Army showed that its capacity must be increased fivefold if it were to perform its mission. No expedient could accommodate so large a group at Fort Harrison, nor was space available at any Army post. Several universities offered to house the school, but the facilities at Harvard proved to be the best obtainable and were accepted. The school graduated its fourth class in Indiana on 10 August and began operation in Massachusetts 2 days later.

---

[1] File 352, OCCh., 9 Dec. 1941, 17 Feb. 1942.

The Harvard location had several advantages, one of which was the cordial and helpful attitude of the university authorities. The great libraries and museums were inspiring to those who found time to visit them, and the historic associations of the old school were frequent reminders of a great past. Every day the students passed the spot where the president of the college, a militia chaplain, led in prayer the troops on their way to fortify Bunker Hill. Drill was on Soldiers' Field, dedicated long ago by the stirring lines of Lowell's "Commemoration Ode." On their way they passed along a street bearing the name of a distinguished chaplain of the Revolution and between buildings where Washington quartered his men and the church in which he worshipped. Assemblies were in the building dedicated to the memory of the Harvard dead of the Civil War.

At first it was necessary to quarter 6 men in the 2-room suites which normally house 2 students, but such crowding was soon relieved as more space could be spared by the university. As messing facilities could not be provided, the students got their meals in public restaurants. The university provided space for offices and classrooms at an annual charge of 30 cents a square foot. Dormitory space cost $3.56 a week for the first 175 students and 75 cents for each man above that number. Other important accommodations were furnished without charge. The 12 sessions beginning in October 1942 had an average attendance of 375 and cost for these facilities about $10.50 a student. The adjutant computed that it cost 4.38 cents to instruct each of the 440 students of the December class for 1 hour.[2]

During 1944 the attendance decreased to less than 200. As military installations were coming to be less crowded, it was determined to move the school to an army post and stop paying rent to a civilian institution. In August of that year it was transferred to Fort Devens, Mass. This made possible such realistic training as ship-to-shore landing and the passage of an infiltration course. In July 1945 another move was made to Fort Oglethorpe, Ga., where the Services of Supply were concentrating their schools. Here the school remained for more than a year. Though each location had its advantages, summer heat in Georgia proved to be as real an impediment to training activities as the snow and frost of a Massachusetts winter.[3]

The first plan for the reactivation of the school proposed sessions consisting of 25 days of instruction, but this was shortened to 4 weeks early in 1942 to conform to the general training plan of the Army. By

---

[2] *Ibid.*, 31 July, 26 Dec. 1942.
[3] *Ibid.*, *passim*.

the end of that year 11 hours of special lectures had been added to the curriculum, and other important subjects were being considered.   The commandant urged that the session be lengthened so that basic matters could be presented more adequately and more time be given to physical conditioning.   The surgeon stated that a less intensive program would reduce fatigue and leave the students with greater resistance to respiratory infections.   By the late summer of 1943 the procurement situation made rapid training less imperative, and it was possible to lengthen the course to 5 weeks.   Soon additional lectures and films crowded the course again, and it was extended to 6 weeks.   Evidently the less intensive program was a boon to some of the students.   The average number of academic failures in the course of 4-, 5-, and 6-weeks' duration varied respectively in about the proportion of 3, 2, and 1.[4]

Four sessions were held at Fort Harrison, 21 at Harvard, 7 at Fort Devens, and 3 at Fort Oglethorpe before the postwar reorganization in January 1946.   So pressing was the need for chaplains during the first year of the school's operation that one class graduated on Saturday and the next began the following Monday.   Frequently new students arrived before their predecessors were able to leave and were quartered with difficulty.   To relieve this inconvenience, sessions were announced to begin on the fifth day after the graduation of the preceding class. This shifted opening dates awkwardly through the week and soon gave place to a schedule by which one term began on Monday and closed on Saturday, the next opening on Thursday and ending on Wednesday.   Later a full week intervened between sessions, and students were directed to arrive 3 or 4 days before the opening date so that their processing might be completed before instruction began.

In the years following the reactivation of the school in 1920, the line officer in command of the post where the school was located was the commandant, and immediate administration was vested in a chaplain known as the director.   This system had worked well in the leisurely years of peace, but emergency conditions in 1942 made a more centralized authority desirable, and a chaplain was made commandant. On 1 December of that year the school became a class I installation. This left the course of instruction under the control of the Chief of Chaplains but gave the commanding general of the corps area where the school was situated a wide authority over general administration.   On 14 April 1943 the War Department established a central headquarters

---

[4] *Ibid., passim.*

for all Army schools at Harvard.   Both of these changes resulted in some interests of the school being merged with those of dissimilar agencies in ways which the commandant believed to be detrimental.[5]

The first allotment of personnel to the school included 14 officers, of whom 6 were chaplains.   The authorized capacity at that time was 75.   When 427 students were enrolled the next year, 33 officers were on the staff.   At first the secretary exercised a wide supervision over the training program, and the duties of adjutant, detachment commander, and supply and medical officers were performed by instructors. Later an assistant commandant and director of training was substituted for the secretary, and a supervisor of training, an adjutant, and an assistant adjutant were appointed.   Some of these officers did some teaching, but their primary duties were administrative.   Five teachers were made assistants to the director of training, and four were named senior instructors in charge of specific courses.   One purpose of this arrangement was to avoid overlapping and to insure a true parallel among sections.   An inspector criticized what he considered an excess of supervision over the work of mature men, saying that uniformity which robbed instructors of their spontaneity and originality was purchased at too high a price.[6]

The number of teachers actually needed for efficient instruction was discussed more than once.   Opinions ranged from the contention that officers should be in the proportion of 1 to every 10 or 12 students to the assertion that abstract ratios are irrelevant but each instructor should teach 2 or 3 parallel sections of his specialty throughout the session.   The latter view was supported by citations of the normal teaching load in civilian colleges and reference to the school in 1918 when instructors had other important duties besides teaching 3 hours a day. During the period when the enrollment approached or exceeded 400, the school was divided into 16 sections.   A different chaplain taught Practical Duties to each section.   Most of them had other classes on some days, and the average teaching load varied from 6 to 8 hours a week.   In the autumn of 1942 one class was so large that there were 31 students to each teacher.   Two years later the enrollment had decreased faster than had been expected, and the ratio of instructors to students was 1 to 6.[7]

---

[5] *Ibid.*, 9 Dec. 1942, 19 Mar. 1943, Aug. 1944; Arthur C. Piepkorn—*A Chronicle of the United States Army Chaplain School during the Second World War: The First Two Years.* Ms, n. d. p. 1.
[6] *Ibid.;* File 352, OCCh., 6 Mar. 1942, 10 June 1943.
[7] *Ibid.*, reports.

During the first sessions of the school, chaplains were needed for duty with troops so urgently that men too old for this service were chosen for instructors.   Only one chaplain in the first faculty was less than 56 years of age.   Most of them were without battle experience since 1918, but some men from the combat areas became instructors during the second year.[8]   Their selection was hampered by the belief that all of the large religious bodies should have representatives on the faculty.   These men acted as centers of more intimate fellowship among the students of their groups and as channels of contact with church agencies.   When an instructor was relieved, his successor was chosen from the same religious body if possible.[9]

When the faculty was enlarged in 1942, the Chief of Chaplains approved a table of organization which authorized field grades for about half the officers.   The next year this was canceled and assignments were made from the bulk allotment of the service command.   In a short time more than two-thirds of the staff and faculty were of company grade.   Among the instructors were men of recognized ability who had relinquished prominent positions in education or other civilian work to enter military service.   Recommendations for the promotion of the more deserving of these men were rejected, one for the fifth time.   Though they did their work faithfully, they could not escape a measure of discontent in this situation.   This prompted the commandant to request a table of organization which would have placed 19 of the 22 officers in field grade.   Though he urged approval as necessary to faculty morale, favorable action was withheld.   The decrease in school enrollment made it possible to transfer some officers to other duties, and a few were relieved to accept important positions in civil life.[10]

For a time students were grouped in sections alphabetically, the senior member acting as section leader.   When advanced instruction was provided for experienced men, they were grouped separately.   For a time rooms were assigned so that senior chaplains would be distributed among those new to the service, as it was believed that they would teach their roommates many things of value through daily association. When these men with prior service were organized in separate sections, they were quartered together.   In February 1943 a new plan of room assignment was adopted as a means of promoting understanding among men of different faiths.   At that time four men were being quartered

---

[8] *Ibid.*, 21 July, 2 Oct. 1943.
[9] *Ibid.*, 9 Dec. 1941, 24 Dec. 1942, 30 Mar. 1943.
[10] *Ibid.*, 24 Aug. 1942, 21 Apr., 16 May 1944, *et seq.*

in most dormitory suites.   So far as it could be arranged, a Catholic, a Jew, a Protestant of one of the liturgical churches, and one from an evangelical body were billeted together.   This plan did much to promote cordiality and personal friendship.[11]

The curriculum as prescribed before the opening of the school consisted of 15 courses varying from 5 to 25 hours and dealing with about the same topics as the extension course.   Equitation was not included, and no specific provision was made for physical conditioning. Significant changes soon were made.   Several short courses dealing with Army routine were dropped, and the hours devoted to Military Law, Map Reading, and Defense against Chemicals were reduced from 65 to 20.   The time saved in this manner was devoted to drill and athletics.   This was primarily for their value in physical development, but these activities became so strenuous that the surgeon blamed the program for a marked increase of skin troubles and injuries.   When this was recognized, the officer in charge adapted the training to the capacity of the students, and broken bones and blistered feet decreased in number.[12]

The transfer to Fort Devens permitted some highly realistic exercises under simulated battle conditions.   Students learned how to leap into deep water and wade ashore, to burrow in the snow, and to creep through wire entanglements and other obstacles.   One incident highly diverting to the students occurred in a drill in personal security during which they were under a quite disquieting fire with live ammunition. After the exercise they turned in their helmets, but one was missing. No one would admit any trick at the sergeant's expense, and a search was made through the trenches.   The helmet was found on the head of a student still lying in a dead faint but otherwise unharmed.

A considerable number of chaplains with prior training and experience were sent to virtually every session of the school.   Primarily this was to prepare them for supervisory duties, but it was recognized that the new citizen army in which they would serve differed in some important respects from the Regular establishment which they had known in times of peace.   Mingling these senior chaplains in classes with men having no knowledge of military affairs soon proved unsatisfactory, though it was argued that they needed the elementary instruction to correct misconceptions.   In 1943 they were placed in separate sections, which constituted 4 of the 16 then composing the school.   Some topics

---

[11] Piepkorn, *op. cit.*, pp. 23, 37–38.
[12] File 352, OCCh., 1 Apr., 1 June, 1 and 31 Aug. 1943.

were treated with more brevity than in the regular course, and a conference for administrative chaplains was added, but the opportunity for free discussion among mature men was the most important change. When the basic course was extended to 6 weeks, a 4-week program for these men with prior experience was established.[13]

There were 8,302 chaplains enrolled in the 35 sessions of the school before the end of 1945, and 8,183 of them graduated. Of the 119 who did not complete the course, 55 were ordered away before the end of the first session. Some of the remaining 64 failed because of sickness or other emergency, but it is estimated that nearly 50 were unsuccessful chiefly for academic reasons. Though the student body was organized in small sections, several or all of these met in one group for instruction in certain subjects. This virtually limited the presentation to lectures and the showing of films. Small classes invited discussion and questions from the students. It is true that the greatest proportion of failures occurred in courses which met in large groups, but it should be noted that these courses dealt with scientific and technical matters quite foreign to the previous education and interest of many of the students.[14]

The proper disposal of men found seriously deficient in their studies was not as simple as in 1918, when candidates could be discharged on recommendation of the faculty. The need for chaplains was so great that men who could not graduate for academic reasons were ordered to duty like the others. A study of the subsequent performance of these men in 1944 showed that their general level of service was very low. Among them, however, was a man who failed in four courses but served well for a year and was rated "Excellent." Another was deficient in five subjects but won high ratings during 3 years and was described by his last commander as the best chaplain he knew. One who had been on duty for 3 years attended the school but failed in four courses. This did not preclude 2 years of efficient service and praise from his superiors.[15] While these examples are exceptional, they show the danger of too great reliance upon formal tests.

More difficult is the evaluation of personality defects which might impair a man's usefulness. In 1942 the faculty agreed that two students lacked essential qualifications and should be discharged, but they were ordered to duty. One who was considered nervously unstable served for 4 years in a combat area where the climate was very try-

[13] *Ibid.*, 6 Jan., 5 and 10 Feb., 19 Mar., 10 Apr., 7 Aug. 1943, 15 May 1945.
[14] *Ibid.*, reports and schedules.
[15] *Ibid.*, 7 Oct. 1942, 26 Aug., 18 Dec. 1944, 9 Feb., 25 June 1945, and personal files.

ing.   He was promoted twice, received a decoration and the highest
efficiency rating, and was recommended for appointment in the Regular Army.   The other served for 6 years.   Several commanders praised
him for certain qualities or habits but mentioned defects, though they
gave him very high ratings as long as he remained on duty.[16]

The school made useful contributions to the training methods of
several foreign armies.   A chaplain of the Free French and three from
the Philippine Army took the course.   A Canadian and two Brazilian
chaplains planned to do so but could not complete the arragements.
The principal chaplains of the Canadian, Brazilian, French, and
British armies or their designated representatives visited the school and
studied its methods during or soon after the war.   These foreign visitors made some helpful contributions from their experience to the plans
and methods of the school.[17]

Different combat arms have distinctive psychological problems
which affect the chaplain's work.   This is especially true of the Air
Force, where fighting conditions sometimes tend toward recklessness
or a degree of fatalism.   The intensive program of the Chaplain
School allowed little time for a study of these matters.   This was considered so important that the Air Force opened its own school at San
Antonio, Tex., in June 1944 to give 2 weeks of special training to graduates of the other school who had been selected for duty with air personnel and a parallel course for enlisted men who were to serve as
chaplains' assistants.[18]

One-third of the course was designed to acquaint students with
the organization and perspectives of the Air Force.   The remainder
was devoted to important practical matters which could not be included in the overcrowded program of the Chaplain School.   Two
instructors taught each subject, with teaching hours varying from 13
to 19 a week as other duties would permit.   Twenty-two sessions were
held, and 1,089 chaplains attended.   Completion of this course was a
prerequisite for oversea assignment.[19]

The course for assistants emphasized the Air Force perspectives
and gave practical training in such matters as choir directing, auto
operation, and office procedures.   Twenty sessions were held, and all
but 6 of the 945 students completed the course.   Seventy-four were

[16] *Ibid.,* 12, 20, 21 May, 2, 3 June 1942, and personal files.

[17] *Ibid.,* 18 Nov., 25 Dec. 1942, 3 Feb., 25 Apr., 25 Sept. 1944, 9 Sept. 1945, 5 Nov. 1947, 13 Aug. 1948.

[18] *Ibid.,* 31 Mar., 12 Apr. 1944; File 210.4, OCCh., 25 Nov., 1 Dec. 1947; *Historical Records of the A. A. F. Chaplain Transition Course,* Ms., OCACh., Vol. I.

[19] *Ibid.,* I and II, *passim.*

members of the Women's Army Corps.   A tabulation of the special qualifications of students shows that 312 were organists, 412 pianists, 570 choristers, and 155 vocal soloists.   An Air Force order prevented personnel trained for duty as chaplains' assistants being assigned otherwise unless declared surplus by the Air Chaplain.[20]

The threatening world situation late in 1940 prompted the War Department to issue Training Circular No. 5, which urged National Guard and Reserve chaplains to attend troop schools and made Regular chaplains available for instructors.   The next year the Chief of Chaplains issued a technical circular for division chaplains concerned largely with plans for local training.   A good number of local schools were conducted.   The chaplains near Boston met at Fort Banks every Tuesday morning for 10 weeks in the summer of 1942.   One division provided 2 hours of instruction on Tuesdays and Thursdays for 2 months, and another had weekly classes during 3 winter months. Many of these local schools used the materials of the Extension Course after correspondence work was suspended early in 1942.[21]

Such a school at Camp Blanding in 1942 ended with an exercise both ingenious and realistic.   All chaplains were provided with maps and other equipment and were required to coordinate their activities to actual troop movements and facts of terrain.   A salvage depot, collecting station, and provost marshal's post were established.   A large number of soldiers, tagged to indicate a variety of simulated wounds, were posted through a wide area, and the chaplains were required to find them and give proper treatment and disposition to all.   This involved selecting a site and laying out a cemetery.   Variety was added by supposed evidence that some men were attempting to desert, and by a gas alarm in the midst of operations.   The final requirement was that chaplains submit burial reports and letters of condolence.[22]

During the early part of the emergency the Chief of Chaplains issued ten technical circulars designed to aid young chaplains in various situations.   The Chaplain's Manual, first published in 1926, was reissued with minor changes in 1937 and 1941.   To combine all of these and other relevant matters in convenient form, the manual was rewritten in 1944.   As the great majority both of chaplains and soldiers had been in the service too short a time for their civilian viewpoint to be radically changed, the manual was written by a Reserve chaplain with long experience in education in the belief that he would understand the mind of the citizen soldier.

---

[20] *Ibid.*, II.
[21] File 352, OCCh., 24 June 1943, 8 July 1944, 14 Aug. 1946.
[22] *Ibid.*, 8 June 1942.

The Chaplain School used a large number of films as teaching material.   During the showing of a medical picture which depicted disease sores and the taking of blood for tests with disquieting realism, one student fainted and needed medical treatment for some time. Notwithstanding this untoward event, belief in the value of appropriate films continued.[23]   *For God and Country* is the title of a picture planned in the office of the Chief of Chaplains but filmed in Hollywood.   Though designed at first for the training of chaplains, it showed religious work in the Army so realistically that it was used extensively by other branches and in many civilian communities.   It was made at less than normal cost through the generosity of both producers and actors.

One of the most striking features of the wartime schools was the indiscriminate mingling of clergymen of many and diverse groups in preparation for a common task of religious ministry.   This can be appreciated only against the background of misunderstanding, distrust, and rivalry which has stimulated and perpetuated the divisions among religious groups.   The close association of students living and working together brought a more adequate mutual understanding of beliefs and practices, of aims and motives.   To some this better acquaintance was a revelation.   In the wartime schools Jew, Catholic, Protestant, liturgist, evangelical, liberal, fundamentalist, and others were thrown into close association.   From this experience many gained a truer concept of the worthy ideals and high devotion which animate all groups and found in it the basis for cordial relations and the practical cooperation so needed in civil life.

---

[23] *Ibid.,* 27 Mar., 26 July 1943, 6 Oct. 1944, 22 May 1945.

CHAPTER XVI

Equipment and Supply

The chaplain who is reported to have said that he was ready for field service if he had a blanket and a hymn book was not representative of the majority of his colleagues. This would be especially true of clergymen of the liturgical bodies who are accustomed to the extensive use of religious symbols and the frequent observance of rites to which various material articles are essential. To some extent, however, practically every chaplain uses some form of professional equipment according to the usages of his church or his personal tastes, and the efficiency of his service depends to a considerable degree upon the availability of such articles when he needs them.

In recent years chaplains have been provided with about the same general equipment as other officers of corresponding rank in the unit to which they may be assigned. The issue of tentage, office and horse furnishings, and similar articles has long been authorized by tables of basic allowances, tables of equipment, and corresponding directives. A significant exception has been that no weapons are provided for chaplains because of the regulation which specifies that they shall not carry them. This rule was intended to conform to the Geneva Convention which names chaplains as noncombatants and protected personnel, though it has been argued with much plausibility that the provision which authorizes medical personnel to carry arms for the protection of the sick and wounded from marauders by implication applies likewise to chaplains.[1]

An inconsistency has been seen in the fact that the chaplain's driver frequently is a member of one of the combat arms and often carries weapons in the field. During the Second World War many chaplains felt that they themselves should be armed for protection against an unscrupulous enemy who often failed to respect the Geneva Cross, the distinctive badge of protected persons. The Chief of Chaplains feared that if armed chaplains were captured, the enemy would punish them for an alleged violation of the Geneva Convention or use

[1] AR 600–40, par. 76; Geneva Convention, articles 8 and 21.

this as an excuse for withdrawing immunities from all chaplains.   On several occasions he found it necessary to remind chaplains in the field of these regulations and the reasons why they should be scrupulously observed.[2]

Until recent years professional equipment and supplies for chaplains have been provided largely from private sources.   The chief exception has been the authorization of a chaplain's fund through which appropriate purchases could be made.   At permanent stations altar guilds and similar benevolent groups frequently provided many useful articles for the use of the chaplain or the furnishing of the chapel. Many times he found it necessary to obtain needed items at his own expense.   During an emergency when many clergymen enter the service direct from civil life, most of them have no equipment suitable for use in camp or field.   Many churches have furnished the most necessary things for their own chaplains, and valuable contributions have been made by benevolent organizations, sometimes interfaith in scope.   The same has been true of a variety of expendable supplies. Before the Second World War the belief that the Army should furnish the basic professional necessities for its chaplains as well as for other professional groups came to be generally accepted, and a beginning was made toward carrying this idea into effect.

The chaplain's outfit is the name which came to be applied to a number of articles designed for field use and adapted to the needs of a majority of chaplains.   The issue of the Chaplain's Flag was authorized before the First World War, but the rest of the outfit was not provided until some years later.   In 1923 the components were a regimental field desk containing a portable typewriter, a folding organ, 300 books of religious and patriotic songs, and chests to contain the books. Soon afterward the Chaplain's Flag was added and the music books became *The Army and Navy Hymnal,* 50 music and 100 word edition. This in turn gave place to the *Song and Service Book for Ship and Field,* 150 copies.   The Chaplain's Scarf was added, and both this and the Flag were provided in different forms for Christian and Jewish chaplains.   At different times the typewriter has been listed as an item for separate issue and as a component of the outfit.   In a few instances chaplains have reported that they have needed parts of the outfit but have requisitioned the whole as the only way to obtain the desired items.[3]

---

[2] Circular Letter, *passim;* TM 16–205, 1944.

[3] *The Chaplain,* WD Doc. 5a (later reissued as TM 16–205): 1926, p. 11; 1937, p. 12; 1941, p. 15; 1944, p. 22; 1947, p. 32.

The changes in the songbooks included in the outfit were made when works better adapted to the needs of chaplains in the field were published. Though a volume of about 300 pages, the *Song and Service Book* was much smaller than the music edition of the *Army and Navy Hymnal*. Necessarily the type was small and the paper thin. A considerable dissatisfaction with this book, too heavy to be carried very far by a chaplain on foot and too small to read easily in a dim light, led the Quartermaster to suspend the purchase of replacements some time after the war, as it was hoped that something better would soon be available.

A small leaflet containing the words of 13 familiar hymns, called *Hymns from Home,* was printed in 1943. Each package of 50 contained one pamphlet with the music. Twelve packages went to each chaplain overseas. The Quartermaster inserted 1 million copies in cartons of emergency rations. Many chaplains used these leaflets in advanced positions until they were worn out or gave them to the men. The initial printing of 3 million copies was quickly followed by an additional 2 million. Soon afterward a different collection was prepared. At the request of the Air Forces, these were printed on blue paper so that they would be less conspicuous from the air.[4]

Some difficulty was experienced with the folding organ, especially in areas where a high humidity caused the wood to swell. The wooden pegs supporting the keys would stick, and notes would continue to sound in spite of all that the harrassed player could do. Among the expedients tried by chaplains on duty in the tropics was the substitution of iron nails for the wooden pegs, enlarging the holes through which they slide with a hot iron, coating them with graphite, and boiling them in oil. The field desk was reported to be needlessly large by some who said those of company size would be easier to carry. The scarf, designed to superimpose a touch of ecclesiastical symbolism upon the uniform, was gratifying to some, but others found it highly incongruous unless worn with other vestments. The Flag was intended to show where the chaplain could be found or where services were being conducted. Later a flagstaff was provided for his car. Sometimes on transports this flag was flown above the colors during services, like the Church Pennant on Naval vessels, though there was no authority for this practice.[5] In the office of the Chief of Chaplains hangs the remnants of a chaplain's flag, a fit symbol of the indomitable spirit with which these men have clung to their posts and done their work even

---

[4] *The Chaplain Serves,* p. 63.
[5] William C. Taggart and Christopher Cross—*My Fighting Congregation,* p. 74.

on the farthest frontiers.   Its blue is faded, its white is soiled, and a third of its length is gone, tattered and blown away by the Aleutian gales.

Early in the Second World War, as was true during the struggle of 1917–18, many chaplains were given articles of primary importance like Mass kits and communion sets by their churches.   Some were not supplied with them or received them only after a long delay; others lost them in the confusion of the battlefront.   The expedients adopted to meet these needs are typical of the resourcefulness of scores of chaplains who found themselves without something which would contribute to the effectiveness of their work.   One bored holes in short pieces of board and used them as communion trays.   Another had no glasses, so cut down and polished 50-calibre shells.   Another used seashells of appropriate size.   Still another describes altar appointments made by a soldier skilled in metal work.   The cross was made from Italian armor plate, mounted on a base constructed from a German range finder.   The chalice was fashioned from a Messerschmitt propeller shaft.   The wafer box and its cover were made respectively from an American and a German shell.   Italian brass, based on British shells, formed the candlesticks.   The whole was described as a striking symbol of the spiritual unity which exists among God's people, whether friends, allies, or enemies.[6]   Such adaptations of the paraphernalia of war to religious ends led more than one chaplain to quote Isaiah 2:4 and Micah 4:3—"They shall beat their swords into plowshares and their spears into pruning hooks."   A chaplain whose church observes communion very frequently wrote:

> My last communion service was held under rather trying circumstances.   It was raining frightfully, and the men stood shivering in the cold damp atmosphere.   We had only a few canteens from which the water had been emptied to use as the cups to place the wine in.   For bread we simply chopped up a bit of crust.   The men sipped the wine from the canteens and broke the bread from a cardboard plate.   But it was a communion service all will remember.[7]

Situations like this soon led to the provision of a portable altar and communion set by the Government and of other articles of a similar nature as speedily as they could be procured and distributed.   One of the early experiments in the adaptability of trucks and trailers to the needs of chaplains in the field produced a vehicle which was de-

---

[6] *The Protestant Voice*, 23 June 1944; *Lutheran Standard*, 12 Feb. 1944; New York *Times*, 3 Feb. 1944.

[7] *Brotherhood and Service News of the Disciples of Christ,* Jan. 1944.

scribed in the following terms: "The traveling church is a model of mobile efficiency.   It consists of a truck and trailer arrangement, with large crosses painted on the sides and back doors to identify it as a religious vehicle.   The ecclesiastical equipment includes a folding altar which may be set up with dignity and decency on the lowered windshield of a jeep; a portable pump organ, weighing 50 pounds; Catholic Mass and Protestant communion kits; bibles, candlesticks and a public address system.   The traveling church can reach about 2,000 people, and its equipment, compact and collapsible, can be on the march on short notice." [8]

Frequently generators were installed so that they could be run by motor vehicles and give power for electric appliances when other sources were not available. The public address systems were helpful not only when crowds were large but when the chaplain had to match his voice against high winds and similar impediments.   It may have been after preparing a traveling church for the road that a chaplain was asked by his assistant, "Sir, didn't Jesus travel lighter than this?" [9]

With the motorization of the Army the chaplain ceased to be a mounted officer except when attached to a mounted or horse-drawn organization.   This made his necessary transportation in the performance of his duties more of a problem than in the earlier days when he had his own horse, assigned or privately owned.   Many have used their private cars on official business.   During the Second World War there were many instances in which chaplains failed to keep appointments because requisitioned cars were late or failed to come.   In other instances helpful commanders assigned a car from the unit pool for the exclusive use of the chaplain only to hear complaints from other officers who had been hampered during busy times by the lack of transportation although the chaplain's car stood idle for long periods. Finally, Circular 81, 1944, authorized a quarter-ton truck and quarter-ton trailer for each chaplain covered by tables of organization and equipment.   Even this did not solve every problem, for chaplains were on duty in situations where the trucks could not be obtained and would have been useless if provided.   For example, some chaplains in Alaska were able to reach detachments of their men only by dog team, airplane, or supply boat making hazardous trips along a rocky coast.

With the construction of many chapels, the equipment of chaplains on posts and stations to a great extent has concerned the furnish-

[8] *Army Day Review,* 4 June 1943.
[9] Christopher Cross—*Soldiers of God,* p. 86.

ing of these buildings rather than of the individuals who served in them.   Many of the earlier structures were provided with ecclesiastical appointments and similar articles through local efforts.   *The Hymnal, Army and Navy* has been issued for use in any room designated as a chapel by proper authority.   Band arrangements of the hymns of all faiths were provided in 1943.   The building of hundreds of chapels in 1941 and succeeding years made imperative the provision of enough furnishings to give these simple structures a dignified and church-like appearance.   Electric organs, altar and pulpit hangings, Bibles, missals, and altar furnishings appropriate for each of the three major faiths were supplied, and numerous other articles have been made available from time to time.   Special purchases at the request of individual chaplains often supplemented the standard equipment supplied to all chapels.

A variety of expendable supplies, especially some items hard to obtain overseas or in isolated locations, were furnished under plans which varied with the movement of troops and the developing supply system of the Army.   Candles, service folders, marriage and baptismal certificates, sacramental wines, and grape juice are typical items.   The selection of the 26 service folders which constitute the series illustrates the meticulous avoidance of all sectarian partiality required by the Chief of Chaplains and observed by his assistants.   Available samples were compared by a representative committee; those submitted by the publishing house of one of the smaller churches were chosen because of superior art work and moderate price; and a chaplain of a widely different church ordered the purchase.   For a time grape juice could be provided only in large containers, with the result that only a part of the contents could be used for the intended purpose.   Experience showed the wisdom of shipping sacramental wine in packages which did not reveal their contents lest the containers should arrive empty. One chaplain proposed that they be labeled "High explosive."

Too much cannot be said in praise of the private agencies which donated a vast quantity and variety of religious supplies.   Among them were many arrangements of Scripture, devotional booklets, and religious periodicals.   To name those great organizations like the Bible societies whose donations were counted in millions would not do justice to the host of small groups and individuals whose smaller contributions were made in the same spirit of helpfulness.   In a few instances, unfortunately, overzealous officers of some of these organizations in raising funds for the support of their work made an improper use of statements by the Chief of Chaplains.   Besides those who had something to sell at a profit, reasonable or otherwise, were some who asked help in obtaining scarce materials for the production of something which they proposed to contribute. In one or two instances when the request came from a reliable organization eager to produce something to meet demonstrated need, the Chief of Chaplains specifically recommended that the necessary materials be allocated.

As the Hebrew or Christian Scriptures are the sacred literature of the three major faiths in America, the provision of these writings for use in chapels and for distribution to the troops became a supply problem of great importance. In former emergencies Bibles and Scripture portions have been donated by private societies, and millions were contributed by such organizations during the Second World War. In addition to complete Bibles in various translations, pocket-size Testaments or other selections were distributed, usually by the chaplains but sometimes by representatives of the societies which supplied them. Some of these were bound in very attractive form and contained maps or other aids. In 1942 one Bible society was printing 9,000 Testaments a day, another 25,000 a week. In 1946, after Army Testaments had been available for 4 years, the former of these organizations supplied chaplains with 22,376 Bibles, 76,828 Testaments, and 86,053 Scripture portions.[10] The oft-told story of the Testament which stopped a bullet and saved a soldier's life probably was the inspiration of a project to place these little volumes between metal covers. The promoters abandoned the project only when experiments by the Ordnance Department demonstrated that the ragged pieces of these plates when shattered by a bullet would be apt to cause a worse injury than the bullet itself.

On 16 October 1940 about 16 million men registered under the Selective Service Act. Ten days later Mrs. Evelyn Kohlstedt, a Christian lady of Ayrshire, Iowa, wrote to President Roosevelt the suggestion that every man in uniform be given a New Testament with an appropriate message from the President. The proposal was not entirely without precedent. In her letter Mrs. Kohlstedt mentioned reading of a similar practice being followed by King George. In 1643 *The Souldier's Pocket Bible,* a compilation from the Geneva version, was issued for the use of Cromwell's troops. On 30 May 1783, Chaplain John Rodgers proposed that Bibles be presented to the American soldiers at the time of their discharge, both for their intrinsic worth and to help dispose of a stock which had been printed during the war by a Mr. Aitkin but which he could not sell without heavy loss in

---

[10] *Arkansas Democrat,* 22 Nov. 1942; Circular Letter, OCCh., 1 June 1947.

competition with those which now could be imported from England. Washington believed this was an excellent plan if it could have been adopted in time.   Mrs. Kohlstedt's proposal received the warm support of the Chief of Chaplains, and authority to put it into operation soon was received.[11]

As there are several excellent translations of the Bible, it was necessary to determine with care the versions to be used.   Single agencies of the Jewish and Roman Catholic faiths could make recommendations for their organizations, but no representative group could act for all of the Protestant bodies.   In this situation it was deemed wise to use the New Testament in the familiar translation commonly known as the King James Version without notes or other aids.   When minor variations in the structure of words were discovered in different printings of this version, the chaplains reading the proofs agreed to follow the style used by the American Bible Society.   Even this did not insure absolute uniformity.   For example, a single adjective appeared in the forms "ahungered," "a hungered," "an-hungered," and "an hungered" in volumes published by this society at various times. A Jewish board made selections from the books of the Law, Psalms, and Prophets sufficient for a volume about the same size as a New Testament.   Catholic authorities recommended an arrangement of daily Scripture readings with notes.   Unfortunately a few of these comments which seemed informative and proper to the editor impressed some readers as tending to create ill will or distrust.   To avoid all chance of giving offense to any person, a new volume containing the four Gospels in the Douay Version was issued.   A later printing consisted of daily readings without comments which could not be objectionable to any reader.[12]

About 11 million Testaments, proportioned to personnel of the 3 major faiths, were printed for distribution to soldiers sufficiently interested to ask for them.   Each contained the following message from the President, dated 6 March 1941:

> As Commander-in-Chief I take pleasure in commending the reading of the Bible to all who serve in the Armed Forces of the United States.   Throughout the centuries men of many faiths and diverse origins have found in the Sacred Book words of wisdom, counsel, and inspiration.   It is a fountain of strength and now, as always, an aid in attaining the highest aspirations of the human soul.

---

[11] File 461, OCCh.; *Cromwell's Soldier's Bible,* reprin , London, 1895; *Writings of George Washington,* XXVII, 1.

[12] File 461, OCCh.

A few objections to this project were made. An atheistic society attacked it as a violation of the constitutional prohibition of an establishment of religion and threatened legal action. A practical objection to the volumes themselves was that they were too large to carry conveniently in the uniform pocket. Later printings were bound in flexible covers which did not protrude beyond the edges of the leaves. Sets of the three Testaments in waterproof containers were placed in the lifeboats of transports. The interest aroused by Captain Rickenbacker's report of the use of a pocket Testament in the group with whom he was adrift for days in the Pacific led to the installation in airplane liferafts of packets containing the Gospel of Matthew, Douay and King James Versions, and a Jewish translation of the Psalms.[13]

Selective service, going into operation late in 1940, brought many chaplains into the new camps, where they found little equipment and some of that ill adapted to their individual needs. To help meet these requirements, appropriations reckoned at $40 a chaplain were made in 1940 for the purchase of religious equipment and supplies and were continued in succeeding years. A wide variety of articles were recognized as appropriate objects for which this fund might be used, as personal services and the purchase of ritual garments were the only ones specifically excluded. Articles purchased through this fund became Government property, subject to ordinary handling and storage, and it was considered inexpedient that items requiring a special blessing according to the usages of some religious bodies should be obtained from this source. A part of the appropriation was used to purchase standard chapel furnishings and the remainder to meet the needs of individual chaplains. In practice they applied to the Chief of Chaplains for authority to buy certain items. If the request was approved, funds were allocated to the local commander and the purchase was made by the supply officer. A few who did not understand the necessary procedure asked for their $40 in cash that they might purchase with greater freedom. In some instances articles for which chaplains had no pressing need were requested lest their claim upon the current appropriation should lapse at the end of the fiscal year. The Chief of Chaplains urged those who could supply their actual needs by other means to do so in order that the fund might be of greater assistance to those with less resources. For some years this money was known as the Chief of Chaplains' Religious Fund, but in 1943 the name was changed to the Chaplains' Activities Fund.[14]

---

[13] *Ibid.*
[14] TM 16–205, 1944, p. 19, 1947, p. 53; Cf. PL No. 800, 8 Oct. 1940, 54 *Stat.* 974.

The Chaplain's Fund was long a recognized institution. It might pertain to a post or to a military unit, and its receipts were derived from profits of the post exchange, offerings at services, or other sources. Expenditures could be made for a wide variety of purposes so long as they were for the general benefit of the men, and the purchase of religious equipment and supplies was among the most appropriate of these. The importance of a fund is illustrated by the situation at Fort Sheridan in 1931. The post had no chaplain's fund, and the commander did not wish to annoy the men with a collection. In order that the Sunday school children might have gifts at their Christmas party, the chaplain spent about $250 of his own money, though he felt this precedent might embarrass his successor if he were a man with heavier financial responsibilities. The Chief of Chaplains concurred in this opinion, saying that a general post subscription should have been taken, even though the poverty-stricken fort could not afford a chaplain's fund.[15]

To bring various welfare funds under a more uniform administration, a revision of AR 210–50 in 1944 abolished chaplains' funds, substituting religious funds as depositories of offertory collections and central post funds as the usual medium through which chaplains and several other officers would obtain equipment and supplies. Few difficulties arose in the application of the latter provision, but certain problems soon appeared in the administration of religious funds. The strict limitation of receipts to offerings at services was intended to guard against the acceptance of donations from business firms or others which might tend to place the chaplain under some degree of obligation to the contributor. This was found to bar legitimate gifts for religious or charitable purposes from persons not attending a chaplain's services, and the regulation was changed to read "voluntary contributions made in connection with religious observance or services."[16]

A more complex problem concerned the making of contributions as an act of worship and of donations for religious and charitable purposes. The Chief of Chaplains felt that the making of offerings was a normal act of worship, for some a necessary part of a religious service, and that the essential element of sacrifice is lacking if funds are used for the benefit of the contributors. The revisers of AR 210–50 in 1944 believed other sources to be adequate for the equipment and supply of chaplains and authorized the making of donations outside the War Department from religious funds. This regulation was de-

---

[15] Personal file, A. V. Simoni, OCCh., 15 and 21 Jan., 3 Mar. 1932.
[16] AR 210–50, 20 Jan. and 13 Dec. 1945.

signed to bring offerings for legitimate charities and religious purposes within the usual rules of accountability, as many chaplains had frequently handled such funds very informally.   Unfortunately a few chaplains accepted considerable donations from the men of their units and used the money in ways which invited criticism.   An example was that of the chaplain in an oversea area who, with the consent of the men, gave a part of their contribution to a local missionary and sent a large sum to a church in America, ostensibly because he exercised his ecclesiastical prerogatives by authority of that church.   Such incidents resulted in a more restrictive regulation; but after prolonged discussion the administration of religious funds was left to Army and Air Force directives.[17]

Finding suitable places for group worship has been a problem for chaplains from the earliest times.   A group of men may be sheltered from the sun by forest trees or from the wind by a hill or cliff, but to protect them from rain, snow, and cold is a different matter.   Lights, seats, and the many adjuncts of worship found in a well-appointed church may not be so necessary, but they are very important.   For many years Army Regulations have made it the duty of post or garrison commanders to set apart suitable rooms or buildings for school and religious purposes.[18]   All too often the best facilities available have been messhalls, warehouses, or similar places where most of the characteristics associated with places of worship were lacking.

The structure built by Washington's Army near Newburgh in the first weeks of 1783 was clearly a public enterprise, for lumber and labor was requisitioned and building supplies were drawn from the quartermaster.   It was designed to accommodate the various brigades in succession at public worship but was used for other assemblies, both military and social.   Assembly tents have been furnished for these purposes since the time of the Mexican War, but many times the supply has been inadequate.   In 1861, by authority of the Secretary of War, McClellan built some chapels of government lumber with volunteer labor.   The Christian Commission erected about 140 chapels in the various Union camps, and many others were made of such materials as could be found, but none of them seem to have been government construction.   A few chapels were built on permanent posts from time to time, often with the help of private donations.   To guard against an excess of zeal placing the Army in an undesirable light, chaplains were long forbidden to solicit funds for the construc-

---

[17] *Ibid.*, 1 June 1944, 20 Jan. and 13 Dec. 1945, 8 Mar. 1947; TM 16–205, 1957, p. 48.
[18] AR 60–5.

tion of chapels without the approval of the Secretary of War.   Notwithstanding several notable enterprises of this nature, there were only
17 permanent chapels at Army posts in 1940, and only $969,542 had
been spent for this purpose since the First World War.[19]

The Act of 31 May 1902 authorized the Secretary of War to
grant to the Young Men's Christian Association a revocable license to
construct and operate on military posts such buildings as their welfare
work for military personnel might require.   During the First World
War several welfare organizations operated a great number of such
buildings in the training camps.   An important part of these buildings was an assembly hall where chaplains could hold services.   While
these facilities were better than those available during any prior time
of major mobilization, they lacked many desirable features and left
the chaplain dependent in some degree upon the courtesy of a civilian
organization.

A similar condition existed at a few permanent posts where chapels had been built on government land by civilian churches under a
similar revocable permit.   These arrangements seem to have caused
no difficulty, and the groups maintaining these chapels no doubt performed an important service.   In most cases the alternative would have
been no chapel and no regular religious ministry, but the implication
of special privilege for a single church led many to question the wisdom
of such a plan.   This matter attracted attention after the Second
World War when a prominent church leader sought first a permit and
then special legislation to authorize his church to take over a government chapel on an important post, enlarge and improve it, and operate it as a chapel of his faith.   A thorough study of the matter, legal
as well as historical, convinced the War Department that such arrangements had been a mistake from the beginning.   Though permits were
revocable, the difficulty of withdrawing one after an organization had
made large investments in a chapel was apparent.   The conclusion
was that existing situations must be respected but that further commitments which would limit the authority of the Government on military
reservations should be avoided.[20]

On 25 September 1940 the Chief of Chaplains recommended to
the General Staff that the plans being formulated for the construction
of training camps should include provisions for a chapel for each division or similar unit.   This proposal was approved, with the proviso

---

[19] *Ibid.; The Army and Navy Chaplain*, Apr.–May 1941, p. 40; *The Military Chaplain*, Oct.–Nov.
1948, p. 23.
[20] 32 *Stat.* 282; file OCCh.

that such buildings should be available for the use of all faiths; but it was pointed out that existing plans called for regimental recreational buildings where services could be held, as it was believed that the men would prefer to attend the ministrations of their own chaplain with their immediate comrades. This consideration strengthened the argument for unit chapels, and the Act of 17 March 1941 appropriated $12,816,880 for the construction of 604 of the mobilization type at an average cost of $21,220. This item was listed with several others in the original form of the bill and was discussed at length in a committee of Congress, but all were combined in a single appropriation in the law as finally adopted.[21]

The main part of these chapels was 81 feet 3 inches long, 37 feet wide, 29 feet 6 inches high to the peak of the roof, with a spire rising 23 feet higher. At one side of the Vestibule was a consultation room, with a cloak room at the other. Above was a balcony where the electric organ was installed. At the back were offices for the chaplains. This allowed seating for about 300 on the main floor and 57 in the balcony. Later modifications extended the vertical part of the steeple to resemble a belfry and placed a window in the balcony for ventilation.[22]

For smaller installations where the large chapels were not needed, appropriate provision was made. Stations having from 300 to 1,000 men were given a combined theater, recreation building, and chapel. A building to serve as theater and chapel, but not for recreation, was authorized for installations with 1,000 to 2,500 men. The mobilization type was designed for regiments or units of 3,000. As these chapels were among the most prominent buildings in a camp, it was natural that they should be located where they would show to advantage. Occasionally two regimental areas met at such a point that both chapels were placed on the same rise of ground and only a few yards apart. In summer when windows were open, the singing of the two congregations was not always in complete harmony.

With the increase of installations overseas, a simpler chapel was designed. Known as the theater-of-operations type, it was 20 by 100 feet and was built at an average cost of $7,000. After some months of experience with the first chapels, it was recognized that there were many situations in the home country where the simpler buildings would meet the need with reasonable adequacy. Revised plans for

---

[21] File 314.7, OCCh.; 55 *Stat.* 34; Hearings before the Subcommittee on Appropriations, H. of R., pp. 81–87, 177.
[22] *The Military Chaplain, loc. cit.;* Plans, OCCh.

later construction allowed one mobilization-type chapel for stations having from 2,500 to 20,000 men and one of the smaller type for each regiment or 3,000 men.   Two of the former were authorized for installations of more than 20,000 men, with the same provision for additional smaller chapels.   On V–J Day there were 1,532 Army chapels in use in the United States.   This number included 145 of the chapel-theater buildings and a number of permanent structures.   There were 162 of the theater-of-operations chapels and 1,137 of the mobilization type.   These were located at 437 camps or stations.   The greatest number of the larger structures seem to have been at Camp Blanding, where 23 were built, though Camp Shelby had 22, besides 6 of the smaller type.   The Chief of Engineers stated in 1946 that the larger chapels had cost an average of $27,000.   Thus the total cost of the 1,299 buildings which were intended for use only as chapels was $31,833,000.[23]

To limit this narrative to government construction would leave the best part of the story of chapel building untold.   Many which were the scenes of devout worship and high inspiration were triumphs of ingenuity and products of sacrificial effort.   Many of these were found in the homeland before more adequate provision were made, but it was overseas, and especially in those regions where materials were scarce and poor, that American resourcefulness met its greatest challenge.   Where weather conditions would permit, charming settings for worship were found in the open air.   One writer describes the "church" in the South Pacific under the cocoanut palms: "The pews may be logs placed on small packing cases, the pulpit just a flattened-out place on the ground, the altar a large packing case, and the nave two rows of giant trees."   Another tells of the stone altar and pulpit built by a chaplain in front of an outdoor movie screen.[24]

Three days before Christmas a chaplain in Tunisia asked for volunteers to prepare a place for worship.   Part of a shed was set apart for this purpose, and the men said, "You go in and write your Christmas sermon.   We will start working on the chapel."   Ammunition boxes were piled and covered with white mattress covers for an altar. A Christmas tree was impossible, but the men gathered palm leaves and other green plants along the edge of the desert and wove them into a backdrop for the altar.   A cross was wound with bandage material, and a pulpit was draped with white.   The candle-lit service on Christmas Eve had deeper meaning for the men because they met

---

[23] *The Army Almanac*, p. 71, Chief of Engineers to C of Ch, 25 Mar. 1946 file, OCCh.
[24] *Virginia Methodist Advocate*, 3 Feb. 1944; *Brotherhood and Service News*, Jan. 1944.

in a place which had been made both comfortable and beautiful by their own exertions. Nor was the element of safety forgotten. One chaplain had an altar at one side of his tent and a foxhole at the other. A chapel on Bataan was said to have the most unusual seating arrangement in the world, a foxhole for every seat. In case of danger all the men had to do was to stiffen their kness and slide into them.[25]

Many other tales are told of chapels built from whatever materials could be found. In Alaska this might be logs cut from the forest; in the Pacific, bamboo and thatch were common; stone was used in some places. One chaplain tells of the lumber obtained by knocking down packing cases and of his elation at finding on the road some 2 by 6 timbers which apparently had fallen from a truck. In another place a lumber barge was wrecked some distance off shore. The men swam out and pushed ashore enough of the drifting lumber for their chapel. One of the finest of these structures was built on Guadalcanal by the natives in gratitude for their liberation and as a memorial to the 1,600 Americans buried nearby. A large party labored for more than 2 months on this remarkable building, 90 by 26, and 26 feet high. Great skill was shown in the weaving of split bamboo and in the decoration of the altar, which was hand carved and inlaid with mother of pearl. At the dedication, the building was presented by Jason, a native Christian, who had been the leader of the workers. Barefoot and clad only in a white loincloth and singlet, he spoke with a simple dignity which many a bishop might envy:

> We want to tell all you people that all we fella' belong Solomon build this church because we want to thank you. We have worked hard and we hope you like this church. And we pray that God will bless all of you, and we hope you will pray for your friends who are lying in this cemetery.
>
> Also, we want to thank all the Americans and allies who have fought to push the enemy out of our land. Now we give this church to you. But this church no belong to you and me. This church belong to God.
>
> And we ask God to bless us all. Thank you.[26]

Several chaplains stress the greater interest taken by the men in the chapel and what it stood for because they had helped to build it. The same was true of ornamentation and furnishings. At an air depot in Alaska a chapel flag was made from salvaged material, the white cross from parachute silk, the blue field of wing fabric rayon, and the gold fringe was sewn on by parachute riggers. The ordnance

---

[25] *The Story of Christian Science Wartime Activities*, p. 177; Cross, *op. cit.*, p. 36.

[26] Wayne M. Daubenspeck, personal file, OCCh.; *Lutheran Standard*, 25 Dec. 1943; *Christian Standard*, 1 Jan. 1944.

shop made a chromium cross for the staff and a base from a thousand-pound bomb fin.   In Europe a chaplain hung in the tower of his chapel a bell from a medieval castle where Hitler, Mussolini, and the King of Italy met in 1938 to plan their wars of conquest.   At that time it was rung to celebrate worldly ambition, but now had been dedicated to a more worthy cause.[27]

A chapel in the Pacific was called the "Church of the Crossroads." This seems to have referred less to shipping lanes than to nationalities and faiths.   On Okinawa, Catholic and Methodist chaplains worked together like brothers building a chapel.   In one place a Jewish artist painted a Madonna and Child; in another, Catholic and Jewish soldiers made a beautiful interior while they lived in the home of the Protestant chaplain.   One chaplain voiced the spirit of the whole chapel program when he said that these buildings were not undenominational they were "all-denominational."   A group of airmen in Africa expressed this attitude well when they named the building which they had constructed "Everyman's Chapel."   In France a chaplain was given a Romney hut for a chapel and began having it furnished and decorated for this purpose.   A German artist, a prisoner of war, was asked to paint a cross and crown of thorns on the central panel of the altar.   Despite difficulties of language he seemed to understand.   The cross was beautifully done in gold with radiating beams of light.   The crown of thorns was very delicately shown around the upright beam of the cross, and close inspection showed that it was a loop of barbed wire.   The chaplain saw in this not an act of mockery but a symbol of the humiliation and pain which were so terribly real to thousands during long periods of captivity and privation.[28]

Chapel construction had scarcely begun before practical questions about the use of the buildings arose.   To forestall some of these, the War Department on 14 July 1941 inserted a section on "Use of Chapels" in Circular No. 140.   It emphasized the fact that Congress had appropriated funds for this construction "for the express purpose of providing adequate facilities for worship and spiritual, moral, cultural, and character building activities" and stressed the responsibility of commanding officers to see that chapels were available to chaplains at all times in carrying out this purpose themselves or with the cooper-

---

[27] George A. Baker, personal file, OCCh.; Cross, *op. cit.,* p. 97; G. E. Mennen, report, Feb. 1944; L. G. Moench, report, June 1943; Ralph K. Wheeler, personal file, OCCh.; *Christian Advocate,* 4 Oct. 1945.

[28] *His Islands,* Feb. 1945; *Christian Advocate,* 28 June 1945; Orlando V. Hayne—*Sir: The Chaplain Wishes to Report,* p. 31; *Sunday Oregonian,* 15 Aug. 1943; *The Military Chaplain,* Oct.–Nov. 1948, p. 25; *Army Day Review,* 6 Apr. 1942, p. 104.

ation of nearby churches. The same directive was later included in AR 60–5. This was clearly intended to guard against the preemption of these buildings for training lectures or similar gatherings unrelated to moral or religious interests.

The Chief of Chaplains elaborated these statements on 1 August 1941 in Technical Circular No. 1. He outlined a program of activities which would keep a unit chapel in use every day of the week and suggested a wide variety of cultural or inspirational gatherings which could properly be included in a chaplain's program. Some chaplains were embarrassed by the desire of their commanders or others to use chapels for social or other secular purposes. Asking what they should do in such situations, they were advised by the Chief to resist as firmly as the situation would permit every proposal which would impair in any degree the distinctive character of the chapel as a place for worship and spiritual culture. He pointed out that the surest defense against such encroachments was to keep the chapel so constantly in use for legitimate purposes that it never would be available for any improper uses. In planning programs of chapel activities, the importance of providing a quiet place for individual meditation and prayer at appropriate times was not overlooked.[29]

As the chapels were definitely intended for the use of chaplains of the three major faiths and for groups having no local chaplains, it was necessary that they be adaptable to the usages of the various religious bodies and that they be free from symbols or other elements which could be offensive to any users of the buildings. To meet the former of these needs, they were provided with an electric organ, a communion rail, pulpit, lectern, ark and a movable altar which could be set up with the symbols of any faith. Naturally, the persons associated with churches which attach importance to religious objects and pictures felt that these would enhance the usefulness as well as the beauty of the simple structures provided by the Government. To others they might be a pleasing adornment; but there was danger that the scene which was an expression of sublime faith to one would imply doctrines or usages which another would believe to be mistaken or harmful. To guard against such causes of friction, the Chief of Chaplains insisted that sectarian pictures or symbols be removed or draped whenever a chapel was not in use by the group to which these objects pertain. Later he required that proposals for permanent objects of this nature be submitted for approval.[30]

---

[29] TM 16–205, 1944, p. 73; Cf. par. 4f, AR 60–5, 19 May 1942.

[30] File 210.4, OCCh.; *The Military Chaplain*, loc. cit.

The inconvenience of observing this rule in some situations led to the suggestion that certain chapels in a camp be set apart for the primary use of one or other of the major faiths.   This was promptly disapproved by the Secretary of War as being contrary to the intent of Congress.[31]   Late in the war when the population in some camps had greatly decreased, there were instances of chapels located close together being used in the proposed way, apparently without objection from any source.   Akin to this project was the desire of some chaplains to give appropriate names to specific chapels, just as hospitals, camps, and streets had long been named in honor of eminent surgeons or great generals.   A few were named for prominent chaplains or religious characters, but it became apparent that this practice would lead to the choice of names having sectarian connotations and would give offense to some of the groups entitled to the use of the buildings.   In consequence the Chief of Chaplains urged that all chapels be designated by number or by some geographic term or the name of the units to which they belonged.

Experience with chapels at stations of varying size and permanence taught several lessons.   These were remembered in the preparation of plans for chapels to be included in any extensive future construction.   The general rule was to provide seats at the ratio of 1 to each 10 men in chapels of 6 sizes, ranging from 150 to 600 seats.   A wing would provide offices and a morning chapel, while a baptistry and a series of Sunday school rooms would be provided in one building on each post.   An interesting feature in these plans is the inclusion of a chapel to seat 186 in camps for prisoners of war.[32]

The years 1939–45 saw more done to provide chaplains with transportation, houses of worship, chapel and field equipment, and a variety of supplies by the Government than during the whole prior history of the Army.   Doubtless this reflects the numerical increase of the adherents of those religious bodies which practice a liturgical form of worship.   Parallel with this has been a tendency toward a greater use of ritual and symbols by some large groups traditionally accustomed to simplicity.   Certainly it indicates growing respect for the convictions of others and a determination that every chaplain shall have every possible aid to enhance the effectiveness of his service.

---

[31] TAG to CG 6 CA, 24 Oct. 1941, AG file 631.4., OCCh.
[32] Plans, OCCh.; AR 415–107, C 2, 15 Dec. 1950.

CHAPTER XVII

Pearl Harbor to Tokyo Bay

A scant quarter-century separated the beginnings of American participation in the two world wars. No drastic change had occurred in the general religious outlook of the people, though there is some indication of one or two trends toward changes of emphasis. Some chaplains seem to have given religious education a larger place in their plans, with evangelism in the narrower meaning of the word being less nearly their sole objective. A parallel tendency was toward a greater use of symbols and ritual by many chaplains of those churches which are not necessarily liturgical in their worship. Except for minor qualifications of this nature, chaplains did substantially the same work, using much the same methods in 1942 as in 1918.

One significant change was the recognition of religious work as the primary task of the chaplains. In 1918 it was so taken for granted that they would frequently serve as defense counsel in courts martial that the instruction in Military Law received major emphasis at the Chaplain School. Many were put in charge of the mess, the exchange, athletics, the mail, and similar matters, and some carried several of these responsibilities for long periods "in addition to their regular duties." An undated chart, published not many years ago by the War Department, lists what were considered the normal activities of a chaplain. Under 5 heads it shows 22 groups of interests, each consisting of from 3 to 10 responsibilities, a total of 142. The chaplain's relation to 5 of these groups is shown as advisory, but only 4 of the others are religious or pastoral in character. This leaves 118 matters for which the chaplain's obligation was more than advisory, and 86 of these lay outside of his professional field. Needless to say, few chaplains included all of these activities in their programs at any one time— if ever.[1]

As early as 1904, Army Regulations gave chaplains a measure of protection from assignment to secular duties. Paragraph 44 specified, "They will not be employed on duties other than those required of them

---

[1] Files, OCCh.

by law or pertaining to their profession, except when the exigencies of
the service, a result of deficiency in number of officers present, require it." This prohibition seems sufficiently definite, except for the
emergency provision; but, with strange inconsistency the revision of
15 April 1917 repeated this paragraph and added another in which it
was stated that further duties for chaplains might include the charge of
recreation, amusement, and the mail, advising men under arrest, and
answering letters of inquiry from the friends of soldiers.

Paragraph 5g of AR 60–5, 15 February 1924, repeated the old
paragraph 44 with only verbal changes but added the proviso that chaplains must not be assigned to duties incompatible with their noncombatant status under the Geneva Convention and specified that they
were not available for detail as post exchange officers or as defense
counsel in courts martial, though they might serve as individual counsel at the request of the accused. Later revisions repeated this directive with only minor changes, such as the addition of athletics, recreation, and morale to the list of responsibilities for which chaplains should
not be available.

Notwithstanding these instructions, there were numerous instances
during the war of chaplains being detailed to these or similar duties.
Some were librarians or postal officers, some organized and supervised
quite comprehensive educational projects. One regimental commander
authorized the chaplain to censor the mail of any soldiers who might
prefer not to have the company officers read their letters. In many
instances a real shortage of officers did exist. In other cases the chaplains had special qualifications or liked the secular duties. Some felt
that their religious work was aided by the secular, as these contacts
widened their acquaintance and extended their friendship with the men.

The Chief of Chaplains discouraged such activities, believing that
the alert and enterprising chaplain could use all his time to advantage
in strictly religious work and that the acquiescence of one chaplain in
assignments to secular duties would tend to impair the protection which
the regulation was intended to give to his colleagues. Commendatory
indorsements by commanding officers revealed the fact that some chaplains did not mention such activities in their monthly reports. This
led to the inclusion in a new printing of Form 3 of a space where the
reporting chaplain showed any detail to secular activities or stated that
there had been none. When assignments which seemed improper
were shown without remedial action by intervening headquarters, the
Chief of Chaplains habitually inquired into the circumstances and requested the chaplain's relief from these duties if an emergency did not

exist.   In general the importance of the chaplain's work was recognized more clearly and he was free to do his primary duty with much less interference of this nature in 1941–45 than had been usual in 1917–18.[2]

Another fact had a vital relation to the work of chaplains. Many writers were surprised by the seriousness of the American soldier.   The oft-quoted statement that there are no atheists in foxholes was paralleled by the soldier who was rescued after many days of drifting among the sharks under the equatorial sun in mid-Pacific and vowed that under those conditions there could be none in rubber rafts.   It was natural that seriousness should increase with the approach to danger and that it should reflect itself in attendance at church.   One chaplain said that men were impressed by the thought that the nearest land was 2 miles away, straight down.   Another held that the men showed gratitude after a battle as much as fear before. Taggart, who had abundant opportunity to know, declared: "Those who turn to religion in combat are not men afraid to die; they are not weak men seeking a haven in religion.   These are strong men with an unfaltering conviction that they are fighting on God's side." [3]

During active military operations one of the chaplain's serious difficulties may be finding a place for group worship.   We read of Air chaplains who held services under the wing of a plane and in a hangar.   In Italy a chaplain had a stable cleaned for a chapel.   His congregation was small but it included a major general, a brigadier, and several privates.   Other inspiring services were held in a cellar, an attic, a royal palace, a cave, and many other unconventional places. Chaplains were welcomed to many churches in the countries where American troops were stationed.   Notable examples are St. Paul's, London, and the Cathedral of Reykjavik.   A week after the occupation of Rome, Chaplain Ryan said a High Mass of Thanksgiving in the presence of more than 10,000 people in the great church of Santa Maria degl'Angeli.   Chaplain Blakeney broke a precedent of more than 900 years on Thanksgiving Day of 1942 when, a nonconformist minister, he conducted the service and preached in Westminster Abbey.   A distinction of a different nature fell to Gibble when he held the first service beyond the Rhine in a railroad tunnel.[4]

---

[2] Correspondence files, OCCh., *passim.*

[3] Stanley High—"The War Boom in Religion," *The Army Reader,* p. 294; Warren J. Clear, Army Hour Broadcast, 12 Apr. 1942; James C. Whittaker—*We Thought We Heard the Angels Sing,* p. 82; Ernie Pyle—*Here is Your War,* p. 12; Thomas R. St. George—*c/o Postmaster,* p. 33; Christopher Cross—*Soldiers of God,* p. 75; William C. Taggart—*My Fighting Congregation,* p. 165.

[4] *Ibid.,* p. 117; TID File 85–A–1, OCCh.; *Chaplains of the Fifth Army,* p. 42; Ms. "History of Chaplains' Work in 88th Division"; *The Chaplain,* 3:12; Ms. "A Most Unusual Chaplain," p. 12.

Several chaplains tell of devices to attract men to their services. One arranged a contest among organizations, highest honors going to a unit having an average of more than 80 percent of its members in church. Another frequently had a young lady to sing or play and tried to have her walk about the camp to attract attention before service. Commanders in their comments upon various chaplains have credited a large attendance at services to publicity, to the chaplain's personal appearance, his untiring efforts and popularity, and to the fact that he "really puts something into his services." One chaplain discovered that about 50 men would attend a battalion service where 40 would come for one in a company or 30 in a platoon. As far as possible he held many services for the smaller units and reached more men.[5]

Elements of special interest appear in the reports of some religious services. After the victorious end of a strenuous campaign in Italy, the 88th Division held a great service of thanksgiving. Eleven thousand men met on a mountainside, sang patriotic hymns, listened to a moving address by their commanding general, then separated for the distinctive services of the three faiths. On Easter Sunday, a Jewish chaplain found himself on a long air journey with a plane load of men representing at least five Christian bodies. Asked by the men to conduct Easter services, he preached on the idealism of Easter and the Passover. Hale took his "portable" Christmas program to six bodies of troops separated by many miles among the mountains of Italy. Besides a good choir, he had the usual Christmas decorations and pageantry. In one place the building would not nearly hold the crowd, so the manger scene, tree, and other accessories were set up in the open air, and the soldiers stood in 8 inches of snow while they sang their carols and paid homage to the Bethlehem Babe.[6]

Applegate carried Christmas cheer to advance posts by air. Arriving in a Santa Claus suit, he brought to each a phonograph and records, candy, fruit, cake, and a small tree but did not fail to express the deeper meanings of the occasion. Few stories are more moving than Peterson's account of the Christmas cheer which he and his associates took to the forgotten patients of the Leper Colony on the Island of Chacachacare. Interesting the men in the project, he soon had enough contributions to fill 430 bags with small conveniences and delicacies. Though the cost was only 85 cents a bag, being remem-

---

[5] High, *loc. cit.;* Gary Bousman—"The Human Side of the Chaplaincy," *Advance,* 3 Apr. 1943; Form 3's, OCCh.; Herbert W. Wicher—Ms. personal narrative, OCCh.

[6] *Chaplains of the Fifth Army,* p. 51; Cross, *op. cit.,* p. 167; *Chaplains' Work in 88th Division,* p. 12.

bered with kindness at Christmas was worth many times this sum to the lepers, children and adults alike. Those who made the gifts and did the work found in this service the inspiration of worship.[7]

A chaplain in Alaska planned to visit a distant outpost which could be reached only by a supply boat which was supposed to sail once a week. Three weeks in succession he took the long journey to the port only to find that stress of weather or other reasons would prevent the sailing of the boat. At the fourth attempt he got away, taking an organ, songbooks, altar equipment, and religious literature. Though he could spend scarcely an hour at the outpost, the worship and his friendly interest were highly appreciated by the men. Some chaplains were snowbound in blizzards or had their vehicles break down miles from any shelter. These are typical of the difficulties encountered in taking the facilities for worship and some conveniences to men in places hard of access. In Attu a chaplain set out to reach a forward position in a blinding snowstorm. Half way to his objective he fell exhausted and was unable to rise although he removed his pack. As the hill was very steep, he managed to slide 8 or 10 rods, where he landed in "the swellest foxhole in Attu." As he had his sleeping bag with him, he made himself at home and slept till noon of the next day.[8]

Some enterprising chaplains found means to avoid obstacles which they could not overcome. One in South America arranged for time on the local radio and flashed his messages across the jungle and mountains. In Italy chaplains of all faiths joined in a series of vespers broadcast over the Army radio. On Easter morning in 1944 one of the most unusual services was conducted by the chaplains of the 349th Infantry. Loudspeakers and the necessary accessories were set up during the night. As the position was near the German line, the service began with an explanation and an Easter message in German. An impressive feature of the English service was the singing of "I Know That My Redeemer Liveth" from Handel's great oratorio by Charlotte Johnston, an Army nurse. Numbers of soldiers left their foxholes and gathered around the field altar, but not a shot came from the German lines until the service was ended.[9]

Several chaplains told of services or other religious rites observed in spite of serious difficulties, physical or otherwise. One heard the confession of a military policeman while he was directing traffic. At

[7] *The Churchman,* 1 Apr. 1944; Harold C. Peterson to C of Ch, 5 Aug. 1946, OCCh.
[8] Charles M. Buck, personal file, OCCh.; File 23, OCCh.
[9] Cross, *op. cit.,* p. 154; *Chaplains of the Fifth Army,* p. 60; *Chaplains' Work in 88th Division,* p. 4.

a communion in the Sahara 400 men participated, though the wind coated the wafers with red and dyed the wine a deeper shade.   In a Christmas service one chaplain had just begun his sermon when an air attack began and the men dived into their foxholes.   He played Christmas carols on the organ till the all-clear signal came an hour later, then finished his sermon.   Huntington led a service in the Solomons at a time when hostile planes flew over at unpredictable intervals.   Five times they were interrupted, and the men had to rush out and fire at the Japanese.   Nevertheless, the service, that began with 75, had lost only one at the benediction.[10]

Many tales are told of worship in unusual situations.   A chaplain on one transport had the Chaplain's Flag hoisted during the service and used the loudspeaker of the ship.   Soon a destroyer drew alongside and held this position, with the personnel of both vessels listening to the service.   Anderson and Smith gained the name of "railroad Chaplains," as they served the men scattered in small groups along important railroad lines.   The former had a baggage car with seats for 50.   His men were located in 17 camps along a railroad in France. When the chaplain's car was pushed into any siding, it was time for church.[11]

Smith had a caboose on the railroad over which vital supplies were carried from the Persian Gulf to the hard-pressed Russians, and on its side was painted "Faith" in English and Persian.   This vehicle was furnished with an organ and hymn books, games, magazines, a small library, and both equipment and supplies for hot lunches. The latter was especially appreciated when a wreck occurred on the line.   When the caboose arrived at a station, the chaplain hung out his flag as a welcome to all.   The caboose went with the first trainload of supplies for the Russians after the Americans took over the operation of this line.   On the way the fireman of the second engine became very ill.   The chaplain cared for him as best he could; the colonel fired the engine; and the train went through.[12]

After the attack on Pearl Harbor, Finnegan was busy among the wounded for many hours.   Some were unconscious, some bandaged beyond recognition.   He gave comfort and cheer to all and invited confessions from those whom he found to be Catholics.   Going among the beds for the last time late at night, he spoke a few words to a man whose face was swathed in bandages.   Thinking that he had not seen

---

[10] Notes by Terrance Finnegan; "A Sahara Communion," *The Lutheran*, 29 Dec. 1942; Cross, *op. cit.*, pp. 107, 152.

[11] File 119b, OCCh.; Cross, *op. cit.*, p. 26.

[12] Washington *Times-Herald*, 16 July 1944; Files, OCCh.

him before, he asked him to go to confession.   With a chuckle the man said, "Now look, Father, don't you think twice is enough for one day?" [13]

The care of the dead and burial with appropriate honors did much to promote morale and *esprit de corps*.   The Arabs were much impressed when a chaplain and party made a long journey into the Atlas Mountains to bring out the bodies of airmen.   In Australia such a party climbed in the rain through briars and jungle vines until noon of the second day to reach and bury the bodies of seven who had been killed on a high mountain.   The next year the guide of this party wrote to the chaplain that he had cleared away the brush, built a fence around the graves, and planted roses.   Taggart found that two of the men killed in a crash were Jewish.   He telephoned for a Jewish prayerbook, and at the funeral was able to read both Jewish and Christian services.   Ernie Pyle told of visiting a German cemetery with a sergeant.   They noted the graves of several Americans among those of German soldiers.   They were alike in size and the care which had been bestowed upon them.   On the crosses above them was printed "Amerikaner," followed by the serial number.   With deep feeling the sergeant remarked, "They respect our dead the same as we do theirs." [14]

For the month of July 1944 Wallace Hale, serving on the Italian front, reported the burial of 414 Americans and 168 of the enemy. The next month these numbers were only 68 and 35, but in September they rose to 314 and 30.   On 14 July his burials were 41 Americans and 11 of the enemy, and on the 18th they were 42 and 12.   Notwithstanding the magnitude of this melancholy task, he gave each man a separate and appropriate service.   In the summer of 1945, 21 persons were killed when their plane crashed into the cliffs bordering a deep valley in New Guinea.   A few days later Catholic and Protestant chaplains flew to the scene.   Though landing was impossible, crosses and a Star of David were dropped, to be placed by the Filipino paratroopers who were to dig the graves.   While the plane circled above the spot, the chaplains recited the funeral rituals of their faiths.   As there was no Jewish chaplain within a thousand miles, one of them read the burial service of that faith in honor of the Jewish girl among the victims.[15]

---

[13] Cross, *op. cit.*, p. 26.

[14] N. C. W. C. News Service, 10 May 1943; Cross, *op. cit.*, p. 72; Taggart, *op. cit.*, p. 150; Pyle, *op. cit.*, "The End in Sight."

[15] Wallace M. Hale, Form 3; New York *World-Telegram*, 8 June 1945; Ms. "History of Chaplains' Activities in the Pacific," p. 283.

Few activities by chaplains equaled in pathos or in devotion those of the American chaplains who were prisoners of war as they sought to comfort and inspire their fellow captives.   Several of them were captured in the first place because they remained with the wounded who could not be moved, rather than find safety in retreat.   Matthews had such an experience late in 1944.   In his first prison camp he was told that he might conduct services but must submit his sermons to the Germans for approval.   This he resisted so effectively that his captors did not insist.   At his second camp there were other chaplains who complied with this demand on the principle of meeting the prison authorities half way.   He was unwilling to do this, so refrained from preaching, though he held a number of small teaching services sur-reptitiously.   He did not know of the experience of the British Chaplain Hullah, held by the Germans for 4 years.   When he asked if he might comment on the Scripture lessons instead of preaching, he was told that there would be no objection.   This opened no small door of opportunity.   Matthews was the only chaplain among 3,000 men at his next camp and was allowed such freedom that he held an Easter sunrise service for a great body of men.   When they were marched hastily to the south to avoid liberation by the pursuing Americans in the spring of 1945, he held services when they were allowed to rest. About noon on 29 April they were overtaken by Patton's tanks. Three hours later they joined in a great service of thanksgiving, not forgetting the comrades who had died that they might be free.[16]

More American chaplains were made prisoners in the Orient than in Europe, and with few exceptions they endured a longer captivity. The spirit of these men is shown in a prayer attributed to Dawson just before the fall of Bataan: "Oh God, I pray Thee that if this garrison does have to surrender, that I may go with them and be strong enough to keep Thee in their midst."   Chaplains of all faiths vied with each other in striving to measure up to this ideal.   For a time the Japanese would permit no religious services, as they regarded the chaplains as propaganda agents.   When they did allow Mass and preaching, they required sermons to be submitted in advance for approval.   The censor's knife sometimes wrought sad havoc in the chaplain's line of thought, but the alternatives were to conform or to have no services.   James E. Davis had a more encouraging experience.   He was captured at Guam on December 1941 and soon was transferred to the Zentsuji Prison

---

[16] *The Chaplain,* Apr. 1946; Bruce B. Matthews to CofCh, 17 Feb. 1947, file, OCCh.

Camp in Japan. Here he was allowed to conduct services regularly till the end of the war.[17]

Several chaplains succeeded in carrying some hymnals or Bibles and communion elements through the notorious Death March. Some Catholic chaplains, being better supplied, shared the latter with their Protestant associates, but the supply soon was exhausted. A Belgian priest in Manila was allowed to bring a supply into camp for the Christmas midnight Mass, which was attended by Catholics, Protestants, Jews, Greek and Russian Orthodox, Chinese, and some of the Japanese guards. A chaplain regularly accompanied work details which were sent away from the camp for several days at a time. Though he had to work with the men from dawn till sunset, he managed to say Mass in the morning and the Rosary at night. Borneman tells of times when their captors tried to suppress all religious gatherings, but the men managed to hold Bible classes along the drainage ditch where they worked.[18]

The survivors of Cabanatuan Prison Camp will long remember the memorial service on 30 May 1943. About 2,000 prisoners were allowed to go under heavy guard to the outside of the cemetery where many hundreds of their comrades had been buried. The chaplains and choir were allowed inside the fence. The senior Protestant and Catholic chaplains and a Jewish cantor each conducted the services of his faith. The choir sang "Rock of Ages," "Soldier, Rest," and "The Recessional." The Japanese general commanding all prison camps in Luzon and the major in charge of Cabanatuan sent wreaths, some thought in derision but others believed with sincere respect. Then Chaplains Brown and O'Brien placed a pitiably small bunch of flowers at the foot of a cross in the center of the cemetery. They were little blossoms found in remote corners, but they were the best that the prisoners had to give. Oliver declared that they were the most beautiful floral offering he ever had seen. A year later a similar service was held. Many had been laid beside their comrades during the year, and only 300 were at the service. Again the Japanese officers sent wreaths, and the guards stood uncovered during the exercises. The choir sang "Sleep, Comrade, Sleep" and "Finlandia," and the prisoners placed a wreath made of weeds and a few flowers. Again it was the perfect tribute, for they gave all they had.[19]

---

[17] *The Army and Navy Chaplain*, Apr.–May 1946, p. 6; Cross, *op. cit.*, p. 36.
[18] *Ibid.* pp. 54, 62; Calvin Ellsworth Chunn—*Of Rice and Men*, pp. 89–90.
[19] *Ibid.;* Alfred C. Oliver—"An Army Chaplain," *The Military Chaplain*, Jan. 1951, p. 14.

Under the leadership of the senior chaplain, a church was organized in Cabanatuan.   A committee of chaplains prepared a constitution and declaration of faith in terms appropriate for virtually all Protestants.   Members were pledged to the basic principles of Christian living and to affiliate with a church in their home communities on their return to the United States.   A large number of men became members of this organization.   Some were already members of churches at home, and it was specified by the constitution that such a relation would not be affected by their connection with the camp church, but many others first entered the organized fellowship of the Christian faith in the religious associations of Cabanatuan.   The records of this church were buried to prevent their destruction by the Japanese.   After the liberation they were recovered and preserved among the archives of the Army.[20]

One of the most remarkable events in the history of the military chaplaincy is the 6-day conference held in Prison Camp No. 1, Cabanatuan, 6–11 September 1943.   Its most striking feature is that it resembled so closely a meeting of chaplains in a home camp or of the ministers of a single faith in some American city.   Though many of these men had endured the rigors of imprisonment for more than a year and the future seemed to hold only a distant hope, they discussed with scholarly thoroughness the ways in which they could be more useful, not only in their present situation but in the normal sphere of chaplain duty in times either of peace or war.   Besides soul-searching messages in which they stimulated each other to a deepened loyalty, they studied a number of proposals and made recommendations to the Chief of Chaplains and to the leaders of the various churches for changes in administration or other matters which would enhance the effectiveness of chaplains' work.   Several of these proposals have since been adopted.   One is at a loss whether to admire the more the courage of these men exerting themselves to prepare for greater usefulness in the years of peace which they might never see or the attempt to leave some record of what they had learned during their long ordeal which might be a help to those who would follow them.   Of the 33 chaplains who at some time were in Prison Camp No. 1, 18 did not live to regain their freedom.[21]

On the Sunday nearest the Fourth of July a chaplain in Cabanatuan had the congregation sing "God Bless America" but was warned that he would be punished severely if the offense were re-

[20] Files, OCCh.; Data from Chaplain Oliver; Cross, *op. cit.*, p. 65.
[21] Data supplied by Chaplain John Borneman.

peated.   On that great day when the Rangers broke in and the
prisoners started on their hasty march to freedom, Filipino women
along the way held up two fingers in token of victory and sang "God
Bless America."   A man clad only in a pair of ragged pants walked
with the chaplain.   He said that he had lost everything in prison,
including his health, "but I didn't lose God." [22]

Those who endured even for a short time the rigors of a prison
can appreciate the scene described by Hayne when he visited Dechau
on the first of May 1945.   Asking to be taken to the section where
the clergy were confined he was led to a closely fenced area where
he found 350 packed into accommodations intended for 150.   Here
were men of education and character from every country the Nazis
had overrun and from the Fatherland itself.   Their first request was
that he would conduct a memorial service for the Americans who had
fallen in the liberation of this camp.   Years before they had given up
one third of their living space that they might have a chapel for Catholic and Protestant worship.   Into this sacred place they brought
their guest.   With the aid of a dilapidated harmonium made in Boston, they sang the great hymns of the centuries with a depth of feeling
few of them ever had experienced.   Humbled in the presence of these
men, some of whom had endured 11 years of suffering for their faith,
the chaplain spoke of the worth of the freedom for which many of
their associates had died and all had sacrificed so much.   At the end
of the service he asked that his assistant might take a picture of the
group and was moved almost to tears by the joy and pride of these
noble men who had received only indignity and humiliation for so
many years. [23]

One field of service in which the chaplains made an inestimable
contribution to better international relations was that of ministration
to prisoners of war.   Hayne told of the Nazi pilot, shot down and seriously injured, who was virulent in his denunciation of the Americans,
then showed fear that the plasma being injected into his arm was poison.   He could scarcely believe the chaplain's assurance that it was
good American blood and that his captors were trying to save his life
and restore him to health.   Finally the chaplain told him that he must
sleep, saying that he hoped he would awake thinking differently of the
Americans.   For the first time the pilot smiled and said, "Perhaps I
will." [24]

---

[22] *The Army and Navy Chaplain*, Jul.–Aug. 1945, p. 4.
[23] Orlando V. Hayne—*Sir, The Chaplain Wishes to Report*, pp. 17–19.
[24] *Ibid.*, p. 4.

Because of his knowledge of the German language, Hoffman was given the task of questioning prisoners in Tunisia. He was the more ready to do this because he thought his presence might insure proper treatment for them. On the Italian front he saw a party of civilians come to kill a wounded German with knives. The vigorous chaplain threw them out and set a guard. The prisoner was most impressed by the fact that these same people had cheered him and his comrades a few days before.[25] How deeply such acts of kindness were appreciated is shown by a letter from Anton Egger, a German clergyman who spent some time as a prisoner in American hands. The following paragraph is translated from a letter written on 1 December 1946 after his return to Innsbruck:

> Writing from home, I should at least like to try to thank you, worthy gentlemen, for all the goodness you showed me and many other comrades during the time of our capture. In many letters which I have received from friends made during the time spent at Camp Maxey reference is made time and again to the fact that the religious service and our beautiful chapels were our chief comfort in the frequent difficult days of our absence from our homes and loved ones. And that we had these fine opportunities was chiefly your handiwork, worthy gentlemen! When, after my return home, I myself told my bishop about Camp Maxey and could report to him how manifold were the opportunities for personal counseling, and when I reported that I could daily celebrate Mass, pray the breviary, and deliver addresses and study—he was very amazed and pleasantly surprised. Finally, since I have come in contact with many who had to undergo the same misfortune of capture, but in other lands and at other places—I really learned to appreciate how fortunate I was. So, once more, I wish you a heartfelt "May God reward you!" [26]

Skelton relates an interesting incident about a German prisoner in Oklahoma. This man told the chaplain that he wished to make a profession of faith and join the church. As the church of his choice and his boyhood association was the Baptist, it would be necessary for him to be voted into membership by a congregation and baptized by immersion. Arrangements were made with a Baptist church in a nearby city. The German was proposed for membership at an evening service and accepted. A few days later he was immersed in the baptistry of the church and formally received into its membership. Later he was given a certificate by which his membership could be transferred to a Baptist church in Germany or elsewhere.[27]

[25] Albert J. Hoffman—Ms. autobiography, pp. 9, 14, OCCh.
[26] Ms., OCCh.
[27] Harold E. Shelton to CofCh, 6 Aug. 1946.

At many posts where prisoners were confined, both in America and Europe, earnest efforts were made to give them the services of chaplains who spoke their language. Clergymen among the prisoners were frequently employed in this way. In the United States they worked under the supervision of the post chaplains of the camps where the prisoners were detained. A report of prisoner-of-war chaplains' activities of the European Theater of Operations, dated 25 October 1946, shows the magnitude of this project. At that time 102 Catholic and 287 Protestant chaplains had been repatriated, 37 of the former faith and 35 of the latter were still serving German prisoners of the Americans in France, Belgium, and England, and 13 other Catholic chaplains appear in the records of the Provost Marshal. During a period of less than 5 months for which reports were available at that time, these chaplains had reported 13,407 services or other assemblies of a religious nature, attended by 488,049 men, and individual services, such as confessions or hospital visits, to an additional 146,872.[28]

In August 1945 a larger measure of organization and supervision was given to the religious work among German prisoners held by American forces in western Europe. Chaplain Norman Adams was put in charge, with headquarters in Paris. This involved responsibility for the work in about 130 camps and among half a million men. Four other chaplains were soon detailed to aid in the supervision. The general plan called for 1 Catholic and 1 Protestant chaplain for each 2,000 men. In some situations it was necessary for German chaplains to serve as many as 4 camps, and these might be 10 or 15 miles apart. An interesting outgrowth of this situation was a number of arrangements by camp commanders for German chaplains to say Mass and hear confessions for American troops in places where there was a shortage of American chaplains.[29]

Gerecke performed a notable service for the war criminals during the Nurnberg trials and executions. Some were morose or arrogant, others courteous or reverent. In several instances the former attitude gradually modified into the latter. On 14 June 1946, more than 6 months after the chaplain began these duties, 21 prisoners, among them Goering and Ribbentrop, sent a letter to the chaplain's wife. They understood how natural it was for her to wish to have her husband at home again but begged that she would not urge his return for a little while. His kindness had sustained them in the months that were past, and no one else could help them spiritually in the time

[28] Adrian W. Van Hal—*Historical Report of POW Chaplains' Activities Among Prisoners of War in ETO under American Jurisdiction, passim.*
[29] *Ibid.*

that remained.   The chaplain found Goering engrossed in the problem: "Can a Christian be a loyal citizen?"   The chaplain's comments were summed up in "Render unto Caesar the things that are Caesar's," balanced by "We must obey God rather than man."   He was moved to pity at the last to see the marshal's self-control break down when his little daughter sent him the message that she would meet him in heaven.[30]

Japanese prisoners condemned to death for crime were usually polite and appreciative of any kindness.   They were deprived of belts and other articles which might serve as a means of suicide and sometimes had to hold their clothes to keep them from falling off.   They were greatly comforted at the time of execution when the chaplains gave them safety pins to save their self respect.   When the chaplains explained their belief in a forgiving Heavenly Father and prayed for the divine mercy upon those about to die, they invariably thanked them and accepted their ministrations with apparent reverence.[31]

Though the status of a military prisoner differs immeasurably from that of the heroes of Cabanatuan, they have several common problems and offer an infinite variety of opportunities for helpfulness to any chaplain.   Some are confirmed criminals serving long sentences in permanent institutions, but the great majority are confined for short periods in guardhouses or stockades for acts in violation of military discipline, some of which would not be disapproved in civil life.   Many are first offenders, sometimes smarting from a sense of what seems to them injustice, and they must be saved from the feeling that they are marked men who never will be trusted again and need help to become good soldiers and citizens.   A garrison commander said that he had his chaplain interview every man who got into trouble with military rules so that he could "temper justice with mercy in proper cases." [32]

One chaplain learned the story of a sergeant whom he found in the stockade awaiting trial for bootlegging and embezzlement.   He admitted the former but positively denied the latter, which was based upon an alleged sale of Army supplies for his private gain.   In furnishing their home he and his wife had bought on credit a radio, refrigerator, rugs, and other furnishings, as well as a car.   His pay proved insufficient for the periodic payments on these accounts in addition to normal living costs, and he resorted to illicit means to in-

---

[30] Henry F. Gerecke, reports and oral statement; *The Lutheran Chaplain*, 4 Apr. 1947.

[31] Statement by Martin C. Poch.

[32] R. B. Stanton, Form 3, July 1943, 1st Ind.

crease his income. When his arrest stopped his pay, his wife and four small children were in distress. The military authorities found work for her in the camp laundry, but she had to hire a woman to take care of her children while she was away. One of the welfare organizations gave her $5. The chaplain arranged for a daily milk supply to be left at the house and for further leniency from the creditors, interested some officers' families in seeing that the children did not suffer, and took the family to the stockade so that they might see the father. Within a few months he was acquitted of the more serious charge, had served a lenient sentence for the other, was restored to duty, and was supporting his family from his honest income.[33]

The same chaplain told of the simple-minded boy who was serving a term for going home without leave. He received a letter from the prisoner's father, inclosing a dollar and asking him to buy snuff with it for his son. After some inquiry he learned that choice copenhagen could be bought for 11 cents a can, so he took the prisoner nine cans and a postal card for his change. Six weeks later came another dollar for more snuff, which he purchased and delivered. Expressing his gratitude, the boy said: "Do you know, Chaplain, they're very decent to us here. The prison officer gives us all the breaks he can. The food and the beds are as good as on the outside, and the work is no harder. I'm perfectly willing to stay here as long as they want me to."

At a large station hospital the chaplain found that the officer in charge of the prison ward would not allow ordinary periodicals to be given to the inmates on the theory that the purpose of imprisonment was deterrent and its effectiveness would be impaired by making the detention less disagreeable. The chaplain believed this policy to be based on a false psychology and that wholesome reading was much better than idleness but was loath to embarrass an earnest officer trying to perform a difficult task. Accordingly he compromised upon religious literature and saw that the prisoners had a variety of the publications of the several faiths.

A chaplain with many years of experience in penal institutions, civil as well as military, declared that he had found education for a definite purpose, such as learning a trade, the most effective continuing influence for the rehabilitation of men serving considerable periods of confinement. As director of education in a large disciplinary barracks his aim was to promote self discipline by encouraging the men not only to be good but to be good for something. With this purpose

---

[33] Observation of the author here *et. seq.*

firmly established, they were receptive to religious motivation.   Another chaplain found that many of the prisoners felt it would be hypocritical for them to attend church and made it his primary object to convince them that real progress toward respectable living could be made while they were serving time.   Another said that his recommendation carried much weight when a prisoner was considered for clemency or restoration to duty.[34]

At one of the large training camps a Reserve chaplain who had been a professor of history arranged with the prison officer to come to the stockade one evening a week and give an entertaining talk on the great characters of American history.   The officer welcomed the proposal, saying that it would have a wholesome effect and that he would try to give it the character of a reward for the good conduct of the prisoners.   The streets of the camp were named for the great soldiers of '76 and '61, and the chaplain need but point through the fence to have his theme.   Though these informal addresses were short and were well spiced with anecdote and humor, the simplest account of men like Washington and Lee could not fail of a strong moral impact.   Usually the chaplain spoke for about 20 minutes, then sat on the barracks steps for 2 hours and listened to the troubles of the men. After some months, but before the supply of military heroes on the street signs was exhausted, he was ordered to staff duties in Washington.   No farewell was more cordial than that of the prisoners when he told them that he would not see them again.

On these occasions his attention had been attracted by one of the prisoners who showed capacity for leadership, unofficially forming and dismissing the men on several occasions and attending to other matters when the sergeant was busy.   As his story was told to the chaplain, he had deserted a prior enlistment when very young and had not been apprehended.   When he reenlisted and his identity was discovered, he was charged with fraudulent enlistment, as the Statute of Limitations barred prosecution on the prior offense.   It appeared that he had answered truthfully all questions asked him at the time of his induction.   When asked if he had his discharge papers with him, he had replied in the negative.   Thus the charge of fraud could not be sustained.   Soon after his release he was riding in a bus which left the road and stopped in a precarious position partly under water on the steep bank of a deep river.   If the mud yielded and the bus slid farther, there would be no survivors.   This man and an officer broke out

---

[34] Harry A. Shuder to CofCh, 9 Oct. 1945; Charles J. Fabing, Form 3, Dec. 1946; John G. Bishop, 5 Oct. 1945, File 352, OCCh.

a window.   The private ordered the lieutenant through the opening but remained inside until the two had helped every passenger to safety. When the chaplain learned of this deed and of the Soldier's Medal which it brought, he was satisfied that these, rather than the stockade record, were the true measure of the man.   How his contacts with this man were related to his courage in the time of testing he never knew.

Brink told of the disillusioned and cynical soldier he found in the guardhouse and of the steps in his transformation.   Later he asked the chaplain to bring him the Bible his mother had sent him.   It was clean, for it never had been opened, but they read from it together. When word came that his mother was seriously ill, the prisoner had the chaplain send a cable which he said she would understand.   It read: "I have found your Bible again."   Months later the chaplain received a message from a chaplain at a distance, saying that Sergeant Blank was recovering from wounds and asked that his Bible be sent to him.   Now it was soiled and thumbed, but through it the chaplain could see two pictures: one of a manly corporal asking for baptism as an expression of his faith, the other of a sergeant leading his squad through a deadly fire to knock out an enemy gun.[35]

A fortunate series of events beginning on Christmas Day in 1943 made Edwin L. Kirtley acquainted with a family living in Hawaii who had spent several years as missionaries in the Marshall Islands. Knowing that he probably would go with a force soon to be sent for the liberation of those islands, he decided to learn what he could from these new friends about the people and their language.   They were able to supply him with a primer, a songbook, and a New Testament in Marshallese; photographs of themselves and of some of the natives which would be an effective introduction; and much useful information.[36]

The chaplain began by comparing Scripture texts in the two languages, identifying what seemed to be the important words, and studying how they were used in other passages.   Within 12 days he had a lexicon of 600 words in both languages.   Later he was gratified to learn that he had made only six errors.   Next he worked out the main principles of grammar and some common idioms and prepared a series of useful phrases which were printed for the use of the troops. On the voyage two interpreters drilled him in pronunciation, and he was able to converse in Marshallese by the time the expedition reached the islands.[37]

---

[35] Eben Cobb Brink—*And God Was There*, pp. 21–23.
[36] Edwin L. Kirtley to author, 16 Apr. 1956, and inclosure.
[37] *Ibid.*

The first of the frightened natives whom he encountered were delighted by a friendly greeting in their own language. It was possible to learn where most of the natives had taken refuge, and these areas were avoided in the bombardment of the Japanese positions. After the main defenses were taken, the chaplain went with the expedition sent to other islands to overcome any Japanese forces that might remain and to bring the natives to a place of safety until they could live in their own homes again. On the passage between two islands the chaplain began to hum a hymn tune. In a moment a group of refugees joined, singing lustily in their own language. Soldiers took up the melody, and before the next island was reached, 6 or 7 great hymns had voiced in 2 languages the common faith and joy. On one island nearly a hundred people were found. They and their village were neat and clean. As soon as they learned that the Americans would do them good and not harm and that the chaplain was a friend of their former missionaries, they welcomed them cordially. A woman brought out some Christian songbooks and a Bible in Marshallese, and the group joined the chaplain in reciting the Shepherd Psalm. The troops were much impressed by the high standard of life to which these people had risen. One was heard to remark: "I certainly believe in foreign missions now." The chaplain's knowledge of the native language is credited with saving many lives, both Marshallese and American.[38]

Perhaps the most striking fact in the whole history of religious work in the Army is the mutual respect and cooperation among chaplains of all faiths. While it was the unchanging ideal that every man should receive the ministrations of a clergyman of his own faith, there were many situations in which this was impossible. Virtually all the religious bodies of the country had recognized that a man with the education and character required for appointment to the chaplaincy could contribute to the spiritual strength of any man of religious earnestness. On the battlelines and in the hospitals the chaplains themselves learned that even more than this was true.

McGinnis was the only chaplain with his unit and many weekends was unable to get the help of either Jewish or Protestant chaplains. On these occasions he would appear just before the movies began on Saturday night and announce: "Tomorrow is Sunday. I am a Catholic chaplain, but I will do my darndest to give the Protestants a Protestant service at 0900, the Jews a Jewish service at 1000, and the Catholics a Catholic service at 1100. I will see you tomor-

---

[38] *Ibid.*

row." The men would cheer the chaplain and turn out in large numbers for all his services the next morning.[39]

On the eve of the Jewish holidays in 1941 a man came into the office of a Methodist chaplain in one of the great eastern camps and asked his help. He was of the Jewish faith but by some error had been listed as a Catholic in the orderly room, and he could not get a pass. The sergeant had agreed that he might go if he would get a certificate from the Jewish chaplain that he had been trained in the Jewish faith. He did not know where to find the rabbi, and the time was short. They found the Jewish chaplain and explained their problem. With a look of forced seriousness on his face he asked: "Do you expect me to convert a Catholic into a Jew in five minutes?" Fortunately nothing so drastic was necessary. The man got his certificate and started for home with his friends.

A few weeks later came Thanksgiving. The Methodist chaplain arranged a program and presided. His Jewish colleague made the opening prayer. A psalm was read by a Lutheran chaplain and the President's proclamation by his Catholic colleague. The company sang "Come, Ye Thankful People, Come," "Holy God, We Praise Thy Name," and "Now Thank We All Our God." The address was by a professor from the State University, and a Baptist chaplain pronounced the benediction.

When the Chaplain's Manual was revised in 1944, it contained suggestions for services on special occasions like Thanksgiving or Memorial Day. The thought was that these should be so free from any sectarian elements that people of all faiths might participate with reverence. Evidently the author believed that this would be achieved by avoiding any word or action which would be actively offensive to any person and was not aware that some religious bodies have rules forbidding their members to join in the worship of other groups. Some time later the matter was studied in the office of the Chief of Chaplains. In view of the position taken by some individuals and groups, it was recommended to all chaplains that in assemblies of this nature in which persons of all faiths were expected to join, the distinctly religious elements be limited to the invocation and benediction and the music to patriotic airs.[40]

In September 1943, Rosh Hashana was celebrated in the Yukon for the first time since 1904. The ceremonial wine was contributed by a Catholic chaplain, the prayers were read by a Special Service

---

[39] Cross, *op. cit.*, pp. 123–24.
[40] TM 16–205, p. 35.

officer, and a Protestant chaplain preached the sermon. A Baptist chaplain led volunteer workers in rebuilding a little Catholic church in Normandy which had been ruined by German artillery. A Methodist chaplain led a worship service for Jewish men which one said was just like the synagogue at home. In all seriousness he added: "Look, Chaplain, if the Methodists don't give you a break after the war, you come around and see me. I think we can get you a job in our synagogue in the Bronx." The same chaplain saved their torahs, candlesticks, and sacred vessels for the Jewish congregation of Sousse during the Tunisian campaign. These had been collected as the armies approached, but the bombardment had wrecked the town before they could be taken to a place of safety. The chaplain saved them from souvenir hunters, found the chief rabbi, and arranged to have them moved to a hiding place in the mountains.[41]

During a heavy bombardment a Jewish chaplain found himself in a foxhole with 13 men. Though there was not a Jew among them, they asked him to pray. This he did, reciting the Twenty-third Psalm, and bringing comfort and renewed strength to all. A colleague in New Guinea said that friendliness and tolerance were increased by the primitive conditions under which they lived. He added, "There are no bigots in foxholes." The lovers of freedom and justice saw more than the vindication of an injured people in the Jewish service in the Zeppelin Stadium at Nurnberg. The chaplain proclaimed those principles of righteousness which had rung true through three millenia and more on the very spot where Hitler often had preached his doctrine of the master race with all its odious implications. Above him towered a huge swastika, the emblem of Nazi oppression. After the service, explosives were placed and this symbol of cruelty and greed was blown to splinters.[42]

Most religious bodies in America came into existence because people at some time disagreed about matters of belief or practice so earnestly that separate organization seemed necessary. The advancement of these organizations and the propagation of distinctive beliefs frequently led to misunderstanding, distrust, and rivalry. This made it inevitable that some clergymen should carry with them into the military service at least a few convictions which seemed prejudices to other chaplains. When they stood up for what they conceived to be their rights, others thought them disagreeably aggressive.

Several complaints about the religious literature distributed in

[41] Cross, *op. cit.*, pp. 158, 160–62.
[42] J. Kaufman—*American Jews in World War II*, pp. 312–15.

Army chapels reached the Chief of Chaplains. These involved publications of several groups. Though some protests were against interpretations of history where the facts themselves are in dispute, they usually grew out of doctrinal expositions which were illustrated and emphasized by showing the errors and follies of others. The Chief of Chaplains repeatedly warned against controversial literature, which arouses antipathy and ill will though it convinces no one, and insisted that individual chaplains must assume full responsibility for the propriety of the literature distributed by them.[43]

In a few places some friction arose over the use of chapels by various groups. Generally this concerned ornamentation or the display of symbols. Early complaints about scenes with sectarian implications being painted on chapel walls led the Chief of Chaplains to direct that all such adornments be of such a nature that they could be removed or covered with drapes when the chapel should be in use by other faiths. As this did not end all complaints on sectarian or artistic grounds, he required photographs or drawings of proposed decorations to be submitted for approval before installation.[44]

The rule that chapels must present a neutral appearance when not in use was included in the Manual and in Army Regulations, but this did not solve the problem in all particulars. Certain symbolic articles or pictures are very important in Catholic worship or private devotions. Others are highly considered in the usages of some of the Protestant bodies but are matters of indifference to other groups. It would be a convenience to the Catholics if the Stations of the Cross or similar aids to devotion could be on display at all times for the benefit of those who might care to go to the chapel in their free time for prayer and meditation. The same would be true of other symbols for many Protestants but to a considerably lesser degree. Moreover, what gives a chapel used by all faiths a truly neutral appearance? Some would feel that symbolism cannot go beyond a Bible open at the Hebrew Scriptures, literature sacred to all three faiths.

A deplorable incident occurred at one of the camps when plans were made for an Easter sunrise service with music by a military band. One bandsman demurred on the ground that he had conscientious scruples against participation in a Protestant service, and the Catholic chaplain supported him in his protest. Unpleasant insinuations were made at headquarters. One officer thought the man was shirking a duty for which he was trained and paid because he did

---

[43] TM 16–205 (1944), pp. 72–73.
[44] *Ibid.*

not want to rise before dawn on even one Sunday. Another could not see how playing an instrument could compromise any reasonable sense of obligation and felt that the chaplain was actually inciting a soldier to insubordination. To end the controversy, the senior Protestant chaplain asked the commander to revoke his order for the participation of the band in the service. Even this did not remove all sense of resentment, for the Catholic chaplain complained several times that the adjutant and others treated him with a reserve which showed that they misconstrued his motives.[45]

Another episode is typical of the very few clashes which occurred among chaplains of various faiths over matters of belief or practice. On an important anniversary in the calendar of his church a chaplain preached a historic sermon on the developments which made this anniversary important. Chaplains of a widely different faith obtained a copy of the outline and sent it to a high official of their church, charging that its historic statements were false, that certain key words were insulting to their church, and that such a sermon tended to engender ill will among military personnel. The Chief of Chaplains hinted that both parties might have exercised more courtesy and charity and recognized that agreement about the historic facts never could be reached and that it is not the province of a military authority to interfere with the doctrinal freedom of a chaplain in his own pulpit.[46]

Early in the war it was stated that a few Protestant chaplains had impersonated Catholic priests and heard the confessions of the sick and wounded. This was pressed as a reason why special insignia should be authorized for Catholic chaplains. This proposal was presented to the President and referred through the Chief of Staff to the Chief of Chaplains. He opposed it vigorously on the ground that the change of insignia would create another barrier where too many existed already. He knew of no instances of deliberate impersonation, though any chaplain ministering to the wounded and dying might listen to any statement they cared to make and speak words of comfort and assurance. The few cases of mistaken identity of which he had learned could be remedied much more easily than by a change of insignia.[47]

At a recent chaplains' conference Earl Weed told of his embarrassment during the First World War when he tried to minister to a wounded man who recognized his insignia and said, "Father, I want

---

[45] Files, OCCh.
[46] *Ibid.*
[47] *Ibid.*

absolution." Saying that he was not a Catholic priest and could not give formal absolution, he recited some great passages of Scripture and prayed, but the man turned away in disappointment. Soon afterward he met Chaplain O'Flaherty, told him of the experience, and asked: "Isn't there *something* that a Protestant chaplain can do to help a wounded Catholic boy?" The chaplain looked at him for a moment as the rain poured from their helmets, then handed him a rosary and prayer book, saying: "Have him say these beads if he is able. If not, help him to say the prayer of contrition and tell him that Father O'Flaherty said if he does this with sincerity he will get absolution." Early in the Second World War, Chaplain Weed printed a small leaflet containing prayers of the three major faiths chosen for this purpose by leaders of these groups, with suggestions of how they could be used most effectively by chaplains of other faiths to give comfort to wounded men. Privately supplied, this leaflet was given to all chaplains on duty, and many found it helpful in the crises of battlefield and hospital.

When a chaplain seeks to minister to a wounded man, it is important that he should have a clear record of any earlier ministration he may have received from any other chaplain. On 7 June 1944 General Eisenhower ordered that this should be noted on the bottom of the Field Medical Record and the Emergency Medical Tag. Because the space was limited, he authorized the use of these abbreviations: Ex—Extreme Unction has been given; Cfes—Confession has been heard; Cmun—Communion has been given; Adm—Administered to by a chaplain. This led to the proposal that space be provided in these forms for this notation. Forwarded to the Surgeon General as a request of the Chief of Chaplains, this recommendation was approved. A large supply of these forms were on hand at that time, but he directed that the desired matter be included when the next printing should take place.[48]

An incident told by Lenk is typical of thousands in which chaplains were sympathetic friends to the wounded and dying. The chaplain knelt beside a man whose throat was wrapped in a blood-soaked bandage. As soon as he recognized the chaplain, he smiled and gave him his fountain pen. For an instant the chaplain did not understand, but the surgeon whispered: "He has lost his voice and wants to write a note." The chaplain gave him a piece of paper, and he wrote: "Padre, tell my wife and baby I love them. I am not afraid to die." [49]

---

[48] Letter orders, Hq. ETO, 7 June 1944; James H. Grady to CofCh, 26 Jan. 1945, *et seq.*
[49] *Chaplains of the Fifth Army*, p. 82.

There were 8,896 chaplains on duty at some time during the war.[50] The Adjutant General's Final Report of Battle Casualties for World War II shows that 204 chaplains were battle casualties from 7 December 1941 through 31 December 1946. The report lists 51 chaplains killed in action, 76 wounded in action of whom 10 died of wounds, 54 captured of whom 17 died while prisoners of war, and three reported missing in action but later returned to duty. In addition there were 46 chaplains who died of nonbattle causes: 20 in accidents, 23 from disease, and 3 from other causes. The quality of service was such that 1,783 chaplains received 2,453 decorations.[51] From the magnitude of the struggle and the great number involved, it follows that these totals greatly exceed those of any previous war; though the proportion of chaplains who gave their lives was less than in the Civil War or the Revolution. The record of heroic action and devoted service which these men made on every continent and ocean testifies that they were not unworthy heirs to the tradition sustained by the best of their predecessors through the centuries.

[50] Data furnished by CofCh, 30 Jan. 1956.
[51] *Ibid.*

CHAPTER XVIII

Counseling and Welfare

Every experienced chaplain knows that some of his most important duties are not religious or but incidentally so. These may relate to virtually any matter of importance to a soldier or his family and may range from considerations of life or death to those which are ridiculously trivial. Chaplains have learned, however, that the latter type may have gained a false perspective in the mind of the men concerned and should be treated with respect. A few tried to laugh the men out of trifling grievances or anxieties. One distributed a printed card bearing numbered spaces, each entitling the bearer to one cry on the chaplain's shoulder. Another went about camp with a towel on each shoulder, symbolizing his readiness to serve in this manner. These may have served a good purpose, but the danger was that men with real problems would be repelled from consulting the chaplain lest they fail to get a sympathetic hearing.

"Tell it to the chaplain" has gained a currency almost equal to "you're in the Army now." By implication it is a compliment to the patience and universal kindness which every chaplain is expected to have. The expression can mean anything from "go jump in the lake" to a literal "I don't know." One first sergeant used the phrase so freely that a group of recruits, taking it literally, overwhelmed the chaplain with petty problems. Troubles of this nature are usually dissipated easily by a friendly talk, and a sympathetic interest often makes lighter the actual burdens which cannot be removed. One chaplain was deeply gratified when a soldier told him that in their regiment the rule was not "take your troubles to the chaplain" but "go to the chaplain with your problems and he will help you before you get into trouble." [1]

It was typical American humor when the surgeon and chaplain who traveled in the same jeep painted on the side "Body and Soul."

---

[1] Cary Bousman—"The Human Side of the Chaplaincy," *The Advance*, 1 Apr. 1943; Verne H. Warner—*The Messenger*, 29 June 1943; Truman H. Tobias, Form 3, May 1943.

This partnership works both ways, and neither sphere is exclusive.[2] The same is true of disciplinary matters involving either police action or legal process. So many of the problems brought to chaplains grow out of the violation of regulations or laws that they have found a cooperative relation with the provost marshal and the judge advocate very helpful. Often the chaplain has been able to learn underlying facts which clarified the case, sometimes revealing extenuating facts. At other times men have given incriminating information to chaplains. An important legal question, not definitely clarified until recent years, concerned the circumstances under which a chaplain might be required to reveal such facts to a court-martial or other official agency.

An interesting case involving this question arose in the Pacific area in 1943. An Air officer left a sum of money at headquarters for safe-keeping. When the custodian was to be transferred to a distance, he turned it over to another officer at the base. The latter denied ever having received it when the owner asked for it some time later. A board of officers took up the matter, but before they reached a decision, the money was turned over to a responsible officer by Chaplain Scanlon. He refused to tell the board where he got the money on the ground that is was a privileged communication and that his influence with the men would be destroyed if they found that he could not be trusted to hold in confidence what they might tell him. He admitted that the facts and money had not been given him in the confessional but maintained that they were none-the-less privileged.[3]

The board found the second officer responsible for the money, and he was charged with embezzlement and perjury and brought to trial. The chaplain was called as a witness but refused to state who had given him the money for the same reasons as on the earlier occasion. He was warned that his refusal subjected him to prosecution, but he stood his ground. Preparations were made to try him under the 96th Article of War, but these were cut short by an order from higher headquarters forbidding the proceedings against the chaplain and directing the court to continue without his testimony. The general directed further that in the future in his command any confidences given to chaplains in the performance of their duties should be privileged.[4]

Both parties to this disagreement seem to have misunderstood some points of applicable law. The chaplain may have remembered

---

[2] Harry C. Butcher—*My Three Years with Eisenhower*, p. 767.
[3] John Patrick Crehan—"Privileged Communications," *The Infantry Journal*, July 1949, pp. 13–15.
[4] *Ibid.*

imperfectly a provision of paragraph 46½ of Army Regulations as corrected in 1917. This made it the duty of chaplains to counsel enlisted men under arrest before trial and added, "Communications, verbal or written, between the chaplain and enlisted man subject to trial or discipline shall be treated as confidential and privileged." When the new system of regulations was adopted, the substance of this paragraph appeared in AR 60–5, 5d, 15 February 1925, but the statement about privileged communications was omitted. The same was true of later revisions, including two published in 1941. Had the chaplain cited regulations, he could have shown only that the type of information he refused to divulge, if given by an enlisted man, would have been privileged 20 years before.

The legal advisor to the board of officers showed a degree of confusion when he stated that attorneys and physicians were the only professional groups to whom this immunity extends. The *Manual for Courts Martial* of 1928 made it clear that information gained by an Army surgeon or civilian physician in the performance of his professional duties is not privileged. Later decisions of the Judge Advocate General reaffirmed this rule.[5]

The general's order and similar cases involving the same principle called attention to the importance of this matter, and the right claimed by the chaplain was soon fortified in regulations. Change 1 in paragraph 5d of AR 60–5, 25 September 1946, as a matter of policy, gave information acquired in this manner a privileged status. Later differences of opinion about the exact meaning of this directive led to its revision and publication as paragraph 6d(2) of AR 60–5, 12 December 1946. This stated plainly that a communication to an Army chaplain in his capacity as a clergyman, whether formal or otherwise, is a privileged communication, and he will not be required to disclose such information to a court-martial or similar body unless this privilege is expressly waived by the person concerned. This principle was included in the 1951 revision of the *Manual for Courts Martial* and applied to all the armed forces.[6]

Problems concerning marriage and family relations were among those most frequently brought to the chaplain for help. As many soldiers were away from home for the first time and were thrown upon their own responsibility in personal matters, some of them felt the need for guidance by disinterested persons of experience. Others needed it

---

[5] *Manual for Courts Martial*, 1928 ed., pp. 131–32; JAG's Dep't, Board of Review, *Holdings, Opinions, and Reviews*, XXXV, 130.

[6] "Rules of Evidence," *Manual for Courts Martial*, 1951 ed.

without recognizing the fact.   This made it important for chaplains to discourage hasty action in situations where they had no opportunity to advise more fully.   Though he may not have emphasized the most vital point, one chaplain was at least stressing the need for thinking twice when he placed the photograph of a beautiful movie star on the bulletin board and wrote under it: "Unless the girl you want to marry is as good looking as this, don't see me." [7]

Frequently men approached their chaplain after their decision had been made, either to get his approval or to discuss secondary considerations.   In some units marriage was permitted only with the consent of the commanders, and some officers would not give this approval unless the chaplain concurred.   In addition to the many practical considerations which would be important in all contemplated marriages, two were of especial concern to many chaplains.   In foreign countries they frequently found that men were not recognizing the full implication of differences of nationality and culture, and sometimes of language and religion.   The latter was very important in any country, especially when the proposed marriage was of a Catholic and Protestant.   To help the young people realize the factors which might lead to future discord, some chaplains gave them leaflets written by clergymen of both faiths which pointed out these dangers and discouraged this type of marriage.[8]

A New York chaplain, on duty in a southern State, was approached by a couple who wished to be married at once.   The girl had come for the weekend, bringing a New York license, and they proposed that the chaplain use his home address and certify that the marriage was performed in New York.   This he declined to do, urging them not to begin their married life with deceit and falsehood.   A kindly corporal at headquarters tried to help and took the perplexed couple to the county seat to obtain a local license.   Here the ceremony was performed by a magistrate.   In order that they might take a short trip, the bridegroom borrowed some money from the corporal.   On his return to camp this well-meaning man's satisfaction in having carried through this project in spite of the limitations of Saturday afternoon was dampened by the discovery that the required permission of the commanding officer had not been obtained and that the young husband had been absent without leave from his unit for some days.   Unfortunately the chaplain was not able to follow the case beyond this point.

---

[7] Washington *Star*, 19 Dec. 1943.

[8] James A. Burris, report, July 1946; Montgomery *Advertiser*, 20 Dec. 1942.

While some cases were more complicated, others were solved with less effort and perplexity. One chaplain was called to the hospital to see a patient whose need for the chaplain's services was urgent. His girl had sent back his ring, but he was confident that if he could get to his home 700 miles away he could make both her and a certain sailor see the error of their way. What he wanted of the chaplain was his help in getting a furlough. He was finally convinced that it would be better to remain where he was and try the effectiveness of correspondence. The next day the chaplain visited the hospital and noticed a soldier and a local girl revealing every sign of a deep and lasting affection. A second glance showed that the man was the heart-broken lover of the day before. Though he knew that time is a great healer of such wounds, he never had realized that 24 hours can accomplish so much.[9]

Even more diverse are the many troubles of families already established which come to the chaplain's attention. A father consulted the chaplain of his son's regiment about the hostile attitude of his son. The chaplain got father, mother, son, and daughter together and drew from them enough information to reveal the cause of the trouble. Though the boy was more than 18, the family treated him as a child, a fact which he had begun to resent. A better understanding all around soon ended the estrangement. Another case is typical of many. A newly married soldier told his chaplain of his troubles with his wife. After a thorough inquiry the chaplain went to her home town and interviewed the wife. As a go-between friendly to both, he soon saw harmony restored.[10]

One chaplain followed a practice designed to perpetuate the sacred associations of the weddings. Whenever he performed the marriage ceremony in the chapel at the Arizona Air Field where he was stationed, he had a complete recording made. This he presented to the couple with the request that they play it over on each wedding anniversary.[11]

The actual performance of the marriage ceremony by chaplains for military personnel frequently involved perplexing questions. The fact that a military reservation is definitely under Federal jurisdiction suggested that a marriage could be performed on the post without reference to the laws of any State. However, as Federal legislation had not provided specifically for this situation, chaplains were directed to

[9] Willard B. Smith—"What Does a Chaplain Do?," TID file 85–A–1, OCCh.
[10] *Ibid.*; *The Polar Tech*, 3 Sep. 1943.
[11] Williston Wirt, Form 3, June 1944.

waive this dubious prerogative and conform in all particulars to the laws of the State wherein their station was located. For their assistance the Chief of Chaplains prepared a compendium of the marriage laws of the several States, but this work was not published, as the Judge Advocate General pointed out that changes were being made by various States and it soon would be so out of date as to be dangerously misleading. Instead, a technical circular was issued to remind chaplains of the many details which are important in the laws of some States in order that they might inform themselves fully concerning the laws in force wherever they might be stationed.

Almost as soon as troops began to be sent overseas, there arose cases of couples who wished to be married although it was impossible for them to meet for the ceremony. This led to a considerable legal discussion. On the one hand it was argued with some plausibility that many States accord legal recognition to the relationship known as a common law marriage and that a more definite commitment is involved in any of the expedients sometimes used when both parties cannot be present at a single place. The most common of these arrangements seems to have been the proxy marriage. The usual plan was to perform identical ceremonies at the same time with an agreed proxy acting for the absent person in each place. An alternative was to establish telephonic communication between the parties so that the one at a distance could make the necessary pledges during the ceremony as if he were present. Another method which many believed more likely to be declared valid if brought to a judicial test was the written marriage contract. The document would set forth all the essential commitments of a marriage, and the agreement would be complete at the time and place it was signed by the second party.

Early in the war some marriages of this nature were recognized by the Federal authorities as a valid basis for monetary allowances to the brides, but this policy was reversed when a legal study of the matter raised a serious question about their general validity. The courts of some States in deciding cases in which this point was not involved had used language which seemed to imply the legality of such marriages. However, this was no guarantee that they would be sustained if challenged in other States. The Judge Advocate General reported that no assurance could be given on the basis of legislation or court decision that these arrangements would be held valid in any State. The Chief of Chaplains conveyed this information to all chaplains on duty, urging that they be very cautious about involvement in so dubious a matter.   In 1945, Minnesota enacted temporary legislation validating absentee marriages in cases of pregnancy, requiring a combination of a written contract and a proxy ceremony.[12]

Though the chaplains' relation to recreation and entertainment was supposed to be advisory only, there were many situations early in the war when they did much more than advise.   A chaplain in Alaska took a leading part in providing a suitable recreation building in Anchorage.   He had an old sawmill rebuilt to cut the lumber, selected the trees to be felled, and supervised the construction of a fine building.   He established a library and provided magazines, scriptures, radios, phonographs, and games.   Three times a week he showed moving pictures or gave lectures or educational talks.   This is typical of the many ways in which chaplains worked for the comfort and welfare of the troops before the development of a body of trained special service officers provided other leadership in this important field.[13]

The chaplain's advisory responsibility sometimes compelled him to protest against certain books in the library or periodicals in the post exchange or to condemn features which occasionally crept into the camp shows.   Unfortunately this negative function was more conspicuous and tended to hide the many positive contributions to the high quality of such activities.   A group of soldiers in England, where its tragic background could be appreciated, saw the film *Mrs. Miniver.* They were much impressed by its effective use of the psalm beginning, "He that dwelleth in the secret place of the Most High shall abide under the shadow of the Almighty," and came to their chaplain asking where they could find it.   He provided them with copies of the New Testament and Psalms and was convinced that the picture and their later reading were powerful influences in their lives.[14]

The United Service Organizations exerted themselves to keep the camp shows which they sponsored on a high level of propriety.   Entertainers who had speaking parts were pledged not to depart from the approved scripts.   Nevertheless, a few of them introduced objectionable jokes or similar matter into some programs in the belief that this was a good way to hold the interest of their soldier audiences. Complaints came from various sources, but a majority were registered by chaplains.   Some were indefinite and useless, but whenever the Chief of Chaplains transmitted specific information of actual impro-

---

[12] *Decisions of the Judge Advocate General,* 13 Sep. 1942, II, 222, 24 March 1944, III, 467; *Decisions of the Comptroller General,* Vol. 24, Feb. 1945; WD Bulletin 33, 6 Dec. 1946; *Laws of Minnesota,* 1945, p. 786.

[13] H. W. Bacon, Form 3, July 1943, 1st Ind.; *The Living Church,* 10 Jan. 1943.

[14] Eben Cobb Brink—*And God Was There,* pp. 25–26.

prieties to the director, the offending entertainer was immediately ordered home and dismissed.   How sadly the taste and intelligence of a large proportion of the American soldiers were underestimated by some players was demonstrated by the great popularity of the Shakespearian plays when they were given in many overseas camps by some of the country's foremost actors and by the appeal of musical programs of an equally high order.[15]

In Europe a chaplain established a rest center in an ancient castle. While several other features attracted the men, a daily rendition of light classical music by a talented pianist from one of the companies had a strong appeal.   At an installation on a Florida beach a chaplain sponsored a Sunday afternoon program of recorded classical selections known as "Music under the Palms."   Interest was enhanced by informal discussions of music after the concert led by two chaplain's assistants who were noted musicians and teachers.   A Negro chaplain in the Pacific organized a glee club of 25 voices which sang for services, in the hospital, and over the radio.   Just before Christmas 8 officers and 22 Newfoundland girls made recordings of the traditional music of the season under the direction of an American chaplain. This was broadcast several times by a Newfoundland station and shortwaved twice as part of the oversea program of an American station.[16]

Before such facilities were provided by other agencies in some installations, chaplains found means to maintain recreation rooms where various programs were carried out.   Many other comforts and conveniences were highly appreciated, but coffee and doughnuts in the hour before "Taps" were very popular.   At one chapel annex the Red Cross served them to all comers for 13 hours daily, and the Central Post Fund paid the bill.   Another chaplain lost nothing in popularity when he induced the cooks to make 750 doughnuts one dark and unpleasant night and distributed them among the men in the gun implacements.   Many chaplains found a healthy interest in hobbies, some of which had a considerable educational value.   One of the most popular of these was the taking and developing of pictures, but others worked in wood and metal, and one regimental chaplain developed a shop for the repair of watches and eye glasses.[17]

Until the assignment of special service officers to some transports

[15] File 250.1, OCCh., *passim.*

[16] Reports of Elburn S. Moore, Sep. 1945, Wallace C. Fiske, Sep. 1943, Curtis O. Greenfield, Oct. 1943, Gomer S. Rees, Dec. 1943.

[17] Reports of T. J. DuBose, Oct. 1945, Richard B. Cheatham, Nov. 1944, Forest R. Stickler, Jan. 1945, Vernon F. Perry, June 1945, French E. Taylor, Feb. 1946, Ralph E. Gebhard, July 1945, Gordon L. King, Aug. 1945, Lewis A. McGee, June 1944.

late in the war, this was one field to which the exclusion of chaplains from secular duties did not apply.   Scores of voyage reports show that the responsibility of the transport chaplain for entertainment and recreation was as pressing as his religious duties.   These duties were expressly charged to him prior to 22 August 1942 by AR 30–1155 and after that date by AR 55–355.

The programs carried out on some ships show great ingenuity and resourcefulness.   One chaplain arranged portable microphones so that men who could not be at the chief center of entertainment could contribute their part to amateur shows.   Some were able to have surprisingly good orchestras playing by the second or third day at sea, though others felt it safer to depend upon recordings.   Athletic events, such as boxing, were generally popular when space and other considerations would permit.   When they could be shown, moving pictures were of great value; and the daily paper, giving world news obtained by radio, was of universal interest.   Lectures on the country to which the troops were going never failed of a good hearing on the outward voyage, and frequently the interest warranted regular classes in the geography and history of these lands.   Just before his unit sailed for Alaska, one chaplain was able to arrange for an illustrated lecture on that country by Father Hubbard, the famous "Glacier Priest."[18]

Some enterprising chaplains had their programs organized and in full operation before the ship left port.   Former teachers would be assigned to conduct classes for men with educational deficiencies or who wished an introduction to a foreign language.   Someone with journalistic experience would be put in charge of the newspaper, and similar delegations of responsibility would be made as capable personnel could be found.   In some instances chaplains felt that they relinquished too much of their control over such activities and thus failed to guard against occasional items or incidents which some of the auditors would consider in poor taste.   One chaplain had great difficulty getting the needed help with the ship's paper.   At last a little girl of 11 volunteered and was appointed "Inquiring Reporter."   She proved to be a very helpful addition to the staff, and her column was an important feature of the publication to the end of the voyage.[19]

When chaplains could not be given office space to which the men could come freely, they found other means of making themselves accessible.   One estimated that 300 men came to his office some days with

---

[18] Raymond Collier to CofCh, 23 July 1942; File of Voyage Reports, OCCh, *passim;* Joseph D. Duchek, Form 3, Aug. 1946.

[19] Voyage Reports, OCCh., *passim.*

some kind of problem. Naturally his interviews with most of them had
to be very brief.   A few chaplains complained of the unfriendly attitude of the ship's officers, but nearly all enjoyed a cordial support like
that of the officer who said to his chaplain: "I am your commanding
officer; you are the chaplain of this ship.   Whatever you do, though
it be right or wrong, I will back you up 100 percent; and if you are
wrong, I will deal with you individually later." [20]

The soldier who told his chaplain that he was "un-financed" was
not alone in his difficulty, but few have been such victims of circumstances as the man who asked for a Red Cross emergency loan very
soon after payday.   Asked what he had done with his $30, he replied:
"I spent 10 dollars for booze and 12 shooting craps, and I'm afraid I
wasted the rest."   Whatever the reason, situations of actual need were
sure to arise.   Normally they were met by the loan service of the Red
Cross or by the Army Emergency Relief.   In rare cases these were not
accessible and the chaplain had to find means of meeting the need.
Some maintained informal loan funds where the price of a railroad
ticket could be obtained without delay when the necessity arose.   In
other situations men needed help in sending their money home, and
the chaplains were able to do this for them.[21]

On the eve of sailing, Armitstead arranged for a civilian priest to
hear confessions in his office, and more than a hundred men came.
Twelve hours after rising, these men had received nothing to eat. The
Red Cross had plenty of food on the pier but could not give any to
men on a ship.   The situation was relieved in a measure when one of
the chaplains purchased 500 candy bars at the post exchange.   Redfern was commended by his commander for his thoughfulness about
the little comforts for the sick in the hospital.   Schwegler was credited
with a "distinct therapeutic benefit" to the patients where he worked.
Oliver was confined in a solitary dark cell on half of the rice ration for
persistently protesting to the Japanese Commandant against his treatment of prisoners in violation of the Geneva Convention.   For refusing
to tell how the medicines which were keeping some of the prisoners
alive were smuggled into the camp, he was beaten unconscious three
times.   A blow from a rifle butt broke a bone in his neck and necessi-
tated the wearing of a support as long as he lived.[22]

---

[20] *The Story of Christian Science Wartime Activities*, p. 173; Arthur J. Estes, Form 3, Aug. 1946;
F. E. Maples, N. D.

[21] Willard B. Smith, *loc. cit.*; *History of Chaplains' Activities in the Pacific*, p. 318.

[22] Johnson N. Armitstead, voyage report; Edgar F. Redfern, Form 3, June 1943, 1st Ind.;
H. G. Schwegler, Form 3, June 1943, 1st Ind.; Christopher Cross—*Soldiers of God*, p. 57; "Beaten
by Japs," *The Army and Navy Chaplain*, Apr. 1945.

One chaplain took photographs of the men of his battalion in many situations and, when considerations of security would permit, sent copies to relatives if he had occasion to write to them.   Often these were published in hometown papers.   They were especially appreciated by the families of the men who died in service.   To a chaplain stationed in Hawaii fell the sad duty of informing the families of members of the 100th Battalion killed or missing in action.   This unit was composed entirely of Americans of Japanese ancestry.   For their magnificent record in Italy during the 20 weeks beginning about the first of March 1944, they are said to be the most decorated unit that ever fought for the United States.   Day after day the chaplain delivered the messages of condolence from the Secretary of War, 27 one day and 28 another.   A few times he had the joyous experience of bearing a second message stating that the man previously reported missing had been found alive and well.   No such happy sequel followed his mission to the home of a widow whose two sons, her only children, were with Clark.   One day he bore the message that one son had been severely wounded.   The next he had to tell her that the other had been killed.[23]

Another matter of vital concern to chaplains was sex morality and its correlative, venereal disease.   Though their objective in relation to the latter was identical with that of the medical officers, there were times when the two were not in full agreement about specific methods.   In some places prophylactic stations were conspicuously maintained near houses of prostitution on the principle that if men would go there they should be encouraged to take prompt treatment afterward.   Most chaplains felt that this implied, if not the sanction of immorality by the Army, at least that it was taken for granted.   In opposition they made every appeal to the pride and moral sense of the men to keep themselves from evil and at the same time avoid all danger of infection.   In some places the stations were made less conspicuous to outsiders while the men were told where they could be found but warned that they would be much safer to avoid all need for their services.

Another example of differing opinions about how to attain a common end grew out of the order in some units that every man going on pass should take a venereal prophylactic unit.   The chaplains believed that this degraded the men who had no intention of wrongdoing and weakened the influences tending to restrain all who left camp. Believing this to be psychologically as well as morally unsound, the

---

[23] Douglass Hall to CofCh, 30 Apr. 1947; Frank A. Spear to CofCh, 16 Apr. 1947.

Chief of Chaplains arranged with the Surgeon General to have the following change made in AR 40–210 on 1 May 1943:

> While insuring ready availability of venereal prophylactic units to prevent disease in accordance with the foregoing, no authority is contained herein for forced issue of units to individuals who do not wish to draw them or buy them.

The difficulties frequently met in attempts to regulate situations of this nature are well illustrated by the story of a house of prostitution in an oversea colonial dependency of one of the allied powers. Being regulated and frequently inspected, the danger of contracting a disease there was much less than in the slum resorts of the nearby town. The institution was legal under local civil law. Not only American military and naval forces were stationed at the base but also those of two friendly powers. Policies for dealing with the situation differed. Strict orders from the Secretary of War, applicable to military personnel, were to some extent neutralized by the divergent policies of other authorities. Full agreement about the practical effectiveness of the differing policies was not reached while the base continued in operation.[24]

A remarkable example of what can be accomplished by substituting higher interests for those which tend to degrade was worked out by the chaplain of an oversea unit in which the venereal rate was alarming. With the cooperation of 60 men and officers, steps were taken to bar objectionable entertainment from the base. Next a school was established, offering 18 courses ranging from music appreciation to agriculture. Soon 380 men were enrolled, studying with enthusiasm. In 2 months there were no cases of venereal disease. Realizing that this enthusiasm would wane with some, the chaplain directed his efforts toward strengthening the home ties of the men as an aid in holding the ground already won.[25]

These incidents reemphasize the fact that great numbers of soldiers away from home need a friend whom they can trust and to whom they can turn in times of perplexity or distress. Many chaplains have been perplexed themselves by some of the situations referred to them, but agreement is all but unanimous that such ministrations to individuals are highly valuable and rewarding. Those who have shown themselves most successful have been ingenious and resourceful, but it is equally significant that they have been men of unfailing kindness and patience and have been able to see matters from the soldier's point of view.

---

[24] Files, OCCh.
[25] *The Story of Christian Science Wartime Activities*, p. 178.

CHAPTER XIX

Cold War

The decade following the surrender of Germany and Japan was a unique period in American military history. The tasks and programs of Army chaplains involved factors equally unusual. They were stationed in nearly all parts of the world and must remain in some of these areas for long periods. Many unpredictable forces were at work in some regions, and military commitments involved much more than the occupation of conquered territories during their readjustment to a peaceful economy. The conflict in Korea and operations under the sponsion of the United Nations constituted an episode of major importance but did not destroy the general continuity of military tasks and problems in other parts of the world. To fulfill their responsibilities in so complex a situation, the chaplains had to be very resourceful in dealing with present conditions while they prepared for an uncertain future.

When combat ceased in the late summer of 1945, there were 8,141 chaplains on duty in an army of more than 8 million. Virtually every soldier was eager to return to his home, now that his military task seemed finished, and some chaplains were as impatient of delay as the men in the ranks. Certain organizational changes adopted during the war to meet temporary situations had revealed permanent values and had to be adapted to the Army of the future. Personnel, training, and equipment for that army each demanded puzzling decisions. More immediate was the necessity that every chaplain who remained on duty during the period of transition should be untiring in his efforts to conserve spiritual values among men awaiting their turn to go home and those remaining for service as occupation troops. This required as complete devotion and a greater ingenuity than service on the battlefield.

The most conspicuous change in organization during the war was the grouping of arms and services in the three great divisions: the Army Ground Service, and Air Forces. On 13 May 1946, Executive Order 9722 directed the Secretary of War to redistribute within the War Department those agencies which had been grouped in the Army Service Forces.[1]   This did not greatly affect the administration of the chaplaincy, for the Ground and Air Forces continued as the coordinate combat branches and some contemplated changes were deferred until Congress could enact legislation which was expected to effect an important reorganization.

The National Security Act of 26 July 1947 placed the Army, Navy, and Air Forces on a parity within the new Department of Defense.   During the period of adjustment in which an independent organization for the Air Force was being developed, Army chaplains continued to serve air personnel.   Many of these, besides numbers of Reserve chaplains not on duty, were transferred permanently to the Air Forces within a few weeks after this was authorized by a joint Army and Air Force regulation on 16 May 1949.   Charles I. Carpenter, who had been reassigned as Air Chaplain after a tour of duty overseas, became the first Chief of Air Force Chaplains.[2]

The Army and Air Force Chaplain Board was an important agency during this period of readjustment.   It established policies for the procurement and transfer of chaplains and their call to active duty, for obtaining equipment and disposing of surplus, and for the administration of the Chaplain School and of religious funds pertaining jointly to the offices of the two chiefs.   One chaplain from each office constituted a subcommittee to act for the board on appointments, active duty, ecclesiastical indorsement, educational qualifications, and procurement matters concerning the civilian churches.[3]

The unification of the services naturally led to the formation of a joint agency to consider matters of concern to all chaplains.   On 18 July 1949, the Armed Forces Chaplain Board was established in the office of the Secretary of Defense.   It was composed of the 3 chiefs and of 1 other chaplain from each service, and it was directed that the chairmanship rotate annually among the chiefs.   The responsibilities of the board were grouped in three broad fields: personnel, equipment, and civilian relations.   It was directed to establish policies to govern procurement, standards, requirements, assignment, and training of military chaplains, including the civilian components; to establish and maintain a close and harmonious relationship with civilian church organizations and the clergy; and to establish policies for the procurement of supplies, equipment, and facilities.   Within a few weeks of its estab-

---

[1] *Federal Register,* 15 May 1946, p. 1.
[2] 61 *Stat.* 495; File 334, OCCh.
[3] *Ibid.*

lishment the board reported agreement on policies for dealing with several of the more important of these matters.[4]

A very different task was assigned to the Chaplain Board of the Army, which became an important agency in the years following the war. It was activated at the Chaplain School in October 1945 under the provisions of AR 400–5 and ASF Circular 364, 1944, and was definitely established the first of the following February. Necessarily its purposes were stated in general terms. It was to study and report on such matters as might be referred to it by the Chief of Service and to originate recommendations for the improvement of the chaplaincy.[5]

At first the board was composed of instructors at the Chaplain School, the plan being that three should be permanent and others associate members. Experience soon showed that board activities frequently would be crowded aside by other duties under such an arrangement. In June 1946 the War Department was reorganized, and the board became a distinct class II installation. This placed it directly under the administrative authority of the Chief of Chaplains. The membership was increased from 3 to 5, and work on a comprehensive program began.[6]

During the succeeding 10 years many and varied matters were assigned to the board for study and recommendation. These concerned nearly every phase of a chaplain's qualifications, training, assignment, equipment, duties, and assistants, and most of them were directed toward some deficiency which had been revealed by the exigencies of war or the reorganization which followed. Assigned tasks were especially numerous in 1952 when 146 projects were referred, and some of these were as extensive as the revision of the chaplain's manual, plans for the training of chaplains' assistants, and the preparation of a manual for hospital chaplains. In 1954 the board was directed to revise the Character Guidance Discussion Topics. This soon grew into a major task, as it was believed that some of this important material could be presented more effectively with an opportunity for discussion than solely by lecture methods. The preparation of aids for effective discussion became an important part of the board's work.[7]

The final collapse of the Axis powers came sooner than had been expected by some military planners. This intensified in some degree the surplus of personnel and equipment which follows when complete

---

[4] *Ibid.*
[5] *Ibid.;* File 352, OCCh.
[6] *Ibid.*
[7] President of Board to Author, 29 March 1956.

victory results from a supreme and prolonged military effort.   The chaplaincy, like other services, had to deal with this situation.   Enough chaplains must be kept on duty to serve the troops who would continue in service and those awaiting discharge.   Among those holding temporary commissions were men of experience and demonstrated ability who would be highly desirable additions to the Regular Army. Many others who did not consider such an appointment were needed in the Reserve components if they were to be developed and maintained as really valuable parts of the Army.   As several thousand chaplains wished to be relieved as soon as possible, their readjustment to civil life presented serious difficulties.

    After the termination of active combat, the discharge of chaplains progressed so rapidly that only 4,481 were in service on 8 February 1946.[8]   This shows that in this short period 3,660 clergymen returned to a civilian status, and many others were to follow.   A good proportion of these men were able to return to the positions they had left when they entered the service or to other appropriate employment.   Most of the religious groups which had endorsed men for the chaplaincy helped them find positions after discharge, and some gave financial aid until such arrangements could be made.   The establishment of the chaplain service in the Veterans Administration gave a considerable number the opportunity to continue a ministry to their late comrades, and others found similar openings in State or other institutions.

    Some were able to devote a semester or a year to specialized study. A number of universities and theological seminaries made special provision for the needs of the returning chaplain.   Harvard was one of the first to announce such a plan.   Qualified chaplains were accepted for study toward the Master's degree in theology without some of the usual prerequisites.   Such concessions were not regarded as acts of kindness to worthy men whose studies had been retarded by military service but a recognition that they had gained skills and understandings of great professional value from their war experiences.   The Jewish Theological Seminary went even further, offering to accept theses based upon chaplains' experiences while in service in partial fulfillment of the requirements for the degree of Doctor of Hebrew Letters.[9]

    The Act of 28 December 1945, fixed the number of officers in the Regular Army at 25,000, and this authorization was doubled on 8 August 1946.   As appointments would be prorated among all branches, this created vacancies for a considerable number of chaplains.   The men

---

[8] File 326, OCCh.; *Watchman Examiner,* 4 April 1946.
[9] File 370.01, OCCh.

who had served during the war already possessed valuable experience, and those who met the specific requirements were invited to apply. They must be college and seminary graduates between the ages of 26 and 45 and must be indorsed specifically for appointment to the Regular Army. Applicants were graded according to a composite score in which their efficiency ratings while on duty and the estimate of the screening board were important. Active duty already performed was credited both for present appointment and future promotion. During 1946–47, selections were made in several increments. A number of Jewish chaplains chosen at this time were the first to be appointed to the Regular Army. When the separation of the Air Force from the Army was completed in 1948, the former received 141 of the Regular chaplains, while 212 remained with the Army. The Officer Personnel Act of 1947 authorized the permanent rank of major general for the Chief of Chaplains and in effect established the grade of brigadier general for another chaplain of the Regular Army. These provisions were reenacted in the Army Organization Act of 1950.[10]

At the time of the Japanese surrender the appointments of about 200 clergymen were being processed. As their active services would not be needed in the new situation, they were offered commissions in the Officers Reserve Corps. Some hundreds of chaplains on duty held Reserve appointments from before the war. Many of them had received promotions in the Army of the United States, and the same was true of some Regular chaplains. Because of legal restrictions upon the number in the various grades, it was necessary for some to be reassigned to duty in their lower permanent grades. The majority of chaplains held temporary commissions which would expire 6 months after the official end of the war unless terminated sooner by the Government. With the development of plans for the reorganization of the reserve components, it was determined that these temporary appointments should terminate at the end of June 1953. A decision of the Comptroller General raised a question about the validity of the rights normally acquired through active duty as this concerned those serving under these temporary commissions during some years before that date. A ruling published late in 1955 held that these rights did not accrue after 30 June 1948 to officers holding only these temporary appointments.[11]

Planning for a more efficient reserve organization after 1945 did not contemplate radical changes but included some proposals which

[10] 59 *Stat.* 664; 60 *Stat.* 925; File 210.1, OCCh.; 61 *Stat.* 884, 885, 912; 64 *Stat.* 267.
[11] Dep. Def. Cir. 32–53, 20 Dec. 1955.

were significant.   One suggestion referred to the Chief of Chaplains for comment was that the tables of organization should provide for four general officers.   This was disapproved on the ground that these chaplains would outrank those of the Regular Army with the exception of the Chief of Chaplains and possibly one other and that no appropriate assignments for them would exist.   The Armed Forces Reserve Act of 1952 was the product of mature study.   It authorized the giving of commissions for an indefinite period rather than for a specific number of years, clarified the relation to the National Guard of the United States of Federally recognized officers of the National Guard of the various States, and abolished some distinctions among Reserve personnel by stating that the Army Reserve includes all Reserve officers and enlisted men other than those who are members of the National Guard of the United States.[12]

A new method of interesting young men in the chaplaincy was authorized by SR 140–105–4, 20 April 1953.   This permitted the appointment of qualified students in recognized theological seminaries as Reserve second lieutenants and their assignment to the Chaplains' Branch, with the provision that they could be regularly commissioned as Reserve chaplains in the grade of first lieutenants on the completion of a normal theological course of 90 hours.   Donald E. Ausland, a theological student in St. Paul, was appointed a second lieutenant on 13 August 1953, being the first prospective chaplain to receive a commission under the provisions of this regulation.   By the spring of 1956 nearly 150 young men had accepted such an appointment.[13]

On 21 April 1956 there were 1,216 chaplains on duty.   They were commissioned in these components: 230 in the Regular Army, 79 in the National Guard of the United States, and 907 in the United States Army Reserve.   The fact that less than one-fifth of the chaplains serving American troops were Regulars shows the continuing importance of the other components.   These numbers also show that only one-fourth of the increase resulting from the Korean conflict were still on duty.[14]

The end of hostilities brought a material change in the immediate purpose of chaplain training.   Instead of the task of introducing a large number of civilian clergymen to Army life in a very brief time, plans must be directed to the needs of those serving occupation troops and a peacetime army.   It was evident that some chaplains would

---

[12] 66 *Stat.* 487, 498.
[13] *The Military Chaplain,* Jan. 1954, p. 24; data from CCh.
[14] *Ibid.*

profit by an acquaintance with certain techniques which are taught in some but not all theological seminaries. Others could prepare intelligently for the executive duties to which they might be assigned by a study of administrative methods and problems. These and similar matters must be considered in relation to the chaplains entering the Regular Army, those likely to continue on duty only for another year or two, and those who would constitute the Reserve component in the years ahead.

Because of the impending deactivation of Fort Oglethorpe, the Chaplain School was moved to Carlisle Barracks, Pa., in December 1946. A month later it was combined with the Army Information, Adjutant General, and Military Police Schools to form an administrative school center at that post. The commanding general of the Army Ground Forces was made responsible for administration and operation through the general in command of the center. This officer was to exercise normal command except in relation to personnel, curriculum, and academic matters. He was authorized to combine facilities such as personnel and those for recreation and printing. The chiefs of these administrative services were to designate the commandant, staff, and faculty of their respective schools and to relieve any of them except for disciplinary reasons. Likewise they had charge of curriculum, academic standards, records and reports, budget and fiscal matters, and the selection of those who were to attend the various sessions of the schools.[15]

The chief purpose for which the school center was established was to carry on economically the activities of the constituent schools until the need for their future services could be foreseen more clearly. Cooperation among the various groups in the center was excellent, and difficulties were few and easy of adjustment. An example was the proposal to save space and personnel by bringing together in one place the records of the several schools. The commandant of the Chaplain School pointed out that this would be a false economy as applied to his school, because it would remove to a great distance certain files which were consulted almost daily, often about questions which could not be foreseen but must be answered without delay, perhaps while someone in Washington held the telephone line. By 1 July 1948 it was deemed that the school center had accomplished its mission and need not be continued, and command responsibility was transferred to the commanding general of the Second Army. The Chaplain School remained

---

[15] WD Cir. No. 24, 28 Jan. 1947.

as a class II activity, with responsibility for the usual academic and fiscal matters vested in the Chief of Chaplains.[16]

After consulting a number of supervisory chaplains about how the training program could be related most helpfully to the type of actual problems which they had encountered, the Chief of Chaplains decided upon a course to continue for 12 weeks. It was to include most of the subjects taught in the wartime school but gave more time to those considered most important. New topics included Staff Procedure, Counseling, and Music Appreciation, and within 2 years, courses in Marriage Counseling, Religious Drama and Pageantry, Voice Culture, and Pulpit and Radio Techniques were added. Before the end of 1948 this course had been given 6 times to a total of 258 chaplains, including most of those recently integrated into the Regular service.[17]

As early as 1946 it was proposed that specialized instruction by experts in certain fields be provided for supervisory chaplains, with the expectation that they would transmit to their associates the essentials of a number of valuable techniques through their training programs. At a conference on curriculum early in 1948 the Chief of Air Force Chaplains urged that a series of scholarly conferences of this nature be arranged. He proposed that 2 weeks be devoted to intensive study of practical fields such as Counseling or Religious Education. Courses given in October and November were based upon this plan. Students were enthusiastic about this instruction by eminent teachers; and a plan for 1949 proposed that 6 subjects be taught in courses lasting 2 or 3 weeks, those of greater interest being repeated to a total of 14 such sessions. It soon was seen that so many chaplains could not be spared from other duties; and 6 subjects, each limited to a course of 2 weeks, were offered in a total of 10 sessions. Counseling, Religious Education, Religion and Modern Culture, The Administrative Chaplain, Essentials of Worship, and Pulpit, Radio, and Television Techniques were the titles of these courses.[18]

Instruction in these subjects soon brought the criticism that the school was being turned into a theological seminary. A bishop of one of the large churches declared that the school did not exist to teach clergymen as such but to instruct them in military subjects and complained to the Armed Forces Chaplain Board. The commandant of the school declared that this specialized instruction was meeting a demonstrated need and carefully avoided any sectarian emphasis; but

---

[16] File 352, OCCh.; DA Cir. 64, 10 Mar. 1948.
[17] File 352, OCCh., *passim.*
[18] *Ibid.*

when plans for 1951 were submitted to the Chief of the Army Field Forces, he disapproved courses in the fields of microphone techniques, counseling, and religious education on the same grounds that they had been criticized by the bishop. Notwithstanding the apparent soundness of this theory, it was recognized that advanced instruction in a number of such practical fields would enable many chaplains to perform their duties more effectively, and it was soon reestablished in the program of the school. Courses announced for junior chaplains in 1955 included a substantial introduction to the psychology and methods of counseling, and the advanced course devoted 20 hours to the cultivation and use of the voice in various situations.[19]

Many Reserve chaplains were eager to attend the school but could not be away from other duties for the duration of the basic course. The same was true of some on active duty. To meet this situation, an associate basic course of 4 weeks was established. It devoted 20 hours to basic military subjects, 10 to Music for Chaplains, the same to Microphone Techniques, and 25 each to Practical Duties, Army Morale, Personal Counseling, and The Administrative Chaplain. Though the plan was to limit classes to 50 men so that there would be opportunity for students to participate in discussions, many were able to attend only the July–August session, and considerably more than that number were allowed to enroll. Seven sessions were held in 1947–48, with 277 chaplains attending. For the benefit of young men with no military experience who were being appointed to the Reserve, 5 sessions of a 6-week course were announced as part of the program for 1949.[20]

A similar program was continued in the following years. The last group of Air Force chaplains to attend this school was graduated in April 1953, and the plan of instruction was directed more specifically toward Army personnel. The courses announced for 1955 show the adaptation of the training program to the needs and opportunities of various chaplains of all components. A basic course of 9 weeks gave a general introduction to the chaplain's status and duties. The course for company officers devoted 12 weeks to a thorough grounding for these junior chaplains. An advanced course continued for 16 weeks and was concerned with the needs of chaplains of field grade. For the benefit of chaplains unable to attend the longer sessions, associate courses both advanced and for company grade chaplains offered half as long programs as the general courses with those titles. In the Fiscal

---

[19] *Ibid.*
[20] *Ibid.*

Year 1952, 297 Army and 248 Air Force chaplains completed one of these courses. The next year these totals were 195 and 167. In the 2 succeeding years, 281 and 293 Army chaplains were in attendance. In 1954 a chaplain of the Army of Venezuela took the 12-week course. The next year three Canadian chaplains were in the student body.[21]

The cost in time and money of bringing Reserve chaplains from distant parts of the country to the school led the commandant to suggest an ingenious alternative. It was that schools be held in 10 localities for 3 consecutive weeks, with the students allowed to return to their parishes for the weekends. Two instructors from the school were to teach intensively either 2 or 3 of the basic subjects during the first week at 1 post, then go on to the second place and repeat the course while 2 other instructors were giving different courses at the first. A third team would begin the circuit the third week. In this way 6 men traveling once around the 10 installations would present the substance of the course in 3 weeks of instruction brought so near to the Reserve chaplains that they could participate without excessive travel or other inconvenience. He reckoned the total cost to the Government at $89 for each student, a small fraction of what it would cost to bring them to the school. The Chief of Chaplains approved the plan but felt that it should be deferred because the military situation of the world was very uncertain at that time.[22]

The grading system of the school during this period was the subject of some critical discussion. Percentage values were applied to the five customary efficiency ratings and were interpreted rigidly. This resulted in some being separated by very narrow numerical margins but at a point on the scale which gave one a higher-named grade than another. Striking examples are found in the records of 1948. Two April students 9½ percent apart were reported *Excellent* though the better of these ratings lacked only one-half of 1 percent of that of a *Superior* student. In June, one man missed an *Excellent* grade by three-tenths of 1 percent, though his standing was much nearer that of the lowest *Excellent* than of any other in his own group. In August one man fell short of a *Superior* rating by two-tenths of 1 percent, and in the next class an *Excellent* and a *Superior* grade differed by only one-tenth of 1 percent.[23]

Several inquiries from civilian schools where chaplains had requested credit for work done in the Chaplain School led to an attempt

---

[21] Data furnished by Chaplain School, 15 March 1955.
[22] File 352, OCCh., *passim*.
[23] *Ibid.*

to evaluate the courses in the usual academic units.   The Chief of Chaplains recommended that graduation from the 6-week course be considered the equivalent of 6 semester hours in college.   As the study was about half professional and half military, he suggested that wherever applicable these credits be considered to be 3 hours in practical theology and 3 in military science.   For the 12-week course he proposed that 12 hours of credit be allowed, divisible in the same proportion.[24]

Experience with extension courses for the training of Reserve officers during the years between the World Wars revealed several facts which were helpful when such a course was planned for chaplains after 1945.   Chaplains of the reserve components were admonished in 1930 that the officers of only two other services were as recreant as they in taking this form of training.   As National Guard chaplains had a notably higher average than their Reserve colleagues, it seemed evident that their interest was stimulated by association with organizations which were carrying on some form of group activity.   Some means of stimulating interest in all Reserve chaplains seemed desirable.[25]

In the earlier period of extension course work a number of enlisted men and civilians had enrolled.   When some of the latter wished to do so in 1946, the commanding general of the Army Ground Forces ruled that regulations would not permit this unless they were War Department employees who needed this knowledge for their work.   A similar question arose when many officers were assigned to extended active duty in foreign countries.   In 1925 the Judge Advocate General held that it would be a violation of international law for them to take extension courses while stationed abroad.   In 1948 this opinion was modified by the ruling that the consent of a friendly foreign government would remove this impediment and that permission to station troops within its territory was tantamount to such consent.   When members of the Philippine Scouts applied, it was thought at first that they might enroll only if they were American citizens, but soon it was decided that they might do so if they were on active duty in the Army of the United States.   This ruling concerned very few chaplains after the Second World War.[26]

Early in the planning period the Chaplain Board proposed that a common subcourse on the chaplain be included in the series designed for lieutenants so that all Reserve officers might be acquainted with

---

[24] *Ibid.*

[25] File 352.6, OCCh., 1930.

[26] *Ibid.*, 1928, 1946, 1948.

the chaplain's functions and know how to utilize his services in promoting discipline and morale.   Though this plan was disapproved, it was ordered that an appropriate lesson on this subject be prepared for inclusion in a subcourse on staff functions.   The fact that officers of the Engineer and Medical Service Corps and the Judge Advocate General's Department were enrolled in the chaplains' extension course in 1948 emphasized a common interest.[27]

In general the revised extension course for chaplains followed the pattern of the interbellum years.   That announced for 1955–56 offered courses aggregating credits of 230 and 364 hours respectively for study by lieutenants and captains.   The former included 76 and the latter 68 hours devoted to professional subjects, while the remainder dealt with military matters.   The corresponding courses in 1931 had allowed 65 and 78 hours for professional studies where the total hours were only 165 and 136.   The more recent program offered a series of 235 hours for majors, but this included no professional subjects.   Students who had passed certain subjects in the resident school within 4 years might be excused from taking parallel subcourses in the extension course but must substitute an equal number of hours made up of optional subjects to gain credit for the series.

In the spring of 1956 the school was preparing 12 subcourses to make the extension program parallel more closely that of the resident school.   At that time the extension department was administering 63 subcourses and grading a monthly average of 750 lessons for the 689 students enrolled.[28]

The systematic training of chaplains' assistants at the school was recommended by the Chief of Chaplains in the autumn of 1944.   After a thorough study of the program and methods being used for this purpose by the Air Force at that time, it was determined to plan a 3-week course of instruction for assistants to chaplains of all branches of the Army.   The proposal was disapproved by higher authority in 2 successive years, and a conference of training officers in the spring of 1948 concluded that so little interest in the plan was evinced by chaplains in the field that only on-the-job training should be attempted at that time.   By 1950 the situation had changed, and on 7 February a class of 67 men and 2 women completed a 4-week course.   There were 62 men and 5 women in the next class, and 3 women were among the 42 students who composed the next.   The schedule for the fiscal year 1951 included 2 courses for assistants to Army chaplains and 2 for wel-

[27] *Ibid.*, 1946–48.
[28] James B. Murphy to Author, 15 March and 10 April 1956.

fare specialists, as assistants to Air chaplains were called.   These programs did not differ radically.   They included instruction in administrative procedure, casualty assistance, music, typing, motion picture projection, and motor operation.   In the fiscal year 1952, 135 assistants and 369 welfare specialists attended, and the next year these totals were 94 and 251.   Only Army personnel were in the school in 1954, and the training of assistants at the school ended with the 82 who took the course that year.[29]

The unification of the Army, Navy, and Air Force in the Department of Defense naturally raised the question of the practicability of training chaplains for the three services in a unified school.   In fact, this had been mentioned as one of the anticipated economies by one or more of the chiefs of chaplains when their opinion of the pending legislation was asked.   In support of separate schools it was contended that each service had its distinctive psychology and traditions, its own organization and terminology, and that a joint training program would necessarily include much matter which would be useless to a part of the student body.   The contrary argument held that the task of all chaplains is essentially the same and that the time which would be given to instructing some chaplains in matters useful only in another service would be negligible when compared with the duplication of equipment and effort which separate training would entail.[30]

Early in 1948 several naval officers visited the Chaplain School and agreed that nearly all of the subject matter included in the Associate Basic Course would be appropriate for chaplains of the Navy. None doubted that chaplains of all services would profit by the specialized instruction being planned at that time.   Two Navy chaplains attended the intensive course in Counseling given in October 1948 and said that it had great practical value for them.   On 23 August 1950 the Armed Forces Chaplain Board recommended the establishment of a unified school.   The Army and Air Force concurred in the general plan, but an assistant secretary of the Navy stated that chaplains coming into the Regular Navy are fully educated, needing only some instruction in naval organization, administration, and discipline, which would be useless to chaplains of other services.   On 3 January 1951 the Secretary of Defense informed the Armed Forces Chaplain Board that the establishment of a unified chaplain school was not favorably considered.[31]

---

[29] *Ibid.;* File 352, OCCh., 1944–50; *The Military Chaplain,* Spring 1950, p. 15.

[30] File 352, OCCh., *passim.*

[31] *Ibid.*

Before the end of the war the Command and General Staff Schools offered a series of short and intensive courses primarily to qualify officers for staff positions in the higher echelons of the Regular Army. At different times these courses were of 5-, 9-, and 10-weeks' duration. Beginning in the spring of 1943, a few chaplains were sent to these courses to enhance their qualifications for supervisory duties, and this policy was continued for several years. Although not limited to chaplains of the Regular Army, these assignments were given only to men likely to render a considerable period of service. A few other chaplains of unusual promise were sent to civilian seminaries or universities for a year or less of specialized study in the years after the war.

The procurement of those articles of equipment for chaplains which cannot be manufactured quickly or which can be produced to advantage only in large quantities necessarily involved the placing of orders for goods to meet anticipated needs for a considerable period. This was notably true of the Army Testaments. The reduction of the Army, coming sooner than had been expected, left a large surplus in stock. After reserving 50,000 of the Jewish, 150,000 of the Catholic, and 400,000 of the Protestant versions to meet anticipated needs in the new situation, the Chief of Chaplains announced on 6 October 1946 that about one million Testaments would be given to religious, educational, eleemosynary, and similar institutions without charge. Several thousand requests were received for a total about seven times the number available, a few from persons who hoped to obtain large quantities for sale at a profit. In distribution, the greatest weight was given to demonstrated need and the probability of most extensive use. In January 1949 the Chief of Chaplains was able to announce that all surplus Scriptures had been allocated and that it had been possible to comply with about one-sixth of the requests received by him. The actual surplus of the 3 versions was: Jewish 140,905, Catholic 238,060, and Protestant 712,428.[32]

About this time occurred a curious but revealing episode. A widely read periodical sponsored by one of the larger churches published a statement that thousands of Bibles were being burned at a camp in process of deactivation and inferred that this represented the settled policy of the Army. Immediately a flood of protests from public officials and private citizens descended upon the Chief of Chaplains and other War Department agencies. One man, who doubtless felt

---

[32] File 461, OCCh., 29 April 1947.

that nothing should be wasted, urged that these English Scriptures be sent "to the Japanese or Chinese, or perhaps to the Russians." [33]

As soon as the identity of the camp could be learned, a thorough investigation was made by the supervising chaplain, the camp commander, and the Inspector General. These facts were ascertained: No Bibles had been burned, but a dozen or fifteen so torn and soiled as to be unfit for use in the chapel had been placed in a fill and covered with earth. A quantity of donated Testaments were on hand. So were a few Army Testaments, as less than full cartons of 50 could not be returned to the quartermaster. When asked by an assistant what should be done with these when the chapel was closed, one of the chaplains had replied, "I don't know; we may have to burn them." The assistant got permission to give them to a nearby church and told the minister that otherwise they would have been burned. The casual remark of the chaplain, taken in cold literalness by the assistant, seems to have been the basis of the whole matter. In support of the original complaint and its implications, a freight handler in the Middle West forwarded several tracts and donated Testaments which were somewhat crumpled but usable when he found them in a bale of waste paper from a different camp. When the facts had been fully established, the editor published a full correction, giving it greater prominence than he had accorded to the first item.[34] An officer of the War Department stated his opinion that this episode, though costing the Government thousands of dollars, had been a salutary demonstration of the respect of military authorities for sacred things.

For some time prior to 1945 a fund donated by interested friends was maintained in the Office of the Chief of Chaplains and was used for the general benefit of the chaplaincy. In that year a revision of AR 210–50 specifically authorized such a fund and provided that it might receive contributions and the unexpended balances of the religious funds of deactivated installations and organizations. It was named the Chief of Chaplains' Religious Fund, a title which had been borne some years before by the appropriations later renamed the Chaplains' Activities Fund. Grants were made to the religious funds of newly established units which needed religious supplies but had not been in operation long enough to acquire a working balance in their religious funds. With the partial separation of the Air Force from the Army in 1948, it was agreed that 60 percent of the money on hand in

---

[33] *The Christian Advocate,* 25 April 1946.
[34] *Ibid.,* 15 Aug. 1946.

the Chief of Chaplains Religious Fund should remain with the Army and the balance should be for the use of the Air Force.[35]

When a large number of camps were dismantled after the war, many·chapels became surplus.   It was determined that they should be sold under terms which required their continued use as shrines, memorials, or places of worship.   The disposal procedure was that the War Assets Administration should advertise locally such chapels as had become available for sale, the cost of removal being considered in fixing the price.   At the end of a month all applications were forwarded to the Chief of Chaplains, by whom the awards were made.   At first it was intended that those sold to religious bodies should be distributed on a proportionate basis, but it soon became apparent that such a plan would be impracticable.   As many more than half of the chapels to be sold were in the 10 southeastern States, moving costs alone dictated that most of them would go to the religious bodies most numerous in that section.

In making awards, every factor was considered, but especial weight was attached to demonstrated need or the opportunity for exceptional usefulness.   The church which had lost its building by fire or the vigorous society in a new development with only building plans had very strong claims.   Few complaints were made about the fairness of the allotment, and these came from persons who saw only a local distribution.   It was natural that the predominant group in one State or section should receive the greatest number, while the majority of buildings in another locality went to a different body because its more numerous congregations could demonstrate the need for more buildings and the opportunity to use them constructively.   Some applicants tried to reenforce their claims with recommendations from many sources, but the committee firmly resisted every influence which might bias their judgment.   On one occasion a senator called the chairman of the committee and scolded him severely for awarding a chapel in his State to a church instead of to another institution.   Hoping to mollify him, the chaplain read excerpts from various recommendations that the award be made to the church because of a real need.   About the fifth in the file was from the senator himself, and it lacked nothing in its warm support of the application of the church.   An abrupt "Thank you. Good-bye" ended the conversation.

On 1 November 1949, after more than 3 years of chapel disposal, the task was nearly complete, and the secretary summarized the work

---

[35] File 210.4, OCCh., 28 May 1948.

of the committee.   A total of 600 chapels had been awarded and accepted.   These included many reawards, because 221 of the 881 offered had been declined.   Applications totaled 2,264 an average of 3.43 per chapel.   This had involved, besides paper attached to the applications, 3,396 letters and 2,535 telephone communications.   One chapel had been given to a State for the use of the National Guard. The remaining 659 had been sold for $928,543.35, an average of slightly more than $1,409.   Cities, counties, and States received 19 of these chapels, schools and colleges 24, patriotic organizations 9, and the remainder went to congregations of 41 religious organizations located in 42 States, the District of Columbia, Hawaii, and British Guiana.[36]

Many chaplains had spoken enthusiastically about the wholesome influence of visits by prominent clergymen to the forces in distant places, and the converse value of direct reports of the moral welfare of the troops to the church people at home was widely recognized. Having both of these considerations in view, a senator proposed early in 1947 that a representative group of clergymen be invited to make an extended tour of the oversea camps.   The Secretary adopted the suggestion and directed the Chief of Chaplains to select 12 men to compose the party.   As one of the chief reasons for this enterprise was that these clergymen should inform the American public as widely as possible of what they might observe during their trip, the size of the groups represented and their relation to others which could not be included were important considerations.   It was readily agreed that three Catholics, a Jew, and a southern Baptist should be included, and the authorities of these bodies were asked to make the selections.   The several Lutheran churches were asked to confer and agree upon a common representative.   The General Commission on Army and Navy Chaplains was invited to choose five men of its constituent bodies and named an Episcopalian, a Presbyterian, a Methodist, and a northern Baptist.   A prominent leader of the Negro Baptist churches suggested that a bishop of one of the Negro Methodist churches might be the fifth selection, and the bishop himself remarked that something should be done "to give some color to the party."   This delightful pleasantry confirmed the opinion that he should be the fifth man.

While the theological position usually called fundamentalist is held by people of many religious bodies, a number of independent organizations have been established largely to maintain this distinctive

---

[36] Chapel File, OCCh.

emphasis.   Two associations have been formed among these groups, and each accredited a number of the clergymen of its constituent bodies for the chaplaincy during the war.   The Chief of Chaplains felt it proper that these groups should participate in the oversea visitation and, supposing that the two associations had so much in common that they would cooperate in harmony, invited them to confer and select the 12th man of the party.   One attempted to carry out this proposal, but the second refused to have any dealings with the other association.   The former group offered to acquiesce in a selection by their rivals if the man so chosen would report his observations to them after his return.   The Chief of Chaplains felt that this generous spirit and their willingness to comply with his request in the first place entitled them to make the selection.   At this point the Secretary enlarged the delegation to 14, which permitted the inclusion of representatives of both of these bodies and of another man chosen for special reasons. The reports of these men to the American people through pulpit, press, and radio were informative and helpful.

A very important activity of chaplains was given enlarged opportunity and influence early in 1947.   In spite of medical treatment and warning by the surgeons, venereal disease had increased to alarming proportions in certain localities.   This was due in part to the situation in which occupation troops found themselves and to an exaggerated faith in the efficiency of some of the newer drugs.   To meet this situation, the Army utilized all its resources, preventive as well as remedial.   The importance of the chaplain's influence was recognized in an order of 24 January from the Secretary of War which contained the following paragraph:

> The Corps of Chaplains bears a special responsibility for the moral and spiritual welfare of the troops.   To aid the chaplains in meeting this responsibility, commanding officers will allocate appropriate periods in the regular training schedule for instruction in citizenship and morality which all military personnel will attend.[37]

Frequently in the past chaplains had shared time with the surgeon and others in the periodic lectures on venereal disease.   Sometimes the two professional viewpoints reinforced each other and the combined effect was excellent, but this was not always true.   The chaplain who said that all he could think of for such an address was to quote Scripture was as blind to his opportunities as the surgeon whose sole emphasis was upon promptness in the use of prophylactics.   Recognizing

---

[37] Press release, Chaplain School, Sep. 1947.

that Secretary Patterson's order gave the opportunity for a tremendous moral influence outside of the strictly religious program, the Chief of Chaplains determined to spare no effort in making the project a success.

As an aid to all chaplains serving with troops as well as to give balance and continuity to the program, he determined to prepare and distribute a series of lectures on appropriate themes and delegated the task to the Chaplain School.   Martin H. Scharlemann, a chaplain of outstanding ability with a rich background of education and experience was put in charge, with able assistants representing various religious groups.   The first draft of lectures was submitted to the Chaplain Board and to the Information and Education Division for comment, and the final revision was made in the office of the Chief of Chaplains.[38]

As it was intended that these lectures should appeal to the patriotism and honor of the men, their themes were broad and varied. Being compulsory, they could not be sectarian.   Chaplains were urged not to read the lectures to the men but to present the material in their own words, and some questions designed to encourage discussion were appended.   The reviewers used especial care to detect any expression which might seem partisan or controversial to any person, and the elements of literary style received due consideration.   The product commanded the intellectual respect of all hearers and challenged men of all faiths on a common ground of moral responsibility.

The reception of the lectures was gratifying, and the chaplains presented them with enthusiasm.   In 1 month 80 chaplains in Europe gave 499 lectures to an aggregate of 54,441 auditors.   One of these men spoke twice to a total of 1,460; another gave 33 lectures and was heard by 8,816.   Another whose men were scattered in small groups spoke 49 times in a month to an average of 21 men.   At the opposite extreme are a few items showing faithful chaplains doing what they could in unusual situations.   One spoke 5 times to a total of 29; another gave 20 lectures to an average of 5.   Another reported a total of 32 at his 12 lectures; and one made a record hard to surpass when he spoke twice and had 1 auditor each time.[39]

In 1948 after the lecture program had been in operation for many months, Duncan Naylor made a very significant survey of the way it had impressed a representative number of troops.   At two widely separated camps he questioned several hundred men of different units and

---

[38] File 352, OCCh.
[39] Reports, OCCh.

various stages of training, having them answer a list of 30 questions, most of which had 4 alternative answers.   For example: "How much do they help?   A lot_____, Fair amount_____, A little_____, None_____."   Only 1 percent of the men said the lectures were a bore, and nearly all felt their sense of responsibility increased by them in a helpful way.   One-third recommended a change of emphasis, but the advocates of more stress on morals were counterbalanced by those who favored more upon citizenship.   Nearly 9 in 10 said that the lectures helped them decide what was right, and a larger proportion that they helped them to do right.   A majority of the older soldiers thought the lectures should be given once or twice a month.   A larger number thought 2 or 3 times a week would be good, and 38 sturdy souls voted for a citizenship and morality lecture every day.[40]

The commanding general of the Army Ground Forces credited this positive moral training, together with command direction, with much of the success in eliminating vile and obscene language and improving discipline and the whole atmosphere of military behavior among the cadre and trainees of the Universal Military Training Experimental Unit.   He directed the commanding generals of replacement training centers to take a personal interest in building up the highest possible standard of social behavior, including the elimination of obscene language.   Saying that repressive measures alone will not suffice, he declared that military and moral training must be integrated during the recruit's period of adjustment to Army life.[41]

Among the highly successful projects developed in the years after the great war was a series of posters designed to emphasize some obligation of respectable living or to warn against a corresponding danger. Under the direction of a member of the staff of the Chief of Chaplains, an artist of ability executed some admirable pictures with appropriate captions and other wording.   After scrutiny by several agencies, the approved design was printed and exhibited for some weeks in many Army buildings.   By that time another was ready to take its place.

At times the critical examination by officers representing various points of view brought out objections which did not seem convincing to the originators of the posters.   One showed a soldier losing his month's pay to three civilian professionals in a card game.   Another had a great hand pointing a finger at a man in uniform and the words

---

[40] *Ibid.*
[41] Press release, Chaplain School, Sep. 1947.

of one of the Ten Commandments in large print. It was asserted that these pictures dishonored the uniform by singling out the serviceman as the probable transgressor. This objection was not satisfied when it was pointed out in discussion that these pictures were designed expressly for soldiers and their specific purpose was to warn them against the dangers pictured or implied. In commenting upon the poster with the pointing finger, the representative of the Chief of Chaplains remarked, not wholly without guile, that he had seen a very effective recruiting poster in which Uncle Sam pointed a stern finger with the words, "I want you."

"Yes, but that is Uncle Sam," said the major across the table.

There was no rejoinder when the chaplain referred to the Commandment and said, "Yes, but whose finger is this supposed to be?"

The most significant thing that can be recorded about the chaplains in the years since 1945 is that they carried on their normal duties faithfully wherever they were stationed. These varied from services of worship to an infinite variety of helpful acts for individuals. During April 1954, a typical month when active hositilities were not in progress, 1,818,209 persons attended public worship conducted by Army chaplains, and 214,702 were present at services led by visiting clergymen. During the same period 783,080 participated in character guidance discussion groups and 222,930 in the program of religious education. Two years earlier a soldier's mother wrote enthusiastically of a crowded chapel service she attended in a Virginia camp: "Mothers should not worry about their boys' spiritual life if they were like those boys and men were on that day." [42]

Reports tell of the soldier who spent his last 2 weeks in the Army building an artistic altar for a chapel in Alabama, of the quonset hut in Alaska which was transformed into an attractive chapel in 6 days through the labor of a chaplain and 2 men, and of the chaplain who supervised the remodeling of a bombed-out stable in a German city into a chapel with memorial stones sacred to the 3 major faiths set in the altar. These stones were brought from the ruins of Catholic and Protestant churches and of a synagogue, and American troops contributed liberally to the reconstruction of these places of worship for the German congregations. One chaplain entertained the staff of a German orphanage at luncheon and chapel worship while men of the battalion cared for the children. One of the 4-year-olds was adopted by the chaplain. [43]

---

[42] Fact sheet, OCCh., 21 Aug. 1952.
[43] *Ibid.*, 27 May, 15 Aug. 1952.

The generosity of the American soldier in relieving distress has elicited worldwide comment.   It has not been limited to allies and friends, but thousands of displaced people and recent enemies have benefited by their open-handed kindness.   Chaplains have organized and directed such enterprises in most cases, but they never have appealed in vain for support in meeting cases of evident need.   Though giving at Christmas time has been conspicuous, many of these projects involved continuous support of such institutions as orphanages and hospitals.

Christmas in 1952 was a great day in western Europe.   An American unit in France sought out every orphan in the city and gave the group a good dinner, a glorious day, and gifts of clothing and toys. One post in Germany donated several tons of food and a large quantity of clothing to 660 needy families.   A battalion stationed near the eastern border sponsored a party for 1,200 children, made large contributions to 2 orphanages, and sent Santa Claus through 35 villages with candy for the children.   A post in upper Austria divided its gifts between orphanages and old folks' homes.   These are a few of many such expressions of good will toward the unfortunate and needy wherever American troops have been stationed and chaplains have encouraged and guided their spontaneous generosity.[44]

---

[44] *Ibid.*, 4–127–53.

CHAPTER XX

Korea

The conflict in Korea involved some unusual elements which had a significant bearing upon the chaplains and the attitude of the men they served. Some had been stationed in the country during the occupation period when Japanese forces were withdrawn and the local government was set up. Most of them knew that the Korean people had been plundered for centuries by powerful empires on either side before the systematic exploitation that followed annexation by Japan. When liberation from this oppressor led swiftly to a worse tyranny in the north and a brutal attack upon the people of the south who were trying to establish the institutions of a free people, all felt a strong sympathy with the victims of this crowning outrage. The fact that the onslaught was resisted by the forces of many nations acting together to protect the defenseless in place of the unilateral judgment and support of national interest which the world had known for so long gave a special sacredness to the cause.

Some chaplains learned enough about the culture of the Koreans to back these sentiments with an intelligent admiration. The inventiveness which developed a phonetic alphabet and a system of printing with movable type centuries ago likewise produced the ironclad which defeated an invasion fleet from Japan 270 years before the famous encounter in Hampton Roads. Robert Homiston tells of his visit to an aged teacher of philosophy at his hut on a mountainside where he was explaining a metaphysical concept to five students. The old man was gratified to learn that Immanuel Kant had stated the matter in substantially the same way. He entertained his caller with hot water and honey, a special courtesy between philosophers before the time of Socrates. To the American mind, an ancient people who had preserved the great things of the spirit through centuries of vicissitude deserved the opportunity to develop their own institutions in freedom.[1]

Christianity in Korea began with a Catholic mission about 1784, and Presbyterian and Methodist missionaries came about a century later. About 1 million Koreans professed the Christian faith before

---

[1] *The Military Chaplain*, Fall 1950, p. 4.

1945, and attempts by the Japanese to force conformity to the cult of a divine emperor met with small success.   After the liberation of the South, great numbers of Koreans sought to learn about Christian doctrines and practices.   Many crossed the 38th Parallel to escape the oppression in the North.   Some organized congregations migrated in a body.   The chaplains were active in helping these homeless people adjust to life in their new surroundings and soon were regarded as especially benevolent agents of the occupying forces.   A soldiers' Christian society met regularly in one of the churches in Seoul.   Soon the group purchased an electric organ for the church, then raised funds for the expenses of a number of Korean students who wished to study in America.   Many ties like these already existed before the attack of June 1950.   They gave the Koreans a high confidence in the goodwill of their deliverers and predisposed the Americans to more than their usual kindness toward the suffering and needy.[2]

Shortly before the attack upon the Republic of Korea on 25 June 1950, there were 738 Army chaplains on duty, 301 of them at assignments overseas.   This was about 9 percent of those in service on 2 September 1945 and is an index of the reduction in the Army since that date.   Military necessities kept large forces in other localities, but the war in Korea caused the transfer of many troops to the Far East. By the summer of 1951 there were considerably more than 300 chaplains in that command, and a large proportion of these were in Korea. So many chaplains were recalled to active duty to meet present or anticipated needs during the Korean conflict that 1,620 were in service at some time during that period.[3]

Service on the Korean front was very trying, especially during the first winter.   Desperate efforts to retard the devastating rush of the invaders were followed by months of grim endurance as the defenders clung to such positions as they were able to hold while they waited for reenforcements and supplies.   To their own share of hardship and danger the chaplains added a deep sympathy with the troubles and anxieties of the men, the suffering of the sick and wounded and of the people of the country.   By midwinter it was reported that some were weakening physically, especially among those over 40 years of age. Before many weeks had passed, the senior chaplain was urging that replacements be hastened to make possible the rotation of men who

        [2] *Ibid.,* pp. 1–9.
        [3] Reports of CofCh; *The Military Chaplain,* Summer 1950, p. 29; Far East Command reports, File 314.7, OCCh.

were breaking emotionally and becoming incoherent in speech and action.[4]

During the second year of the war it was possible to send more chaplains to the Far East Command, and those suffering the effects of prolonged arduous service could be rotated more promptly. For October 1951, a month with 4 Sundays, 350 chaplains reported services attended by 643,870 persons and pastoral assistance to 380,259. In December, special programs and 5 Sundays combined to carry the total attendance to 1,157,072, but the number of ministrations to individuals showed little change. Several prominent churchmen of the various faiths, including the senior chaplains of some of the allied forces, visited the Far East at this time.[5]

Early in the war, chaplains were requested for the Korean increments in American divisions. To meet this need, the Army employed several missionaries whose regular work had been interrupted by the war, and others familiar with the language were sought for service with prisoners of war. Among the aids to this ministry which were provided were bilingual hymnbooks in English and Korean or Chinese, a life of Christ in Korean and Chinese, and tracts explaining the chief doctrines of the Christian faith. Many individuals and organizations contributed services or funds to provide these and other similar helps.[6]

Plans for a chaplaincy in the Korean Army had been studied even before the war began. With very little delay Chaplains Bennett and Sherry, accompanied by Monsignor George Carroll of the Maryknoll Fathers and Dr. William B. Shaw of the Methodist Mission, laid the proposal before the Korean military authorities. Soon afterward President Rhee approved the project but advised that the chaplains be financed by the interested churches so that the hostility of non-Christian groups would be avoided. A school for chaplain candidates was established, and by the end of October, 55 chaplains were ready for assignment. In 1954 more than 250 were on duty. Though other Korean groups were free to provide chaplains, only the Christian bodies had done so at that time. The plan of organization was very similar to that followed in the armed forces of the United States, with the Army, Navy, and Air Force each having its chief of chaplains. A report for July 1951 shows 513 services conducted by the chaplains of the Korean Army and attended by 34,485 persons. This develop-

---

[4] *Ibid.*
[5] *Ibid.*
[6] *Ibid.*

ment and the potent influence of the Korean chaplains during the war would have been impossible without the warm support of the venerable President of the Republic.[7]

American chaplains in Korea maintained the tradition of industry, devotion, and courage established through the years. One learned that the men of a certain company had not had a real service since arriving in Korea. He drove for 4 hours over the mountains to reach them, distributed religious literature, conducted a service, and arranged to return every Monday for others. Another passed through heavy fire to reach and conduct services for a detached outpost. A colleague made his way along icy slopes to a rescue party pinned down by concentrated fire, gave last rites to the mortally wounded, and helped bring others to a place of safety. One said that sermons are out of place on the firing line but prayer is very helpful anywhere. He told of a short service for a small group in a valley during such heavy artillery fire that he could be heard only part of the time. As they read the Shepherd Psalm together, one man exclaimed: "That's it—the valley of the shadow of death! Did David write the psalm for us?" "Yes," answered the chaplain, "David wrote the psalm for us."[8]

Churchmen visiting the front were impressed by the importance which the officers attached to the chaplains and their work. The commander of a tank company led the singing at morning service, telling the chaplain that he was Sunday school superintendent back home. Albert S. Thompson, a Negro sergeant, gained the name of "The Rev." Though he was not a chaplain's assistant, he assisted in very important ways. He conducted prayer meetings every evening that the men of his company were free and gained their confidence by his kindness and faith. During a sharp action he rushed forward to rescue two wounded men. Singlehanded, he drove back the five enemies who attacked him and brought both men to a place of safety.[9]

Understanding critics have asserted that most American soldiers felt the Korean conflict to be a spiritual war. Not only were they fighting to protect the innocent victims of a cruel and unprovoked attack, but they were giving their lifeblood to establish a better way of settling the disputes of nations than the world had ever known. At the same time they were resisting with all their power a false doctrine which promised the impossible to ignorant and simple-minded people in order to enslave and exploit them and use them to rob other peoples of their freedom and chosen institutions. This sense of moral impera-

---

[7] *The Military Chaplain*, Dec. 1954, p. 14.
[8] DA releases, 16 Oct. 1950, May and Oct. 1953, 15 Aug. 1952.
[9] *Ibid.*, 10 June and 31 Oct. 1952; *The Military Chaplain*, Winter, 1952, p. 24.

tive nerved them to endure more and gave them a deeper confidence in the ultimate triumph of their cause. As one chaplain expressed it, faith had become one of the soldier's most important weapons.[10]

The plight of the wounded has always appealed to the sympathy of chaplains, and this has been especially true in times of disaster when retreating forces have found it necessary to leave in the hands of the enemy those who could not be moved. Several American chaplains remained with the wounded in different localities in Korea before their forces were strong enough to check the advance of the invaders. Meager records seem to show that one or two were slain in cold blood. Others were imprisoned until the end of hostilities unless disease or starvation sooner released them from the squalor, filth, and exposure of the prison pens. Arthur Mills was one who showed the same spirit with less tragic results. During the first month of the war a group of wounded men were isolated, and the American command feared that it would be necessary to abandon them. Exclaiming, "This is the way we did it in the last war," the chaplain jumped into his jeep and drove away. Hours later, to the amazement of his comrades, he reappeared with the jeep loaded with wounded men.[11]

Chief of Chaplains Bennett, who served in the Far East during the bitter first years of the Korean war, spoke with enthusiasm of the work of chaplains of 15 nations in promoting the "spiritually indispensable." A similar diversity of elements in a common service appears in a day in the life of Herbert Brichto, Jewish chaplain of the Seoul area. Starting for a distant post in the morning, his skillful driver maneuvered his jeep through miles of deep ruts and mud until they reached some obstruction which even this nimble vehicle could not surmount. Filling their pockets with supplies, they waded and stumbled on. After service they returned to their mud-bound jeep, set up an altar, and held another Jewish service. The weary return trip was broken by a call at a British service tent for tea and crumpets. Farther along they came upon an upset truck which still held a Negro soldier pinned to the ground. The chaplain comforted him until enough men could be summoned to lift the truck and set him free. A British priest arrived and ministered to the injured man until a Canadian medical officer came and gave first aid. The chaplain rode in the ambulance with the sufferer to the nearest hospital, which was a Norwegian unit 15 miles away, comforting him with prayer and the recital of psalms. After this adventure involving 3 races, 4 nationali-

---

[10] DA release, 30 Aug. 1951.
[11] Ibid., 4 Aug. 1950.

ties, and 3 religions, the chaplain arrived at his quarters in time to celebrate the birth of his little daughter on the other side of the world.[12]

Religious fellowship and inspiration were an immeasurable help to those whose fortune it was to endure the monotony and privation of prolonged periods as prisoners of war. Some of those who were liberated told hero tales of chaplains who had shared their captivity and had been a tower of strength to their comrades. Not only did they carry on religious ministrations as their captors would permit, but they cared for the sick, encouraged the despondent, and brought comfort of body or mind wherever possible. Many prison groups had no chaplain among them. In several instances a devout soldier organized informal devotional meetings or Bible classes which helped to sustain his associates through many trying months.[13]

American chaplains were not unwilling to share the blessings of an uplifting faith with the enemies who had become their prisoners. Many Christians were found among the captured North Koreans who were glad to give expression to their faith as soon as they could do so without peril to their lives. Chaplains arranged a regular ministry by missionaries or others who knew the language, and soon large numbers of the prisoners asked instruction in Christian principles and ideals. Among them was a Buddhist priest who studied with avidity while a prisoner, intending to prepare for the Christian ministry after his release. A correspondent who attended a service in a prison compound described the depth of feeling with which these men sang and prayed in the new freedom which captivity had given them. One of the prison compounds visited by Chief of Chaplains Parker in December 1951 had an organized church. Later he received an artistic plaque laboriously made from old tin cans by men more skillful in the use of tools than of English. It was inscribed: "Well Come Chaplain Parker." [14]

When the lines were established with the appearance of some permanence, a number of chapels were built. One near the front was entirely underground and so protected that it could be used as a shelter from bombs and shells. Another in a safer area was artistically decorated in blue, gold, and white and had stained glass windows and a large bell. One was designed and built by a Lithuanian refugee who had escaped from the Russian armies, studied engineering, became an American citizen, and was now serving with the Signal Corps.

---

[12] *Ibid.*, 27 May 1952; *The Military Chaplain,* Summer, 1952, p. 15.
[13] DA release, 30 Oct. 1953.
[14] *Ibid.*, 13 Feb. and 11 Dec. 1952; *The Military Chaplain,* Fall, 1953, pp. 14–15.

In several places American soldiers labored and contributed to replace Korean churches which had been destroyed. A typical example is the fine granite structure completed in 93 days under the leadership of Silas E. Decker as a memorial to the dead of the I Corps and made possible by a donation of $10,000 by the men.[15]

Human sympathy for suffering and need has seldom gained a finer expression than through the gifts and efforts of the American servicemen. Though they have shown themselves eager to relieve distress everywhere, even among enemies who have just laid down their arms, the tragic plight of the orphans left by the war in Korea moved them to more than their usual spirit of kindness. Many deeds of individual or group generosity are recorded, and usually a chaplain was the guiding spirit in these acts of mercy. Not only did they hold out helping hands to the pathetic victims of the war whom they met on the street or in hospitals or orphanages, but soldiers who had never seen Korea sent money to buy food, clothing, medicine, or shelter. A chaplain in Alaska forwarded $1,271, one in Georgia sent $10,000 and some months later another $3,800 which made possible the construction of a school for the blind and deaf.[16] One signal battalion which had provided much of the food and clothing for an orphanage for many months received a letter of thanks in the name of all the children. Despite its labored English, it left no doubt of their gratitude, and these sentences show a worthy determination to reciprocate in the only way they could:

> We have no way to render our gratitude because we are obliged to you so much favor. We never forget your kindness. But there is only a way to render you some of what we might be wanted from you. It is not else, learn hard, keep good the admonition make ourselves in good Character, and make us in future to serve for others as like as you do for us.[17]

Many heart-warming stories are told of the parties given by various units when orphan groups were fed, entertained, and delighted with gifts which would give comfort and joy for many days to come. Introducing the children to American ice cream was very diverting to the soldiers. In one part of the base section a large number of orphans and other children of the community were introduced to American baseball. It proved so popular that a group of officers got some equip-

---

[15] *Ibid.,* Summer, 1952, p. 28; DA release, Oct. 1953, Jan. 1954.

[16] *Ibid.,* 6 Dec. 1951, 8 Aug. 1952, 6 Oct. 1953.

[17] DA fact sheet 270, n. d.

ment from America, sponsored training and a series of games, and gave many children new ideas of sportsmanship and honor.[18]

Thirteen chaplains died in Korea, and 26 were injured in battle. A total of 567 received 683 decorations in recognition of devoted service. Wendell F. Byrd wrote in his diary: "To me there is something fascinating about the courage of men who can go out through mines facing enemy fire on dangerous missions and raids, then come back to their tents or foxholes and stomach a good meal in a cheerful mood." A few weeks later his duty took him into an advanced position where he was killed by a mine. Emil Kapaun endured the horrors of a winter prison for 6 months, keeping alive a spark of courage in his despondent comrades and bidding them be of good cheer as he was carried away to die. Others who could have escaped stayed with the wounded, and their military record ends with the pathetic words "Missing in action." If all the facts were known, the story of their death might well equal the most honorable of the records of how the most devoted Army chaplains have lived and died.[19]

---

[18] DA release, 28 Nov. 1951, 6 Oct. 1953.
[19] *Ibid.*, 28 Nov. 1951; *The Military Chaplain,* Fall, 1953, pp. 1–3; additional data furnished by CofCh, 30 Jan. 1956.

CHAPTER XXI

Achievements

The chaplain deals with intangibles which can neither be weighed nor valued by any known unit. If it were possible to compute loyalty and human kindness or moral character in terms of spiritual calories or pounds, it would still be futile to ravel the cords which lead individuals and groups and to credit the chaplain with those threads of influence which he has exerted in the resolution of the soldier or the spirit of the regiment. When the spiritual impact of a sunset or a starry sky, a symphony or a throb of sympathy or affection can be measured, it may be possible to compute those potent forces outside the sphere of the physical sciences which the chaplain is in the Army to intensify and direct.

Combined statistics for the 6 years beginning with July 1941 show that religious workers in the Army conducted about 6½ million services with one-third of a billion in attendance. Fifty million were visited in hospitals and five million in guardhouses: One-third of a billion sought pastoral ministrations, and the total receiving some form of religious service was about a billion.[1] Impressive as these figures may be, they reveal the means that were used but not the achievements, effort rather than accomplishment.

Slightly more tangible are statistics of concrete acts by or for individuals like baptisms or confirmations which imply systematic instruction and definite commitment to righteous living. Some have counted their converts with a gratifying confidence, but differing opinions about the efficacy of "foxhole religion" have left a doubt of the permanent value to be accorded to some of the visible results of these efforts. When it is considered that the chaplain who definitely leads one man to higher ideals and loyalties may have started a chain of influence which may bear fruit at another time and place, it is plain that statistics of this nature can show only a part of what really has occurred.

The place that a chaplain gains in the esteem and liking of his

---

[1] Chart prepared by Chief of Chaplains.

men may not seem very important, but it indicates much that is.   One
was "Charlie Chaplin" to the officers of his regiment.   He was the
butt of many a good-natured joke, but his geniality never failed.   The
respect he won from his messmates extended to what he represented;
and when he arranged some special services, many of them were there.
Another was always jolly and joined in the amusements of the men.
Because they liked him, they listened when he gave advice.   Still another chaplain was described as so scholarly and reserved that no one
would approach him if it could be avoided.   During a hard jungle fight
he was active on the front line and in places of greatest danger.   The
men saw their chaplain in a new light, realizing that he was going far
toward making up in devoted helpfulness what he lacked in affability.
These men are typical of the hundreds who found that being respected
and liked by officers and men was not only a steppingstone to more
important matters but was a wholesome influence itself.   Many soldiers
came home with a friendlier attitude toward the clergy than they ever
had felt before.[2]

Many commanders tell of the chaplain's influence being enhanced
when he showed that he "could take it" by participating voluntarily in
strenuous exercises or bivouacs and long marches.[3]   If an element of
danger were involved, the exploit lost nothing in effectiveness unless so
extreme as to appear foolhardy.   Several took the training in parachute jumping, one explaining that paratroopers classified all soldiers
as jumpers or nonjumpers and he wanted to join the inner circle.   Occasionally these adventures exacted a price.   One chaplain was injured
on his first practice jump and returned to America for treatment.
When an insane man ran out of the hospital, broke away from three
men, and threw himself into the frigid waters of an Alaskan inlet,
Charles Culpepper plunged after him fully clothed.   In spite of the
darkness and the violence of the man, the chaplain brought him ashore
in safety.[4]

Other incidents show how resourcefulness or courage can win respect.   One chaplain 49 years old could outmarch most of the men of
the unit and had notable skill in driving a tank or assembling and firing
a gun.   Another operated the steam winch when an emergency crew
had to unload a ship.   Later he explained that he had worked his way

---

[2] Kenneth Gow—*Letters of a Soldier*, p. 167; Olga S. Greenlaw—*Lady and the Tiger*.

[3] Forms 3: Wm. J. Clements, July 1943, C. E. Haterius, June 1943, H. Montgomery, July 1944, *et al.*

[4] *Brotherhood and Service News*, Jan. 1944; Forms 3: Probert E. Herb, June 1943, Stanley P. Gosek, Sept. 1945; Personal file, Charles R. Culpepper.

through college that way.   One found two Germans in a foxhole, dis-
armed them, and marched them in as prisoners.   One captured a German city in the sense that he represented his commander in accepting
the surrender.   Another was accosted by a German who came out of
the woods and wished to surrender.   The chaplain said that he had
not been instructed in this particular duty at the Chaplain School, but
he placed the prisoner on the hood of his jeep and took him to the military police.   Perhaps the record was made by the chaplain in Africa
who was riding to the front with 2 lieutenants when they drove over a
rise and found themselves in the midst of 500 Italians.   The enemy,
however, was eager to surrender and insisted that it be to the chaplain
because of his superior rank.   As his unit was not equipped to take
care of so many, the prisoners were turned over to the British.[5]   In
themselves these incidents are trivial, but the chaplain who shrinks from
neither hard work nor danger has taken a long step toward winning
respect for the principles he represents.

Reports from various installations and units give chaplains a large
measure of credit for reductions in the venereal disease rate, especially
after the systematic lectures on citizenship and morality began in 1947.
In one place the rate dropped at that time to less than one-third of
what it had been.   A commander explained the especially bad situation of his unit but added that the chaplain lectured on morality every
week and interviewed every man infected with venereal disease.   But
for these efforts, he believed, the situation would have been much worse.
These opinions, plus the fact that a large proportion of the men kept
away from all danger of infection, emphasize the statement of Antonio
Villarama, Secretary of Public Health of the Philippines, in 1947:
"The chaplains with their religious and moral weapons can do more
toward preventing venereal disease than the combined efforts of the
physicians.   Venereal disease control must be based upon religious and
moral indoctrination."[6]

Many indorsements on chaplains' reports state that they have done
much for the morale of their regiments.   One commander attributes
this to the chaplain's "stubborn insistence that every soldier get his
every right."   Another stresses his "good cheer and ready help in difficult individual situations."   Another said the morale was high be-

---

[5] *Armored News,* 6 Mar. 1944; *The Daily Alaska Empire,* 7 Jan. 1943; Christopher Cross—*Soldiers
of God,* p. 78; "A Most Unusual Chaplain," p. 13; Charles E. Titus, Form 3, April 1945; Fort
Wayne *News-Sentinel,* 19 Feb. 1944.

[6] Wilber K. Anderson to 3d Army Ch; 14 Oct. 1947, OCCh.; John W. Sparks, Form 3, Oct.
1947; Joseph R. Koch, Form 3, Nov. 1947.

cause the men were "on a sound footing in their religion."   One commander gave credit to the chaplain for a decrease in obscene and vulgar speech.   A chaplain instituted the custom of collecting a penny for every profane word he overheard.   The men entered into the spirit of the rule and made offending comrades take their penalties, though they did not kow how the "Chaplain's Cussing Fund" would be used.[7]

One commander analyzed the work of his chaplain in a way which brought a commendation from the general.   He stated that the troops were largely of Mexican-Indian ancestry with little either of education or religious training.   In his services and elsewhere the chaplain stressed the application of Biblical ethics to life in the Army.   The colonel credited this with a marked decrease in drinking, gambling, and profanity.   Where liquor and gaming had taken 70 percent of the men's pay, this had been reduced to 15.   Emphasis upon responsibility to dependents led the men to send home hundreds of dollars which otherwise would have been squandered, and contributed to habits of thought which would be useful in the coming years.[8]

Every attempt to evaluate the chaplain's work must consider the effect of military life and participation in warfare upon the soldier. The optimist will ask if the chaplains grasped their unparalleled opportunity to lead the impressionable multitude into the higher life.   Those who take the gloomy view will seek for evidence that they snatched a few fragments from the moral and spiritual ruin.   The judgment of people who are supposed to know is contradictory, and generalization is risky.

A wounded marine said that the implications of the platitude about atheists in foxholes were false and dangerous.   He was convinced that war and the military environment tend to weaken the faith and practice of religion "except in those moments of great crises when each individual stands alone."   A soldier warned against attaching too much significance to pictures of large crowds at church because many had nowhere else to go and were there without ethical appreciation or objectives.   In 1918 Dr. Daniel A. Poling had been quite enthusiastic about the wholesome effect upon men and chaplains of some of the things he had seen in France.   Late in 1943 after a tour of the battlefronts of the world, he wrote of the "overwhelming indifference to organized religion" he had seen in many places.   He feared this indif-

---

[7] Forms 3: C. P. Cummings, Aug. 1945, H. D. Bennett, May 1943, Henry J. Louttit, May 1944, H. Duhan, Aug. 1944; *Brotherhood and Service News*, Jan. 44.
[8] Richard J. Egan, Form 3, May 1943.

ference more than positive danger and asked his fellow churchmen what they were going to do about it.[9]

Equally plausible are the judgments of those who reach a more hopeful conclusion. The statisticians have reckoned that soldiers attend church about twice as often as in civil life, and the Chief of Chaplains declared that the churches would not hold them if civilians attended Sunday morning services in the same proportion.[10] Senator Mead was impressed by the throngs he saw kneeling in the Pacific mud and rain, remarking, "This life makes Christians of men." Many chaplains concurred in the opinion of one of their number that the soldiers showed "a renewed and deeper appreciation of the values and purposes of religion." One who held the same view believed the men of his army attended church in about the same proportion as in civil life but hastened to show that mere attendance is no index of more important matters, as many soldiers who are indifferent at other times attend chapel regularly during their first weeks in camp and when their unit is about to start for the war zone. A thoughtful sergeant told Brink that the churches would lose their hold on the returning soldier unless they forgot unnecessary things and just made people think about God. Willetts urged young men of established character to enlist for a term of foreign service as a preparation for civic leadership.[11] Moritz Gottlieb, Special Commissioner for the Jewish Welfare Board, visited Australia and New Guinea late in 1943. After describing what Christian Chaplains were doing for Jewish men and the goodwill which he saw among all chaplains, he wrote:

> "When we have won this war, what a joy to the hearts of mother, father, sister, brother, and all those who had to stay home, to find their men returning from war with a greater sense of spiritual and religious values than the average had before going away to war. Yes, that will be one of the great, if not *the greatest and most lasting, values* that can come from this war. That can be the guiding spirit of the new Postwar world we all look forward to. A world of great understanding and greater tolerance—a world being built on the age old hope of *Peace on Earth, Good Will Toward All Men.*"[12]

How did their military experiences affect the chaplains themselves? Hayne said they taught him patience. Tubesing learned understand-

---

[9] Elisha Atkins—*Religion of Soldier and Sailor*, p. 101 ff.; *Time*, 21 Feb., 3 Jan. 1944.

[10] U. S. Congress, House, *Hearings . . . Pursuant to H. R. 465*, Pt. I, pp. 493–98.

[11] James M. Mead—*Tell the Folks Back Home*, pp. 210, 201; *Messages from William Jewell Chaplains;* Eben. Cobb Brink—*And God Was There*, p. 86; Benjamin D. Willetts—*Trailing a Chaplain*, p. 26.

[12] *History of Chaplains' Activities in the Pacific*, pp. 454–55.

ing and compassion in "the finest institution for learning in existence." After 38 months of service Jordan believed that no amount of formal schooling could train a minister to be a pastor so well as a tour of duty with the Army. Others found their own faith deepened and enriched as they ministered to men of other faiths. Some felt a new reality and directness in preaching out of doors or in mess halls where no conventionalized symbols nor obstruse practices diverted attention or clouded the stark realities of life.[13]

A relevant question has been asked repeatedly but never answered conclusively. Has their experience in the chaplaincy tended to unfit some men for the parish ministry by making them chafe under the necessity of devoting valuable time and effort to trivial matters? It is true that a considerable number of the men who have served as chaplains during each of our major wars have become college presidents or professors, administrators of religious or welfare agencies, editors or authors, public officials, or, especially since the Second World War, chaplains in the Regular Army. Most of these men have been reticent about their motives, and conclusions must be advanced with caution. There seems no doubt that a considerable number of men, already restive under some of the distasteful demands of parish duty, found this aversion intensified when they returned to civil life and took the opportunity to find other employment. Others returned to the pastorate with a firm determination that vital matters should not be hampered by customs or projects of slight importance. A few made places for themselves in new fields of usefulness. How many gained from their army experience the broader outlook and vigor which qualified them for administrative and similar work must be left to conjecture. The same is true of the proportion who would have been called to these positions in the normal processes of civilian life.

More tangible are the indications that thousands of chaplains came to know their colleagues of other groups better than ever before. Almost without exception this brought enhanced respect for the men and for the ideals toward which they worked. A degree of cooperation seldom equaled among civilian clergy became the normal rule for chaplains. One declared that many soldiers would expect this unity when they returned to their homes and would be lost to the church if they failed to find it.[14] At the end of the First World War, Poling expressed this faith in the men he had seen working together in France:

---

[13] Orlando V. Hayne—*Sir: The Chaplain Wishes to Report*, p. 8; *American Lutheran;* Sept. 1942; *Brotherhood and Service News,* Jan. 1944; Brink, *op. cit.,* p. 76; *Army Chaplain,* Jan.–Feb., 1940, p. 94.

[14] Hayne, *op. cit.,* p. 7.

> "I wish that every pastor in America could have at least 6 months in actual service overseas . . . . These men who have heard the great spiritual voice of Civilization in her rebirth, who have toiled and listened through long and terrifying days that crowded out of their lives the petty and superficial things . . . will not return to be contented with the ancient walls of ecclesiasticism and sectarian differences. They, with the hundreds of thousands they have ministered to, will strike mightily against the props of outgrown systems . . . They will save us from ourselves, and together we shall set Christ free in his own temple.[15]

Twenty-five years saw only a beginning of the realization of this hope, but the men of 1942 started on a higher level than their forerunners of 1918. There were four times as many of them to learn the meaning of cooperation without compromise, and they had four times as long for the lesson. The full consequences of these closer ties of understanding and friendship cannot be seen for many years, but there are thousands of clergymen and millions of veterans who have seen something better than distrust and competition actually at work among the religious leaders of all faiths.

Still another question cannot be ignored. To doubt or even reject some facet of a moribund sectarian dogma cannot be compared with the abandonment or temporary lapse from an accepted standard of moral conduct. It was reported that the chaplain of Tappan's Confederate regiment became so excited during a Kentucky fight in 1861 that he not only shot 2 Yankees and killed 1 with a knife but ran after the retreating enemy shouting imprecations unfit to print. Many saw in this a good chance to tease the chaplain, but to some the profanity, not the bloodthirstiness, was evidence of moral instability.[16] It is true that in every war a few chaplains have been caught in the mesh of unusual temptation and have failed in some important particular to be true to their sense of duty. The same is true of civilian clergymen in time of peace. Each sphere of activity has its peculiar temptations, and each affords certain wholesome sustaining influences which the other lacks. Many chaplains have testified that the challenge of the service left them stronger than ever before. Their confidence seems to overbalance the few who are known to have failed in some time of crisis, but this is a matter not susceptible of proof.

Many contacts between chaplains and civilian churches have left permanent ties of friendship. Some have gone further and linked many soldiers to the institutions of their home communities. Through a

---

[15] Daniel A. Poling—*Huts in Hell,* pp. 159-60.
[16] Bell Irvin Wiley—*The Life of Johnny Reb,* p. 188.

Christmas party for 500 children and helping in the local church, Atkinson gained the warm gratitude of the English village where he was quartered.   Scharlemann found a Waldensian church without a pastor near where he was stationed in Italy.   Within 3 weeks he had mastered enough of their language so he could preach to them in Italian, and he continued this service for 18 months.   During the war the Chief of Chaplains sent certificates suitable for framing as expressions of appreciation to churches and other institutions which had given clergymen to the chaplaincy.[17]

A service to the churches which many chaplains performed faithfully was to keep them informed of the activities or other forms of religious interest manifested by men of their congregation or community. This was especially important when men made specific commitments to religious life or resolved to devote themselves to work in this field. Frequently chaplains reported to the Chief of Chaplains the names of men who had determined to enter the ministry, priesthood, or rabbinate.   Such information was transmitted to the pastors of these men with the request that appropriate encouragement and guidance be given them as a courtesy to the military service.   Some chaplains were able to give these young men an introduction to their theological studies or practical experience in leading choirs or teaching classes.   After the end of hostilities in Europe, a course in theology was given as part of the Information and Education program.   A chaplain was one of the chief instructors and was privileged to teach 35 men in the first session and 45 in the next.[18]   Thus the ministry of religion recruits itself and the chaplaincy lives on, holding high the standard of loyalty and reverence, righteousness and service, in every time of crisis.

---

[17] Elbert L. Atkinson—"Information and Experiences of Chaplain's Activities," pp. 4, 6; Release, Chaplain School, Sept. 1947.

[18] Troy E. Brooks, Form 3, Oct. 1944, *et al.;* Edmund L. Malone, Form 3, Sept. 1945.

Bibliography

MANUSCRIPT SOURCES

Of supreme importance among the sources of material for this study have been the unpublished records, reports, and correspondence concerning chaplains to be found in the Office of the Chief of Chaplains, other Army and Air Force files, the national and State archives, and the records of religious organizations. Most of these are classified by subject and number and can be located with comparative ease. Some exist in multiple copies and can be found in several places. Because they are not classified in the usual manner or for other patent reasons, the following are listed separately:

Conyngham, D. P., Esq.—*The Soldiers of the Cross.* (Accounts of the activities of priests and nuns in the Union and Confederate armies and hospitals, compiled about 1870), archives, Notre Dame University.

Dabney—List of 128 chaplains in Lee's army, library of Union Theological Seminary, Richmond.

Hayne, Orlando V.—*Sir: The Chaplain Wishes to Report,* OCCh.

History of Chaplains' Work in the 88th Division, n. d., OCCh.

Historical Records of the A. A. F. Chaplain Transition Course, 2 vols. OCAFCh.

Hoffman, Albert J.—*Autobiography.*

(Honeywell, Roy J.)—*History of Military Training: The Corps of Chaplains, 1941–45,* OCCh.

Lipsey, R. C.—*The Chaplain's Book,* Camp Heldesheim, Germany, May 1, 1945–May 31, 1945, OCCh.

Records of the New Hampshire Chaplains' Association, State Library, Concord.

(Piepkorn, Arthur C.)—*A Chronicle of the Training School for Newly-Appointed Chaplains and Chaplain Candidates during the First World War,* n. d., OCCh.

(Piepkorn, Arthur C.)—*The U. S. Army Chaplain School in France: 1918–1919,* n. d., OCCh.

454841 O—58——23

(Piepkorn, Arthur C.)—*A Chronicle of the United States Army Chaplain School during the Second World War: The First Two Years*, n. d., OCCh.

Tetreau, Elzar D.—*Pen Sketches and Diary of a Chaplain of Infantry* (1918–19), OCCh.

Van Hal, Adrian W.—*Historical Report of P. O. W. Chaplains' Activities among Prisoners of War in E. T. O. under American Jurisdiction*, OCCh.

Willetts, Benjamin D.—*Trailing a Chaplain*, OCCh.

Kirtley, Edwin L.—Account of his experiences in learning and using the language of the Marshall Islanders in 1944, sent to the author, 15 April 1956.

PERIODICAL SOURCES
(Listed by author when name is known)

Alexander, Jack—"He's Our Guy" (Albert J. Hoffman), *Saturday Evening Post,* CCXVII, 9.

Arnold, William R.—"The Army Chaplain," *Army and Navy Journal,* LXXX, 81, LXXXI, 76, LXXXII, 104.

Arnold, William R.—"Faith under Fire; What Kind of Boy will the Army Send Back?" *Woman's Home Companion,* LXXI, 24.

Arnold, William R.—"Our Fighting Troops Receive Spiritual Encouragement from Army Chaplains," *Victory Bulletin,* V, 7.

Arnold, William R.—"Wanted: Army Chaplains," *Christian Advocate,* CXVIII, 1233.

Arnold, William R.—"We Are Strong in Spirit," *Country Gentleman,* CXII, 10.

Aveling, Francis—"Brother Chaplains," *Catholic World,* CVIII, 145.

Bateman, Cephas C.—"The Army Chaplain: His Work and Worth," *Journal of the Military Service Institution of the United States,* Mar.–Apr. 1905.

Bateman, Cephas C.—"Evolution of the Army Chaplains' Corps," *Army and Navy Register,* 26 June 1920, p. 805.

Bell, B. J.—"The Church's Work for Men at War," 1919.

Bernstein, P. S.—"Jewish Chaplains on Land and Sea," *Opinion,* XIII, 6–8.

Blied, Benjamin—"Catholic Charity in the Army, 1861–65," *Social Justice Review,* XXXIII, 166.

Book, J. D.—"Tell It to the Chaplain!" *Churchman,* CLVI, 19.

Braley, Berton—"Priest—and Soldier, Too" (W. R. Arnold), *Extension,* XXXVII, 6.

Bousman, Gary—"The Human Side of the Chaplaincy," *Advance,* 3 Apr. 1943.

Bousman, Gary—"Three Years an Army Chaplain," *Chicago Theological Seminary Register,* XXXIV, 15.

Brasted, Alva J.—"In Defense of Chaplains," *Army Ordnance,* XV, 352.

Brasted, Alva J.—"Religion of Our Soldiers," *Religious Education,* XXXVIII, 188.

Brickner, B. R.—"How I Found Your Boy Overseas," *Think,* X, 24.

Brock, H. I.—"At the Front the Church is Universal," *New York Times Magazine,* Aug. 22, 1943.

Brown, R. M.—"We Have Met the Enemy," *New Yorker*, XXIX, 58.

Burke, A. B.—"The Army Goes to Church," *Coronet*, XI, 3.

Chase, R. H.—"It Makes Christians: A Fighting Army Chaplain Tells What Happens to Men's Moral Values in the Stress of Battle," *Life*, XV, 57.

Clark, J. R.—"Chaplains in Combat," *Christian Century*, LXIII, 1435.

Cleary, W. D.—"United States Chaplains Go to School," *America*, LXIX, 347.

Crehan, John Patrick—"Privileged Communications," *The Infantry Journal*, July 1949, p. 13.

Cullon, Peter E.—"A Remarkable Group of Gee Eyes," *The Army and Navy Chaplain*, Oct.–Nov. 1947, p. 1.

Crowell, A. A.—"Parachute Parson" (Raymond S. Hall), *Flying*, XXXIII, 43.

Dame, Lawrence—"Army Chaplains Get Tough," *Magazine Digest*, XXVII, 83.

Day, Richard—"The Work of a Chaplain," *Christianity and Crisis*, IX, 30.

Devan, S. A.—"The Armed Forces Practise Ecumenicity," *Christendom*, VII, 450.

Doherty, Eddie—"Front-Line Chaplain" (Albert J. Hoffman), *Sign*, XXIV, 121.

Donovan, S. P.—"Making Our Service Men Spiritually Alert," *Homiletic and Pastoral Review*, XLII, 505.

Dowe, R. M., Jr.—"Ordeal of Chaplain Kapaun," *Saturday Evening Post*, Jan. 16, 1954, p. 20; Reprinted, *Reader's Digest*, Apr. 1954, p. 140; Discussion, *Saturday Evening Post*, Feb. 27, 1954.

Earley, S. B.—"Catholicism in the Services," *America*, LXX, 453.

Edmundson, C. F.—"Faithful unto Death: A True Tale of Munda," *American Legion Magazine*, XXXVII, 9.

Fahringer, F. H.—"Glimpses of a Chaplain's Work," *Baptist Leader*, V, 12.

Flynn, Fabian—"D Day and After," *Sign*, XXIV, 61.

Fulton, H. K.—"Training Army Chaplains," *Outlook*, CXX, 167.

Gaskill, Gordon—"Soldiers without Weapons," *American Magazine*, CXXXVII, 37.

Gerecke, Henry F.—"Assignment with the International Military Tribunal as Spiritual Advisor," *The Army and Navy Chaplain*, July–Aug. 1947, p. 2.

Gilkey, J. G.—"The Church and the Chaplaincy," *Christianity and Crisis*, IV, 3.

Glenn, C. L.—"The Importance of the Chaplaincy," *Christianity and Crisis,* II, 5.

Glenn, C. L.—"What the Chaplains Need," *Christianity and Crisis,* III, 3.

Goldman, R. I.—"A Social Worker Assists an Army Chaplain," *Family,* XXV, 188.

Gregory, W. E.—"The Chaplain and Mental Health," *American Journal of Sociology,* LII, 420.

Hamilton, C. G.—"The Chaplain's Job," *Christian Century,* LVIII, 906.

Hershey, S., and Tennant, H.—"Are the Churches Failing Our GI's?", *American Mercury,* LXXVII, 3.

High, Stanley—"The War Boom in Religion," *American Magazine,* CXXXIV, 51.

Hoffman, B. H.—"Meet an Army Chaplain" (Clyde Hahn), *Ladies Home Journal,* LXII, 133.

Hoffman, Catherine—"Tabernacles and Tents," *Extension,* XXXVI, 6.

Hoke, Donald E.—"Top Brass Chaplain," *Christian Life,* Feb. 1951, p. 19.

Holloway, Vernon H.—"A Review of American Religious Pacifism," *Religion and Life,* Summer, 1950, p. 367.

Honeywell, Roy J.—"The Chapel and the Rum," *Quartermaster Review,* Sep.–Oct. 1953, p. 33.

Iley, C. H.—"Chaplain of the Spars," *Christian Advocate,* CXIX, 1181.

Kennedy, R. C.—"How Good Were Our Army Chaplains?", *Christian Century,* LXIII, 716.

Kilde, Clarence—"The Chaplain's Devotional Materials for His Men," *Christianity and Crisis,* V. 5.

Kilde, Clarence—"A Chaplain's Ministry and His Resources," *Christianity and Crisis,* IV, 6.

Korn, Bertram W.—"Jewish Chaplains during the Civil War," *American Jewish Archives,* I, 7.

La Tour, Cy—"Man's Man—A Soldier's Pal," *Churchman,* CLV, 10.

Lavine, H.—"Chaplain Heroes," *Newsweek,* XL, 74.

Levinger, L. J.—"Christian and Jew at the Front," *Biblical World,* LIII, 477.

Leonard, A. W.—"Visiting Our Chaplains," *Christian Advocate,* CXVIII, 430.

Lowell, C. S.—"I Was A Chaplain," *Christian Century,* LXI, 773.

Lucas, J. G.—"When the Chaplain Comes Home," *Woman's Home Companion,* LXXII, 31.

Mears, J. G.—"Chaplains Labor to Uphold Army Morals and Morale," *America,* LXV, 539.

Mears, J. G.—"The Chaplains Swing Along with the Lads in the Camps," *America,* LXV, 514.

McGurn, Barrett—"Soldier-Priests," *Sign,* XXI, 666.

Meehan, T. F.—"Chaplain Service in the Navy and the Army, A Review of Notable Developments since the Revolution," *America,* LIX, 562.

Metzger, Charles H.—"Chaplains in the American Revolution," *Catholic Historical Review,* XXXI, 31.

Moffatt, Cleveland—in *Leslie's Weekly,* 22 Sep., 27 Oct., 1898.

Oliver, Alfred C.—"An Army Chaplain," *The Military Chaplain,* Jan. 1951.

Oliver, Alfred C.—"The Men of Bataan and their Chaplains," *Living Church,* CX, 21.

Olsson, K. A.—"Mission of the Chaplain," *Christianity and Crisis,* III, 4.

Payton, J. S.—"Three Faiths—One God," *Christian Advocate* CXVIII, 613.

Plumb, Robert J.—"Chaplain of Arnold's Expedition to Quebec," *The Chaplain,* July–Aug. 1949, p. 12.

Plumb, Robert J.—"Chaplain of the Revolution," *The Chaplain,* Sep. 1948, p. 8.

Poletti, Adrian—"Bomber Base in England," *Sign,* XXIII, 677.

Poling, Daniel A.—"Strong Man of God," *Sign,* XXIV, 547.

Pool, David deS.—"The Jewish Chaplain," *Contemporary Jewish Record,* V, 235.

Poole, L. D.—"An Air Force Chaplain in the Marshalls," *America,* LXXI, 571.

Pugh, W. B.—"A Chaplain's View from the Front," *Expositor and Homiletic Review,* XLV, 505.

Pugh, W. B.—"Visiting Overseas," *Religious Digest,* XVI, 81.

Rabe, Gerald—"A Chaplain Faces the Front," *Christian Family and our Mission,* XL, 86.

Rabe, Gerald—"Notes in the Diary of an S. V. D. in Khaki," *Christian Family and our Mission,* XXXIX, 338.

Ribalow, H. U.— ·Warriors of the Spirit," *Congress Weekly,* X, 6.

Richards, B. G.—"The First Jewish Chaplain," *Congress Weekly,* IX, 8.

Richmond, H. R.—"A Rabbi Recalls Pearl Harbor," *Opinion,* XIII, 22.

Rogers, E. K.—"Doughboy's Chaplain," *Expositer and Homiletic Review,* XLVI, 7.

Rothschild, J. J.—"Nothing Will be the Same," *Jewish Veteran*, XIV, 4.

Ryan, G. A.—"Manpower on the Spiritual Front," *Ecclesiastical Review*, CIX, 1.

Sandrow, E. T.—"The Chaplain Will Also Return," *Reconstructionist*, X, 9.

Shaw, J. R.—"Jungle War," *Christian Century*, LX, 1411.

Singer, H. D.—"Your Kids Taught Me about Religion," *Saturday Evening Post*, Sep 5, 1953, p. 30.

Stack, K. G.—"God and Guadalcanal," *Extension*, XXXVIII, 12.

Staples, C. A.—"A Chaplain of the Revolution" (Enos Hitchcock), *Unitarian Review*, XXXV, 267.

Strahan, Speer—"Holy Communion in Hawaii," *Commonweal*, XXXV, 396.

Stratton, David H.—"The Army and the Gospel in the West," *The Western Humanities Review*, VIII, 3.

Stroup, R. C.—"A Soldier Looks at the Church," *Harper's Magazine*, CLXXXIX, 397.

Tepper, Irving—"A Jewish Chaplain in North Africa," *Contemporary Jewish Record*, VI, 239.

Toulin, Isaac—"D-Day for the Soul," *Jewish Veteran*, XIV, 4.

Toulin, Isaac—"Liberation through Chaplain's Eyes," *Jewish Veteran*, XIV, 10.

Toulin, Isaac—"Why Is This Night Different?", *Jewish Veteran*, XIII, 4.

Waring, G. J.—"The Chaplain's Duties, *Catholic Mind*, XV, 441.

Washburn, H. B.—"The Army Chaplain," *Papers of the American Society of Church History*, Ser. 2, VII, 1.

Washburn, H. B.—"Army and Navy Commission in Action," *Churchman*, CLV, 13.

Werner, Alfred—"Overseas Chaplains in Action," *National Jewish Monthly*, LVII, 258.

Whaling, M. C.—"A Place for the Chaplain," *Christian Family and our Mission*, XXXVIII, 49.

Whelton, Paul—"Harvard Trains 5000 for Army Chaplain Jobs," Hearst newspapers, 11 Oct. 1942.

Wirt, Williston—"Sky-Circuit Sky Pilot," *Advance*, CXXXVI, 11.

Wittles, D. G.—"Are the Chaplains Doing a Job?", *Saturday Evening Post*, CCXVII, 12.

Wilson, Robert R.—"Status of Chaplains with Armed Forces," *Journal of International Law*, June 1943, p. 490.

GOVERNMENT PUBLICATIONS

American State Papers: *Documents Legislative and Executive of the Congress of the United States,* Washington, 1832 *et seq.*

The United States Army Chaplaincy, W. D. Pamphlet 16–1, (reprint of Thompson—*American Army Chaplaincy*)

Official Opinions of the Attorneys General of the United States.

The Chaplain's Manual:

> Waring, George J.—*Chaplain's Duties and How Best to Accomplish his Work,* 1912.
>
> *The Chaplain, His Place and Duties,* 1926, revised and published as—
>
> *Training Manual No. 2270–5, The Chaplain,* 1937, revised again as—
>
> *Technical Manual 16–205, The Chaplain,* 1941. Rewritten and published under the same number and title in 1944 and again in 1947.

The Chaplain Serves, 1943. Reprint with additions, 1944.

Congressional Globe, Sketches of debates and proceedings to 1872.

Congressional Record, Proceedings and debates from 1873 to date.

Congress of the United States, House and Senate, *Hearings.*

Decisions of the Comptroller General.

Decisions of the Judge Advocate General.

Heitman, Francis Bernard—*Historical Register and Dictionary of the United States Army from its Organization, September 29, 1789, to March 2, 1903,* 2 vols., Washington, 1903.

Heitman, Francis Bernard—*Historical Register of Officers of the Continental Army during the War of the Revolution, April 1775 to December, 1783,* new ed., Washington, 1914.

Manual for Courts Martial, 1928.

The Medal of Honor of the United States Army, Washington, 1948.

Session Laws of the State of Minnesota passed during the Fifty-Fourth Session of the State Legislature at the Session Commencing January 2, 1945.

Journal of the Congress of the Confederate States of America, 1861–1865, 9 vols., Washington, 1904.

Journals of the American Congress from 1774 to 1788, 4 vols., Washington, 1823.

Journals of the Continental Congress, 1774–1789, 34 vols., Washington, 1934.

Judge Advocate General's Department, Board of Review, *Holdings, Opinions and Reviews.*

The Public Statutes at Large of the United States of America, 1850 et seq.

Stryker, William S.—*Official Register of the Officers and Men of New Jersey in the Revolutionary War,* Trenton, 1872.

United States Code, 1940 Ed., 3 vols. and later supplements.

The War of the Rebellion: A Compilation of the Official Records of the Union and Confederate Armies, 4 series, 70 vols. in 128, Washington, 1880–1901.

Military Records of various states in the Civil War:

> *Report of the Adjutant General of the State of Illinois,* 9 vols., Springfield, 1900.
>
> *Report of the Adjutant General of the State of Indiana,* 8 vols., 1865.
>
> *Roster and Record of Iowa Soldiers in the War of the Rebellion, together with historical sketches of Volunteer Organizations, 1861–1866,* 6 vols., Des Moines, 1908.
>
> *Report of the Adjutant General of the State of Kentucky,* 2 vols., Frankfort, 1866.
>
> *Maine in the War for the Union: A History of the Part Borne by troops in the supression of the American Rebellion,* by William E. S. Whitman and Charles H. True, Lewiston, 1865.
>
> *Massachusetts Soldiers, Sailors, and Marines in the Civil War,* 9 vols., compiled and published by the Adjutant General, Norwood, 1931.
>
> *Michigan in the War,* compiled by Jno. Robertson, Adjutant General, Revised Ed., Lansing, 1882.
>
> *History and Roster of Maryland Volunteers, War of 1861–65,* Baltimore, 1898.
>
> *Minnesota in the Civil and Indian Wars, 1861–1865,* St. Paul, 1890.
>
> *Official Register of Missouri Troops for 1862,* Adjutant General's Office, State of Missouri, St. Louis, 1863.
>
> *Records of Officers and Men of New Jersey in the Civil War, 1861–1865,* 2 vols., compiled in the office of the Adjutant General, Trenton, 1876.
>
> *New York in the War of the Rebellion, 1861 to 1865,* 6 vols., compiled by Frederick Phisterer, 3d Ed., Albany, 1912.

Official Roster of the Soldiers of the State of Ohio in the War of the Rebellion, 1861–1866, Cincinnati, 1886.

Bates, Samuel P.—*History of Pennsylvania Volunteers, 1861–65,* 5 vols., Harrisburg, 1870.

Annual Report of the Adjutant General of the State of Rhode Island and Providence Plantations for the Year 1865, 2 vols., Providence, 1893.

Report of the Adjutant General of the State of Tennessee of the Military Forces of the State, 1861–66, Nashville, 1866.

Revised Roster of Vermont Volunteers and Lists of Vermonters who served in the Army and Navy of the United States during the War of the Rebellion, 1861–65, Montpelier, 1892.

Roster of Wisconsin Volunteers, War of the Rebellion, 1861–1865, 2 vols. Madison, 1886.

WORKS BY OR ABOUT CHAPLAINS

Memorial and Letters of Rev. John R. Adams, D. D., 1890, private print.

Anderson, Stanley E.—*Shepherds to 24,000,000 Service Men*, Butler, Ind., 1955.

Atteridge, Andrew Hilliary—*The Catholic Chaplains in the Great War*, London, (1917).

Avery, David—*Narrative of the Rise and Progress of the Differences which have Issued in a Separation between the Minister and People of Bennington*, Bennington, 1783.

Axton, John T., Jr.—*Brief History of Chaplains in the U. S. Army*, Fort Leavenworth, 1925.

Barnes, L. C.—*The John Gano Evidence of George Washington's Religion*, Bulletin of William Jewell College, Sept. 15, 1926.

Bennett, William W., D. D.—*A Narrative of the Great Revival which prevailed in the Southern Armies during the late Civil War between the states of the Federal Union*, Philadelphia, 1877.

Betts, Alexander, D. D.—*Experiences of a Confederate Chaplain, 1861–1865*, edited by W. A. Betts.

Biederwolf, William Edward—*History of the 161 Regiment, Indiana Volunteer Infantry*, Logansport, Ind., 1899.

Bittle, Celestine N.—*Soldiering for Cross and Flag: Impressions of a War Chaplain*, Milwaukee, (c. 1929).

Boardman, Benjamin—"*Diary of the Reverend Benjamin Boardman*," Proceedings of the Massachusetts Historical Society, Series 2, VII, 400–13, May 1892.

Bowman, B. L., D. D.—*Transport Chaplain, A Chronological History of a Chaplain in World War II*, Sarasota, Fla., 1947.

Brace, Frederic R.—*Brief Sketches of the New Jersey Chaplains in the Continental Army and in the State Militia during the War of Independence*, Patterson, 1909.

Bradford, J. H.—*The Chaplains in the Volunteer Army*, Washington, 1892(?)

Bradley, Rev. George S., Chaplain 22d Wisconsin—*The Star Corps; or, Notes of an Army Chaplain during Sherman's Famous "March to the Sea,"* Milwaukee, 1865.

Brasted, Alva Jennings—*Service to Service Men*, Minneapolis, 1941.

Brink, Eben. Cobb—*And God Was There*, Philadelphia, c. 1944.

Bristol, Frank Milton—*The Life of Chaplain McCabe*, New York, 1908.

Brown, William Young—*The Army Chaplain: his Office, Duties, and Responsibilities, and the Means of Aiding him*, Philadelphia, 1863.

"Chaplains for the Mexican War—1846," *Woodstock Letters*, XV, 198–202, XVI, 33–39, 225–29.

American Chaplains of the Fifth Army, Milan, 1945.

Chapman, Robert B.—*Tell it to the Chaplain*, New York, 1952.

Cleaveland, John—"Journal," *Salem Historical Collections*, XII, 85–103, XIII, 53–63.

Clyde, Rev. John C., D. D.—*Rosbrugh: A Tale of the Revolution*, Easton, Pa., 1880.

Corby, Very Rev. W.—*Memoirs of Chaplain Life*, Notre Dame, Ind., 1894.

Costen, William Hilary—*The Spanish-American War Volunteer*, Middletown, Pa., 1899.

Cross, Christopher—*Soldiers of God*, New York, c. 1945.

Cross, The Rev. Jos., D. D.—*Camp and Field: Papers from the Portfolio of an Army Chaplain*, Columbia, S. C., 1864.

Cutler, William Parker and Julia Perkins—*Life, Journals, and Correspondence of Rev. Manassah Cutler*, 2 vols., Cincinnati, 1888.

Denison, Rev. Frederic, A. M.—*A Chaplain's Experience in the Union Army*, Providence, 1893.

Denison, Rev. Frederic—*Sabres and Spurs: The First Regiment Rhode Island Cavalry in the Civil War*, Central Falls, 1876.

Denison, Rev. Frederic—*Shot and Shell: The Third Rhode Island Heavy Artillery Regiment in the Rebellion, 1861–1865*, Providence, 1879.

Denison, Rev. Frederic—*Army Hymns*, Providence, 1863.

Drumm, William M.—*Hospital Chaplains*, 1943.

Duffy, Francis P.—*Father Duffy's Story: A Tale of Humor and Heroism, of Life and Death with the Fighting Sixty-Ninth*, Garden City, c. 1918.

Eastman, W. R.—"The Army Chaplain of 1863," *Personal Recollections of the War of the Rebellion*, 4th Series, New York, 1912.

Eaton, John, Ph. D., LL. D., and Ethel Osgood Mason—*Grant, Lincoln and the Freedman, Reminiscences of the Civil War*, New York, 1907.

Emerson, Daniel—"A Journal of my Procedure with the Army to Crown Point," in Emerson, Benjamin K.—*The Ipswich Emersons*, Boston, MCM.

Evans, Israel—*A Discourse Delivered at Easton on 17 October 1779 to Officers and Soldiers of the Western Army after Return from the Expedition against the Five Nations*, Philadelphia, 1779.

Fallows, Alice—*Everybody's Bishop, being the Life and Times of the Right Reverend Samuel Fallows, D. D.,* New York, (1927).

Federal Council of Churches of Christ in America—*Survey of the Moral and Religious Forces in the Military Camps and Naval Stations in the United States,* May 1, 1918.

Fithian, Philip V.—*Letters to His Wife, Elizabeth Beatty Fithian, with a Biographical Sketch by Frank D. Andrews,* Vineland, N. J., 1932.

Flick, E. M. E.—*Chaplain Duffy of the Sixty-ninth Regiment,* New York, 1935.

Frank, Emma L.—*The Chaplaincy in the Armed Services, A Preliminary Bibliography,* Oberlin, 1945.

Friedman, L. M.—"Abraham Lincoln and Jewish Army Chaplains," in his *Jewish Pioneers and Patriots,* New York, 1943.

Fuller, Richard F.—*Chaplain Fuller: Being a Life Sketch of a New England Clergyman and Army Chaplain,* Boston, 1863.

Gano, John—*Biographical Memoirs of the Late Rev. John Gano of Frankfort (Kentucky), Formerly of the City of New York,* New York, 1806. Pages 92–116, which contain an account of his services in the Revolution, were reprinted in the *Historical Magazine,* V (Nov. 1861), 330–35, under the title, "A Chaplain of the Revolution; Memoirs of the Rev. John Gano."

Garrett, Ray Ellis—*William Edward Biederwolf, A Biography,* Grand Rapids, 1948.

Germain, Aiden H.—*Catholic Military and Naval Chaplains, 1776–1917,* Washington, 1929.

Gracy, Samuel L.—*Annals of the 6th Pennsylvania Cavalry,* Philadelphia, 1868.

Grant, D. F.—*War is my Parish,* Milwaukee, 1947.

Guild, R. A.—*Chaplain Smith and the Baptists; or the Life, Journals, Letters, and Addresses of the Rev. Hezekiah Smith, D. D., of Haverhill, Mass., 1737–1805,* Philadelphia, 1885.

Hammond, Rev. J. Pinkney, M. A., Chaplain U. S. Army—*The Army Chaplain's Manual. Designed as a Help to Chaplains in the Discharge of their Various Duties, both Temporal and Spiritual,* Philadelphia, 1863.

Headley, J. T.—*The Chaplains and Clergy of the Revolution,* New York, 1864.

Hickcox, Percy M.—*Mine Eyes Have Seen,* Boston, 1950.

Hitchcock, Enos—"Diary of Enos Hitchcock, D. D., A Chaplain in the Revolutionary Army," with a memoir, W. B. Weeden, Ed.,

Publications of the Rhode Island Historical Society, New Ser., VII, July 1899, 106–34, Oct. 1899, 147–94.

(Hodgman, Stephen A.)—*The Nation's Sin and Punishment,* 1864.

Holman, C. T.—*Personal Problems of Men in the Armed Forces,* New York, 1944.

(Hudson, Henry N.)—*A Chaplain's Campaign with General Butler,* New York, 1865.

Humphreys, Charles A.—*Field, Camp, Hospital and Prison in the Civil War, 1863–1865,* Boston, 1918.

Jenkins, B. A.—*Father Meany and the Fighting 69th,* New York, 1944.

Johnson, Lorenzo D.—*An Address to the Pastors and People of these United States on the Chaplaincy of the General Government,* Washington, 1857.

Johnson, Lorenzo D.—*Chaplains of the General Government, with Objections to their Employment Considered,* New York, 1856.

Jones, Rev. J. William, D. D.—*Christ in the Camp, or Religion in Lee's Army,* Richmond, 1887.

Kimball, Clyde—*A Diary of My Work Overseas,* Nashua, N. H., 1947.

Leonard, Abiel—*A Prayer Composed for the Benefit of the Soldiery of the American Army,* Cambridge, 1775.

Leonard, A. W.—*The Chaplaincy from the Standpoint of the Government and the Church,* Washington, 1941.

Lev, Aryeh, Ed.—*What Chaplains Preach,* New York, 1942.

Levinger, Rabbi Lee J., M. A.—*A Jewish Chaplain in France,* New York, 1922.

Lothrup, S. K.—"Life of Samuel Kirkland," Sparks, Ed., *Library of American Biography,* 2 Ser., XV, Boston, 1848.

Lyle, W. W.—*Lights and Shadows of Army Life, or Pen Pictures from the Battlefield, the Camp, and the Hospital,* 2d Ed., Cincinnati, 1865.

Marks, Rev. J. J., D. D.—*The Peninsula Campaign in Virginia, or Incidents and Scenes on the Battle-Fields and in Richmond,* Philadelphia, 1864.

McCarthy, Chaplain George T.—*The Greater Love,* Chicago (1920).

M'Clure, Alexander Wilson—*The Lives of John Wilson, John Norton, and John Davenport,* Boston, 1846.

McElroy, Rev. Thomas—"The War Letters of Father Peter Paul Cooney of the Congregation of the Holy Cross," *Records of the American Catholic Historical Society of Philadelphia,* XLIV, 47–69 (March 1933), 151–69 (June 1933), 220–37 (Sept. 1933).

Moore, Frank, Ed.—*The Patriot Preachers of the American Revolution*, New York, 1862.

Mullins, Chaplain G. G.—*My Life is an Open Book*, St. Louis, 1883.

Murray, John—*The Life of John Murray*, Boston, 1833.

Murray, Nicholas—"Memoir of the Rev. James Caldwell," *Proceedings of the New Jersey Historical Society*, III, 79.

Nance, Ellwood C.—*Faith of our Fighters*, St. Louis, 1944.

Nave, Orville J.—*Nave's Handbook of the Army Chaplaincy*, Los Angeles 1917.

Noll, Rev. Arthur Howard, Ed.—*Doctor Quintard, Chaplain C. S. A. and Second Bishop of Tennessee, Being his story of the War (1861–1865)*, Sewanee, 1905.

Nygaard, Norman E.—*Keep 'Em Flying: Sermons to Men in the Air Forces*, New York, 1945.

History of Chaplains' Activities in the Pacific. (Hq. USA, PAC).

Pauly, Karl B.—*The Man and his Record*, New York (1944). *Bricker of Ohio:*

Pepper, Capt. George W.—*Personal Recollections of Sherman's Campaigns in Georgia and the Carolinas*, Zanesville, 1866.

Pitts, Charles F.—*Chaplains in Gray: The Confederate Chaplains Story*, Nashville, 1957.

Plater, Charles D.—*Catholic Soldiers*, by 60 Chaplains and many others, 1919.

Poling, Daniel A.—*Huts in Hell*, Boston (1918).

Poling, Daniel A.—*Your Daddy Did not Die*, New York, 1944.

The Priest Goes to War, 1945.

Rickard, Harry C.—*Hospital Chaplain (Europe 1944–47)*, Boyce, Va., 1954.

Rogers, Rev. J. B.—*War Pictures. Experiences and Observations of a Chaplain in the U. S. Army in the War of the Southern Rebellion*, Chicago, 1863.

Rogers, William—*The Journal of a Brigade Chaplain in the Campaign of 1779 against the Six Nations, under Command of Major General John Sullivan* (R. I. Historical Tracts, Ser. I, No. 7), Providence, 1879. Reprinted in *Journals of the Military Expedition of Major General John Sullivan against the Six Nations of Indians in 1779 with Records of the Centennial Celebrations*, Auburn, N. Y., 1887.

Sheldon, George, Ed.—*What Befell Stephen Williams in his Captivity*, (Includes Williams' narrative and notes), Deerfield, 1889.

Smith, Mary P. Wells—*The Boy Captive of Old Deerfield,* Boston, 1929.

Sperry, W. L., Ed.—*Religion of Soldier and Sailor,* 4 vols., Cambridge, 1945.

Stearns, Gustav—*From Army Camps and Battle-Fields,* Minneapolis, 1929.

Steward, Theophilus Gould—*Active Service, or Religious Work among U. S. Soldiers,* New York (189?).

Steward, T. G.—*The Colored Regiments in the U. S. Army,* Philadelphia, 1904.

Styles, William A. L., M. D.—*Pioneer Military Chaplains.*

Summerbell, Captain Carlyle—*A Preacher Goes to War,* 1930.

Taggart, Chaplain William C., and Cross, Christopher—*My Fighting Congregation,* Garden City, 1943.

Thompson, Donald A.—*American Army Chaplaincy, A Brief History,* Washington, 1946. Reprinted as *United States Army Chaplaincy,* W. D. Pamphlet 16–1.

Thorne, John Calvin—*A Monograph on the Rev. Israel Evans, A. M., Chaplain in the American Army during the entire Revolutionary War, 1775–1783, the Second Settled Minister of Concord, New Hampshire, 1789–1799,* Concord, 1902 (reprinted 1907).

Thornton, Francis B.—*Sea of Glory: the Magnificent Story of the Four Chaplains,* New York, 1953.

Todd, Charles Burr—*Life and Letters of Joel Barlow,* New York, 1886.

Todd, William C.—*Rev. Stephen Peabody and Wife of Atkinson, N. H., An Old-Time Pastor,* Boston, 1894.

Trumbull, Benjamin—"A Concise Journal or Minutes of the Principal Movements toward St. John's, of the Siege and Surrender of the Forts There in 1775," *Collections of the Connecticut Historical Society,* VII (1899), 139–73.

Trumbull, Benjamin—"Journal of a Campaign at New York, 1776–7," *Collections of the Connecticut Historical Society,* VII (1899), 175–218.

Trumbull, H. Clay—*War Memories of an Army Chaplain,* New York, 1898.

Van Dewater, George R.—*New York and the War with Spain.*

(Van Dewater, G. R.)—*History of the 71st Regiment, New York Volunteers.*

Waring, George J.—*United States Catholic Chaplains in the World War,* New York, (1924).

White, Henry Clay—*Abraham Baldwin, One of the Founders of the Republic and Father of the University of Georgia, the First of American State Universities,* Athens, Ga., 1926.

Williams, Michael—*American Catholics in the War,* New York, 1921.

Wise, John—*Two Narratives of an Expedition against Quebec, A. D. 1690, under Sir William Phips,* Cambridge, 1902.

Ylvisaker, Nils M.—*Trumpets of God,* Minneapolis, 1945.

Young, A. H.—"The Rev. John Ogilvie, D. D., an Army Chaplain at Ft. Niagara and Montreal, 1759–1760," Ontario Historical Society, *Papers and Records,* XXII (1925), 296–337.

Zabriskie, Alexander C.—*Bishop Brent: Crusader for Christian Unity,* Philadelphia, (1948).

Zunder, Theodore Albert—*The Early Days of Joel Barlow, a Connecticut Wit,* New Haven, 1934.

UNSIGNED ARTICLES ABOUT CHAPLAINS

"Army Chaplains," *Life*, XIII, 89.

"Army Chaplain Heroes," *Army and Navy Register*, LXIII, 1.

"Chaplaincy in the Army," *Danville Quarterly Review*, III, 255.

"Chaplains Courageous," *Time*, LX, 51.

"He's in Korea," *Christian Century*, LXIX, 975.

"Student Chaplains," *Time*, LVII, 111.

"Where Are the Chaplains?" *Newsweek*, XL, 68.

"Church in Uniform," *Time*, LVI, 68.

"Sky Pilots," *Newsweek*, XXXV, 72.

"Chaplains for Security," *Newsweek*, XXVIII, 88.

"Chaplains Have Much Work Still to Do," *Christian Century*, LXIII, 1331.

"Holy Joes," *Newsweek*, XXVI, 91.

"What the War Does to Chaplains," *Christian Century*, LXII, 541.

"Four Chaplains: Each Awarded Posthumous Distinguished Service Cross," *Time*, XLIV, 73.

"No Sects in the Sky," *Newsweek*, XXV, 86.

"Chaplains of the ROK's," *Time*, LXI, 60.

"Lace-Curtain Chaplain," *Newsweek*, XLII, 80.

"No Priest Chaplains to Spare," *America*, LXXXIX, 65.

"Our Service Men Need Chaplains," *Christian Century*, LXX, 405.

"Procurement of Military Chaplains," *America*, XC, 309.

"A Mighty Fortress," *Newsweek*, XXIV, 50.

"Foxhole Religion," *Christianity and Crisis*, IV, 5.

"Chaplains in Bataan," *Time*, XXXIX, 52.

"Chaplains Bolster Morale of American Soldiers," *Forth*, CVII, 8.

GENERAL WORKS

Andrews, Charles T.—*The Colonial Period of American History,* 4 vols., New Haven, 1934–38.

The Army Almanac.

Army Day Review.

The 120th Field Artillery Diary.

The 139th Field Artillery.

Atkins, Elisha, in *Religion of Soldier and Sailor,* 4 vols. (W. L. Sperry, Ed.), Cambridge, 1945.

Babson, John James—*History of the Town of Gloucester, Cape Ann, Including the Town of Rockport,* Gloucester, 1860.

Backus, William W.—*A Genealogical Memoir of the Backus Family,* 1889.

Baker, Ray Stannard—*Woodrow Wilson: Life and Letters,* 8 vols. Garden City, 1927–39.

Baldwin, Alice M.—*The Clergy of Connecticut in Revolutionary Days,* New Haven, 1936.

Baldwin, Alice M.—*The New England Clergy and the American Revolution,* Durham, N. C., 1928.

Bancroft, George—*A History of the United States from the Discovery of the American Continent,* 10 vols., Boston, 1834–75.

Banks, Charles Edward—*The History of Martha's Vineyard, Dukes County, Massachusetts,* 3 vols., Boston, 1911–25.

Barber, Thomas H.—*Along the Road,* New York, 1924.

Bassett, John Spencer—*A Short History of the United States,* New York, 1930.

Beatty, John—*Memoirs of a Volunteer, 1861–1863,* (edited by Harvey S. Ford), New York (1946).

Appleton's Cyclopedia of American Biography.

The Cyclopedia of American Biography, New York, 1915.

Dictionary of American Biography, 20 vols. (edited by Allen Johnson and Dumas Malone), New York, 1943, supplementary vol. (edited by Harris E. Starr), 1944.

Dictionary of National Biography, 21 vols., Oxford, 1921.

Encyclopedia of American Biography, New Series, 16 vols., New York, 1943.

Lamb's Biographical Dictionary.

The National Cyclopedia of American Biography, 36 vols., New York, 1932.

Boynton, Maj. Edward C.—*General Orders of Geo. Washington, Commander-in-Chief of the Army of the Revolution, issued at Newburgh on the Hudson, 1782-1783,* Newburgh, 1883.

Bradley, Omar N.—*A Soldier's Story,* New York, 1951.

Bradley, Thomas D.—*A Condensed History of the Ancient and Honorable Artillery Company, 1635-1889,* 1889.

Brodhead, John Romeyn, Ed.—*Documents Relating to the Colonial History of the State of New York,* 10 vols., Albany, 1853.

Broun, Haywood—*The A. E. F.; With General Pershing and the American Forces,* New York, 1918.

Burch, John P.—*Charles W. Quantrell: A True History of his Guerrilla Warfare on the Missouri and Kansas Border during the Civil War of 1861-1865, as told by Captain Harrison Trew* (Kansas City, 1923).

Burke, John J.—*The Catholics at War,* New York (1942).

Burnett, Edmund C., Ed.—*Letters of Members of the Continental Congress,* Washington, 8 vols., 1921.

Burt, Col. Silas W.—"Memoirs of the Military History of the State of New York during the War for the Union," in *New York and the War with Spain,* by the State Historian of New York, 1903.

Butcher, Henry C.—*My Three Years with Eisenhower, 1942-1945,* 1946.

By Their Side—A Memorial, War Service of the National Lutheran Council, 1940-1948.

Cambridge Medieval History.

Carman, Harry J., and McKee, Samuel—*A History of the United States,* Vol. I, Boston & New York (1931).

Carter, Russell G.—*The 101st Field Artillery.*

Cathcart, William—*Baptist Encyclopedia,* Philadelphia, 1881.

Catholic Builders of the Nation, A Symposium on the Catholic Contribution to the Civilization of the United States, 5 vols. Boston, 1923.

Chase, Ellen—*The Beginnings of the American Revolution,* 3 vols., New York, 1910.

The Story of Christian Science Wartime Activities, 1939-1946, Boston, 1947.

Chunn, Maj. Calvin Ellsworth—*Of Rice and Men. The Story of Americans under the Rising Sun,* Los Angeles & Tulsa.

Clare, Thomas H.—*Lookin' Eastward,* New York, 1945.

Connecticut Men in the Revolutionary War.

Corning, Amos Elwood—*Washington at Temple Hill,* Newburgh, 1932.

Cromwell's Soldier's Bible, reprint, London, 1895.

Curtis, Edward E.—*The Organization of the British Army in the American Revolution,* New Haven, 1926.

Davis, Jefferson—*The Rise and Fall of the Confederate Government*, 2 vols., New York, 1881.

Delaware Archives, 5 vols., 1911.

Detrick, Charles R.—*History of the Operations of the First Regiment, California Volunteer Infantry, in the Campaign in the Philippine Islands.*

Dexter, Franklin B.—*Biographical Sketches of the Graduates of Yale College with Annals of the College History*, New York, 1885.

Durkin, Joseph T., Ed.—*John Dooley, Confederate Soldier, His War Journal*, Georgetown, 1945.

Eckenrode, H. J.—*The Revolution in Virginia*, Boston, 1916.

Egle, William H.—*History of Pennsylvania*, Harrisburg, 1876.

Elmer, Ebenezer—*Journal.*

Encyclopedia Britannica, 11th Ed., 1910, 14th Ed., 1929.

History of the 101st U. S. Engineers.

An English Combatant—*Battlefields of the South, from Bull Run to Fredericksburg with Sketches of Confederate Commanders, and gossip of the Camps*, New York, 1864.

Faust, Karl Irving—*Campaigning in the Philippines*, San Francisco, 1899.

Fichter, Joseph H.—*James Lainez, Jesuit*, St. Louis & London, 1944.

Fiske, John—*The Beginnings of New England*, Boston (1889).

Fiske, John—*Dutch and Quaker Colonies in America*, 2 vols., Boston (1899).

Fiske, John—*New France and New England*, Boston (1902).

Flick, Alexander C., Ed.—*A Short History of the State of New York*, New York (1901).

Foote, William H.—*Sketches of North Carolina, historical and biographical*, New York, 1846.

Force, Peter, Ed.—*American Archives*, Series 4, 6 vols., 1837, Series 5, 3 vols., 1853.

Fox, Dixon Ryan—*Ideas in Motion*, New York and London, 1935.

Fox, Lt. Col. William F.—*Regimental Losses in the American Civil War, 1861–1865*, Albany, 1889.

Frank, Tenney—*Roman Imperialism*, New York, 1914.

Franklin, Benjamin—*Benjamin Franklin's Autobiography*, New York.

Freeman, Douglas Southall—*Lee's Lieutenants: A Study in Command*, 3 vols., New York, 1942.

Freeman, Douglas Southall—*R. E. Lee: A Biography*, 4 vols., New York and London, 1940.

French, Allen—*The First Year of the American Revolution*, Boston and New York, 1934.

Ganoe, William Addleman—*The History of the United States Army*, New York and London, 1942.

Gerand, Rt. Rev. Philias S.—*The History of the City of Ogdensburg,* Ogdensburg, 1927.

Gow, Kenneth—*Letters of a Soldier,* New York (1920).

Grant, U. S.—*Personal Memoirs of U. S. Grant,* 2 vols., New York, 1885.

Greenlaw, Olga S.—*The Lady and the Tigers,* New York, 1943.

Gregg, John A.—*Of Men and of Arms,* Nashville, 1945.

Gregory, Marian—*Memories of Service in France.*

Haldeman, I. M.—*A History of the First Baptist Church in the City of New York.*

Hanson, Marcus Lee—*The Immigrant in American History,* 1942.

Harte, Bret—*The Poetical Works of Bret Harte,* Boston, 1872.

Hatch, Louis Clinton, Ed. in Chief—*Maine: A History,* 3 vols., New York, 1919.

Hatch, Louis Clinton—*The Administration of the American Revolutionary Army,* New York, 1904.

Catalogus Senatus Academici, Universitate Harvardiana.

Hatfield, Edwin F.—*History of Elizabeth, New Jersey, including early history of Union County,* New York, 1868.

Hatfield, Edwin F.—*Revolutionary History of Elizabeth,* 1926.

Heath, William—*Memoirs of Major-General Heath,* Boston, 1798.

Herrick, Rev. H. N., D. D., and Sweet, William Warren—*A History of the North Indiana Conference of the Methodist Episcopal Church,* Indianapolis, 1917.

Hershner and Liest—*History of St. John's Reformed Church in Lower Heidelberg.*

Hesseltine, William Burt—*Civil War Prisons: A Study in War Psychology,* Columbus, 1930.

History of Hingham.

Hodgman, Stephen A.—*The Nation's Sin and Punishment,* New York, 1864.

Holman, C. T.—*Personal Problems of Men in the Armed Forces.*

Holmes, Fred L.—*George Washington Traveled this Way,* Boston (1935).

Hubbard, William—*Narrative of the Troubles with the Indians in New England,* Boston, 1677.

Hughes, Rupert—*George Washington,* 3 vols., New York, 1926–1930.

Hutchison, David—*The Foundations of the Constitution,* New York, 1928.

The Writings of Thomas Jefferson, Andrew A. Lipscomb, Ed., 20 vols., 1903.

Judy, William Lewis—*A Soldier's Diary,* Chicago, 1930.

Kramer, Harold M.—*With Seeing Eyes,* Boston (1919).

Karraker, William A.—*The American Churches and the Spanish-American War,* Chicago, 1943.

Kaufman, I.—*American Jews in World War II, The Story of 500,000 Fighters for Freedom,* 2 vols. (1947).

Le Roy, James A.—*The Americans in the Philippines,* 2 vols., Boston and New York, 1914.

Lexikon für Theologie und Kirche, Michael Buchberger, Ed., 10 vols., Freiburg, 1930–1938.

Lossing, Benson J.—*The Pictorial Fieldbook of the Revolution,* 2 vols., New York, 1850.

Lot, Ferdinand—*L'Art Militaire et Les Armees au moyen age en Europe et dans le Proche Orient,* 2 vols., Paris, 1946.

Marshall, Edward—*The Story of the Rough Riders,* New York, 1899.

Proceedings of the Massachusetts Historical Society.

Massachusetts Soldiers and Sailors in the Revolutionary War, 17 vols., Boston, 1896–1908.

Mayo, Margaret—*Trooping with the Troops,* New York (1919).

McCallum, Lee—*Our Sons at War.*

McCormac, Eugene Irving—*James K. Polk: A Political Biography,* Berkeley, 1922.

McGiffert, Arthur Cushman—*Jonathan Edwards,* New York, 1932.

Mead, James M.—*Tell the Folks Back Home,* New York and London (1944).

Morris, B. F.—*Christian Life and Character of the Civil Institutions of the United States,* Philadelphia, 1864.

Moss, Lemuel—*Annals of the United States Christian Commission,* Philadelphia, 1868.

New Hampshire State Papers.

New York Archives.

Nickerson, Hoffman—*The Turning Point of the Revolution, or Burgoyne in America,* Boston and New York, 1928.

Nicolay, John G., and Hay, John, Editors—*Complete Works of Abraham Lincoln,* 12 vols., New York (1905).

Noyes, Harriette Eliza—*A Memorial History of the Town of Hampstead, New Hampshire,* Boston, 1899–1903.

O'Hara, Edward H.—*World War at its Climax,* East Aurora, N. Y. (1922).

Oman, Sir Charles—*A History of the Art of War in the Sixteenth Century,* New York (1937).

The New Oxford Classical Dictionary.

Palfrey, John Gorham—*History of New England,* 5 vols., Boston, 1864.

Parkman, Francis—*France and England in North America; a Series of Historical Narratives,* Boston:
> *Montcalm and Wolfe,* 2 vols., 1884.
> *Lasalle and the Discovery of the Great West,* 12th ed., 1880.
> *The Old Regime in Canada,* 8th ed., 1880.
> *Count Frontenac and New France under Louis XIV,* 7th ed., 1880.
> *Pioneers of France in the New World,* 17th ed., 1880.
> *The Conspiracy of Pontiac and the Indian War after the Conquest of Canada,* 2 vols., 9th ed., 1880.
> *The Jesuits in North America in the Seventeenth Century,* 14th ed., 1880.
> *Half Century of Conflict.*

Pennsylvania Archives, 119 vols., Harrisburg, 1874–1935.

Pershing, John J.—*My Experiences in the World War,* 2 vols., New York, 1931.

Perry, Arthur Latham—*Origins in Williamstown,* 2d ed., New York, 1896 (contains John Norton's narrative of his captivity—*The Redeemed Captive*—with notes).

Pickering, Octavius—*The Life of Timothy Pickering,* 4 vols., Boston, 1867–1873.

Polk, James K.—*Polk: The Diary of a President, 1845–1849,* Edited by Allan Nevins, London and New York, 1929.

Possidius—*Sancti Augustini vita scripta a Possidio episcopo,* Princeton, 1919.

Proehl, Frederick C.—*Marching Side by Side,* St. Louis, 1945.

Pyle, Ernie—*Here is Your War.*

Raikes, George Alfred—*The History of the Honorable Artillery Company,* 2 vols., 1878.

Ranlett, L. F.—*Let's Go!,* Boston and New York, 1927.

Reid, W. Max—*The Mohawk Valley: Its History and its Legends,* New York and London, 1907.

Rice, Philip Sidney—*An American Crusader at Verdun,* Princeton, 1918.

Riedesal, Friederike Charlotte Luise (von Massow) freifrau von—*Letters and journals relating to the War of the American revolution and the capture of the German troops at Saratoga,* Trans. by William L. Stone, Albany, 1867.

Roberts, Oliver Ayer—*History of the Military Company of Massachusetts now called the Ancient and Honorable Artillery Company of Massachusetts, 1637–1888,* 4 vols., 1895–1901.

Roosevelt, Theodore—*The Rough Riders and Men of Action,* New York, 1926.

Root, Mary P.—"Patron Saints," in *Chapter sketches,* Connecticut Daughters of the American Revolution, New Haven (1901).

Rusk, Ralph L.—*The Life of Ralph Waldo Emerson,* New York, 1949.

Saffell, William Thomas R.—*Records of the Revolutionary War,* New York, 1858.

Sandburg, Carl—*Abraham Lincoln: The War Years,* 4 vols., New York (1939).

Scott, Col. Robert L., Jr.—*God is My Copilot,* New York, 1943.

Service with Fighting Men, 2 vols., New York, 1922.

Shaler, U. S.—*Kentucky: A Pioneer Commonwealth,* Boston, 1885.

Shanks, Major General David S.—*As They Passed Through the Port,* Washington (1927).

Shannon, Fred Albert—*The Organization and Administration of the Union Army, 1861-1865,* 2 vols., Cleveland, 1928.

Shipler, Guy E., Ed.—*War Work in the Diocese of New York.*

Smith, Justin H.—*The War with Mexico,* 2 vols., New York, 1919.

Sozomen, Hermias—*Ecclesiastical History, A. D. 324 to 440,* London, 1855.

Sparks, Jared, Ed.—*The Library of American Biography,* 25 vols., Boston and London, 1834-1848.

Spellman, Francis J.—*Action this Day,* New York, 1943.

Sprague, William B.—*Annals of the American Pulpit,* 9 vols., New York, 1857-1865.

Stackpole, Everett S.—*History of New Hampshire,* 4 vols., New York.

St. George, Thomas R.—*% Postmaster,* New York (1943).

Stidger, William L.—*Soldier Silhouettes on our Front,* New York, 1918.

Strickland, Riley—*Adventures of the A. E. F. Soldier* (Austin, 1920).

Sullivan, Vincent F.—*With the Yanks in France,* New York (1921).

Swan, Captain Carroll Judson—*My Company,* Boston and New York, 1918.

Sweet, William Warren—*The Story of Religions in America,* New York and London (1930).

Sweet, William Warren—*The Methodist Episcopal Church and the Civil War,* Cincinnati (1912).

Temple, Josiah Howard—*North Brookfield, Massachusetts,* Boston, 1887.

Thucydides—*The Peloponnesian War,* Modern Library Edition, Crowley Tr.

Trumbull, James Russell—*History of Northampton, Massachusetts,* 2 vols., Northampton, 1898.

Tyler, Lyon G.—"The College of William and Mary, its Work, Discipline, and History," *Bulletin of the College of William and Mary,* X, No. 4.

Waldo, Fullerton L.—*America at the Front,* New York (1918).

Writings of George Washington from the original Manuscript sources, 1745–1799, John C. Fitzpatrick, Ed., 39 volumes, Washington, 1931–44.

Whittaker, James C.—*We Thought We Heard the Angels Sing,* New York, 1943.

Wiley, Bell Irvin—*The Life of Johnny Reb: The Common Soldier of the Confederacy,* Indianapolis and New York, c. 1943.

Williams, John—*The Redeemed Captive Returning to Zion* (includes Stephen Williams' narrative of his captivity), Northampton, 1853.

Williams, Stephen West—*Genealogy and History of the Family of Williams in America,* Greenfield, Mass., 1847.

Wilson, Henry—*Military Measures of the United States Congress, 1861–1865,* New York, 1866.

Index of Chaplains

	Pages
Abiather	1, 2
Adams, Amos	49
Adams, John R	127, 137, 144, 147, 148
Adams, Norman	283
Allen, Michael M	107
Allen, Moses	50, 61
Allen, Thomas	33, 51
Ambrose, Thomas L	123
Ames, Sylvanus	49
Anderson, Walter R	276
Applegate, Joseph M	274
Armitstead, Johnson N	304
Arnold, William R	201
Atherton, Hope	12
Ausland, Donald E	312
Avery, David	46, 56, 57, 58, 61
Axton, John T	201
Backus, Simon	20
Baker, Nathan	96
Balch, Benjamin	52
Baldwin, Abraham	42, 58
Baldwin, Charles W	176
Baldwin, Ebenezer	49
Ball, Dabney	93
Balmaine, Alexander	47
Barber, Lorenzo	96, 98, 113
Barclay, Thomas	15
Barlow, Joel	42, 61
Barnum, Caleb	49
Bartlett, George W	123
Barton, Thomas	21
Barton, William	58
Bateman, Cephas C	168
Beatty, Charles	26
Beecher, James	100
Beecher, Thomas	100
Benedict, Abner	52
Bennett, Ivan L	201, 331, 333
Bennett, R. B	96, 98
Benton, Orlando N	123
Berry, T. W	172
Betts, Alexander D	118, 127, 143, 146, 150
Biederwolf, William E	160, 161, 165
Bittle, Celestine N	170, 189, 191, 194
Blair, Samuel	56
Blakeney, James	273
Boardman, Benjamin	56, 57
Borneman, John K	279
Bowles, John R	116
Bradley, George S	91, 93, 94, 129, 147
Brainard, John	26
Brasted, Alva J	173, 239
Brent, Charles	178, 199, 213
Brichto, Herbert	333
Bricker, John	176
Brink, Eben. Cobb	87, 341
Brown (f. n. u.)	105
Brown, Ralph W. D	279
Brown, Thomas	27
Brown, William Y	172, 201
Brownlow, William G	90
Brudenell (f. n. u.)	72
Bucher, John Conrad	43
Buckminster, Joseph	56
Butler, Francis E	123
Byrd, Wendell F	336
Caldwell, James	47
Carnes, John	56
Carpenter, Charles I	231, 308
Chenoweth, John F	177
Christy, B. F	96, 128, 134
Cleaveland, Ebenezer	56, 57
Cleaveland, John	24, 29, 32, 33
Clemens, Joseph	173
Coffin, Enoch	15
Coffin, Moses	20
Cohee, Ora J	239
Cooke, Noah	56, 58
Cooney, Peter	145, 146
Corby, William	110, 132, 136, 137, 140, 146
Cordell, John	50
Costen, W. Hilary	160
Crawford, William	25
Cross, Joseph	89
Culpepper, Charles R	338
Cutler, Manassah	54
David, Ebenezer	49, 56
Davis, James E	278
Davis, Thomas	51
Davitt, William F	196
Dawson, William	278
Dean, John Marvin	212
Decker, Silas	335
Denison, Frederic	113, 134, 136, 140, 142, 144, 145, 147
Densmore, George W	123
Devan, S. Arthur	226

Pages

De Veaux, John A_____ 237
Dillon, James_____ 145
Duffield, George_____ 50, 54
Duffy, Francis P_____ 187, 194, 198
Dunbar, Samuel_____ 6, 29
Dwight, Daniel_____ 17
Dwight, Timothy_____ 54

Eakin, Samuel_____ 55
Easterbrook, Edmund_____ 197, 200, 201
Eaton, John_____ 101, 130
Eddy, John W_____ 123
Edwards, Timothy_____ 15
Egan, C. L_____ 147
Eliot, John_____ 41
Elliot, John_____ 41
Ellis, John_____ 56, 57
Emerson, Daniel_____ 21
Emerson, John_____ 13
Emerson, Joseph_____ 21, 49
Emerson, William_____ 49
Evans, Israel_____ 57, 61, 66

Fallows, Samuel_____ 100
Fealy, Ignatius_____ 177, 179
Finnegan, Terrance_____ 276
Fischel, Arnold_____ 107
Fiske, A. S_____ 138
Fithian, Philip V_____ 34, 49, 61
Fleming, Robert_____ 177, 179
Forbes, Eli_____ 26, 27
Forster, Jacob_____ 56
Foster, Daniel_____ 123
Frankle, Jacob_____ 107
French, Jonathan_____ 28
Frye, Jonathan_____ 18
Fuller, Arthur_____ 96,
      103, 122, 134, 136, 142, 145

Gache, Henry_____ 133
Gano, John_____ 55, 56, 58, 70
Gardner, Ozem B_____ 124
Gerecke, Henry F_____ 283
Gibble, William T_____ 273
Gilbert (f. n. u.)_____ 165
Gillen, Paul_____ 127
Gordon, William_____ 33
Gotthelf, Bernhard H_____ 107
Graham, John_____ 25
Granbery, John C_____ 144
Griffith, David_____ 46
Gros, Johann Daniel_____ 44

Hale, John_____ 13
Hale, Wallace M_____ 277
Hall, Francis B_____ 124
Hall, James_____ 52
Hammond, J. Pinkney_____ 172
Haney, Milton M_____ 96, 98, 124

Pages

Harrison, Samuel_____ 116
Hart (f. n. u.)_____ 164
Hawley, Joseph_____ 20
Hayne, Orlando V_____ 281, 341
Hitchcock, Enos_____ 57
Hitchcock, Gad_____ 29, 33
Hoffman, Albert J_____ 282
Hoge, Moses D_____ 137, 141
Homiston, Robert_____ 329
Howell, Horatio S_____ 123
Hudson, Henry N_____ 114
Humphries, Charles A_____ 93,
      103, 128, 135, 137, 140, 142, 144, 147
Hunt, Robert_____ 10
Hunter, Andrew_____ 34, 51, 52, 56, 58, 61, 116
Hunter, William_____ 116
Huntington, Park_____ 276
Hurt, John_____ 51, 52, 56, 58

Ireland, John_____ 108

Jackson, William_____ 116
Jefferson, Matthew M_____ 176
Johnson, Stephen_____ 32
Jones, David_____ 46, 52, 57, 78
Jones, Isaac F_____ 212
Jones, J. William_____ 88, 100,
      103, 105, 127, 128, 137, 138, 144, 146, 149
Jordan, Galen E_____ 342

Kapaun, Emil_____ 336
Keith, Robert_____ 61
Kirkland, Samuel_____ 28, 44, 58, 68
Kirkpatrick, (f. n. u.)____ 28
Kirtley, Edwin L_____ 287
Knox, George_____ 123

Lacy, Beverley T_____ 138, 143, 149, 198
La Loutre, Louis J_____ 10
Langdon, Samuel_____ 18, 61
Las Cases, Bartolome_____ 10
Lemon, Orange V_____ 120
Lee, Edwin_____ 226
Lenk, Joseph A_____ 293
Leonard, Abiel_____ 56, 57, 73
Lev, Aryeh_____ 237
Linn, William_____ 61
Lotbiniere, Louis_____ 45, 58
Lyth, John_____ 47

Mansfield, Isaac_____ 56, 57
Marks, J. J_____ 90,
      93, 126, 129, 135, 137, 141, 146, 150
Martin, John_____ 46
Mason, John_____ 58
Matthews, Bruce B_____ 278
McCabe, Charles C_____ 93,
      105, 126, 129, 142, 147, 150
McCalla, Daniel_____ 50
McCarthy, George T_____ 185, 187, 192

Pages

McClintock, Samuel _____ 54
McElroy, John _____ 84
McGill, John _____ 118
McGinnis, James S _____ 288
McKinnon, William C _____ 163, 164
McMullen, J. P _____ 125
McMurdie, Robert _____ 40
Melsheimer, Frederick _____ 73
Mendoza, (f. n. u.) _____ 10
Miller, Frank L _____ 237
Miller, Henry _____ 44
Miller, Luther D _____ 201
Mills, Arthur _____ 333
Mines, John F _____ 97
Moody, Paul D _____ 212, 226
Moody, Samuel _____ 20, 198
Mullins, George G _____ 157
Murray, John _____ 43

Nave, Orville J __ 154, 157, 161, 166, 169, 173
Naylor, Duncan _____ 325
Neill, Edward D _____ 100
Nevelling, John _____ 55
Newell, (f. n. u.) _____ 24
Noble, Oliver _____ 56
North, (f. n. u.) _____ 97
Norton, John _____ 19

O'Brien, James W _____ 279
O'Flaherty, Colman E _____ 196, 293
Ogilby, (f. n. u.) _____ 195
Ogilvie, John _____ 16
Oliver, Alfred C _____ 279, 304
Ouellet, Thomas _____ 133, 135, 146, 148

Parker, Roy H _____ 201, 334
Payne, Josiah _____ 56
Peabody, Stephen _____ 55
Pepper, George W _____ 89, 136, 148
Peterson, Harold C _____ 274
Phinehas _____ 2, 3
Picquet, Francois _____ 27
Picton, Thomas _____ 80
Pierce, Charles C _____ 154, 156, 162, 172
Pierpont, John _____ 105
Pile, William A _____ 100
Pillsbury, Caleb _____ 91, 92
Plumb, William _____ 46, 58
Poling, Daniel A _____ 196, 240, 340, 342
Pomeroy, Benjamin _____ 8, 31
Pruden, Aldred A _____ 174, 179
Pugh, William B _____ 226, 237

Quintard, Charles _____ 88, 89,
     132, 137, 138, 139, 142, 146, 148, 150

Randolph, John A _____ 180
Rawson, Grindall _____ 13
Redfern, Edgar _____ 304
Rey, Anthony _____ 84

Rice, George _____ 165
Ripley, Hezekiah _____ 51
Rixey, George F _____ 237
Rodgers, John _____ 61, 259
Rogers, J. B _____ 129, 135, 144
Rogers, William _____ 40, 58, 68
Ronan, Edwin _____ 213
Rosbrugh, John _____ 50
Rossiter, (f. n. u.) _____ 46
Rouband, Pierre _____ 10
Ryan, Patrick J _____ 210, 273

St. Pierre, Paul de _____ 46
Sanders, Levi W _____ 123
Sandford, David _____ 55
Sarner, Ferdinand L _____ 107
Scanlon, Gerald _____ 296
Scharlemann, Martin H _____ 325, 344
Schliemann, J. C _____ 165
Schwegler, H. G _____ 304
Scully, Thomas _____ 134, 143, 145, 146
Sheeran, James _____ 135, 145, 146
Sherrill, Henry K _____ 226
Sherry, Robert _____ 331
Simpson, G. W _____ 172
Skelton, Harold E _____ 282
Smith, (f. n. u.) _____ 179
Smith, Cotton Mather _____ 33
Smith, Elias _____ 56
Smith, Hezekiah _____ 56, 57, 58
Smith, Joseph _____ 15
Smith, Robert _____ 51
Smith, Stanley E _____ 276
Smith, Symon _____ 16
Smith, William _____ 26
Spring, Samuel _____ 55, 61, 68
Springer, John M _____ 96, 98, 123, 125
Stearns, Gustav _____ 187, 189
Steel, John _____ 28
Steward, Theophilus G _____ 160, 172
Stiles, Joseph C _____ 105, 149
Stone, Samuel _____ 11, 12
Storaasli, Gynther _____ 231
Streit, Christian _____ 43
Summerbell, Carlyle _____ 187, 194
Sweetland, Eleazer _____ 56

Taggart, William C _____ 273, 277
Taladrid, Damasio _____ 145
Tate, James _____ 58
Tetard, John Peter _____ 44
Tetreau, Elzar _____ 185, 194
Thaxter, Joseph _____ 46
Thomas, John M _____ 176
Thompson, Charles _____ 50
Trecy, J. F _____ 128, 134
True, Henry _____ 18

Pages

Trumbull, H. Clay_____ 102,
    134, 135, 136, 137, 139, 141, 144, 147, 150
Tubesing, Karl A_____ 341
Turner, Henry M_____ 116

Underdue, James_____ 116

Van Dewater, George R_____ 158, 161

Walther, John L_____ 123
Waring, George F_____ 173, 201, 225
Warring, William_____ 116
Weed, Earl_____ 293

Pages

Weld, (f. n. u.)_____ 25
West, Samuel_____ 51
Whalen, Charles_____ 46
Whitehead, John M_____ 124
Whittlesay, Eliphalet_____ 100
Willetts, Benjamin D_____ 341
Williams, Stephen_____ 19
Wilmer, James J_____ 78
Wilson, John_____ 12
Wise, John_____ 13, 15, 32
Wolfe, Joseph L. N_____ 192, 194

Yates, Julian E_____ 201

General Index

Pages

Abercromby, James_____ 24
Absence without leave_____ 67
Acland, Harriet_____ 72
Air chaplain_____ 231, 308
Air chaplain school_____ 250
Assistants_____ 318
Attendance at services__ 58, 135, 187, 327, 337

Balaam_____ 6
Bellomont, Earl of_____ 16
Bibles, distribution of_____ 61, 141, 259, 301
Bradstreet, Simon_____ 13
Brinkley, Daniel_____ 179
Burials_____ 137, 162, 191, 277
Butler, Benjamin F. (Secretary)_____ 79
Butler, Benjamin F. (General)_____ 114

Cabanatuan_____ 279
Casualties among chaplains_____ 18, 47,
        78, 84, 122, 196, 212, 294, 336
Catholic chaplains____ 45, 108, 163, 225, 288
Catholic soldiers_____ 391, 393
Champlain, Samuel_____ 10
Chapels_____ 61, 126, 263, 322
Chaplaingrams_____ 242
Chaplain boards_____ 308, 314, 319
Chaplain School_____ 28,
        171, 174, 180, 204, 243, 313
Chaplains:
    As combatants_____ 18, 20,
        47, 51, 52, 98, 124, 165
    Assignment_____ 37, 71, 81, 104
    Numbers_____ 20, 28,
        30, 56, 120, 168, 175, 180, 209,
        214, 243, 307, 310, 316, 330.
    Opposition to_____ 84
    Qualifications_____ 42,
        104, 107, 222, 249
    Release when captured_____ 51, 97, 153
    Schoolmasters_____ 80
    Supervisory_____ 198, 213
Character guidance_____ 309, 324, 339
Charity_____ 328, 335
Chiefs of Chaplains_____ 201
Christian Endeavor_____ 239
Churches in 1775_____ 34
Church membership_____ 282
Church, prisoners of war_____ 280
Church relations_____ 170, 215, 228, 237, 323
Civilian Conservation Corps_____ 210, 212

Civilian universities_____ 205, 310
Conscientious objectors_____ 105
Corps of Chaplains_____ 201

David_____ 1, 2
Davis, Jefferson_____ 93, 94, 95
De Monts_____ 10

Edwards, Jonathan_____ 8
Efficiency ratings_____ 200
Eggar, Anton_____ 282
Extension courses_____ 207, 317

Fetiales_____ 4
Films, training_____ 252
Flag, chaplain's_____ 254
Franklin, Benjamin_____ 26
French chaplains_____ 46
Funds_____ 261, 321

Gambling_____ 59, 145, 156, 161, 340
Geneva Convention_____ 8, 253, 272, 304
Grant, Ulysses S_____ 101, 115
Gregg, John A_____ 237
Guardians of America_____ 239

Harvard_____ 13, 18, 21, 73, 172, 173, 244
Holy Name Society_____ 238
Hospital chaplains_____ 41, 111
Howe, Julia Ward_____ 92, 142
Hubbard, Bernard_____ 303
Hymnal_____ 254, 258, 331

Insignia_____ 157, 178, 292

Jackson, Stonewall_____ 118, 130, 143, 150
James, Jesse_____ 124
Jason_____ 267
Jewish chaplains_____ 107, 171, 179, 289, 333
Jewish Welfare Board_____ 184,
        186, 219, 225, 227, 341
Johnston, Charlotte_____ 275
Justinian_____ 3

Keppel, Frederick_____ 177, 180
Knights of Columbus_____ 184, 189
Knox, Henry_____ 70, 76, 77
Kohlstedt, Evelyn_____ 259
Korean culture_____ 329
Korean chaplains_____ 331

Lainez, James_____ 6
Languages_____ 44, 287

Pages

Lee, Robert E_____ 89, 130, 131
Leonard, Adna W_____ 226, 237, 240
Liquor, sale of_____ 159, 166
Lincoln, Abraham_____ 2, 101, 111, 130
Lossing, Benson_____ 66
Louisbourg, chaplains at_____ 20

Maccabaeus_____ 3
Madison, James (Rev.)_____ 34
Maine, the_____ 158
Manual, chaplain's_____ 172, 251, 289
Marriage, absentee_____ 300
Marriage, counseling_____ 190, 298
Martin of Tours_____ 5
Massachusetts, Fort_____ 19
Medal of Honor_____ 124
Medical tag_____ 293
Mexican War_____ 80
Military academy_____ 80
Mohawks, missionary to_____ 17
Moses_____ 1, 2, 3

Naval chaplains at the Chaplain
  School_____ 319
Negro chaplains_____ 116, 220, 302
Negro troops_____ 100, 159, 167, 220

Offerings_____ 146, 262
Outfit, chaplains_____ 254

Pacifistic groups_____ 203
Pay of chaplains_____ 17, 35,
    37, 44, 76, 77, 79, 86, 104, 111,
    117, 119, 127, 152, 167.

Pequots_____ 12
Philippine chaplains_____ 213
Pickering, Timothy_____ 66, 75
Post chaplains_____ 80, 152
Posters_____ 326
Prisoners, military_____ 68, 284
Prisoners of war, American_____ 142,
                          147, 150, 334
Prisoners of war, enemy_____ 99, 282, 334
Privileged communications_____ 296

Profanity_____ 25, 38, 59, 144, 168, 340, 343
Putnam, Rufus_____ 70, 75

Quebec_____ 13, 50
Queen Anne's Chapel_____ 15, 16

Rank_____ 110, 177, 178, 202, 312
Ratio of chaplains_____ 121, 170, 217
Ratisbon, Council of_____ 7
Reports_____ 111, 232
Riedesel, Frederika_____ 72
Red Cross_____ 162, 184, 235, 302, 304
Reserve chaplains____ 202, 206, 223, 308, 311
Roberdeau, Daniel_____ 38, 59

Sabbath_____ 58, 130
Salvation Army_____ 184, 192
School in France_____ 180
Schools, local_____ 207, 251, 316
Schuyler, Peter_____ 16
Secular duties_____ 46, 161, 193, 271
Service Men's Christian League_____ 240
Sherman, William T_____ 94, 155
Spellman, Francis J_____ 236

Temperance_____ 79, 144, 166, 168, 233
Temple, The_____ 61, 69
Testaments, Army_____ 259, 320
Thompson, Albert S_____ 332
Thucydides_____ 3, 4
Transportation_____ 117, 127, 257
Trumpets_____ 4

Uniform of chaplains_____ 86, 110, 157, 178
United Service Organizations_____ 301
Utley, William L_____ 91

Venereal disease_____ 195, 305, 339

Wally, John_____ 14
Washington, George_____ 2, 5,
    23, 35, 41, 55, 58, 60, 67, 70, 73, 130
Wilson, Joseph Ruggles_____ 122

Young Men's Christian Association___ 159,
                     183, 189, 240, 264